# HUMAN RIGHTS: CONCEPT AND STANDARDS

# Human Rights: Concept and Standards

*Edited by*
JANUSZ SYMONIDES

**Ashgate**

DARTMOUTH

Aldershot • Burlington USA • Singapore • Sydney

UNESCO

Publishing

Published by
Dartmouth Publishing Company Limited
Ashgate Publishing Limited
Gower House
Croft Road
Aldershot
Hants GU11 3HR
England

Ashgate Publishing Company
131 Main Street
Burlington
Vermont 05401–5600
USA

Ashgate website: http://www.ashgate.com

Published jointly with the United Nations Educational, Scientific and Cultural Organization
7, place de Fontenoy, 75352, Paris 07 SP

**British Library Cataloguing in Publication Data**
Symonides, Janusz
   Human rights : concept and standards
   1. Human rights
   I. Symonides, Janusz   II. UNESCO. Secretariat
   341.4'81

**Library of Congress Cataloging-in-Publication Data**
Human rights : concept and standards / edited by Janusz Symonides.
   p.  cm.
   Includes bibliographical references.
   ISBN 0-7546-2023-9 (hb.) – ISBN 0-7546-2025-5 (pbk.)
   1. Human rights.   2. Civil rights.   I. Symonides, Janusz.
JC571.H4694415   2000
323–dc21
                                         00-20743

Ashgate ISBN 0 7546 2023 9 (Hbk)
        ISBN 0 7546 2025 5 (Pbk)
UNESCO ISBN 92-3-103589-4

Typeset by Manton Typesetters, Louth, Lincolnshire, UK.
Printed in Great Britain by MPG Books Ltd, Bodmin, Cornwall.

# Contents

## PART II   CIVIL, POLITICAL, ECONOMIC, SOCIAL AND CULTURAL RIGHTS

### 3   Civil and Political Rights

*Manfred Nowak*

### 4   Economic and Social Rights

*Asbjørn Eide*

# Preface

At the end of the twentieth century, human rights have frequently been qualified as the 'common heritage' or as the 'common language' of humanity. Indeed they do not belong to the domestic jurisdiction of states and are internationally protected. Today they create a body of universal standards and  values at the service of human dignity, equality and non-discrimination, and human freedoms.

During the half-century since the adoption of the United Nations Charter in 1945 and the Universal Declaration of Human Rights in 1948, a comprehensive international human rights law embracing many international instruments has been created. An analysis and presentation of the conceptual framework and adopted human rights standards is the main objective of this volume. Its content is divided into four parts.

The first part, comprising two chapters, deals with the concept of human rights. It presents the evolution and expansion of this concept and its philosophical formulations and  theoretical reflection on the nature and sources of human rights. International standards in the next two parts are grouped, first, from the point of view of categories of human rights: civil, political, economic, social and cultural, and then in relation to the protection of certain categories of vulnerable persons.

Parts II and III should be read in conjunction with the first volume of this manual, *Human Rights: New Dimensions and Challenges*, because the human rights presented therein, such as the right to development, are not repeated in this second volume.

The presentation of international human rights law in this volume is based on the fundamental assumption proclaimed by the Vienna Declaration and Programme of Action (June 1993):

> 5. All human rights are universal, indivisible and interdependent and interrelated. The international community must treat human rights globally in a fair and equal manner, on the same footing, and with the same emphasis.

The last chapter (Part IV) discusses the relationship between human rights and humanitarian law. The existence of armed conflicts, both international and internal, does not in any way liberate belligerents from respect for human rights. Respect and knowledge of humanitarian standards are a guarantee for the observance of human rights. For this very reason, the United Nations World Conference on Human Rights (Vienna, 1993), in the part of its final document concerning human rights education, calls for the inclusion of humanitarian law in the curricula of all institutions of learning in both formal and non-formal settings.

This volume does not intend to give a comprehensive picture of the implementation and violations of human rights in the world; these can be found in annual reports of non-governmental organizations, in reports and resolutions of the United Nations system and documents of regional organizations as well as in reports of the treaty bodies and judgments of human rights tribunals. Nevertheless, it raises many questions linked with the observance of adopted standards and discusses the main obstacles to their full implementation, as well as the causes of their violation. To consider human rights instruments without their social context and to limit the analysis to purely legalistic aspects could, and not without justification, be qualified as scholastic, abstract and, as a result, a futile exercise.

By the same token, though it is not an objective of this volume to provide a detailed presentation of all monitoring and enforcement procedures, or to give practical advice and detailed instructions on how to defend human rights – these will be included in the next volume – nonetheless, human rights instruments are presented together with their implementation provisions.

The impressive number of human rights treaties, declarations and recommendations adopted by the United Nations system and regional organizations raises a serious question about the scope of human rights education. An attempt to make all these standards and all theoretical questions linked with their adoption and implementation known to a general public may be qualified as an impossible task. However, the most important standards should be known to all. Bearing this in mind, UNESCO has published in dozens of languages many popular teaching aids, such as *Human Rights: Questions and Answers*, addressing these rather general needs.

The book is prepared for the more specialized readers: human rights activists, teachers, students and journalists, as well as various professional groups like decision makers, law enforcement personnel, and those in public administration, army or police, who all deal with human rights questions. Bibliographies at the end of each chapter facilitate further study and reflection. As this volume is also addressed to members of the academic community, it contains certain topics, such as academic freedom, which might be of interest to them.

Though the main objective of all the contributors to this volume is to present international standards, nevertheless the reader may also find references to national constitutions and laws. This permits a better understanding of the extent to which international norms are already incorporated in domestic law, how they are interpreted and understood, and how national and regional particularities are reflected in national standards.

A question which cannot be left unanswered concerns the further development of human rights law. Do we need new human rights, a 'horizontal' broadening of their catalogue? It is true that law has to reflect changing social reality and relations, that the international community cannot close its eyes to new challenges, including those caused by the unprecedented progress of science and technology. Therefore the process of development and adjustment of international human rights law is endless. New human rights instruments will be adopted. However, they should not be concentrated on new rights: this may hardly be considered as a priority because, paradoxically, they may even turn attention away from the effective implementation of existing rights. Therefore the precedence should be given to the consolidation of existing standards. There is, however, a need for a 'vertical' development of human rights law linked to the elucidation and reinforcement of already existing norms, to their monitoring and enforcement. The fact that the United Nations Commission on Human Rights has on its agenda several additional protocols to already existing human rights treaties seems to support this thesis. This is why the contributors to this volume, showing areas in which further development, such as in the case of economic, social and cultural rights or the protection of certain categories of vulnerable persons and groups, is absolutely necessary, take rather a balanced approach as far as the need for new rights is concerned.

JANUSZ SYMONIDES

# About the Contributors

**Thomas Buergenthal**  Lobingier Professor of Comparative Law and Jurisprudence. Presiding Director of the International Rule of Law Center, George Washington University Law School, Washington DC. Former Judge and President of the Inter-American Court of Human Rights. Member of the United Nations Human Rights Committee. Honorary President of the Inter-American Institute of Human Rights, San José, Costa Rica.

**Erica-Irene A. Daes**  Visiting Professor at the European University Institute, Doctor of Law. Chairperson/Rapporteur of the United Nations Working Group on Indigenous Populations. Member and Special Rapporteur of the United Nations Sub-Commission for the Promotion and Protection of Human Rights. Winner of the United Nations Human Rights Award 1993.

**Asbjørn Eide**  Director of the Norwegian Institute of Human Rights, Oslo. Member of the United Nations Sub-Commission for the Promotion and Protection of Human Rights. Chairman of the United Nations Working Group on the Rights of Minorities. United Nations Special Rapporteur on the Right to Food as a Human Right.

**Héctor Gros Espiell**  Professor of International Law. Associate Member of the Institute of International Law. Member of the UNESCO International Bioethics Committee. Former Minister of External Relations, Uruguay. Former President of the Inter-American Court of Human Rights. Former Ambassador and Permanent Delegate of Uruguay to UNESCO.

**Hurst Hannum**  Academic Dean and Professor of International Law at The Fletcher School of Law and Diplomacy of Tufts University. Former Executive Director of The Procedural Aspects of International Law Institute, Washington, DC. Jennings Randolph Peace Fellow of the United States Institute of Peace, 1989–90.

**Yuri Kolosov**   Professor of International Law at the Moscow State Institute of International Relations. Former member of the United Nations Committee on the Rights of the Child. Holder of the UNESCO Chair for Human Rights and Democracy (Moscow).

**Sedef Koray**   Associate of the Centre for Studies on Turkey, University of Essen. Specialist in questions concerning migrant workers, multi-cultural society and ethnic relations.

**Manfred Nowak**   Assistant Professor, Institute for Constitutional and Administrative Law, University of Vienna. Director, Ludwig Boltzmann Institute of Human Rights, Vienna. Member and adviser to Amnesty International, International Commission of Jurists.

**Faruk Şen**   Professor, Director, Centre for Studies on Turkey, University of Essen. Specialist in questions concerning migrant workers, ethnic minorities and Islam in Europe. Author of many publications on these subjects.

**Jerome J. Shestack**   Chairman of the International League for Human Rights. Former United States Ambassador to the United Nations Commission on Human Rights. Senior United States Delegate to the Conference on Security and Co-operation in Europe. Former member of the Executive Committee of the American Society of International Law.

**Janusz Symonides**   Professor of International Law and International Relations, University of Warsaw. Former Vice-Chancellor of Nicolaus Copernicus University, Torun, Poland and former Director of the Polish Institute of International Relations, Warsaw. Director of the Department for Peace, Human Rights, Democracy and Tolerance, UNESCO.

**Katarina Tomaševski**   Professor of International Law and International Relations, University of Lund. Lecturer at the Centre for African Studies, University of Copenhagen. United Nations Special Rapporteur on the Right to Education.

# PART I
# THE CONCEPT OF HUMAN RIGHTS

# 1 International Human Rights in an Historical Perspective

THOMAS BUERGENTHAL

## Introduction

The subject of this chapter is the historical evolution of international human rights law and the institutions established for its implementation. Here, therefore, we shall deal neither with the history of human rights in general nor with those historical movements and philosophical principles which gave rise over the past two centuries to national constitutional norms and mechanisms for the protection of the rights of the individual and of groups.[1]

It is, of course, true that the evolution of international human rights law cannot be conceptually divorced from the much older domestic constitutional law norms intended to safeguard the rights of the individual against arbitrary state action. As a matter of fact, much of substantive international human rights law, namely the nature or contents of these rights, has its conceptual source in the principles of domestic constitutional law embodied in the fundamental laws of various countries. Their historical and philosophical origins can, in turn, be traced back to such great milestones of human freedom as the American Declaration of Independence and the French Declaration of the Rights of Man and of the Citizen, among others. These instruments, and the national constitutions which inspired them, greatly influenced the contents of much of modern international human rights law. One cannot, for example, read Article 1 of the Universal Declaration of Human Rights, 'All human beings are born free and equal in dignity and rights', without recognizing the debt this formulation owes to the American and French Declarations and to the idea of human freedom they articulate.

The modern international human rights revolution begins with the adoption of the Charter of the United Nations.[2] While it is certainly true that international law recognized some forms of international human rights protection prior to the Charter, the process which ushered in 'the internationalization of human rights and the humanization of international law', as it has been characterized elsewhere,[3] begins with the establishment of the United Nations.[4] The result has been a worldwide movement in which states, intergovernmental and non-governmental organizations are the principal players in a continuing struggle concerning the role the international community should play in promoting and protecting human rights.

The idea that the protection of human rights knows no international boundaries, and that the international community has an obligation to ensure that governments guarantee and protect human rights wherever they may be violated, has gradually captured the imagination of mankind. The end of the Cold War has deideologized the struggle for human rights and reinforced the international human rights movement. Today, violators of human rights can no longer count on one or the other superpower to shield them from international condemnation, a practice which in the past had a very detrimental effect on the development and application of human rights law.

This is not to say that massive violations of human rights are no longer being committed, or that the international institutions designed to prevent such violations are all in place and working effectively. Many governments still violate human rights on a large scale and many more would prefer never to have to account for their actions. But the fact is that they are increasingly being forced by a variety of external and internal factors to answer for their behaviour to the international community. This reality limits their freedom of action, and in many, albeit not all, cases contributes to an improved human rights situation.

What we have here is a dynamic and continuing process which has its normative basis in the Charter of the United Nations. The Charter in turn has given rise to a vast body of international and regional human rights law and the establishment of numerous international institutions and mechanisms designed to promote and supervise its implementation. In this chapter we shall describe the evolution of this process, as well as the law and institutions it has produced. To do so we need to look first at some relevant historical antecedents of modern international human rights.

## Historical Antecedents

### The General Rule

Human beings as such had no rights under traditional international law, which was defined as the law which governed relations between states. The traditional definition was expanded somewhat after the First World War, when it came to be recognized that some newly created intergovernmental organizations could, in some limited circumstances, also enjoy rights under international law and, to that extent, be subjects of international law. Since individual human beings were not deemed to have any rights under traditional international law, they were said to be objects rather than subjects of that law. To the extent that states had any international legal obligations concerning the treatment of individuals, they were obligations owing to the states whose nationality the individuals possessed.[5]

These theories about the nature of international law had a number of consequences as far as individual human beings were concerned. First, it was for the state of the individual's nationality to protect him or her from acts by other states which violated international law. Individuals therefore depended on the states of their nationality to vindicate these rights on the international plane, because private persons had no standing to do so themselves. They also had no standing to compel their states to espouse these claims. Second, because only a state whose nationality the individual possessed could be considered aggrieved, a stateless person enjoyed no protection at all under traditional international law. Third, since individuals had no rights under traditional international law and enjoyed only such protection as the state of their nationality was willing to extend to them, they had no rights and no recourse on the international plane against abuses committed against them by their own governments. Finally, because the treatment by states of their own nationals was not a matter to which international law applied, the entire subject was deemed to fall within the domestic jurisdiction of each state, barring other states from interceding or intervening on their behalf.

As traditional international law evolved over time, it gradually expanded its reach by grafting some exceptions on the principles described above. These exceptions had their source in the international law doctrines and treaty arrangements to be discussed below. Although these exceptions did not nullify the basic rule that individuals as such were not subjects of international law and hence had no rights under that law, they did make international law applicable under certain circumstances to the manner in which governments treated human beings. Where that was so, the doctrine of non-intervention in the domestic jurisdiction of states could no longer be validly invoked to prevent diplomatic intercession or even action by other states.

*Special Rules and Regimes*

First, one of the early exceptions recognized by traditional international law had its legal basis in the doctrine of humanitarian intervention. Under this doctrine, which can be traced back to Hugo Grotius and other early international lawyers, the use of force by one or more states to stop the maltreatment by a state of its own nationals was deemed to be lawful when that conduct was so brutal and large-scale as to shock the conscience of mankind.[6] Although greatly misused in the past and frequently invoked as a mere pretext for the occupation or invasion of weaker countries,[7] this doctrine was the first to acknowledge some limits on the freedom states enjoyed under international law in dealing with their own nationals.[8] Contemporary arguments about the rights of international organizations or groups of states to use force, if necessary, to put an end to massive violations of human rights continue to be justified from time to time by reference to this doctrine.[9]

Second, it is a basic principle of international law that a state may limit its sovereignty by treaty and thus internationalize a subject which would otherwise not be regulated by international law. For example, if one state concludes a treaty with another state in which they agree to treat their respective nationals in a humane manner, they have to that extent internationalized that particular subject.[10] Between these two states, neither can henceforth lawfully assert that its treatment of its own nationals is a subject which falls exclusively within its domestic jurisdiction.[11] This principle has been extremely important in the development of international human rights law and the gradual internationalization of human rights.[12] Although the internationalization process continues to this day every time a human rights treaty enters into force, it began in the nineteenth century with the conclusion of treaties to ban the slave trade and to protect various minorities, particularly Christians, in the Ottoman Empire.[13] These agreements were relied upon by the states comprising the Concert of Europe to provide the legal basis for their diplomatic (and at times even military) interventions on behalf of the Christian populations in the Turkish Empire.[14]

Third, although the Covenant of the League of Nations, which established the League in 1920, did not deal with human rights as such, it contained two provisions (Articles 22 and 23) which anticipated some aspects of modern international human rights protection. The League also played an important role in supervising the implementation of post-First World War minorities treaties, which established another exception to the aforementioned general rule. Article 22 of the Covenant established the Mandates System of the League. Under this provision, the former colonies of the states which had lost the First World War were transformed into so-called 'Mandates' of the League and placed under the administration of various victorious powers. The latter agreed to administer these territories pursuant to ' ... the principle that the well-being and development of [the native] peoples form a sacred trust of civilization' and undertook to provide the League with annual reports bearing on the discharge of their responsibilities. These reports were reviewed by the Mandates Commission of the League. Although this body had no real power when first established, its authority to supervise the administration of the Mandates grew with time.[15] Had the Second World War not led to the demise of the League, the Mandates Commission might well have transformed itself into an important institution for the protection of the rights of the native populations in the mandated territories.[16] The reporting requirements found in many present-day human rights treaties hark back to the practice of the Mandates Commission.

The Member States of the League of Nations agreed in Article 23(a) of the League Covenant, 'subject to and in accordance with the provisions of international conventions existing or to be hereafter agreed upon', to 'endeavour to secure and maintain fair and humane conditions of labour for men, women and children, both in their own countries and in all countries to which their commercial and industrial relations extend'. Article 23 also envisaged the establishment of international organizations to promote this objective. That function was assumed by the International Labour Organisation (ILO), which came into being at about the same time as the League and immediately embarked on the task of drafting and promoting the adoption of treaties dealing with fair labour standards. The establishment of the ILO and the functions assigned to it foreshadow modern international human rights concerns with economic rights.

The League of Nations also played a very important role in developing an international system for the protection of minorities.[17] While this subject was not regulated by the Covenant, the League derived its powers in this field from a series of post-First World War treaties. That war produced a substantial redrawing of the political map of Europe and of the Middle East. A number of new states came into being and others regained their independence. Some of these countries, notably Albania, Bulgaria, Czechoslovakia, Hungary, Poland, Romania and Yugoslavia, included pockets of national, linguistic and religious minorities. These groups had good historical reasons to fear for their survival as minorities. The governments of the victorious nations – the so-called 'Principal Allied and Associated Powers'

– therefore required the new states to conclude special treaties for the protection of some of these minorities.[18]

The first treaty to establish this protective regime was the treaty between the Principal Allied and Associated Powers and Poland, signed at Versailles on 29 June 1919. It served as a model for those that followed. In these treaties, the states to which the minorities system applied undertook not to discriminate against members of the protected minorities and to grant them special rights necessary for the preservation of their national, religious or linguistic integrity, including the right to the official use of their languages, to maintain their schools and to practise their religions.

To ensure compliance, the treaties contained provisions similar to Article 12 of the Polish Treaty, which declared that 'Poland agrees that the stipulations in the foregoing articles, so far as they affect persons belonging to racial, religious or linguistic minorities, constitute obligations of international concern and shall be placed under the guarantee of the League of Nations.' The League of Nations agreed to serve as guarantor of the obligations the parties assumed in these treaties. It exercised that function by developing a system for dealing with petitions by minorities charging violations of their rights. That system was relatively effective and quite advanced for its time. The petitions were reviewed by a Committee of Three of the League Council, the states concerned were given an opportunity to present their views and, when appropriate, the Permanent Court of International Justice was asked to render advisory opinions on disputed questions of law.[19]

Although some isolated minorities arrangements of the League era survive to this day, the League's minorities system as such died with it. As we shall see, there has been a renewed interest in recent years in the protection of minorities.[20]

Fourth, traditional international law recognized very early in its development that states had an obligation to treat foreign nationals in conformity with certain minimum standards of civilization or justice. Since this obligation was owed to the state of the individual's nationality rather than to the individual victims, only the state of their nationality was considered to have a cause for action under international law against the offending state.[21] When damages were awarded, however, the successful state as a rule used these funds to compensate its nationals for the damages they had sustained, even though under international law it was free not to do so.[22]

The substantive law applicable to claims by states on behalf of their nationals was derived for the most part from so-called 'general principles of law recognized by civilized nations'.[23] These principles had their source in natural law and various domestic legal doctrines applicable to the treatment of individuals. International arbitrators and tribunals drew on this body of law and doctrine to give substance to concepts such as 'denial of justice', 'minimum standards of justice' and so on. When modern international law came to recognize that individuals, irrespective of their nationality, should enjoy certain basic human rights, the substantive principles of the law of state responsibility provided a reservoir of norms which could be drawn upon in codifying international human rights law. Today, because of the dramatic evolution and extensive codification of human rights law, human rights law nourishes the law of state responsibility.[24]

Fifth, although international humanitarian law can today be defined as the human rights component of the law of war, humanitarian law predates the emergence of international human rights law. Its modern development began with a series of Swiss initiatives undertaken in the nineteenth century.[25] They produced the Geneva Convention of 1864, which was designed to protect medical personnel, hospital installations and wounded or sick combatants. The Geneva Convention of 1864 was followed by the Hague Convention No. III of 1899, which established comparable humanitarian rules applicable to naval warfare. These treaties have been revised, amplified and modernized from time to time and now comprise a vast body of law applicable to almost all aspects of modern armed conflict. Much of that law is today codified in the four Geneva Conventions of 1949 and the two 1977 Additional Protocols to these Conventions.[26] Various provisions of these Protocols mirror the principles which are proclaimed in modern international human rights instruments,[27] while the derogation clauses of the principal human rights conventions incorporate by reference the obligations assumed by the States Parties in various humanitarian law treaties.[28] Thus, although humanitarian law is much older than modern international human rights law and influenced the latter, modern humanitarian law draws heavily on human rights law.

As we have seen in the preceding pages, traditional international law developed various doctrines and institutions which were designed to protect different groups or categories of human beings: minorities, certain native populations, foreign nationals, victims of massive violations, combatants and so on. That law, and the legal principles it gave rise to, laid the conceptual and institutional foundation for the development of modern international human rights law. What distinguished the latter from its precursors, however, is that modern international human rights law has gradually transformed the individual from a mere object of international law to a subject having international rights and obligations.

## Modern International Human Rights Law

The historical evolution of international human rights law over the past 50 years reveals an evolutionary process which can be divided into a number of stages.[29] It would be a mistake to assume, however, that each of these stages can be neatly separated from later or even earlier developments in this field. The fact is that there is considerable overlap between these stages. They are, however, useful guideposts when tracing the historical evolution of modern international human rights law.

### *The Normative Foundation*

The first stage in this process begins with the entry into force of the Charter of the United Nations and continues at least until the adoption in 1966 of the International Covenants on Human Rights. By this time, the Universal Declaration of Human Rights had been adopted by the United Nations, as had the Genocide Convention and the Convention on the Elimination of All Forms of Racial Discrimination, to mention only the principal human rights instruments. During this same period, the European Convention of Human Rights entered into force, the Organization of American States proclaimed the American Declaration of the Rights and Duties of Man, and UNESCO and the ILO, respectively, adopted the Convention against Discrimination in Education and the Convention concerning Discrimination in Respect of Employment and Occupation.

In short, this period witnessed the normative consolidation of international human rights law. It is true, of course, that this process continues to this day. It is equally true, however, that in these first 20 years following the establishment of the United Nations the process had become irreversible. Two very important factors explain this development. First, the human rights provisions of the Charter, supplemented by the Universal Declaration of Human Rights, and other human rights instruments, came to be accepted as defining the basic human rights obligations that the member states of the United Nations had accepted by ratifying the Charter. That is to say, while some states still argued in the early days of the United Nations that the Charter imposed no human rights obligations whatsoever on them, that view was no longer tenable by the end of the 1960s. Second, once it was acknowledged that the Charter, a multilateral treaty, had created some human rights obligations for the member states, it followed as a matter of international law that human rights had, to that extent, been internationalized and removed from the protective domain of a subject which is essentially within their domestic jurisdiction.[30]

It should now be asked how these development came about. The idea that the United Nations should become the international protector of the rights of the individual grew out of the tragic experience of the Second World War and the horrendous violations of human rights committed in the Holocaust. Many wartime leaders believed that the rise of Hitler could have been averted had there existed in the 1930s a strong international organization with authority to address human rights issues. To them, it was critical that the experience with the League of Nations, which was weak and lacked the power to deal with human rights issues, must not be repeated.[31]

One would therefore have expected the United Nations Charter to contain provisions establishing an effective international system for the protection of human rights. That did not happen because of opposition from the major powers: the United States, the Soviet Union, France and the United Kingdom. These states all had serious human rights problems of their own at the time,[32] and were therefore not prepared to agree to strong commitments in that area. Although various smaller countries favoured the inclusion of a bill of rights in the Charter, they lacked the political influence to prevail. That explains why the human rights provisions of the Charter, as adopted in San Francisco, were deliberately weak and vague.

The three major human rights provisions of the Charter are Articles 1(3), 55(c) and 56.[33] The first of these provisions recognizes that one of the 'purposes' of the United Nations is international cooperation in solving various international problems, including 'humanitarian' problems' and 'in promoting and encouraging respect for human rights and fundamental freedoms for all without distinctions as to race, sex, language or religion'. This provision is amplified by Article 55(c), which reads as follows:

> With a view to the creation of conditions of stability and well-being which are necessary for the peaceful and friendly relations among nations based on respect for the principles of equal rights and self-determination of peoples, the United Nations shall promote: ...
>
> (c) universal respect for, and observance of, human rights and fundamental freedoms for all without distinction as to race, sex, language, or religion.

Article 56 imposes the same obligations on member states by providing that 'all Members pledge themselves to take joint and separate action in co-operation with the Organization for the achievement of the purposes set forth in Article 55'.

These provisions did not establish an immediate obligation to guarantee or observe human rights, nor did they define what was meant by 'human rights and fundamental freedoms'. They imposed the much vaguer obligation to 'promote ... universal respect for, and the observance of, human rights' and to take 'joint and separate action in co-operation with the Organization' to achieve this purpose. The only unambiguous provision in these articles is the prohibition of discrimination.

Despite their vagueness, the human rights provisions of the Charter had a number of important consequences.[34] First, as we have already noted, the Charter internationalized the concept of human rights. This did not mean that, as soon as the Charter entered into force, all human rights issues were *ipso facto* no longer matters essentially within the domestic jurisdiction of states. It meant instead that states had assumed some international obligations relating to human rights, although their full scope remained to be defined, and that, as far as these obligations were concerned, the states could no longer claim that human rights as such were essentially domestic in character.

Second, the obligation of the member states of the United Nations to cooperate with the Organization in the promotion of human rights provided the United Nations with the requisite legal authority to undertake a massive effort to define and codify these rights. The foundation of this codification effort was laid by the proclamation in 1948 of the Universal Declaration of Human Rights. Adopted as a non-binding United Nations General Assembly resolution, the Declaration was designed, as its preamble indicates, to provide 'a common understanding' of the human rights and fundamental freedoms referred to in the Charter and to serve 'as a common standard of achievement for all peoples and all nations'. But the Declaration not only gave meaning to the phrase 'human rights and fundamental freedoms' used in the Charter, over time, it came to be accepted as a normative instrument in its own right which, together with the Charter, spelled out the human rights obligations incumbent upon all United Nations member states.[35]

The success of the United Nations' effort is reflected in the adoption of the International Bill of Rights[36] and in the vast number of international human rights instruments in existence today. The entry into force of each new treaty in this field has further internationalized the subject of human rights as between the parties to them. It has also endowed the individuals to whom these treaties apply with international legal rights. The state practice spawned by the vast network of human rights treaties continues to create a growing body of customary international law on the subject. Hence a definition of international law which did not today recognize the individual as the direct beneficiary of international human right law and, to that extent, a subject of international law, would be blind to current legal and political realities.

## Institution Building

The second stage in the evolution of international human rights law began in the late 1960s and continued for the next 15 to 20 years. This period might be denominated 'the era of institution building'. During these years we find two distinct developments taking place within the United Nations framework. The first focused on the nature of the human right obligations which Articles 55 and 56 created for member states. Only after this issue had been resolved could the United Nations begin to create institutions and mechanisms to enforce their obligations. From a strictly legal point of view, the answer to the question concerning the obligations of member states turned on the meaning of the phrase 'to promote ... universal respect for, and observance of, human rights and fundamental freedoms'.

It could certainly be argued that this provision did not require states at the time of their ratification of the Charter to stop any and all violations of human rights. It was much too vague for that. If this were true, how long could a state go on violating human rights before running afoul of the Charter, or were there at least some human rights violations which had to stop? It took the United Nations a long time to provide some clear answers to these questions. They were eventually provided and grew out of the United Nations' struggle to put an end to apartheid. Apartheid came gradually to be characterized as a pervasive violation of all basic human rights, a governmental policy implemented on a massive scale against a large segment of the population.[37] In this context, the meaning of the obligation expressed by the words 'to promote', regardless of how vague in the abstract, became concrete, in that a United Nations member state which embarked on or maintained such a policy could certainly not be deemed to be 'promoting human rights and fundamental freedoms' and was, therefore, in violation of its Charter obligations.

This principle was formally established with the adoption of ECOSOC resolution 1235 (XLII) of 6 June 1967. It authorized the United Nations Commission on Human Rights 'to make a thorough study of situations which reveal a consistent pattern of violations of human rights, as exemplified by the policy of apartheid as practised in the Republic of South Africa ... and racial discrimination as practised notably in Southern Rhodesia'. This resolution was followed by ECOSOC resolution 1503 (XLVIII) of 27 May 1970, which empowered the United Nations Sub-Commission on the Prevention of Discrimination and Protection of Minorities to develop a mechanism for dealing with communications from individuals and groups revealing 'a consistent pattern of gross and reliably attested violations of human rights'. The Sub-Commission and the Commission on

Human Rights implemented this resolution by establishing a procedure for dealing with such communications.

These two ECOSOC resolutions continue in force to this day and serve as the foundation of the United Nations Charter-based system for the protection of human rights. They have given birth to an ever-expanding institutional mechanism within the United Nations framework for dealing with large-scale human rights violations which embrace the mushrooming system of rapporteurs and special missions as well as the Office of the United Nations High Commissioner for Human Rights. All of these developments have their juridical basis in the Charter, complemented by the Universal Declaration of Human Rights. This Charter-based institutional framework, developed in the late 1960s to respond to the scourge of apartheid, has been used since the early 1980s to deal with all types of massive violations of human rights.[38]

The period here under consideration also saw the emergence and consolidation of universal and regional treaty-based institutions for the protection of human rights. In the mid-to-late 1970s, the United Nations Human Rights Committee[39] and the Committee on the Elimination of Racial Discrimination (CERD)[40] came into being with the entry into force of the International Covenant on Civil and Political Rights and the International Convention on the Elimination of All Forms of Racial Discrimination. The entry into force in 1978 of the American Convention on Human Rights brought with it the establishment of the Inter-American Commission and Court of Human Rights.[41] Although the European Convention of Human Rights came into effect as early as 1953, it was not until the late 1960s and early 1970s that the institutions it created, particularly the Court, began to play an important role in the implementation of the Convention.[42] In 1978, moreover, UNESCO adopted a special mechanism for dealing with human rights violations falling within its sphere of competence.[43] ILO institutions for dealing with human rights issues[44] predate those referred to above, whereas those established under the African Charter on Human and Peoples' Rights did not come into being until after the entry into force of that instrument in 1986.[45]

The establishment of these and related institutions also contributed to the emergence of non-governmental human rights organizations and laid the basis for their growing significance. Although some of these groups existed much earlier, their number and strength, and their activism, begin in this period.[46] The creation of the intergovernmental human rights institutions referred to above provided the non-governmental organizations with their *raison d'être* for filing human rights complaints and mounting human rights enforcement campaigns. In earlier times their principal role consisted in the promotion of normative instruments.

There are a number of interrelated political reasons for some of these developments. The end of the colonial era and the vast expansion which the United Nations underwent in the late 1950s and early 1960s resulted in the admission to the United Nations of many newly independent states committed to putting an end to apartheid. That could only be achieved by developing and strengthening United Nations mechanisms for dealing with this serious human rights problem. By supporting these steps as far as apartheid was concerned, the Soviet Union and its allies gave the Western democracies an opening to press for the expansion of the jurisdiction of these United Nations human rights institutions to embrace all massive violations of human rights, and not only apartheid.

These diverse efforts by the West, the East and the non-aligned nations focused a great deal of public attention on United Nations human rights activities which, in turn, produced worldwide expectations about the UN role and that of other international organizations in addressing human rights violations. Many states now find it increasingly difficult for political and propaganda reasons not to pay at least some lip service to international human rights efforts, making it harder for them to oppose the establishment of various international and regional human rights institutions. The entire subject gained in significance with President Jimmy Carter's widely proclaimed commitment to making human rights the centrepiece of US foreign policy and his willingness to act on this commitment. While it is open to debate how much the Carter administration actually achieved in improving the human rights situation in the world, it cannot be doubted that President Carter did succeed in placing human rights firmly and irrevocably on the international political agenda.

Human rights thus gained a political respectability as an important element in the contemporary *realpolitik* equation. By addressing an issue of genuine concern to peoples all over the world, the promotion of human rights had become a political force difficult for many governments to ignore. Ironically, the more each side of the ideological conflict and the non-aligned nations sought to exploit human rights for their own political ends, the more the idea about genuine international human rights protection captured the imagination of humankind, making many institutional developments in this field possible. And this despite the fact that a large number of governments would have preferred to keep human rights off the international agenda altogether.

## Implementation and the Post-Cold War World

The institutions referred to in the preceding section did not come fully into their own until the mid-to-late 1980s, when they could begin to focus on effective measures to ensure state compliance with their international obligations.[47] This process continues to this day. It is one thing to establish institutions on the international plane to promote and protect human rights; it is quite another to give them the tools to achieve their objective. Moreover, states are more likely to agree to the creation of human rights institutions than to cooperate with these institutions when such states or their allies are charged with human rights violations. It must be recognized, at the same time, that the political factors which permitted the creation of human rights institutions in the first place – the human rights movement inspired by the ideas which captured the imagination of mankind – make it increasingly difficult for many states not to comply with their human rights obligations.

During the period under consideration, the world underwent dramatic changes to which the human rights revolution contributed significantly and from which it also benefited significantly. The end of the Cold War freed many nations in Europe from communist rule, permitting them to embark on a process of democratic transformation. What is more, it liberated international efforts to promote human rights from the debilitating ideological conflicts and political sloganeering of the past. These developments have enabled the United Nations to focus increasingly on obstacles to the implementation of human rights.[48]

The end of the Cold War and its effect on human rights is reflected in part in the text of the 1993 Vienna Declaration and Programme of Action, adopted at the World Conference on Human Rights held in Vienna in June 1993.[49] The pervasive scope of the Declaration, evidenced by the fact that it addresses most, if not all, modern human rights concerns, is one of its striking features, as is the fact that it does so, on the whole, in a politically balanced and serious manner. While it does not come up with solutions to the many intractable problems facing the international community in this field, the Vienna Declaration identifies them and in the process demonstrates that there are few, if any, human rights issues today which are not of international concern. The catalogue embraces civil and political rights, economic, social and cultural rights, the right to development, the rights of refugees and internally displaced persons, humanitarian law issues, the rights of minorities and of indigenous peoples, the rights of women, the rights of the disabled, and so on. It is in this context that the statement in paragraph 4 of the Declaration that 'the promotion and protection of all human rights is a legitimate concern of the international community' gains its true significance. Put another way, the dividing line between domestic and international human rights issues is no more, not because this is what has been decreed by some super-legislature, but because it no longer has a factual or legal justification. Moreover – and this is much more important – the international community is today free to say so.

This same idea also finds expression in another, equally important, principle proclaimed in the Vienna Declaration. Paragraph 5 of that instrument declares:

> All human rights are universal, indivisible and interdependent and interrelated. The international community must treat human rights globally in a fair and equal manner, on the same footing, and with the same emphasis. While the significance of national and regional particularities and various historical, cultural and religious backgrounds must be borne in mind, it is the duty of States, regardless of their political, economic and cultural systems, to promote and protect all human rights and fundamental freedoms.

The recognition of the universal character of human rights and the concomitant rejection of cultural relativism, which has traditionally sought to justify violations of human rights by reference to some special religious or cultural imperatives, lay the foundation for global efforts to improve the human rights situation of all human beings.

Read together, paragraphs 4 and 5 of the Vienna Declaration do away with two major impediments to the implementation of human rights which prevented effective international action in the past: the artificial distinctions between domestic and international human rights concerns, on the one hand, and cultural relativism, on the other. The Vienna Declaration also addressed a third obstacle: the myth that all governments, whether democratic or not, can protect human rights and that a state's form of government could not be deemed to affect its compliance with international human rights standards. This legal and political fiction, another product of the Cold War, forced the international community for decades to close its eyes to massive human rights violations having their source in political systems antithetical to the protection of human rights and the rule of law. In paragraph 8, the Vienna Declaration put this myth to rest by proclaiming that 'democracy, development and respect for human rights and fundamental freedoms are interdependent and mutually reinforcing'. This provision declares further that 'democracy is based on the freely expressed will of the people to determine their own political, economic, social and cultural systems and their full participation in all aspects of their lives'. Paragraph 8 concludes by urging the international community to 'support the strengthening and promoting of democracy, development and respect for human rights and fundamental freedoms in the entire world'.

The notion that genuine democracy and the protection of human rights go together, a concept that could not have been proclaimed during the Cold War, found expression earlier in the East–West context with the adoption in 1990 of the Copenhagen Concluding Document of the Conference on Security and Co-operation in Europe. Whereas this document laid the foundation for the establishment of a democratic European public order,[50] the Vienna Declaration can be read to have done the same for the world as a whole. This is not to say that all nations of the world have now become democracies, or even that they are close to this goal. Unfortunately for the enjoyment of human rights, neither is the case as yet. It does mean, however, that the absence of democracy in a state is today in itself a violation of the human rights of its population and that the international community has the right for that very reason to concern itself with efforts designed to remove obstacles to its democratization.[51]

While the removal of these political myths and legal fictions has enabled the international community to focus more realistically on the task of getting governments to comply with their international human rights obligations, genuine progress in this area will be slow. Today it is increasingly recognized that the task is a very difficult one, even with the best intentions of governments. The underlying causes of many human rights violations are deep-rooted. They cannot be overcome by governmental decrees alone. Poverty, corruption, disease, lack of educational resources, economic and political under-development, and so on are but a few factors which contribute to violations of human rights, and these are problems that cannot be solved overnight. Solutions often cannot be obtained without financial and human resources which are scarce and require international cooperation. The fact that various international lending institutions, such as the World Bank and some regional development banks, have begun to channel some of their resources into efforts to develop and strengthen national institutions capable of promoting the rule of law in the administration of justice, democratic pluralism and a higher standard of education, in addition to higher standards of living, is an important step in the process of implementing human rights. It would be a mistake not to recognize, however, that this will be a long and arduous process.

In some regions of the world, considerable progress has neverthe-less been made as far as the implementation of human rights is concerned. During the period under consideration here, the human rights system established under the European Convention of Human Rights gained institutional maturity. In fact, by the time the Soviet Union collapsed, the European Court of Human Rights had for all practical purposes become the constitutional court of Western Europe. The recent accession of most of the former Eastern and Central European allies of the Soviet Union to the European Convention has the potential of transforming the Court into the constitutional court of all Europe. This process may take longer, however, than one might

assume at first glance because these newer members face many political, economic and social problems[52] of a type and seriousness few,
if any, of the Western European members confronted when they first
joined the Convention system.

The inter-American human rights system, which came into being
later than its European counterpart, was unable for many years to
play a major role in improving the human rights situation in the
Americas. For decades the region was in the grips of oppressive
regimes which engaged in massive violations of human rights behind a veil of impunity sustained at the height of the Cold War by
super-power protection. With the onset of the process of transition to
democracy in that region, which began in the mid-1980s, the inter-
American human rights system could at last focus on implementation.
The judgments of the Inter-American Court of Human Rights in the
late 1980s, exposing the heinous practice of disappearances for all
the world to see,[53] opened the way for the Court and the Inter-
American Commission on Human Rights to play a much more active
role in protecting human rights in the Americas. Unlike Western
Europe, however, the Americas is a region which is still very much in
the process of development, with serious social and economic problems, poverty and corruption. In some countries, moreover, the
military may no longer be in power, but it is still a real force to be
reckoned with. In short, transition to democracy has a long way to go
in the region, which is not to say that there has not been impressive
progress in the past few years. When all is said and done, the assumption of many human rights activists in the 1960s and 1970s that
the only obstacles to the effective protection of human rights and
genuine democracy in the region were oppressive military regimes
has been only partially borne out by the experience of the last ten
years. It is probably true, however, that the process is now on the
whole irreversible and that, while the human rights problems of the
region cannot be solved by merely substituting a freely elected government for a military regime, the inter-American human rights
system has in recent years been able to point to some real successes.[54]

The same cannot as yet be said of the African human rights system, which still faces many of the problems which afflicted the
inter-American system two decades ago as far as repressive regimes
are concerned. It faces even greater economic, social and political
obstacles. The poverty, corruption, underdevelopment, disease, tribal
conflicts and many other scourges which affect African society today
make the task of the African Commission on Human and Peoples'
Rights extremely difficult. The liberation of South Africa from apartheid – in itself probably the greatest victory to date of the human
rights revolution – and that country's emergence as the foremost
democratic nation of Africa, as well as the promising trends towards

democracy in the region, cannot in the long run but strengthen the role of the African Commission.

The African Commission, the human rights organs of the inter-American system and the treaty bodies established within the United Nations framework all suffer from a very serious lack of financial resources. This fact has very harmful consequences for their ability to discharge their responsibilities. The real tragedy here is that, at precisely the moment in history when conditions are on the whole more favourable than ever for the implementation of human rights at the global and regional levels, the institutions assigned to the task of promoting and supervising this process are not able to do so satisfactorily for financial reasons. In this connection, it must be kept in mind that, while resources are scarce everywhere, the real reasons for at least some budget-cutting activities affecting human rights bodies have more to do with a desire of some governments to limit the power of these institutions than with genuine budgetary concerns. Given the current human rights revolution, it is today politically easier to cut the budget of a human rights body by pointing to a lack of funds than to suggest that its activities are not important. Some of the financial problems facing human rights institutions can certainly be attributed to these political machinations.

*Individual Responsibility, Minority Rights and Collective Humanitarian Intervention*

International human rights law has traditionally focused on the responsibility of governments, rather than that of individuals, for violations of human rights. The assumption here was that governments have a duty not only not to violate human rights, but also to control all activities taking place within their territory, to punish human rights violations and to ensure that its own officials do not violate human rights. Although the war crimes trials following the Second World War, the Geneva Conventions on humanitarian law, and some international human rights treaties, notably the Genocide Convention, established individual international criminal responsibility for some of the most egregious violations of human rights, including genocide, crimes against humanity and war crimes,[55] international human rights law and efforts to enforce it have for the most part focused on the behaviour and obligations of governments.

This focus has shifted to some extent in recent years. For one thing, it has become increasingly clear that some governments are simply not able to protect those within their jurisdiction from violations of human rights committed by powerful groups within the state. This has been true of terrorist groups, criminal organizations and, in certain countries, the military establishment and its allies operating outside the sphere of civilian control. Here the watchword is impunity; that is, individuals belonging to these groups have in certain countries been able to commit large-scale violations of human rights while enjoying a *de facto* immunity from prosecution for what, in theory at least, are criminal acts under the law of the state where these acts are committed. It is obvious, therefore, that potential violators will not be deterred from engaging in massive human rights abuses if they know that they will always enjoy domestic impunity and that, at most, only the state will be held internationally responsible for their acts.

These realities are increasingly forcing the international community to explore ways, not only to hold the state responsible, but also to act directly against individuals the state is too weak or unwilling to punish. While various principles of international criminal law have theoretically always permitted the imposition of individual responsibility for international crimes, including some grave violations of human rights, no international tribunals with jurisdiction to apply that law have existed in the decades since the Nuremberg and Tokyo War Crimes Tribunals were dissolved. This situation has changed in the past few years with the establishment by the United Nations of the International Tribunal for the Former Yugoslavia and the International Tribunal for Rwanda, with jurisdiction over crimes against humanity, genocide and war crimes committed in those territories.[56] The United Nations is now also in the process of establishing a permanent international criminal court. Moreover, some international investigatory bodies, such as the United Nations Truth Commission for El Salvador,[57] while not international tribunals with criminal jurisdiction, are being created in large measure to pierce national veils of impunity and to fix individual responsibility. The international community is also beginning to develop legal doctrines which would bar governments from granting amnesties to gross violators of human rights, a practice that has tended to be imposed on weak governments by military regimes or other powerful groups before turning over power to civilian authorities.

These responses to new international realities, while still in a formative stage, suggest that the concept of international responsibility for massive violations of human rights is expanding to include individuals and groups in addition to governments. If individuals are deemed to have ever greater rights under the international law of human rights, it makes sense to impose corresponding duties on them not to violate those rights and to hold them internationally responsible for the violation of internationally protected human rights. This approach may in the long run serve as a greater deterrent against human rights violations than the imposition of economic sanctions against a state whose government may either have been powerless at a given time to prevent the violations or have come into power subsequent to their commission.

The international law concepts of state continuity and state responsibility, while valid principles, can in today's world have unjust consequences. They may force newly elected governments of impoverished countries to pay compensation for human rights violations committed by their repressive predecessors, without giving them the international support, tools and remedies to make it possible for the responsible individuals to be held internationally liable for their misdeeds. In the absence of such remedies, a newly established democratic government, with economic resources seriously depleted by an oppressive regime, may be made to pay compensation for the human rights violations committed by that regime while its former leaders – those responsible for the violations – live in luxury, frequently abroad, and thus go unpunished. An effective international system to hold these individuals personally liable as a matter of international law and bar domestic amnesties granted under duress would go a long way to deter human rights violations and to ensure a more just approach to this entire problem. The fact that the international community is today moving in this direction is a welcome development.

In recent years we have also seen a renewed interest by the international community in the establishment of international norms and institutions for the protection of the rights of individuals belonging to national, racial, ethnic, linguistic or religious minorities. Here it is worth recalling that the United Nations Charter contains a broad non-discrimination clause but makes no reference to minority rights as such. The same is true of the Universal Declaration of Human Rights, which does, however, contain an equal protection clause[58] as well as a non-discrimination provision which is more extensive in scope than that of the Charter.[59] The International Covenant on Civil and Political Rights, adopted in 1966, contains one rather general provision on the subject.[60] It is true, of course, that, to the extent that the Genocide Convention criminalizes acts designed to eradicate national, ethical, racial or religious groups as such, it can be characterized as an instrument for the protection of the rights of minorities, albeit one which is very limited in scope.[61] On the whole, however, there was relatively little interest in the international community during the formative years of the United Nations and other post-Second World War international and regional organizations in the establishment of international systems for the protection of the rights of minorities. The absence of an appropriate clause on this subject in the United Nations Charter can be attributed, in part at least, to the opposition of some Eastern and Central European nations. These countries believed that various irredentist movements in the 1930s, which had been encouraged by Hitler and his allies, had their source in the League of Nations minorities system. Whether true or not, the omission of any reference to minorities in the United Nations Charter and the Universal Declaration is related to these sentiments.[62]

The break-up of the Soviet empire, the inhuman policies of 'ethnic cleansing' accompanying the dissolution of the former Yugoslavia and the threats of similar practices in other parts of the world have again focused international attention on the need for the international protection of minorities. Efforts to lay the normative foundation for a system which would accomplish this objective have been initiated in the United Nations with the adoption by the General Assembly of the 1992 Declaration on the Rights of Persons Belonging to National or Ethnic, Religious and Linguistic Minorities;[63] in the Council of Europe, with the adoption in 1994 of the Framework Convention for the Protection of National Minorities;[64] and in the framework of the Organization on Security and Co-operation in Europe (OSCE), with the 1990 Copenhagen Concluding Document and a number of later OSCE instruments on the subject, followed in 1992 by the establishment of the Office of the OSCE High Commissioner for National Minorities.[65]

Considering that we live in a world in which extreme nationalism and various forms or racial, ethnic and religious intolerance are on the rise, it is safe to predict that international efforts to protect minorities will increasingly occupy the attention of the international community and result in greater legislative and institutional activities in this area. We may thus be coming full circle from the minorities system established by the League of Nations, its abandonment by the founders of the United Nations, to the realization that current international realities require a revival of the ideas which gave rise to the League system, and the promulgation of a new body of international human rights law on the subject.

The United Nations Security Council is today also increasingly taking action to deal with large-scale human rights violations by authorizing enforcement measures under the powers that Chapter VII of the United Nations Charter confers on it. This chapter applies to situations determined by the Security Council to constitute a 'threat to the peace, breach of the peace, or act of aggression'.[66] Such action has been taken by the Security Council in some of its decisions relating to the Kurds in Iraq, to Somalia and to the former Yugoslavia and Haiti, among others. While it is still too early to assert that these and related cases have now firmly established the principle that massive violations of human rights will be deemed by the Security Council to constitute a sufficient legal basis for action under Chapter VII, it is clear that the Security Council is moving in that direction.[67] What we are seeing here is the emergence of a modern version of collective humanitarian intervention which has its basis in the convergence of two important developments: the growing power of the Security Council in the post-Cold War era and the increasing unwillingness of the international community to tolerate massive violations of human rights. Only time will tell whether this ultimate weapon of the international community for dealing with truly egregious violations of human rights will in fact be used to advance the cause of human rights rather than some extraneous political objectives, a practice which brought the old doctrine of humanitarian intervention into bad repute.

### Conclusion

Over the last 50 years, the individual human being has gradually acquired an increasing number of internationally recognized human rights and obligations. Human beings have to this extent become subjects of international law in their own right. This development gives meaning to the proposition that the last half-century has witnessed the internationalization of human rights and the humanization of international law. What we have here is a still evolving process which began with the adoption of the United Nations Charter and continues to this day with the developments described in the preceding pages.

The past 50 years have also seen a vast expansion of the meaning of international human rights. It began with basic civil and political rights, on the one hand, and economic, social and cultural rights, on the other, and continues to evolve into a greatly enlarged catalogue of new or related rights. Moreover, the international law concept of domestic jurisdiction which, in the past, shielded oppressive governments against international condemnation, has become an anachronism lacking current significance as far as the promotion of human rights is concerned. One need only compare the contents of the Universal Declaration of Human Rights with that of the 1993 Vienna Declaration and Plan of Action to recognize the dramatic conceptual changes which have taken place in the international human rights field. It is today also clear that democratic pluralism as a form of government is rapidly becoming a basic principle of the public order to which the international community aspires. What started out as a half-hearted effort to pay propagandistic lip service to the concept of human rights has gradually produced a world movement of great political significance.

Of course, there is still a wide chasm between proclamations of lofty principles and genuine observance of human rights in many parts of the world. None of this should surprise, considering the problems many countries face and the obstacles which must be overcome in order to translate international norms into real safe-guards against violations of human rights in general and in specific regions in particular. In short, the normative and institutional achieve-ments in the field of human rights should not blind us to the fact that the effective implementation of human rights takes time and vast resources and that, while it is possible by government fiat to put an end to some violations of human rights, this is not true of many serious abuses endemic to certain societies, regions or countries. It is nevertheless undeniable that the international community is taking important steps in the right direction as far as implementation is concerned, and that it has had some notable successes. The end of apartheid, the demise of the Soviet empire, and the process of transi-tion to democracy which has been set in motion in a number of regions of the world, while not attributable exclusively to the human rights revolution, would certainly not have taken place without it.

Recent efforts by the international community to hold individuals, and not only states, internationally responsible for human rights violations, and the new emphasis on the protection of the rights of minorities, are a welcome development, as is the role the Security Council is beginning to play under Chapter VII of the United Na-tions Charter in dealing with massive violations of human rights. The same is true of the involvement of international lending institu-tions in the task of promoting human rights. These and some other recent activities which space did not permit us to explore fully in this chapter all point to a genuine maturing of the international commu-nity's approach to human rights.

## Notes

1 On this subject generally, see H. Hamburger, 'Droits de l'homme et relations internationales', *Recueil des Cours*, 97, 1959, 293; F. Hartung, *Die Entwicklung der Menschen- und Bürgerrechte von 1776 bis zur Gegenwart*, 2nd edn, Berlin, Musterschmidt, 1954. See also H. Gros Espiell (1988, p.65), in which the author describes the history of human rights in Latin America.
2 L.B. Sohn, 'The new international law: protection of the rights of individuals rather than States', *American University Law Review*, 32, (1), 1982.
3 T. Buergenthal, 'Human rights: a challenge for the universities', *UNESCO Cou-rier*, 31, (25), October 1978, 28.
4 Scholarly efforts to develop an international law of human rights predates the UN Charter by many years. See, for example, M. Mandelstramm 'La Declara-tion des droits internationaux de l'homme', *Revue de droit international*, 5, (59), 1930; B. Scott, 'La Declaration internationale des droits de l'homme', ibid., 79. See also L.B. Sohn, 'How American international lawyers prepared for the San Francisco Bill of Rights', *American Journal of International Law*, 89, 1995, 540.
5 See, for example, L. Oppenheim, *International Law: A Treatise*, Vol. 1, 2nd edn, London, Longmans, Green and Co., 1912, p.362.
6 See A. Rougier, *'La théorie de l'intervention d'humanité'*, R.G.D.I.P., 17, 1910, 468;

E.C. Stowell, *Intervention in International Law*, Washington, DC, 1921, p.53; Sohn and Buergenthal (1973, p.137).

7   Ian Brownlie, 'Humanitarian intervention', in J.N. Moore (ed.), *Law and Civil War in the Modern World*, Baltimore, Johns Hopkins University Press, 1974, p.217.

8   See generally F.R. Teson, *Humanitarian Intervention: An Inquiry Into Law and Morality*, Dobbs Ferry, New York, Transnational Publishers, 1988.

9   See, for example, R. Lillich, 'Intervention to protect human rights', *McGill Law Journal*, **15**, 1969, 205. But see T.M. Franck and N. Rodley, 'After Bangladesh: the law of humanitarian intervention by military force', *American Journal of International Law*, **67**, 1973, 275, who question the soundness of this argument as far as unilateral military action by individual states is concerned.

10   See L. Henkin, 'Human rights and "domestic jurisdiction"', in T. Buergenthal (ed.), *Human Rights, International Law and the Helsinki Accord*, Montclair Allanheld, Osmun and Co., 1977, p.21.

11   'Advisory Opinion on Nationality Decrees Issued in Tunis and Morocco', P.C.I.J., ser. B, no. 4, 1923.

12   T. Buergenthal, 'Domestic jurisdiction, intervention and human rights', in P. Brown and D. MacLean (eds), *Human Rights and U.S. Foreign Policy*, Lexington, Massachusetts, Heath, 1979, p. 111.

13   See, for example, Treaty of Paris of 30 March 1856; Treaty of Berlin of 13 July 1878.

14   See Sohn and Buergenthal (1973, pp.143–92).

15   See generally ibid., pp.337–73.

16   After the Second World War, the UN Trusteeship System was given supervisory powers over the remaining Mandates and other non-self-governing territories. Among the last of these territories to gain independence (in 1990) was Namibia. It had been administered by South Africa under the South-West Africa Mandate. South Africa had for many years refused to comply with UN General Assembly and Security Council Resolutions calling on it to relinquish control over Namibia. The bitter dispute between the United Nations and South Africa concerning Namibia generated considerable litigation before the International Court of Justice. For an analysis of these cases and the relevant resolutions, see L.B. Sohn, *Rights in Conflict: The United Nations and South Africa*, New York, Transnational Publications, 1994, pp.24–31, 148–9. See also Egon Schwelb, 'The International Court of Justice and the human rights clauses of the Charter', *American Journal of International Law*, **66**, 1972, 337.

17   See generally Sohn and Buergenthal (1973, p.213).

18   See generally H. Hannum, *Autonomy, Sovereignty and Self-Determination: The Accommodation of Conflicting Rights*, Philadelphia, University of Pennsylvania Press, 1990; rev. edn, 1995, p.51.

19   See generally J. Stone, *International Guarantees of Minority Rights: Procedure of the Council of the League of Nations in Theory and Practice*, London, H. Milford, Oxford University Press, 1932.

20   See below, 'Individual Responsibility, Minority Rights and Collective Humanitarian Intervention'.

21   'Mavrommatis Palestine Concessions (Jurisdiction)', P.C.I.J., ser. A, no. 2, 1934.

22   For the relevant legal doctrines, see E.M. Borchard, *The Diplomatic Protection of Citizens Abroad or the Law of International Claims*, New York, 1916; Chittharanjan Felix Amerasinghe, *State Responsibility for Injuries to Aliens*, Oxford, Clarendon Press, 1967.

23   See I.C.J. Statute, Article 38 (1)(c).

24   Here it should be noted, as the *Restatement of the Foreign Relations Law of the United States (Third)* (1987) puts it, that 'the difference in history and in juris-

prudential origins between the older law of responsibility for injury to aliens and the newer law of human rights should not conceal their essential affinity and their convergence' (Introductory Note to Part VII, Vol. 2, p.145). The *Restatement* goes on to point out that, 'as the law of human rights developed, the law of responsibility for injury to aliens, as applied to natural persons, began to refer to violations of their "fundamental human rights", and States began to invoke contemporary norms of human rights as the basis for claims for injury to their nationals' (ibid., p.1058). See generally F.V. Garcia-Amador, L.B. Sohn and R. Baxter, *Recent Codification of the Law of State Responsibility for Injuries to Aliens*, Dobbs Ferry, New York, Oceana, 1974.

25 See P. Boissier, *History of the International Committee of the Red Cross: From Solferino to Tsushima*, Geneva, Henry Dunant Institute, 1985.

26 See Yoram Dinstein, 'Human rights in armed conflict: international humanitarian law', in T. Meron (ed.), *Human Rights in International Law: Legal and Policy Issues*, Oxford, Clarendon Press, 1984, p.345; M. Bothe, K.J. Partsch and W. Solf, *New Rules for Victims of Armed Conflicts: A Commentary on the Two 1977 Protocols Additional to the Geneva Conventions of 1949*, The Hague, Martinus Nijhoff Publishers, 1982.

27 See generally T. Meron, *Human Rights and Humanitarian Norms as Customary Law*, Oxford, Clarendon Press, 1989.

28 See International Covenant on Civil and Political Rights, Article 4; European Convention of Human Rights, Article 15; American Convention on Human Rights, Article 27. See also, T. Meron, *Human Rights in Internal Strife: Their International Protection*, Cambridge, Grotius Publications, Cambridge University Press, 1987, p.23.

29 On this subject generally, see Nikken (1987).

30 Although Article 2(7) of the Charter, which deals with non-intervention in matters that are essentially within the domestic jurisdiction of states, was frequently invoked in the early days of the UN by some states seeking to limit UN discussion of human rights cases, this provision has gradually faded away as a major obstacle to UN consideration of human rights issues. (See Henkin, 1990, p. 51.) See also F. Ermacora, 'Human rights and domestic jurisdiction (Article 2(7) of the Charter)' *Recueil des Cours*, 124, 1968, 371.

31 As early as 1941, President Franklin D. Roosevelt, in his famous 'Four Freedoms' speech, called for 'a world founded upon four essential freedoms'. These he identified as freedom of speech and expression, freedom for every person to worship God in his own way, freedom from want, and freedom from fear. Roosevelt's vision of 'the moral order', as he characterized it, became the clarion call of the nations that fought the Axis in the Second World War. See A.N. Holcombe, *Human Rights in the Modern World*, New York, New York University Press, 1948, pp.4–5; L.B. Sohn, 'The Human Rights Movement: From Roosevelt's Four Freedoms to the Interdependence of Peace, Development and Human Rights', Harvard Law School Human Rights Program, Edward A. Smith Lecture, 1995.

32 The United States still had *de jure* racial discrimination, the Soviet Union its Gulag, and France and the UK their colonies.

33 For the drafting history of these provisions, see, J. Robinson, *Human Rights and Fundamental Freedoms in the Charter of the United Nations: A Commentary*, New York, Institute of Jewish Affairs of the American Jewish Congress and World Jewish Congress, 1946; L.B. Sohn, 'A short history of United Nations documents on human rights', in *The United Nations and Human Rights*, pp.39, 43–59 (18th Report of the Commission to Study the Organization of Peace, 1968).

34 For the relevant UN practice under these two provisions, see B. Simma (ed.) *The Charter of the United Nations: A Commentary*, Oxford, Oxford University

Press, 1994, pp.776–95. See also J.P. Cot and A. Pellet, *La Charte des Nations Unies*, 2nd edn, Paris, Economica, 1991, pp.865–93; H. Hannum, 'Human rights', in O. Schachter and C. Joyner (eds), *United Nations Legal Order*, Vol. 1, Cambridge, Cambridge University Press, 1995, p.319.

35   For the different theories which explain the normative status of the Universal Declaration, see L.B. Sohn, 'The new international law: protection of the rights of individuals rather than states', *American University Law Review*, **32**, (1), 1982, 16–17; P. Alston and B. Simma, 'The source of human rights law: custom, *jus cogens* and general principles', *Australian Year Book of International Law*, **12**, 1992, 82; T. Buergenthal, *International Human Rights in A Nutshell*, 2nd edn, Saint Paul, West Publishing, 1995, p.33.

36   The International Bill of Rights consists of the Universal Declaration of Human Rights and the International Covenants on Human Rights. On this subject generally, see T. Buergenthal, *supra*, note 35, p.28.

37   See generally L.B. Sohn (1994).

38   See H. Tolley, Jr., *The U.N. Commission on Human Rights*, Boulder, Westview Press, 1987; P. Alston, 'The Commission on Human Rights', in P. Alston, *The United Nations and Human Rights: A Critical Appraisal*, New York, Oxford University Press, 1992, pp. 126, 138; A. Eide, 'The Sub-Commission on Prevention of Discrimination and Protection of Minorities', in P. Alston, *supra*, p.211.

39   D. McGoldrick, *The Human Rights Committee: Its Role in the Development of the International Covenant on Civil and Political Rights*, Oxford, Clarendon Press, 1994; M. Nowak, *UNO-Pakt über bürgerliche und politische Rechte und Fakultativprotokoll: CCPR-Kommentar*, Kehl, N.P. Engel, 1989.

40   K.J. Partsch, 'The Committee on the Elimination of Racial Discrimination,' in P. Alston, *supra*, note 38, p.339.

41   Although it is true that an Inter-American Commission on Human Rights was established by the Organization of American States in 1960, that body did not begin to play a significant role until the mid to late-1960s. See T. Buergenthal, 'The inter-American system for the protection of human rights', in Meron (1984, p.438); T. Buergenthal (1995, p.174).

42   On the European Convention of Human Rights, see generally Frowein and Peukert (1985); Macdonald *et al.* (1993). See also J.G. Merrills, *The Development of International Law by the European Court of Human Rights*, New York, Cambridge University Press, 1988.

43   UNESCO Doc. 104 EX/Decision 3.3, 1978. On this subject, see P. Alston, 'UNESCO's procedure for dealing with human rights violations', *Santa Clara Law Revue*, **20**, 1980, 665.

44   See generally F. Wolf, 'Human rights and the International Labour Organisation', in Meron (1984, p.273).

45   See C. Flinterman and E.A. Ankumah, 'The African Charter on Human and Peoples' Rights', in Hannum (1992, p. 152); U.O. Umozurike, 'Six years of the African Commission on Human and Peoples' Rights', in U. Beyerlin *et al.* (eds), *Recht zwischen Umbruch und Bewahrung (Festschrift für Rudolf Bernhard)*, Berlin, Springer, 1995, p.635.

46   See T. Buergenthal, note 41, (1984, p.318).

47   For a most useful assessment of this subject within the UN framework, see the individual articles on different UN institutions in P. Alston, *supra*, note 38.

48   For a much more sceptical view of this subject, see D.P. Forsythe, 'Human rights after the Cold War', *Netherlands Quarterly of Human Rights*, **11**, 1993, 393.

49   UN Secretary-General, *Report of the World Conference on Human Rights*, UN Doc. A/Conf. 157/24, 1993. See also A.A. Cancado Trindade, 'Memoria da Conferencia Mundial de Direitos Humanos (Vienna, 1993)', *Boletim da Sociedade Brasileira de Direito Internacional*, 87/90, 1993, 9.

50 T. Buergenthal, 'The CSCE rights system', *George Washington Journal of International Law and Economics*, **25**, 1993, 333, 355–6.
51 On this subject generally, see T.M. Franck, 'The emerging right to democratic governance', *American Journal of International Law*, **86**, 1992, 46.
52 See Menno T. Kamminga, 'Is the European Convention of Human Rights sufficiently equipped to cope with gross and systematic violations?', *Netherlands Quarterly on Human Rights*, **12**, 1994, 153.
53 See, for example, *Velasquez Rodriguez v. Honduras (Merits)*, Inter-American Court of Human Rights, Ser. C: Decisions and Judgments, No. 4, 1988. See also H. Gros Espiell, 'Los métodos de interpretación utilizados por la Corte Interamericana de Derechos Humanos en su jurisprudencia contenciosa', in *La Corte y el Sistema Interamericano de Derechos Humanos*, San José, Costa Rica, Instituto Interamericano de Derechos Humanos, 1994, p.223.
54 See generally Buergenthal and Shelton (1995).
55 On this subject generally, see Y. Dinstein, 'International humanitarian law', in I. Cotler and F.P. Eliadis (eds), *International Human Rights Law: Theory and Practice*, Montreal, Canadian Human Rights Foundation, 1992, p.203; M. Cherif Bassiouni, *Crimes Against Humanity in International Criminal Law*, Dordrecht, Martinus Nijhoff Publishers, 1992; T. Meron, 'War crimes in Yugoslavia and the development of international law', *American Journal of International Law*, **88**, 1994, 78.
56 T. Meron, 'International criminalization of internal atrocities', *American Journal of International Law*, **89**, 1995, 554.
57 T. Buergenthal, 'The United Nations Truth Commission for El Salvador', *Vanderbilt Journal of Transnational Law*, **27**, 1994, 497. See also UN Security Council Res. 1012 of 28 August 1995, mandating the Secretary-General to establish a special commission of enquiry for Burundi with broad investigatory and quasi-judicial powers.
58 Universal Declaration of Human Rights, Article 7.
59 Compare Article 2 of the Universal Declaration of Human Rights with Articles 1(3) and 55(c) of the UN Charter.
60 International Covenant on Civil and Political Rights, Article 27. It reads as follows: 'In those States in which ethnic, religious or linguistic minorities exist, persons belonging to such minorities shall not be denied the right, in community with the other members of their group, to enjoy their own culture, to profess and practise their own religion, or to use their own language.' For an analysis of this provision, see L.B. Sohn, 'The rights of minorities', in L. Henkin (ed.), *The International Bill of Rights: The Covenant on Civil and Political Rights*, New York, Columbia University Press, 1981, p.270.
61 Y. Dinstein, 'Collective human rights of peoples and minorities', *International and Comparative Law Quarterly*, **25**, 1976, 102, 105.
62 See H. Lauterpacht, *International Law and Human Rights*, New York, Praeger, 1950, p.424; H. Hannum, *supra*, note 18, pp.56–7.
63 UN General Assembly Res. 47/135 of 18 December 1992. See generally P. Thornberry, 'The UN Declaration: background, analysis and observations', in A. Phillips and A. Rosas (eds), *The UN Minority Rights Declaration*, Turku/Åbo, Åbo Akademi Univ., 1993, p.11.
64 Council of Europe, Doc. H., 1994. See H. Klebes, 'The Council of Europe's Framework Convention for the Protection of National Minorities', *Human Rights Law Journal*, **16**, 1995, 92. See also D. Thürer, 'Region und Minderheitenschutz – Aufbauelemente einer europäischen Architektur?', in U. Beyerlin *et al.*, *supra*, note 45, p.337.
65 See D. Chigas, 'Bridging the gap between theory and practice: the CSCE High Commissioner on National Minorities', *Helsinki Monitor*, **5**, 1994, 27; Buergenthal (1995, p.170).

66 UN Charter, Article 39.
67 J. Delbrück, 'A more effective international law or new world law? Some aspects of the development of international law in a changing international system', *Index to Legal Periodicals*, **68**, 1993, 705, 707; R. Higgins, *Problems and Process: International Law and How We Use It*, Oxford, Clarendon Press, 1994, p.254.

## Bibliography

Alston, P. (1990), *The United Nations and Human Rights: A Critical Appraisal*, New York, Oxford University Press.

Buergenthal, T. (1995), *International Human Rights in a Nutshell*, 2nd edn, Saint Paul, Minnesota, West Publishing Co.

Buergenthal, T. and D. Shelton (1995), *Protecting Human Rights in the Americas: Cases and Materials*, 4th edn, Kehl/Strasbourg/Arlington, N.P. Engel.

Buergenthal, T., C. Grossman and P. Nikken (eds) (1990), *Manual Internacional de Derechos Humanos*, San José, Costa Rica, Instituto Interamericano de Derechos Humanos.

Cançado Trindade, A.A. (ed.) (1994, 1995) *Estudios Basicos de Derechos Humanos*, Vol. 1 and Vol. 2, San José, Costa Rica, Instituto Interamericano de Derechos Humanos.

Cohen-Jonathan, G. (1989), *La Convention européenne des droits de l'homme*, Paris, Economica.

Frowein, J. and W. Peukert (1985), *Europäische Menschenrechts Konvention: EMRK-Kommentar*, Kehl, N.P. Engel.

Gros Espiell, H. (1985, 1988), *Estudios sobre Derechos Humanos*, Vol. 1, Caracas, Editorial Juridica Venezolana and Vol. 2, Madrid, Editorial Civitas.

Hannum, H. (ed.) (1992), *Guide to International Human Rights Practice*, 2d edn, Philadelphia, University of Pennsylvania Press.

Henkin, L. (1990), *The Age of Rights*, New York: Columbia University Press.

Macdonald, R., F. Matscher and H. Petzold (eds) (1993), *The European System for the Protection of Human Rights*, Dordrecht, Martinus Nijhoff Publishers.

Meron, T. (ed.) (1984), *Human Rights in International Law: Legal and Policy Issues*, Oxford, Clarendon Press.

Meron, T. (1987), *Human Rights Law-Making in the United Nations: A Critique of Instruments and Process*, Oxford, Clarendon Press.

Newman, F. and D. Weissbrodt (1990), *International Human Rights: Law, Policy and Process*, Cincinnati, Anderson Publishing Co.

Nikken, P. (1987), *La Protección Internacional de los Derechos Humanos: Su Desarollo Progresivo*, Madrid, Editorial Civitas.

Sohn, L.B. (1994), *Rights in Conflict: The United Nations and South Africa*, New York, Transnational Publications.

Sohn, L.B. and T. Buergenthal (1973), *International Protection of Human Rights*, Indianapolis, Bobbs-Merril.

Thornberry, P. (1991), *International Law and the Rights of Minorities*, Oxford, Clarendon Press.

Van Dijk, P. and G.J.H. Van Hoof (1990), *Theory and Practice of the European Convention of Human Rights*, 2nd edn, Deventer, Kluwer.

Vasak, K. (1978), *Les Dimensions internationales des droits de l'homme* (English edition, *International Dimensions of Human Rights*, Paris, UNESCO.

# 2 The Philosophical Foundations of Human Rights

JEROME J. SHESTACK

## Introduction[1]

Fifty years ago there was no body of international human rights law to speak of. There were, to be sure, philosophies and theories, but the international rules that reflected them were absent. Today, through the United Nations and its half-century of enactments, an impressive body of human rights doctrine is embodied in international law.

Having come this far legally, why then should we still be concerned with the philosophical foundations of human rights? To philosophize, Plato taught, is to come to know oneself. Others say that the special function of philosophy is to discover true propositions or, at least, to deepen our understanding of truth. Still others see the philosopher as a judge, assessing the varieties of human experience and pronouncing on the claim to knowledge.[2]

But are there particular reasons for reflection on the philosophy of human rights? With due allowance for philosophical ardour, we suggest there are.[3]

First, the justification of moral principles is an attempt to make coherent sense about the principles which govern and should govern the ways human beings treat one another. Our own attitudes towards the subject are likely to remain obscure unless we try to understand the philosophies which shape them. Moral principles influence, if not determine, the right modes of individual conduct and social institutions. Piaget's statement that 'morality is the logic of action' contains a striking insight.

Second, if we understand the moral force of human rights principles, we can reinforce the authority of the international law of human rights, which is particularly valuable for an arena still lacking in

31

formal enforcement mechanisms. Put another way, we further fidelity to human rights law by understanding the moral justifications that underlie human rights laws.

Third, understanding the philosophical foundations of human rights helps us devise a translation formula which will permit men and women to speak to each other across the gulfs of creed and dogma, a necessary exercise if there is to be universal recognition of human rights principles.

Fourth, understanding the moral philosophy of human rights also helps us to delineate the structures of human thought in a manner which reveals the implications of thinking and speaking about rights in a particular way, the relationships of rights to one another, the hierarchical ordering of rights and the nature of the conflicts or tension among rights.

So let us take for granted that we can benefit from reflecting on the philosophical foundations of human rights. What then is the segment of philosophy we examine when we delve into human rights? The answer is that human rights are a set of moral principles and their justification lies in the province of moral philosophy. It is that field we explore here.

It bears emphasis, at this point, that, while the modern human rights theories we discuss have been articulated largely by Western philosophers, the moral concepts are not exclusively Western and find counterparts in non-Western thought as well. Of course, the truth of a philosophical principle should not depend on its geography but on the soundness of its foundation. Self-determination, for example, is a Western-originated concept,[4] yet it has spawned the birth of many Third World states. It is significant that the key human rights instruments starting with the Universal Declaration of Human Rights were not drafted by Western states alone and, in any event, the instruments have been endorsed by nations around the world. It is hoped that the theories and concepts dealt with here will be appraised objectively in the calculus of reason.

We shall approach our task, first, by addressing the historical sources of human rights justifications, then surveying key modern human rights theories and analysing some of the current conflicts in human rights theory. At best, we can only touch on the teachings in a field which is complex, vast and, too often, obscure.

## The Nature of Human Rights

One of the initial questions in any philosophical inquiry is what is meant by human rights. The question is not trivial. Human beings, as Sartre said, are 'stalkers of meaning'. Meaning tells us 'why'.

Particularly in the international sphere, where diverse cultures are involved, where positivist underpinnings are shaky and where implementation mechanisms are fragile, the issue of definition can be crucial. Indeed, some philosophical schools assert that the entire task of philosophy centres on meaning. How we understand the meaning of human rights will influence our judgments on such issues as which rights are regarded as absolute, which are universal, which should be given priority, which can be overruled by other interests, which call for international pressures, which can demand programmes for implementation and which will be fought for.

We turn first to the question, what do we mean by human 'rights'? Let us focus initially on the word 'human'. To speak of 'human' rights requires a conception of what rights one possesses by virtue of being human. Of course, we are not speaking here of human rights in the self-evident sense that those who have them are human, but in the sense that, in order to have them, one need only be human. Put another way, are there rights that human beings have simply because they are human beings and independent of their varying social circumstances and degrees of merit? The answers which individuals and states provide to this question have great bearing on their attitudes and their vigour with respect to protecting human rights.

Some scholars identify human rights as those which are 'important', 'moral' and 'universal'. It is comforting to adorn human rights with those characteristics, but such attributes themselves contain ambiguities. For example, when we say a right is 'important' enough to be a 'human' right, we may be speaking of one or more of the following qualities: (1) intrinsic value, (2) instrumental value, (3) value in a scheme of rights, (4) importance in not being outweighed by other considerations, or (5) importance as structural support for the system of the good life. 'Universal' and 'moral' are perhaps even more complicated words. What makes certain rights universal, moral and important, and who decides? This is another way, perhaps, of getting at the question of what is the source or authority for human rights, or how they can be established or justified.

Approaches to these questions vary widely. Intuitive moral philosophers claim that definitions of human rights are futile because they involve moral judgments which must be self-evident and are not further explicable. Other moral philosophers, faced with the instability of meaning, focus on the consequences of human rights, or what they are for. A refinement on this process, advanced by the prescriptivist school, says that we should not be concerned with what is sought to be achieved by issuing a moral (human rights) utterance but with what is actually done in issuing it: that is what act is accomplished, what facts are brought into existence. We shall explore some of these questions in discussing the various schools of moral philosophy.

The definitional process does not become easier when we examine the second word in the term human 'rights'. Certainly, 'rights' is a chameleon-like term which can describe a variety of legal relationships. Sometimes, 'right' is used in its strict sense of the right-holder being entitled to something with a correlative duty in another. Sometimes, 'right' is used to indicate an immunity from having a legal status altered. Sometimes it indicates a privilege to do something. Sometimes, it refers to a power to create a legal relationship. Although all of these terms have been identified as rights, each invokes different protections and produces variant results.

For example, when we speak of an inalienable right, do we mean a right on which no expectations or limitations are valid? Or do we mean a prima facie right with a special burden on the proponent of any limitation? Or do we mean a principle which must be followed unless some other moral principle weighty enough to allow abridgment arises?

If we classify a right as a claim against a government to refrain from certain acts, such as not to torture its citizens or deny them freedom of speech, religion or emigration, then other complexities arise. If a particular claim stems from a metaphysical concept such as the nature of humanity, or from a religious concept such as the divine will, or from some other a priori concept, then the claim may really be an immunity to which normative judgments should not apply. If, however, the claim is based on certain interests such as the common good, other problems arise, such as the need to determine the common good, or the need to balance other societal interests, which may allow a wide variety of interpretations not supportive of individual human rights demands.

If we speak of the 'rights' in the International Covenant on Economic, Social and Cultural Rights, such as the right to favourable conditions of work, social security, health, education, fair wages, a decent standard of living, and even holidays with pay, what do we intend? Are these rights which individuals can assert? Or are they only aspirational goals? If they are rights, on whom are the correlative duties?

If we speak of privileges, there are other concerns. If the privileges are granted by the state, then presumably the state is entitled to condition them. Does the right of a state to derogate from rights in an international covenant mean that the rights are only privileges? Here, too, the answer is connected to the moral strength and inviolability of the 'right' or 'privilege' that is involved.

The definitional answers to these many questions are complex. And part of the complexity is that in defining we must confront the conflicts between utilitarian and anti-utilitarian philosophy, between values of equality and liberty, between absolute and relativist conceptions of rights, all issues of moral justification.

To summarize at this point, even where international law has established a conventional system of human rights, a philosophical understanding of the nature of rights is not just an academic exercise. Understanding the nature of the 'right' involved can help clarify our consideration of the degree of protection available, the nature of derogations or exceptions, the priorities to be afforded to various rights, the question of the hierarchical relationships in a series of rights, the question of whether rights 'trump' competing claims based on cultural rooting, and similar problems. To be sure, the answer to these questions may evolve over time through legal rulings, interpretations, decisions and pragmatic compromises. But how those answers emerge will be influenced, if not driven, by the moral justifications of the human rights in issue.

We proceed therefore to examine the sources of human rights claims. Where do we derive the moral justifications which can be urged for or against human rights? What is their scope or content and how compelling are they?

## Sources of Human Rights

### Religion

The term 'human rights' as such is not found in traditional religions. Nonetheless, theology presents the basis for a human rights theory stemming from a law higher than the state and whose source is the Supreme Being. Of course, this theory presupposes an acceptance of revealed doctrine as the source of such rights.

If one accepts the premise of the Old Testament that Adam was created in the 'image of God', this implies that the divine stamp gives human beings a high value of worth.[5] In similar vein, the Koran says: 'Surely we have accorded dignity to the Sons of Man.' So too, in the Bhagavad-Gita:

Who sees his Lord
Within every creature
Deathlessly dwelling
Amidst the mortal: That man sees truly...

Put another way, in a religious context, every human being is considered sacred. Accepting a universal common father gives rise to a common humanity and from this flows a universality of certain rights. Since the rights stem from a divine source, they are inalienable by mortal authority. This concept is found not only in the Judaeo-Christian tradition but in Islam and other religions with a deistic base.[6]

Even if one accepts the revealed truth of the fatherhood of God and the brotherhood of all human beings, the problem remains as to which human rights flow therefrom. Equality of all human beings in the eyes of God would seem a necessary development from the common creation by God, but freedom to live as one prefers is not. Indeed, religions generally impose severe limitations on individual freedom. For most religions, the emphasis falls on duties rather than rights. Moreover, revelation is capable of differing interpretations even as to equality, and some religions have been quite restrictive towards slaves, women and non-believers, even though all are God's creations. Thus, at least as practised, there are serious incompatibilities between various religious practices and the scope of human rights structured by the United Nations.

However, religious philosophers of all faiths are engaged in the process of interpreting religious doctrines towards the end of effecting a reconciliation with basic human rights prescriptions. This process is largely through hermeneutic exercise, namely reinterpretation of a religion's sacred texts through both historical explication and a type of prophetic application to modern conditions.

Hence, despite the problems in the theological approach, religious doctrine offers a promising but still largely undeveloped possibility of selecting elements of various religious traditions to construct a broad intercultural rationale which supports the various fundamental principles of equality and justice which underlie international human rights. Indeed, once the leap to belief has been made, religion may be the most attractive of the theoretical approaches. When human beings are not visualized in God's image then their basic rights may well lose their metaphysical *raison d'être*. On the other hand, the concept of human beings created in the image of God certainly endows men and women with a worth and dignity from which can logically flow the components of a comprehensive human rights system.

## Natural Law: the Autonomous Individual

Philosophers and jurists did not leave human rights solely to theologians. In their search for a law which was higher than positive law, they developed the theory of natural law. Natural law theory has underpinnings in Sophocles and Aristotle, but it was first elaborated by the stoics of the Greek Hellenistic period and later of the Roman period. Natural law, they believed, embodied those elementary principles of justice which were right reason, that is in accordance with nature, unalterable and eternal. A classic example is that of Antigone, who defied Creon's command not to bury her slain brother by claiming that she was obeying immutable laws higher then the ruler's command.

Mediaeval Christian philosophers, such as Thomas Aquinas, put great stress on natural law, as conferring certain immutable rights upon individuals as part of the law of God. But there were critical limitations in the mediaeval concepts which recognized slavery and serfdom, thus excluding central ideas of freedom and equality.

As feudalism declined, modern secular theories of natural law arose, particularly as enunciated by Hugo Grotius and Samuel von Pufendorf. Their philosophy detached natural law from religion, laying the groundwork for the secular, rationalistic version of modern natural law. According to Grotius, a natural characteristic of human beings is the social impulse to live peacefully and in harmony with others. Whatever conformed to the nature of men and women as rational, social beings was right and just; whatever opposed it by disturbing the social harmony was wrong and unjust. Grotius defined natural law as a 'dictate of right reason'; that is, an act, according to whether it is or is not in conformity with rational nature, has in it a quality of moral necessity or moral baseness.

Grotius, it should be noted, was also a father of modern international law. He saw the law of nations as embodying both laws which have as their source the will of man and laws derived from the principles of the law of nature. This theory, of course, has immense importance for the status and legitimacy of human rights as part of a system of international law.

Natural law theory led to natural rights theory, the theory most closely associated with modern human rights. The chief exponent of this theory was John Locke, who developed his philosophy within the framework of seventeenth-century humanism and political activity, known as the Age of Enlightenment. Locke imagined the existence of human beings in a state of nature. In that state, men and women were in a state of freedom, able to determine their actions and also in a state of equality in the sense that no one was subjected to the will or authority of another. However, to end the hazards and inconveniences of the state of nature, men and women entered into a 'social contract' by which they mutually agreed to form a community and set up a body politic. However, in setting up that political authority, individuals retained the natural rights of life, liberty and property which were their own. Government was obliged to protect the natural rights of its subjects and, if government neglected this obligation, it would forfeit its validity and office.[7]

In practice, natural rights theory was the philosophical impetus for the wave of revolt against absolutism during the late eighteenth century. It is seen in the French Declaration of the Rights of Man, in the United States Declaration of Independence, and later in the constitutions of numerous states created upon liberation from colonialism and, still later, in the principal United Nations human rights documents.

Natural rights theory makes an important contribution to human rights. It affords an appeal from the realities of naked power to a higher authority which is asserted for the protection of human rights. It identifies with human freedom and equality from which other human rights easily flow. And it provides properties of security and support for a human rights system, both domestically and internationally.

From a philosophical viewpoint, the critical problem which natural rights doctrine faced is how to determine the norms that are to be considered as part of the law of nature and therefore inalienable, or at least prima facie inalienable.

Under Locke's view of human beings in the state of nature, all that was needed was the opportunity to be self-dependent; life, liberty and property were the inherent rights which met this demand. But what of a world unlike the times of Locke, in which there are not ample resources to satisfy human needs? Does natural law theory have the flexibility to satisfy new claims based on contemporary conditions and modern human understanding? Perhaps it does, but that very potential for flexibility has been the basis for the chief criticism of natural rights theory. Critics pointed out that most of the norm setting of natural rights theories contain a priori elements deduced by the norm setter. In short, the principal problem with natural law is that the rights considered to be natural can differ from theorist to theorist, depending upon their conceptions of nature.

Because of this and other difficulties, natural rights theory became unpopular with legal scholars and philosophers.[8] However, in revised form, natural rights philosophy had a renaissance in the aftermath of the Second World War, as we shall discuss shortly.

*Positivism: the Authority of the State*

The assault upon natural law intensified during the nineteenth and twentieth centuries. John Stuart Mill claimed that rights are founded on utility. Karl von Savigny in Germany and Sir Henry Maine in England claimed that rights are a function of cultural variables. But the most serious attack on natural law came from a doctrine called legal positivism. This philosophy came to dominate legal theory during most of the nineteenth century and commands considerable allegiance in the twentieth.

Classical positivist philosophers deny an a priori source of rights and assume that all authority stems from what the state and officials have prescribed. This approach rejects any attempt to discern and articulate an idea of law transcending the empirical realities of existing legal systems. In its essence, this view negates the moral philosophical basis of human rights. Under positivist theory, the source of human rights is to be found only in the enactments of a system of law with sanctions attached to it. Views on what the law 'ought' to be have no place in law and are cognitively worthless. The need to distinguish with maximum clarity law as it is from what it ought to be is the theme that haunted positivist exponents, and they condemned natural law thinkers because they had blurred this vital distinction.

A principal criticism of this theory is that, under positivism, the law is no better than the source of its authority, an authority whose tradition may embody concepts which do not further human rights and which are, indeed, anti-human rights. By philosophically divorcing a legal system from the ethical and moral foundations of society, positive law encourages the belief that that law must be obeyed, no matter how immoral it may be or however it disregards the world of the individual. The anti-Semitic edicts of the Nazis, although abhorrent to moral law, were obeyed as positive law. The same is true of the immoral apartheid practices which prevailed in South Africa for many years. The fact that positivist philosophy has been used to justify obedience to iniquitous laws has been a central focus for much of the modern criticism of that doctrine. Critics of positivism maintain that unjust laws not only lack a capacity to demand fidelity but also do not deserve the name of law because they lack internal morality.

Even granting the validity of the criticism, the positivist contribution can still be significant. If the state's processes can be brought to bear in the protection of human rights, it becomes easier to focus upon the specific implementation which is necessary for the protection of particular rights. Indeed, positivist thinkers such as Bentham and Austin were often in the vanguard of those who sought to bring about reform in the law. A positivist system also offers flexibility to meet changing needs, since it is always under human control.

The methodology of the positivist jurists in the technical building of legal conceptions is also pragmatically useful in developing a system of rights in international law. For example, the human rights treaties adopted by the United Nations reflect a positive set of rights, that is rules developed by the sovereign states themselves and then made part of a system of international law. While many states may differ on the theoretical basis of these rules, the rules themselves remain to provide a legal grounding for human rights protection. On the other hand, in theory, positivism tends to undermine an international basis for human rights because of the emphasis positivists place on the supremacy of national sovereignty without accepting the restraining influence of an inherent right above the state. Under this view, rules of international law are not law but merely rules of positive morality set or imposed by opinion. Furthermore, by emphasizing the role of the nation-state as the source of law, the positivist approach produces the view that the individual has no status in international law.

*Marxism: Man as a Specie Being*

Contrasted with natural law is Marxist theory, an approach which is also concerned with the nature of human beings. However, here the view of men and women is not of autonomous individuals with rights developed from either a divine or inherent nature, but of men and women as 'specie beings'.

While the influence of Marxism has diminished considerably since the fall of communism in Eastern Europe, Marxism, which was a dominant philosophy in much of the world for many years and in variant forms, is not without influence still, particularly in assigning values to social and economic rights.

Marx regarded the law of nature approach to human rights as idealistic and ahistorical. He saw nothing natural or inalienable about human rights. In a society in which capitalists monopolize the means of production, he regarded the notion of individual rights as a bourgeois illusion. Concepts such as law, justice, morality, democracy, freedom and so on were considered as historical categories, whose content is determined by the material conditions and the social circumstances of a people. As the conditions of life change, so the content of notions and ideas may change.

Marxism sees a person's essence as the potential to use one's abilities to the fullest and to satisfy one's needs. Since, in capitalist society, production is controlled by a few, such a society cannot satisfy those individual needs. An actualization of potential is contingent on the return of men and women to themselves as social beings which occurs in a Communist society devoid of class conflict. However, until that stage is reached, the state is a social collectivity and is the vehicle for the transformation of society. Such a conceptualization of the nature of society precludes the existence of individual rights rooted in the state of nature which are prior to the state. Only rights which are granted by the state exist, and their exercise is contingent on the fulfilment of obligations to society and to the state.

The Marxist system of rights has often been referred to as 'parental', with the authoritarian political body providing the sole guidance in value choice. Marxism, as applied in communist doctrine, claims further that, no matter what the actual wishes of men and women may be, their true choice is to choose the goals the state sets.[9] The creation of such a 'specie being' is a type of paternalism which not only ignores transcendental reason but negates individuality. In practice, pursuit of the prior claims of society as reflected by the interests of the communist state has resulted in systematic suppression of individual civil and political rights.

On an international level, Marxist theory has proved incompatible with a functioning universal system of human rights. The prior claims of a communist society do not recognize overruling by international norms. While communist governments may admit a theoretical recognition of the competence of the international community to establish transnational norms, the application of those norms is held to be a matter of exclusive domestic jurisdiction. The repeated assertions over the years by communist states in international fora that their alleged abuse of human rights is a matter of exclusive domestic jurisdiction is not just a matter of protecting sovereignty or avoiding the embarrassment of international examination. It may be such, but it also reflects communist theory on the unlimited role of the state to decide what is good for the 'specie beings'. Be that as it may, the influence of Marxism on human rights concepts has declined, as Marxism itself has ironically become a historical category with lessening philosophical impact.

### The Sociological Approach: Process and Interests

To many scholars, each of the theories of rights discussed so far is deficient. Moreover, the twentieth century is quite a different place from the nineteenth. Natural and social sciences developed and began to increase understanding about people and their cultures, their conflicts and their interests. Anthropology, psychology and other disciplines lent their insights. These developments inspired what has been called the sociological school of jurisprudence. 'School' is perhaps a misnomer, since what has evolved is a number of disparate theories which have the common denominator of trying to line up the law with the facts of human life in society. Sociological jurisprudence tends to move away from both a priori theories and analytical types of jurisprudence. This approach, insofar as it relates to human rights, sometimes directs attention to the questions of institutional development; sometimes focuses on specific problems of public policy which have a bearing on human rights; sometimes aims at classifying behavioural dimensions of law and society. In a human rights context, the approach is useful in that it identifies the empirical components of a human rights system in the context of the social process.

A primary contribution of the sociological school is its emphasis on obtaining a just equilibrium of interests among prevailing moral sentiments and the social and economic conditions of time and place. In many ways this approach can be said to build on William James's pragmatic principle that 'the essence of good is simply to satisfy demand'. This approach also was related to the development in twentieth-century society of increased demands for a variety of wants beyond classical civil and political liberties: such matters as help for the unemployed, the handicapped, the underprivileged, minorities and other elements of society.

It is not possible here to outline the particular approaches of the leading sociological thinkers, but Roscoe Pound's analysis merits special reference. Pound pointed out that, during the nineteenth century, the history of the law was written largely as a record of an increasing recognition of individual rights. In the twentieth century, however, this history should be written in terms of a continually widening recognition of human wants, human demands and social interests. Pound catalogued the interests as individual, public and social. He did not try to give value preferences to these interests. His guiding principle was one of 'social engineering'; that is, the ordering of human relations through politically organized society so as to secure all interests insofar as this was possible with the least sacrifice of the totality of interests.

The approach of Pound and his progeny usefully enlarges our understanding of the scope of human rights and their correlation with demands. His identification of the interests involved takes into account the realities of the social process; he shows us how to focus on rights in terms of what people are concerned about and what they want. He makes us 'result-minded, cause-minded and process-minded'.[10]

However, an approach which merely catalogues human demands is deficient in failing to focus on how rights are interrelated or what the priorities should be. The sociological school does not answer the logical question of how a normative conclusion about rights can be empirically derived from factual premises such as having interests. A descriptive science in the social human rights field is helpful but not enough to satisfy the need of goal identification. The sociological approach thus provides a useful method, but a method in need of a philosophy. Nonetheless, by providing a quantitative survey of the interests which demand satisfaction, this school sharpens perceptions of the values involved and the policies necessary to achieve them.

## Modern Human Rights Theories

### Rights Based on Natural Rights: Core Rights

The aftermath of the Second World War brought about a revival of natural rights theory. Certainly, this was due in part to the revulsion against Nazism which revealed the horrors that could emanate from a positivist system in which the individual counted for nothing. It was not surprising that there should emerge a renewed search for immutable principles which would protect humanity against such brutality.

There is, of course, a large variety of presentations and analyses among scholars addressing theories of moral philosophy.[11] While the new rights philosophers do not wear the same metaphysical dress as the early expounders of the Rights of Man, most adopt what may be called a qualified natural law approach, in that they try to identify the values which have an eternal and universal aspect. They agree that only a positive legal system which meets those values can function as an effective legal system. In a larger sense, the object of much of revived natural rights thought can be viewed as attempts to work out the principles which might reconcile the 'is' and the 'ought' in law.

The common theme which has emerged from a huge family of theories is that a minimum absolute or core postulate of any just and universal system of rights must include some recognition of the value of individual freedom or autonomy. Underlying such foundational or core rights theory is the omnipresence of Immanuel Kant's compelling ethic. Kant's ethic maintains that persons typically have different desires and ends, so any principle derived from them can only be contingent. But the moral law needs a categorical foundation, not a contingent one. The basis for moral law must be prior to all purposes and ends. The basis is the individual as a transcendental subject capable of an autonomous will. Rights then flow from the autonomy of the individual in choosing his or her ends, consistent with a similar freedom for all.

In short, Kant's great imperative is that the central focus of morality is 'personhood', namely the capacity to take responsibility as a free and rational agent for one's system of ends. A natural corollary of this Kantian thesis is that the highest purpose of human life is to will autonomously. A person must always be treated as an end and the highest purpose of the state is to promote conditions favouring the free and harmonious unfolding of individuality. Kant's theory being transcendental, a priori and categorical (all amount to the same thing) overrides all arbitrary distinctions of race, creed and custom and is universal in nature.[12]

In variant forms, modern human rights core theories seem to be settling for concepts of natural necessity, that is, necessity in the sense of prescribing a minimum definition of what it means to be human in any morally tolerable form of society. Put another way, some modes of treatment of human beings are so fundamental to the existence of anything we would be willing to call a society that it makes better sense to treat an acceptance of them as constitutive of man and woman as social beings rather than as artificial conventions. This view does not entail verified propositions, as science

requires. Rather, it views human life as encompassing certain freedom and sensibilities without which the designation 'human' would
not make sense. To use a linguistic metaphor, humanity has a gram-
matical form of which certain basic human rights are a necessary
part. This concept of what we take human beings to be is a profound
one, even if it is deemed self-evident.

To be sure, there is a certain aspect of vindication to many of the
new individualist theories. They can be viewed as saying that, if we
adopt certain human rights (freedom of thought, equality) as norms,
we can produce a certain kind of society; and, if one finds that kind
of society desirable, one should adopt the norms and call them absolute principles. This, of course, is a type of tautology. Then, again,
tautologies can be significant, if society is willing to accept them.

The renaissance of qualified or modified natural rights or core theories has had a seminal influence on conventional international human
rights norms. A reflection of that influence is found in the Universal
Declaration of Human Rights itself, which begins with the following
concept: 'Whereas recognition of the inherent dignity and of the equal
and inalienable rights of all members of the human family is the
foundation of freedom, justice and peace in the world'. In a similar
vein, Article 1 provides: 'All human beings are born free and equal in
dignity. They are endowed with reason and conscience and should act
toward one another in a spirit of brotherhood.' The debt that 'inherent
dignity' and 'inalienable rights' owe to natural law philosophy is obvious. The key human rights treaties also reflect quite directly the moral
universalist foundations we have just discussed.

The philosophical justification and affirmation of the core principles
of human rights as universal principles are, of course, highly significant and reassuring for the vitality of human rights in rules for the
world of nations. Rights which preserve the integrity of the person
flow logically from the fundamental freedom and autonomy of the
person. So does the principle of non-discrimination which must attach
to any absolute concept of autonomy. However, affirming such basic
or core principles is one thing; working out all the other elements of a
complete system of rights such as international law seeks to provide is
something else. What rights derive from those we deem core rights?
How are they developed with generic consistency? By what theory do
we test the legitimacy of an overall system? In the next sections, we
shall discuss some of the leading rights theories which have wrestled
with the methodology and justification of an overall system of rights.

*Rights Based on the Value of Utility*

'Consequentialism' is a school of modern moral philosophy which
embraces the family of utilitarian theories. Generally, it may be

described as holding that actions and other objects of moral assessment are justified only if their consequences have more intrinsic value than alternative actions.[13] Classic utilitarianism, the most explored branch of this school, is a moral theory that judges the rightness of actions which affect outcomes in terms of securing the greatest happiness to all concerned. Utilitarian theory played a commanding role in the philosophy and political theory of the nineteenth century and continues with vigour in the twentieth.

The approach to the problem of rights through theories of values has an obvious attraction. Utilitarian theories have a teleological structure; that is, they seek to define notions of right solely in terms of tendencies to promote certain specified ends. An ontological commitment may not be necessary here (at least, it is not so evident), since values (equality, happiness, liberty, dignity, respect and so on) concern behaviour and are not known in a metaphysical sense but rather are accepted and acted upon.

Jeremy Bentham, who expounded classical utilitarianism, believed that every human decision was motivated by some calculation of pleasure and pain. He thought that every political decision should be made on the same calculation, that is to maximize the net produce of pleasure over pain. Hence, both governments and the limits of governments were to be judged not by reference to abstract individual rights but in terms of what tends to promote the greatest happiness of the greatest number.

Under utilitarian doctrine, all count equally at the primary level and any of us may have to accept sacrifices if the benefits they yield to others are large enough to outweigh them. In short, utilitarianism is a maximizing and collectivizing principle which requires governments to maximize the total net sum of the happiness of all their subjects. This principle is in contrast to natural rights theory, which is a distributive and individualizing principle that assigns priority to the specific basic interests of each individual subject.

Bentham's happiness principle enjoyed enormous popularity and influence during the first half of the nineteenth century, when most reformers spoke the language of utilitarianism. Nonetheless, Bentham's principle met with no shortage of criticism. His 'felicific calculus'; that is, adding and subtracting the pleasure and pain units of different persons to determine what would produce the greatest net balance of happiness, has come to be viewed as a practical, if not a theoretical, impossibility.

Later utilitarian thinkers have restated the doctrine in terms of 'revealed preferences'. Here, the rule–utilitarian guide for governmental conduct would not be pleasure or happiness but an economically focused value of general welfare, reflecting the maximum satisfaction and minimum frustration of wants and preferences.

Such restatements of utilitarian theory have an obvious appeal in the sphere of economic decision making. Even then, there are conceptual and practical problems which plague utilitarian value theory, such as the ambiguities of the welfare concept, the nature of the person who is the subject of welfare, the uncertain basis of individual preference whose satisfaction is at issue, and other problems inherent in the process of identifying the consequences of an act and in estimating the value of the consequences.

For our discussion here, what is particularly relevant is the modern criticism of utilitarianism on the ground that it fails to recognize individual autonomy or, put another way, it fails to take rights seriously. The criticism is along the following lines: utilitarianism, however refined, retains the central principle of maximizing the aggregate desires or general welfare as the ultimate criterion of value. While utilitarianism treats persons as equals, it does so only in the sense of including them in the mathematical equation, and not in the sense of attributing to each individual worth. Under the utilitarian equation, one individual's desires or welfare may be sacrificed as long as aggregate satisfaction or welfare is increased. Utilitarianism thus fails to treat persons as equals, in that it literally dissolves moral personality into utilitarian aggregates. Moreover, the mere increase in aggregate happiness or welfare, if abstracted from questions of distribution and worth of the individual, is not a real value or true moral goal.

Hence, despite the egalitarian pretensions of utilitarian doctrine, it has a sinister side in which the well-being of the individual may be sacrificed for what are claimed to be aggregate interests, and justice and right do not have a secure place. Utilitarian philosophy thus leaves liberty and rights vulnerable to contingencies and therefore at risk.[14] In an era characterized by inhumanity, the dark side of utilitarianism made it too suspect to be accepted as a prevailing philosophy. Indeed, most modern moral theorists seem to have reached an anti-utilitarian consensus, at least in recognizing certain basic individual rights as constraints on any maximizing aggregative principle. In Ronald Dworkin's felicitous phrase, rights must be 'trumps' over countervailing utilitarian calculations.

## Rights Based on Justice

The monumental thesis of modern philosophy is John Rawls's *A Theory of Justice*.[15] 'Justice is the first virtue of social institutions,' says Rawls. Human rights, of course, are an end of justice; consequently, the role of justice is crucial to understanding human rights. No theory of human rights for a domestic or international order in modern society can be advanced today without considering Rawls's thesis, and we discuss this theory here more than any other contemporary ones.

Principles of justice, according to Rawls, provide a way of assigning rights and duties in the basic institutions of society. These principles define the appropriate distribution of the benefits and burdens of social cooperation. Rawls's thesis is that each person possesses 'an inviolability founded on justice' which even the welfare of society as a whole cannot override. 'Justice denies that the loss of freedom for some is made right by a greater good shared by others. Therefore, in a just society the liberties of equal citizenship are settled; the rights secured by justice are not subject to political bargaining or to the calculus of social interests.'

But what are the rights of justice? Put another way, what are the principles of morality or the foundation of rules which would be agreed upon by all members of a society? Rawls assumes that the principles of justice (morality) are not self-evident to our common sense but that they can be formulated through the tradition of the social contract in moral and political philosophy.

To set the stage for ascertaining the principles of justice, Rawls imagines a group of men and women who have come together to form a social contract. He conceives the contractors in an original position. What is this original position? It is one of equality of the contractor with respect to power and freedom. It is taken for granted that all know the general principles of human psychology, sociology, economics, social organization and the theory of human institutions. However, the contractors are under a 'veil of ignorance' as to the particular circumstances of their own society or of their individual race, sex, social position, wealth, talents, opinions, aspirations and tastes. Therefore they are prevented from making a self-interested decision, which otherwise would corrupt the fairness of their judgment. In that hypothetical original position, all of the contractors would consider only their own self-interest, which is to acquire a sufficiency of primary human goods, namely fundamental liberties, rights and opportunities of income and wealth, and as social bases of self-esteem. Hence, in the original position, contractors would choose a basic structure for society fairly, because they would be abstracted from knowing the detailed facts about their own condition in the real world.

Rawls then tries to show that, if these men and women were rational and acted only in their self-interest under a 'veil of ignorance', they would choose principles which would be good for all of the members, not simply to the advantage of some. The answers given by those in the original position may then be taken as a blueprint or as a pattern for the establishment of laws which are worthy of the universal assent of citizens everywhere. In other words, their choices would be the basis for the ordering of a just society in any time or place. Rawls's system thus allows us to derive universal principles of justice (morality) acceptable to all rational human beings.

What particular principles would be chosen? Rawls claims that, if the contractors in the original position are rational and act in a condition of disinterestedness or ignorance of their own status and prospects, they will choose two principles of justice.

Rawls's *First Principle* is that 'each person is to have an equal right to the most extensive total system of equal basic liberties compatible with a similar system of liberty for all' (para. 47). Sensible persons would choose a society founded on such a principle, because under a veil of ignorance they would calculate that such a rule would best allow them to pursue their own interests.

Rawls's *Second Principle* deals with distributive justice. It holds that 'Social and economic inequalities are to be arranged so they are both (a) to the greatest benefit of the least advantaged, consistent with a just savings principle[16] and (b) attached to positions and offices open to all under condition of fair equality of opportunity' (ibid.). The general conception of justice behind these two principles reached in the original position is one of 'fairness'.

Rawls's principles of justice are arranged in a hierarchy. The first priority is that of liberty. Liberty can be restricted only for the sake of liberty. There are two such cases: (1) a less extensive liberty must strengthen the total system of liberty shared by all,[17] and (2) a less than equal liberty must be acceptable to those citizens with the lesser liberty.

The *First Principle* focuses on the basic liberties. Which are they? Rawls does not enumerate them precisely but indicates, roughly speaking, that they include political liberty, freedom of speech and assembly, liberty of conscience and thought, freedom of the person (along with the right to hold personal property) and freedom from arbitrary arrest and seizure. These liberties are all required to be equal by the *First Principle*, since citizens of a just society are to have the same basic rights. Rawls applies a value criterion in determining basic liberties. He believes that a liberty is more or less significant depending on whether it serves the full, informal and effective exercise of the moral powers.

Rawls's *Second Principle* focuses on the problem of distributive justice. Clause (a) states Rawls's *Difference Principle*, a strongly egalitarian conception which holds that, unless there is a distribution which makes both groups better off, an equal distribution is preferred. Thus the higher expectations of those better situated are just only if they are part of a scheme which improves the expectations of the least advantaged. In Rawls's theory, the *Difference Principle* is the most egalitarian principle which it would be rational to adopt among the various available alternatives.

Rawls recognizes that a person may be unable to take advantage of rights and opportunities as a result of poverty and ignorance and a general lack of means. These factors, however, are not considered to be constraints on liberty; rather, they are matters which affect the 'worth' or 'value' of liberty. Liberty is represented by the complete system of the liberties, while the worth of liberty to persons and groups is proportional to their capacity to advance their ends within the framework the system defines. The basic liberties must be held equally. But the worth of liberty may vary, because of inequality in wealth, income or authority. Therefore some have greater means to achieve their aims than others. However, the lesser worth of liberty is compensated for by the *Difference Principle* discussed above. Rawls, in short, builds a two-part structure of liberty, which allows a reconciliation of liberty and equality.

This, of course, is highly abstract philosophy and not easily digested. When one tries to apply Rawls's principles to the non-metaphorical world, some difficult empirical questions arise.

Consider, for example, the basic civil and political liberties identified by Rawls which involve recognition of individual autonomy. The demands made are of a negative sort; they principally involve non-interference with the equal sharing of basic liberties by individuals. Rawls's overriding principle of justice requires that all citizens share these liberties equally, as indeed international law provides. Here the respective positions of modern utilitarian, egalitarian and natural rights philosophy all equally seem to be in general agreement. Moreover, groupings are not empirically difficult. The inclusion of all persons in these liberties does not negate or reduce the share of any; hence there is probably the least chance of a clash with other values. In constructing a rights system, it is therefore appropriate to impose a heavy burden on those who would treat persons unequally by denying any of them basic liberties.

But, in the real world, will there not be clashes between liberty and other interests, such as public order and security, or efficient measures for public health and safety? To solve this conflict, Rawls suggests a *Principle of Reconciliation* under which basic liberties may be restricted only when methods of reasoning acceptable to all make it clear that unrestricted liberties will lead to consequences generally agreed to be harmful for all. *This Principle of Reconciliation* is that of the common interest. Put another way, a basic liberty may be limited only in cases where there would be an advantage to the total system of basic liberty.

With respect to Rawls's *Second Principle* (Clause (b)), the problems are more complex. Here Rawls holds that a condition of distributive justice is fair equality of opportunity. Opportunity, stated as a principle of non-discrimination, is easy to put into legal precept and, in fact, international human rights covenants and many domestic constitutions provide that there should be no discrimination by virtue of sex, race, religion or national origin. However, empirical knowledge tells us that equality of opportunity is not enough because society creates the conditions of the pursuit, thereby affecting the outcome.

For example, a person who grows up under conditions of discrimination and deprivation has less opportunity to get into a college than someone from the mainstream of society with a good elementary and secondary education. Hence, to provide equality of opportunity, it is necessary to compensate for unequal starting points. But the opportunities of others also should be protected. Our object, therefore, is to give those who have had an unequal start the necessary handicap points and yet not denigrate the opportunities of others. Whether we utilize subsidies, special courses, quotas or affirmative action programmes depends on how compelling we view the obligation to provide equality of opportunity. Here there may be substantial differences between a utilitarian and egalitarian approach. In some democratic states, for example, affirmative action programmes for minorities have met a utilitarian backlash. It is not easy to resolve the differences, but understanding the moral conceptions enables us to focus on reconciliation of competing views.

With respect to a more equal apportionment of economic benefits derived under Rawls's *Second Principle* and the *Difference Principle*, even more difficult problems arise since the demands on society are heavier. Economic benefits may range from modest ones, such as free education, aid to the elderly and to the handicapped, social security and so on, to major redistributions of wealth. But obviously, such benefits are not achieved merely by a negative restraint on government; tinkering with distribution is required.

But how much tinkering with the distribution system is suitable, and to what desirable ends? As reasonable moral persons interested in both the well-being of the individual and the common good, we might recognize that certain economic needs of those at the bottom strata of society present so imperative a claim for relief that they outweigh a larger aggregate of benefits to those higher on the economic scale.[18] One's moral theory affects what one is willing to accept as relevant facts, as well as the degree of sacrifice one is willing to accept to further equalitarian goals.

Rawls's *Difference Principle* addresses this issue. But if we acknowledge the claims for more equitable distribution of economic benefits, we still have to decide at what point on the spectrum we draw the line and say that the claims for equality do not outweigh the competing values of liberty or the utilitarian aggregate benefits which will be decreased by meeting the claims. It may be that, in any particular social structure, the inequalities allowed under the *Difference Principle* would produce a minimum distribution of goods and benefits too small to satisfy the reasonable demands of the least advantaged, or too large to command acceptance by the advantaged.

Rawls's thesis presents still more difficult moral issues of distributive justice in the international context. For example, many developing nations are economically disadvantaged and their disadvantages can only be redressed by substantial transfer to them of resources, technology and other benefits from developed countries. The sources of those inequalities compete for dominance in determining the appropriate moral response.

One basis put forward for the disadvantages suffered by developing nations is that developed countries caused the disadvantages through colonialism, imperialism, racism and other exploitation. If developed states accept that claim, the moral response should be that the entity which caused the harm should remedy it or, at least, contribute substantially to the remedy. If, however, the accusation is rejected (as unfair, too old, inaccurate and so on), the moral justification for a response is different. The developed countries may still be willing to help lessen international economic inequality, but that task may be undertaken not out of guilt or the need to make reparations but out of a utilitarian calculus that includes such values as increasing markets, creating alliances or lessening tension. However, the utilitarian calculation may not warrant any substantial reallocation. Or the response may be elicited through the moral obligation to advance a just world order along the Rawlsian *Difference Principle*. But here the Rawlsian concept may impose conditions: for example, in the latter case, donor states may require the receiving states to accommodate certain civil and political liberties which are part of the donors' concept of justice, as a reciprocal element of (or the price for) a more just international system.[19]

These issues are obviously quite complicated, with numerous considerations of *realpolitik* intersecting. But even this short discussion shows that the tough issues of fulfilling economic and social rights, on both a domestic and international level, cannot be divorced from the moral issues which swirl around modern moral and political philosophy. The contribution of moral theories to solutions of problems in the legal and political order may be impeded by lack of comprehension or inept articulation, but the interlacing is not barred by triviality or irrelevance.

Critics of Rawls's theory maintain that it was designed to support the institutions of modern democracy in a domestic state context. But even if that were the case, it does not refute his moral thesis, or an international extension of it. Indeed, even if Rawls's theory was intended as a model for domestic states, its application can further an international just order.[20] This is because, in the real world, state parties only reach questions of international justice after dealing, first, with the basic structure of the state's institutions and, second, with the rights and duties of individual members. If Rawls's moral principles produce justice for individuals in a domestic state, that is a long step towards gaining the domestic state's endorsement of and adherence to international human rights principles. In this regard, the international world order is no greater than the sum of its state parts. Hence, if the Rawlsian moral schemata contributes to a realization of domestic justice by the various state parts, the prescriptions of international human rights will invariably be served.

Rawls himself has suggested that his model can be applied to a world order, if one extends the concept of the original position and thinks of the parties as representatives of different states which must choose together the fundamental principles to adjudicate claims among states (para. 57). However, as Thomas M. Franck has pointed out, once the actors in the original position are representatives of states, the dynamic changes, and it is not clear that they would opt for moral principles which further human rights unless they themselves are representatives of just states.[21] It is a fair point that the implications of Rawls's model on an international level still need to be worked through. In any event, Rawls's moral structure, showing how the values of liberty and equality underlying the nature of the autonomous human can be realized in open institutional forms, should at least be morally compelling for a world in which large segments of humanity suffer oppression and poverty and deprivation of civil, political, social and economic rights.

One cannot cover Rawls's highly complex neo-Kantian theory or deal with the considerable critical analysis of it in a few pages,[22] but even brief discussion shows the importance of his theory for the moral justification of a rights-based system of government under a participatory structure. Rawls effects a reconciliation of tensions between egalitarianism and non-interference, between demands for freedom by the advantaged and demands for equality by the less advantaged.[23] His structure of social justice maximizes liberty and the worth of liberty to both groups. One may also consider whether Rawls's thesis is reflected in the consensus on human rights to be found in the international human rights covenants, and whether, in fact, most of the nations have tacitly agreed to a social contract in this area. Rawls's theory is obviously comforting for the construct of constitutional democracy as well as for the concept of the universality of human rights.

*Rights Based on Reaction to Injustice*

At least brief mention should be made of Professor Edmund Cahn's theory of justice. While Cahn's theory no longer has the influence it once enjoyed, it has a particular appeal to human rights activists. Cahn asserts that, although there may be universal a priori truths concerning justice from which rights or norms may be deduced, it is better to approach justice from its negative rather than its affirmative side.[24] In other words, it is much easier to identify injustice from experience and observation than it is to identify justice. Furthermore, says Cahn, where justice is thought of in the customary manner as an ideal mode or condition (for example, Rawls), the human response will be contemplative and 'contemplation bakes no loaves'. But the response to a real or imagined instance of injustice is alive with movement and warmth, producing outrage and anger. Therefore, he concludes, justice is the active process of remedying or preventing what arouses the sense of injustice. An examination of the instances which will be considered injustice thereby allows a positive formulation of justice.

This concept of the need to right wrong has the capacity to produce action. The practical starting point may well be the strongly felt response to words which move one with emotional force and practical urgency to press for the satisfaction or repair of some need, deprivation, threat or insecurity. Such an approach obviously will find a response in human rights advocates anxious to focus public attention on the injustice of the wide variety of egregious human rights abuses which remain prevalent.

However, when we get to the more sophisticated kinds of entitlements arising from considerations of social justice, there is less agreement on what constitutes injustice, and Cahn's insight offers less help. Here we need an overall structure of the type presented by moral philosophers such as Rawls, Ackerman or Gewirth.[25] Still, Cahn's insight is useful; in the end it may well be that we will secure only those rights for which we are aroused to fight.

*Rights Based on Dignity*

A number of human rights theorists have tried to construct a comprehensive system of human rights based on a value–policy oriented approach founded on the protection of human dignity.[26] Some religious philosophers, finding dignity the inherent quality of the sacredness of human beings, believe that an entire rights system can flow from that concept. A secular exposition of that theory is best presented by McDougal, Lasswell and Chen, who proceed on the premise that demands for human rights are demands for wide sharing in all the values upon which human rights depend and for effective participation in all community value processes. The interdependent values, which can all fall under the rubric of human dignity, are the demands relating to (1) respect, (2) power, (3) enlightenment, (4) well-being, (5) health, (6) skill, (7) affection, and (8) rectitude. The authors assemble a huge catalogue of the demands which satisfy these eight values, as well as all of the ways in which they are denigrated.

McDougal *et al.* find a great disparity between the rising common demands of people for human dignity values and the achievement of them. This disparity is due to 'environmental' factors, such as population, resources and institutional arrangements, and also to 'predispositional factors'; that is, special interests seeking 'short-term payoffs' in defiance of the common interests which would further human rights values. The ultimate goal, as they see it, is a world community in which a democratic distribution of values is encouraged and promoted, all available resources are utilized to the maximum, and the protection of human dignity is regarded as a paramount objective of social policy. While they call their approach a policy-oriented perspective, their choice of human dignity as the super-value in the shaping and sharing of all other values has a natural rights ring to it.

Their approach too has been criticized as having a Western orientation which it does, but that does not mean it is wrong. A more telling criticism is the difficulty in making use of their system. Their list of demands is huge, there is no hierarchical order, both trivial and serious claims are intertwined, and it has a utopian aspect which belies reality. Still, McDougal *et al.* have shown how a basic value such as dignity – a value on which most people would agree – can be a springboard for structuring a rights system. Even if one disagrees with their formulation, they have opened the door to a more simple and useful construction built on their insights.

*Rights Based on Equality of Respect and Concern*

A striking aspect of modern theorists is their pronounced effort to reconcile different theories of rights. In this regard, in our discussion of modern theories, we must consider the work of Ronald Dworkin,[27] who offers a promising reconciliation theory between natural rights and utilitarian theories. Dworkin proceeds from the postulate of political morality; that is, that governments must treat all their citizens with equal concern and respect. In the absence of such a premise, there is a lack of a basis for any valid discourse on rights and claims. So far so good.

Dworkin next endorses the egalitarian character of the utilitarian principle that 'everybody can count for one, nobody for more than one', a practical political application of this principle being participatory democracy. Under this principle he believes that the state may exercise wide interventionist functions in order to advance social welfare.

Dworkin believes that a right to liberty in general is too vague to be meaningful. However, certain specific liberties, such as freedom of speech, freedom of worship, rights of association and personal and sexual relations, do require special protection against government interference. This is so not because these preferred liberties have some special substantive or inherent value (as most rights philosophers hold), but because of a kind of procedural impediment which these preferred liberties might face. The impediment is that, if those liberties were left to a utilitarian calculation, that is, an unrestricted calculation of the general interest, the balance would be tipped in favour of restrictions.

Why is there such an impediment? Dworkin says that, if a vote were truly utilitarian, all voters would desire the liberties for themselves and the liberties would be protected under a utilitarian calculation. However, a vote on these liberties would not be truly utilitarian, nor would it afford equal concern about and respect for liberties solely by reflecting personal wants or satisfactions of individuals and affording equal concerns to others. This is because external preferences, such as prejudice and discrimination against other individuals deriving from the failure to generally treat other persons as equals, would enter into the picture. These external preferences would corrupt utilitarianism by causing the individual to vote against assigning liberties to others.

Accordingly, the liberties to be protected against such external preferences must be given a preferred status. By doing so, we can protect the fundamental right of citizens to equal concern and respect because we prohibit 'decisions that seem, antecedently, likely to have been reached by virtue of the external components of the preferences democracy reveals'.

The argument is attractive because Dworkin (like Rawls, but in a different way) has minimized the tension between liberty and equality. Dworkin does so without conceding a general right to liberty (which might exacerbate the tension) but by specifying particular basic liberties which must be protected to prevent corruption of a government's duty to treat persons as equals.

Dworkin's theory seems to retain both the benefits of natural rights theory without the need for an ontological commitment and the benefits of utilitarian theory without the need to sacrifice basic individual rights. His resplendent universe thus seems to accommodate the two major planets of philosophical thought. Dworkin's theory is also valuable in focusing on the relational rather than the conflicting aspects of liberty and equality. Even if one is not fully convinced at this stage by Dworkin's analysis, one has the feeling that his reconciling approach should work within the institutions of a participatory democracy.

## Theory Based on Cultural Relativism (versus Universalism)

An issue which has an impact on the moral foundations of human rights is the clash between those who evaluate human rights from the perspective of cultural relativism and those who view human rights from the universalist or individualist perspective. This clash immerses one in the vortex of modern human rights politics.

At the outset, we should make clear that the issue is not over the cultural rights dealt with in the International Covenant on Economic, Social and Cultural Rights, which encourages and protects cultural, scientific and educational knowledge and development, rights which are part of the universal system of human rights. Rather, the issue here concerns those practices which contravene universal human rights, and which practices are sought to be justified on grounds of moral or cultural relativism. It is that thesis we address here.

Cultural relativism, as a concept to justify human rights abuses on cultural grounds, has scant claim to moral validity. Still, because cultural relativism has been given the trappings of philosophical credentials even in United Nations circles, we shall analyse the concept seriously and analytically from a philosophical perspective.

As presented earlier, the universalist (foundationalist, individualist) thesis is that human rights are universal, reflecting the autonomous, individual nature of the human being. What is cultural relativism? Essentially, it is an anthropological and sociological concept loosely grounded in the theory of moral relativism. Moral relativism is not very influential in modern philosophy, but 'cultural relativism' has been frequently used as an argument against the universality of human rights.

Cultural relativists,[28] in their most aggressive conceptual stance,[29] argue that there are no human rights absolutes, that the principles which we may use for judging behaviour are relative to the society in which we are raised, that there is infinite cultural variability and that all cultures are morally equal or valid. Put into a philosophical calculus, the relativist says, 'Truth is just for a time or place' identified by the standards of one's cultural peers.[30] Relativism thus shifts the touchstones by which to measure the worth of human rights practice. To suggest that fundamental rights may be overridden or adjusted in the light of cultural practices is to challenge the underlying moral justification of a universal system of human rights.

We discussed earlier the foundations and sources of universalism and how that moral philosophy developed. What are the sources of cultural relativism? Is it a philosophy at all? How should we analyse cultural relativism in the context of international human rights.[31]

Moral relativism, the normative basis of cultural relativism, is said to derive from the famous aphorism (of dubious meaning) of the Greek philosopher Protagoras that 'Man is the measure of all things'. Plato's *Theaetus* states the Protagorean thesis in terms of the community (not the individual) as the measure of all things and Plato fairly decimates the concept. The Protagorean view had, at most, a feeble foothold in philosophical thought until the late eighteenth century, when Johan Gottfried von Herder, dissenting from Enlightenment philosophy, claimed that all nations had a unique way of being; there were no absolute principles but only regional and contingent ones. Condemning universal values, he introduced the concept of *Volksgeist*, the spirit of the people. Herder's view influenced German romanticism and French counter-revolutionary writers who glorified the aggregate of local customs and prejudices, under an umbrella called 'culture'.

From time to time during the nineteenth and early twentieth century, the claims of *Volksgeist* arose mostly in the European political context of ultranationalism versus universalist principles of the Enlightenment philosophy. In time, with the rise of pan-Germanism, culture was reduced to the cult of origins. During the Nazi period, the *Volksgeist* theme revealed and realized its stark and tragic totalitarian potential.[32]

During the nineteenth-century colonial period, many anthropologists, imbued with feelings of Western superiority, viewed other cultures as 'native', 'primitive' or 'barbaric', relegating those cultures to an inferior status. During the post-Second World War period, Western anthropologists and sociologists confessed error and embraced a concept of cultural relativism as a counterpoint to colonialization. In combating colonialization, with its implications of superiority of the colonists, the French anthropologist, Claude Lévi-Strauss and others of his school argued for the separate, independent value of all cultures, and also that the West should stop extending its culture to the rest of the world. The goal of bringing about independence from colonialism was certainly worthy, but the anthropologists and sociologists went further and gave cultural relativism a moral or ethical stance. In restoring to other cultures the dignity stolen from them through Western imperialism, they argued that all cultures were morally equal and that universalist values (such as universal human rights) were dead.[33]

For the new states, the theme of cultural identity was appealing: it helped break with Western imperialism and it permitted the colonialized to affirm their cultural differences, and to turn what colonializers had mocked into a subject of pride. It was logical that most new states wanted to make their own cultural traditions part of national life and to bind individuals to the integrity and cohesion of the socially minded spirit. But in some states, pursuit of cultural identity had deleterious effects. While it was a means of resistance under colonial rule, afterwards it turned out to have a repressive side by creating an obligatory homogeneity and diminishing the place of the individual in the calculus of identity politics.

With this background, let us examine the tenets of cultural relativism, particularly in the context of international human rights. What are the objectives of cultural relativism compared to those of universalism? What are the respective camps defending? A universal moral philosophy affirms principles which protect universal, individual human rights of liberty, freedom, equality and justice everywhere, giving them a non-transient, non-legal foundation. The relativists defend a cultural conditioning which supposedly reflects a set of wants and goods that members of disparate cultural groups share (and which may include various human rights goods), but are not ones arrived at by individual choices or preserved for individuals in the community as a matter of right.[34]

Posing the contrast this way deflates the worth of the cultural relativist position in any objective value comparison with universalist principles. But cultural relativism cannot be dismissed so readily, if only because, in the real world, repressive rulers utilize the relativist claim as justification for their ruling practices. We can all cite examples of repressive rulers who seek to rationalize repressive practices by claiming that the culture of their society accepts those practices over universalist international human rights prescriptions, and that to criticize their society's human rights practices is to impose Western cultural imperialism over their local culture. Thus cultural relativist arguments are used to justify limitations on speech, subjugation of women, female genital mutilation, amputation of limbs and other cruel punishment, arbitrary use of power, and other violations of international human rights conventions. It is no wonder that the doctrine that human rights are contingent on cultural practice has been called the 'gift of cultural relativists to tyrants'.

Philosophical analysis requires scrutiny of the foundation of any thesis. What is the basic tenet of cultural relativism? It is that cultures manifest so wide and diverse a range of preferences, motivations and evaluations that no human rights principles can be said to be self-evident and recognized in all times and all places. Does this relativist thesis withstand scrutiny? We believe it does not. We present the reasons for this conclusion on several levels.

First, John Finnis has cogently shown that those philosophers who have surveyed modern anthropological literature have found that the basic assumption which underlies the relativist approach is unwarranted. As Finnis points out:

> All human societies show a concern for the value of human life [...] in none is the killing of other human beings permitted without some fairly definite justification. In all societies there is some prohibition of incest, some opposition to boundless promiscuity and to rape, some favour for stability and permanence in sexual relations. All human societies display a concern for truth [...] all societies display a favour for the values of co-operation, of common over individual good, of obligation between individuals, and of justice within groups. All know friendship. All have some conception of *meum* and *tuum*, title or property, and of reciprocity [...] All display a concern for powers or principles which are to be respected as suprahuman; in one form or another, religion is universal.[35]

Here, in short, is a universality of basic moral requirements manifested in value judgments.

One, therefore, should not have to probe deeply to conclude that there is a universal cultural receptivity to such fundamental rights as freedom from torture, slavery and arbitrary execution, due process of law and freedom to travel. Moreover, any observer of state practice can cite example after example where repression which one authoritarian government excuses as cultural identity turns out not to be a cultural tradition at all, when a democratic government replaces the authoritarian one. Further, there are many examples of peoples of like cultures living virtually side by side, where one state condemns human rights abuses and a counterpart state creates abuses. Thus most human rights abuses are not legitimately identified with the authentic culture of any society, only with authoritarian rulers of that society.[36]

Indeed, even most confirmed relativist scholars are repulsed at practices which are highly coercive and abusive and accept that at least some human rights values are absolute. This is no more than a recognition, grudging or not, that suffering and abuse are not culturally authentic values and cannot be justified in the name of cultural relativism. In short, it is wrong to say that all cultures are equally valid; some cultures contain evil elements which have no rational, intuitive or empirical claim to moral equivalence with non-abusive cultures.

Second, cultural relativists often incorrectly perceive the attributes of cultural communities. Cultural relativists tend to look at cultures from a static, romanticized perspective in which traditional societies are defined as unchanging holistic entities, unaffected by human history or the dynamics of cultural change.[37] But this view fails to take into account the dynamism of culture which normally offers its members a range of development options, or is willing to accommo-date varying individual responses to its norms, while preserving legitimate values of authentic tradition. Anthropologists acknowledge that culture is flexible and holds many possibilities of choice within its framework. To recognize the values held by a given people at a given time in no wise implies that these values are a constant or static factor in the lives of current or succeeding generations of the same group.

Third, the dynamics of change have been accelerated in this tech-nological, communicative age, with the result that many closed societies, once exposed to individualist benefits, seek to incorporate those values and interests in their culture. In fact, therefore, indi-vidualist values have a great appeal to all cultures once the values are perceived. Of course, a necessary element of bringing about such change is free discourse between cultures, so that the human rights benefits can be known. It is telling that authoritarian rulers try to prevent such discourse, which, at the least, reveals a lack of faith in their normative position.

Fourth, there is still another approach which, in part, renders moot the conflict between universalist and relativist theory. This consists of appreciation of what has transpired in international law. Even as theorists have continued to quarrel with each other, fundamental human rights principles have become universal by virtue of their entry into international law as *jus cogens*, customary law or by con-vention. In other words, the relativist argument has been overtaken by the fact that human rights have become hegemonic and therefore universal by fiat.

The relativist, of course, may reply that international law is not a decisive foundation for the relativist any more than an iniquitous positive law is for the universalist. This argument can be countered in relativist terms. Law creates societal pressure for adherence; ad-herence creates habit; habit creates custom; custom becomes a cultural attribute. Thus the legal standards convert to the very cultural stand-ard which the cultural relativist advocates. To be sure, the normal process is for theory to turn into law, but, conversely, law creates the cultural attributes of a society.[38] In any event, the broad acceptance by many nations across the globe of the principal human rights treaties can be taken, at least on the legal level (if not yet in practice), as a triumph of universalism over relativism.

Finally, it is revealing that the implications of the relativist position for human rights have obviously been troubling to many relativist theorists who, in personal terms, would like to see human rights values firmly ensconced in world affairs. And so they search for justification other than the universalist theories to affirm human rights, a search which in itself speaks for the flimsy, if not spurious, founda-tions of cultural relativism.

For example, Jacob Raz grounds rights in interests which are themselves grounded in values. Richard Rorty argues that human rights activists should rely, not on reason and theory, but on passion and the courage of their convictions. Other theorists produce other rationales. It is still an open question among some theorists whether, at the end of the day, individualists and relativists will recommend the same policies but on different moral grounds. While such reconciliation may not satisfy the universalist thesis, human rights proponents should take comfort from the moral compulsion a good person feels to combat evil and to vindicate human rights. If enough feel that moral compulsion, the universalist goals will have then been fulfilled.

This brief description of modern theories of rights does not even begin to exhaust the complex and daunting literature and complexities of this subject. Moreover, the development of rights theory will certainly benefit from flourishing new philosophical and scientific exploration. Scholars such as Rawls, Ackerman, Coleman, Donagan, Donnelly, Dworkin, Finnis, Gewirth, Heller, Howard, Michelman, Nagel, Nozick, Raz, Richards, Rorty and Sumner, and others in many nations and from diverse backgrounds, are still adding insights to classic moral philosophy and developing or refining their own theories both in domestic and international contexts. It is the natural bent of theory analysis to raise queries and articulate doubts. The field is stirring and the potential for new insight remains large.

Long ago, Hume asked what authority any moral reasoning can have which leads to opinions so wide of the general practice of mankind. It remains a haunting point, as we view the gap between the international law of human rights and current practice. A more promising question may be whether moral reasoning can narrow the gap between moral principle and practice. It is hoped that the discussion here, albeit with all the questions it raises, will affirm faith in the meaningfulness and rationality of a quest for a humane society.

## Notes

1   The discussion here can do no more than alert the reader to some of the principal theories of the moral philosophy of human rights and to encourage further intellectual exploration. The last 15 years alone have produced numerous volumes and articles on moral philosophy, though surprisingly few have dealt directly with human rights. The dense, specialized lexicon which most theorists use unfortunately means that they fail to reach the audience they should seek. This chapter is written for undergraduate and graduate students

who are not specialists in academic philosophy, and an attempt is made to use ordinary language to explain philosophical concepts.

2    A pertinent anecdote is that of Gertrude Stein, who, on her deathbed, asked of her friends: 'What is the answer? What is the answer?' A philosopher friend leaned over and spoke gently in her ear. Gertrude Stein closed her eyes and whispered: 'Then, what is the question? What is the question?' Identifying the pertinent questions is a large measure of the philosophical enterprise.

3    The term 'justification of moral principles' is used here in the sense of 'warranted assertions' containing qualities which go beyond local and transient rightness. I believe that most of what passes for discussion of 'truth' in philosophy is such justification. For an analysis of truth and warranted assertions, see H. Putnam, 'Are legal values made or discovered?', *Legal Theory*, 1, (5), 1995, and comments therein by B. Leiter and J.L. Coleman.

4    In 1918, President Woodrow Wilson was the first to announce to the United States Congress that '"self-determination" is not a mere phrase. It is an imperative principal of action.' For a sprightly account of the Western development of self-determination, see D.P. Moynihan, *Pandemonium: Ethnicity in International Politics*, New York, Oxford University Press, 1993. Compare Wilson's 'self-determination' with Fichte's earlier *selbst bestimmung*. Cultural relativism is another Western concept which has found support among various non-Western states. See discussion later in this chapter.

5    An appealing expression of this comes from the Talmud: 'A man may coin several coins with the same matrix and all will be similar, but the King of Kings, the Almighty, has coined every man with the same matrix of Adam and no one is similar to the other. Therefore, every man ought to say the whole world has been created for me' (*Sanhedrin* 38:1, ed. Soncino).

6    See S. Greenberg, *Foundations of a Faith*, New York, Burning Bush Press, 1967; L. Swidler, *Religious Liberty and Human Rights*, Philadelphia, Ecumenical Press, 1986; A.E. Mayer, *Islam and Human Rights*, London, Pinter Publishers, 1991.

7    Nearly a century later, Rousseau refined the concept of a social contract. He saw the first virtue of the social contract as its capacity to organize in collective defence of liberty and order. Second, the social contract establishes a community with potential for doing justice, thereby giving the citizens the morality which had been wanting in the state of nature. (J.-J. Rousseau, *On the Social Contract*, 1762.) See *The Social Contract and Discourses*, trans. G.D.H. Cole, London, J.M. Dent, 1973.

8    Jeremy Bentham, for example, considered natural rights as so much 'bawling on paper'. Oft-quoted is his colourful attack: 'Right is a child of law; from real laws come real rights, but from imaginary law, from laws of nature, come imaginary rights [...] Natural rights is simple nonsense: natural and imprescriptible rights, rhetorical nonsense, nonsense upon stilts' (Bentham, *Anarchical Fallacies, Works of Jeremy Bentham*, Edinburgh, William Tait, 1845).

9    No attempt is made here to deal with some of the substantial reinterpretation and modification of Marxist theory utilized by various Third World socialist countries. See J. Nyerere, *Essays on Socialism*, New York, Oxford University Press, 1968.

10   R. Pound, *Jurisprudence*, St Paul, Minn., West Publishing Co., 1959.

11   Modern rights theorists display a number of common characteristics. First, they are eclectic, borrowing from each other's insights so that it is somewhat imprecise to characterize their theories as simply utilitarian, naturalist, positivist or any of the other classifications which philosophers use. Second, most rights theorists recognize the need to identify the justifications which can validate the moral principles of human rights. Third, they acknowledge the benefits of constructing an entire system of rights which can satisfy all morally

relevant actions and institutions in consistent and conflict-resolving ways. Unfortunately, many theorists also get caught up in the distinctions and fine-tunings of contractualism, consequentialism, value neutrality, objectivity, relativism, pluralism and other branches of epistemological, metaphysical or ethical philosophy without advancing our understanding of the moral foundations of human rights much beyond the classic theories. In the discussion which follows, there is space to address only the more influential modern theories, and then only in bare-bones outline.

12  Even most positivist and utilitarian philosophers now seem to concede that, unless the idea of Kant's moral, non-legal right is admitted, no account of justice as a distinct segment of morality can be given. Put simply, any society which uses the vocabulary of rights presupposes that some justification is required to interfere with a person's freedom. Without that minimal right of freedom, an important segment of our moral scheme (but not all of it) would have to be relinquished and the various political rights and responsibilities which we talk about could not exist. See H.L.A. Hart, *The Concept of Law*, Oxford, Clarendon Press, 1961. For a modern positivist philosopher's view, see J. Coleman, *Markets, Morals and the Law*, New York, Cambridge University Press, 1988.

13  The term 'consequentialism' was introduced into technical philosophy in 1958 by G.E.M. Anscombe. It has come to describe a whole family of utilitarian-grounded theories, some egoist in principle, some altruistic, some benevolent, and so on. Consequentialist theorists are often at odds with each other. See J. Raz (1986).

14  Some utilitarians, notably J.S. Mill, allow that, in moral and legal practice, justice and rights may be considerations superior to interests and to the liberty to pursue the satisfaction of interests. But they insist that justice and rights are derivative of interests and desires and are to be given context by determining what is necessary to maximize the satisfaction of the latter. That, of course, makes justice and rights contingent and does not satisfy the theories which assign to rights superior moral standing. In other words, so long as utility is what Mill said it is, namely, 'the ultimate appeal on all ethical questions', individual rights can never be secure.

15  Rawls (1971). The essence of Rawls's theory is found in Sections 1–4, 9, 11–17, 20–30, 33–5 and 39–40. References herein are to sections.

16  Rawls's savings principle is a complex restraint on distribution to any one generation by allowing for accumulation of savings to improve the standard of life of later generations of the least advantaged.

17  Examples given by Rawls are restrictions on the scope of majority rule imposed by a bill of rights, and restrictions on the freedom to speak imposed by a system of rules of order.

18  Thus we would hardly dispute that higher taxation of the upper end of the population is desirable in order to provide for the needs of those at the lower end.

19  For example, the 24 industrial nations decided in Brussels on 4 July 1980 to grant economic aid to less developed nations on the basis of a series of criteria, including adherence to the rule of law and 'respect for human rights'. See F.E. Oppenheim, *The Plan of Morality in Foreign Policy*, Lexington, Mass., Lexington Books, 1991. Another condition for transfer of resources from developed to less developed states might be that the receiving states use the resources to increase distributive justice among their own citizens and thereby benefit the poor in those states, for example, extending the lines of Rawls's *'Difference Principle'*.

20  Rawls's later writings more or less concede this. See J. Rawls, 'Kantian constructivism in moral theory', *Journal of Philosophy*, **76**, 1980, 515–72. But

Rawls's later writings do not diminish the force of his theory of justice.

21   T.M. Franck, *The Power of Legitimacy Among Nations*, New York, Oxford University Press, 1990, pp.213–33 and 285.

22   The literature dealing with Rawls's thesis, pro and con, is vast. See, for example, T. Scanlon, 'Rawls's Theory of Justice', *University of Philadelphia Law Review*, **121**, (1020), 1973; R. Wolff, *Understanding Rawls*, Princeton, Princeton University Press, 1977; N. Daniels (ed.) *Reading Rawls*, Oxford, Oxford University Press, 1975; M. Sandel, *Liberalism and the Limits of Justice*, Cambridge, Cambridge University Press, 1982; T.W. Pogge, *Realizing Rawls*, Ithaca, Cornell University Press, 1989. The best of these are Kukathas and Petit (1990) and the excellent collection of essays in Avineri and De-Shalit (1992).

23   One might contrast Rawls's fertile moral landscape with Robert Nozick's theories in *Anarchy, State and Utopia*, New York, Basic Books, 1974. Nozick's system, which he calls 'libertarian capitalism', is a radical extension of classical laissez-faire theory. I have dealt with Nozick's theory elsewhere: see J. Shestack, 'The jurisprudence of human rights', in T. Meron (ed.), *International Human Rights*, Oxford, Oxford University Press,1983.

24   E. Cahn, *The Sense of Injustice, An Anthropological View of Law*, New York, New York University Press, 1949.

25   Alan Gewirth is another influential neo-Kantian philosopher who merits study. Gewirth holds that, in reasoning ethically, an agent abstracts from his or her particular ends and thinks in terms of what generic rights for rational autonomy the agent would demand on the condition of a like extension to all other agents. These rights are those of freedom and well-being, which Gewirth calls generic rights. He frames his moral thesis on the Principle of Generic Consistency: 'Act in accord with the generic rights of your recipients as well as yourself.' From these generic rights flow an entire structure of civil, political, economic and social rights. (Gewirth, 1982.)

26   M.S. McDougal, H.D. Lasswell and L.C. Chen, *Human Rights and World Public Order*, New Haven, Conn., Yale University Press, 1980.

27   R. Dworkin (1978). His later book, *Law's Empire* (1986), seems to amend somewhat his original perspective in order to deal with the value of community. See J.L. Coleman, 'Truth and objectivity in law', *Legal Theory*, **1**, (33), 1995.

28   I use this term to include a broad spectrum of relativist theories (cultural, ethnic, particularist, moral). The various relativist schools vary considerably.

29   R.E. Howard, *Human Rights and the Search for Community*, Boulder, Col., Westview Press, 1995; see also her article, 'Cultural absolutism and the nostalgia for Community', *Human Rights Quarterly*, **15**, (315), 1993; and 'Dignity, community and Human rights' in A.A. An-Na'im (ed.), *Human Rights in Cross-Cultural Perspectives*, Philadelphia, University of Philadelphia Press, 1992. Howard points out that, 'cultural relativists' convert to 'cultural absolutists' when they maintain that there is one universal principle, which is to act in accordance with the principles of one's own group. Howard has written most perceptively in this area.

30   In many ways, the conflict builds on Hegel's distinction between *moralität* (abstract or universal rules of morality) and *sittlichkeit* (ethical principles specific to a certain community).

31   It is not within the scope of this chapter to cover the way in which relativism versus individualism plays out in domestic politics, except for a brief note. In some Western states, in particular, there has developed during the past several decades a communitarian movement, largely in opposition to political liberalism. Normatively, communitarians ally themselves with moral relativism. The liberal individualist response accuses the communitarians of a conservative political ideology which denigrates individual autonomy and freedom of choice.

For examples of the cantankerous and casuistical debate on relativism versus individualism among normally soft-spoken academics, see Avineri and De-Shalit (1992); their introduction is particularly good.

32 In France, for example, the defenders of Albert Dreyfus, in the spirit of the Enlightenment, maintained that 'man is not the slave of his race, language or religion, nor of the course of rivers, or the direction of mountain races'. The Anti-Dreyfusards found Dreyfus guilty by virtue of his ethnicity which they regarded as at odds with the true, ethnically pure, French character. France, as it turned out, by rehabilitating Dreyfus, then opted for a society constituted by a social contract and universal principles rather than one based on the idea of a collective spirit. See A. Finkielkraut, *La Défaite de la pensée*, 1987, English edition, New York, Columbia University Press, 1995.

33 Alain Finkielkraut's satirical but insightful account of how cultural relativism has been played out is summarized in a recent review of Finkielkraut by Paul Berman: 'In our eagerness to repudiate anything smacking of old-fashioned imperialism, we seize on the principles of modern anthropologists, who insist on regarding the culture of one society as fully equivalent to the culture of another. We applaud ourselves for discovering that our own culture is merely one among many, and is not to be seen as anything superior. But, having set out in the morning along that admirably egalitarian path, we find by about noon that we are obliged to describe the democratic notions of human rights and freedom as merely anthropological traits peculiar to our own culture, and, not wishing to impose our local customs on anyone else, we are obliged by nightfall to conclude that human rights and democracy are fine for us and other customs are fine for other people. Freedom for us, oppression for others (for such is their culture, and we must respect it)' (P. Berman, 'In Defense of Reason', Review of Finkielkraut, *New Yorker Magazine*, 4 September 1995, p. 94).

34 One should mention a basic classic dilemma which relativists face. Relativism holds that all cultures are valid and none absolute or false. Universalism holds that its principles are absolute. If that universalist thesis is false, then relativism is refuted. If that thesis is true, then relativism is refuted. A theory which justifies its own rejection is not a strong contender for acceptance.

35 J. Finnis (1980, ch. IV); compare A.D. Rentlen, *International Human Rights: Universalism v. Relativism*, Newbury Park, Calif., Sage Publications, 1990.

36 Related to whether cultural attributes are real or pretextual is the fact that cultural norms are often subject to different interpretations and to manipulation by individuals or groups. For example, male chauvinism of the early nineteenth century made the concept of a woman's place being in the home a cultural attribute of that time in Victorian England.

37 Rhoda Howard points out the tendency of many cultural relativists to present traditional societies in mystical or aggregative terms which ignore or belittle individual preferences. Yet, as communitarian societies have changed, they approach the individualist model in culture as well as politics and economics. See R.E. Howard, *supra*, note 29, *Human Rights Quarterly*, 15, 1993, 315.

38 For example, in the United States in the South, opponents of civil rights laws argued that they were against the southern 'way of life'. But the enactment of the civil rights laws brought about a change in the way of life and the cultural pattern of southern society in a fairly short period of time.

## Bibliography

Ackerman, Bruce (1980), *Social Justice in the Liberal State*, New Haven, Yale University Press.

Avineri, Shlomo and Avner De-Shalit (eds) (1992), *Communitarianism and Individualism*, Oxford, Oxford University Press.

Berting, Jan, Peter R. Baehr, J. Herman Burgers, Cees Flinterman, Barbara De Klerk, Rob Kroes, Cornelis A. Van Minnen and Koo Vanderwal (eds) (1990), *Human Rights in a Pluralist World*, Connecticut, Greenwood Publishing Group.

Claude, Richard Pierre and Burns H. Weston (eds) (1989), *Human Rights in the World Community*, Philadelphia, University of Philadelphia Press.

Donagan, Alan (1977) *The Theory of Morality*, Chicago, University of Chicago Press.

Dworkin, Ronald (1978), *Taking Rights Seriously*, London, Duckworth.

Dworkin, Ronald (1986), *Law's Empire*, London, Fontana Press.

Finkielkraut, Alain (1995), *The Defeat of the Mind*, English edn, New York, Columbia University Press.

Finnis, John (1980), *Natural Law and Natural Rights*, Oxford, Clarendon Press.

Gaete, Rolando (1993), *Human Rights and the Limits of Critical Reason*, Aldershot, Dartmouth Publishing Company.

Gewirth, Alan (1982), *Reason and Morality*, Chicago, University of Chicago Press.*

Heller, Agnes (1987), *Beyond Justice*, Cambridge, Mass., Blackwell Press.

Hurrell, Andrew and Benedict Kingsburg (eds) (1992), *The International Politics of the Environment*, London, Clarendon Press.

Kukathas, Chandran and Philip Pettit (1990), *Rawls: A Theory of Justice and its Critics*, Stanford, Stanford University Press.

Mahoney, Kathleen E. and Paul Mahoney (eds) (1993), *Human Rights in the Twenty-First Century: A Global Challenge*, Netherlands, Martinus Nijhoff International.

Nagel, Thomas (1991), *Equality and Partiality*, New York, Oxford University Press.

Rawls, John (1971), *The Theory of Justice*, Cambridge, Mass., Harvard University Press.

Raz, Joseph (1986), *The Morality of Freedom*, Oxford, Clarendon Press.*

Roberts, Adam and Benedict Kingsbury (eds) (1993), *United Nations, Divided World*, 2nd edn, London, Oxford University Press.

Rorty, Richard (1979), *Philosophy and the Mirror of Nature*, Princeton, Princeton University Press.

Rorty, Richard (1982), *Consequences of Pragmatism*, Minneapolis, University of Minneapolis Press.

Scruton, Roger (1995), *Modern Philosophy*, New York, Allen Lane Penguin Press.*

Sumner, L.W. (1987), *The Moral Foundation of Rights*, Oxford, Oxford University Press.

* Especially recommended.

# PART II
# CIVIL, POLITICAL, ECONOMIC, SOCIAL AND CULTURAL RIGHTS

# 3 Civil and Political Rights

MANFRED NOWAK

## Introduction

Civil and political rights are often referred to as the 'first generation' or 'first dimension' of human rights, which distinguishes them from economic, social and cultural rights as well as from collective or solidarity rights of the 'third generation'. Although only a little can be learnt from this distinction for the interpretation of human rights today, the 'three generations' doctrine, as developed by Karel Vasak, former Director of UNESCO's Division of Human Rights and Peace, illustrates very well how human rights emerged in history. Human rights are a product of revolutionary changes inspired by the political thinking of philosophers and the liberation struggles of oppressed classes and peoples. Typical examples are the bourgeois and socialist revolutions as well as the liberation struggles against colonialism, imperialism, fascism, racism, communism, religious fundamentalism or other ideologies which suppress the liberty and dignity of the human being.

Civil and political rights are the most important and lasting achievements of the American and French revolutions in the late eighteenth century and of other bourgeois revolutions in the nineteenth and twentieth centuries. Based on the rationalistic doctrine of natural law, according to which human beings are born free and equal in dignity and inalienable rights, civil and political rights are the legal expression of two different concepts of freedom:[1] the ancient democratic concept of achieving collective freedom through active participation in the political decision-making process, and the modern liberal concept of achieving individual freedom by creating a private sphere for every human being which is to be protected against any undue interference by the state and other powerful actors, such as religions. In this sense, political rights are the individualistic expression of democracy, the civil rights of liberalism. In the various bills of rights formulated following the American Revolution of 1776 and the French Declaration of the Rights of Man and of the Citizen of 1789, both concepts of freedom are represented. With the rise of liberalism and capitalism in the nineteenth century, the democratic or political element of the 'first generation' gradually lost ground, and the bourgeois concept of human rights seemed to be reduced to mere claims against state intervention.

Typical examples of political rights are the rights to vote, to equal access to public service and to take part in the government of one's country. Civil rights are somewhat more complex and range from the protection of the individual's physical, spiritual, legal and economic existence (rights to life, physical integrity, privacy and dignity; freedom of thought, conscience, religion and opinion; right to nationality and recognition as a person before the law; right to own property) via classical freedom rights (liberty of person, freedom of movement, prohibition of slavery, freedom of expression) to highly detailed procedural safeguards relating to fair trial and the rule of law in general. The category of 'political freedoms' (freedom of expression, media, arts, assembly, association and so on) serves both concepts of democratic and liberal freedom and thereby constitutes the link between civil and political rights.

## Recognition of Civil and Political Rights

Modern international human rights law constitutes a synthesis of various generations, dimensions, concepts and philosophies of human rights. According to its preamble, the Universal Declaration of Human Rights was proclaimed by the General Assembly of the United Nations on 10 December 1948 as a 'common standard of achievement for all peoples and all nations' and as 'the foundation of freedom, justice and peace in the world'. Consequently, the Universal Declaration contains civil, political, economic, social and cultural rights and entitles everyone, in Article 28, 'to a social and international order in which the rights and freedoms set forth in this Declaration can be fully realized'.[2]

During the time of the Cold War, human rights were highly politicized and often misused in the ideological debates. Western states, for example, tried to reduce human rights to the classical concept of civil and political rights as manifested in the European Convention for the Protection of Human Rights and Fundamental Freedoms of 1950, ratified in 1953,[3] the American Convention on Human Rights of 1969, ratified in 1978,[4] various documents of the Conference on Security and Co-operation in Europe/Organization on Security and

Co-operation in Europe (CSCE/OSCE) process[5] and in their success-ful attempt to divide the International Bill of Human Rights into two separate treaties, the International Covenant on Economic, Social and Cultural Rights and the International Covenant on Civil and Political Rights of 1966, both ratified in 1976.[6]

Socialist states, on the other hand, while maintaining the rhetoric of the interdependence of all human rights, advocated the predomi-nance of economic, social and cultural rights, and bear a good share of the responsibility for the fact that the development of effective mechanisms for the international protection of civil and political rights (as well as other human rights) was blocked within the United Nations for decades.

For quite a long time, the newly independent states in Africa and Asia tended to view violations of human rights in their region prima-rily as a result of colonialism. However, with the adoption of the African Charter of Human and Peoples' Rights of 1981, ratified in 1986,[7] the African states not only recognized their regional responsi-bility for the protection of human rights but, for the first time, formulated a human rights treaty which accords equal emphasis to all three 'generations'.

The Asian States which are the only ones which have failed so far to develop a binding regional treaty and implementation mechanism for the protection of human rights, are at the same time most outspo-ken in criticizing the universality of human rights, and of civil and political rights in particular. This controversy dominated the prepa-rations for the Second World Conference on Human Rights in Vienna and almost blocked the adoption of a final document based on con-sensus. Nevertheless, the Vienna Declaration and Programme of Action of 1993[8] reaffirmed the universality, indivisibility and interde-pendence of all human rights, as well as the legal opinion that international measures for the protection of human rights are no longer an undue interference in the internal affairs of states.

In other words, although the ideological and political debates about human rights continue after the end of the Cold War, there is an emerging consensus that all human rights are equally important, indivisible, interdependent and interrelated. The division into differ-ent 'dimensions' or 'generations' has, therefore, lost much of its theoretical and practical importance. Above all, the fact that a given human right belongs to one or another category of human rights tells us very little about its content and the corresponding obligations of states. The prevailing view among Western scholars, governments and courts for many years, that civil and political rights primarily entail obligations on states to refrain from interfering, whereas eco-nomic, social and cultural rights create duties of positive state action, can no longer be upheld. In principle, all human rights, although to varying degrees, contain state obligations of conduct and/or result and need to be respected, protected and ensured by all appropriate means. The precise content and extent of state obligations must, however, be established on a case-by-case basis for each human right separately.

The following identification, description and analysis of civil and political rights are based on the most important and universally accepted international treaty in this field, the United Nations Covenant on Civil and Political Rights which has been ratified by more than 140 states of all geopolitical regions in 1999. The Human Rights Committee, an 18-member expert body elected by States Parties, is entrusted with monitoring states' compliance with their international obligations, with means of examining state reports under Article 40 of the International Covenant on Civil and Political Rights, and individual complaints in accordance with its First Optional Protocol. Since its establishment in 1977, the Committee has had ample opportunity to apply and interpret all provisions of the Covenant, above all by the adoption of general comments under Article 40(4) and by deciding on individual complaints. All general comments and most decisions are adopted by consensus and therefore reflect a truly universal interpretation of civil and political rights by a body of highly competent and independent human rights experts. References to the regional human rights treaties cited above, to the relevant case law by regional human rights bodies, and to special human rights treaties, such as the International Convention on the Elimination of All Forms of Racial Discrimination, the Convention on the Elimination of All Forms of Discrimination against Women, the Convention against Torture and the Convention on the Rights of the Child, will only be made in important cases or for comparative purposes.

## Obligations of States

Article 2 of the International Covenant on Civil and Political Rights obliges all States Parties to respect all the Covenant's rights and to ensure them for all individuals without any discrimination.[9] The obligation 'to respect' indicates the traditional duty of states to refrain from restricting the exercise of civil and political rights. The precise substance of this obligation not to interfere depends, however, on the formulation of each right. Only a few rights, such as the prohibition of torture, are absolute; that is, states must refrain from practising torture under all circumstances, even in the event of a national emergency or the threat of a terrorist attack. Most provisions, such as the guarantees of political freedoms, contain explicit limitation clauses; that is, states have a fairly broad power 'margin of appreciation' to restrict the exercise of these rights in the interest of public safety, public order and morals, national security or for the protection of the human rights of others. Such limitations must, however, be provided by domestic law and must be necessary, that is proportional, reasonable and non-arbitrary. In other words, limitation clauses provide states with an opportunity to balance universal human rights with national peculiarities and cultural and religious values, but states are under an obligation to prove to the international community that these restrictions are necessary and reasonable. In this context, the European Court of Human Rights developed the formula of a 'pressing social need' to be shown by the respective government.

In addition to these limitation clauses, states also have other means to escape their obligations to respect civil and political rights. In time of public emergency which threatens the life of the nation (for example, war, internal armed conflicts, terrorism, natural disasters), they are authorized by Article 4 of the International Covenant on Civil and Political Rights to take temporary measures derogating from most of their obligations. At the time of ratification or accession they may also enter reservations, even to the extent of fully excluding the application of certain rights. In practice, states tend to make use of these rights quite frequently, but the Human Rights Committee and regional human rights bodies stressed their authority to monitor reservations and emergency powers of states.[10]

The obligation to ensure indicates the duty of States Parties to guarantee by means of positive action to all human beings the actual enjoyment of their civil and political rights and the opportunity to exercise them. Again the precise extent of this obligation depends on the formulation of each right. In principle, it means to enact domestic laws and to adopt the necessary administrative and judicial measures to give effect to each right, to provide for effective judicial and other remedies against violations of civil and political rights, and to safeguard certain rights institutionally by way of procedural guarantees or the establishment of relevant legal institutions. For instance, the right to a fair judicial hearing in criminal cases or suits at law requires states to establish a sufficient number of courts and tribunals and to regulate their procedure in a manner that at least fulfils the minimum guarantees set forth in Article 14 of the International Covenant on Civil and Political Rights, Article 6 of the European Convention of Human Rights or Article 8 of the American Convention on Human Rights (for example, the right to the free assistance of an interpreter or the right to appeal a criminal judgment to a higher tribunal). Persons who are deprived of their liberty by arrest or detention are entitled to habeas corpus proceedings before a court and, in the case of unlawful detention, to compensation. Aliens may be expelled only after a proceeding which affords certain minimum guarantees. The right to vote means that states must establish democratically elected bodies (such as parliaments) and hold regular elections which guarantee free and secret exercise of the ballot. The right to marry obliges states to recognize marriage as a legal institution and to provide therein for the formal contraction of marriage, the rights and duties of spouses, reasons for divorce, and so on.

The obligation to ensure also includes the obligation to protect the individual's enjoyment of civil and political rights against private interference. The obligation to protect thus refers to the so-called 'horizontal effects', that is, to legal effects which human rights produce on the horizontal level between private parties. The fact that international human rights law establishes legal obligations only for states does not mean, of course, that individuals have no duty to respect human rights of their fellow human beings. The precise substance of such duties needs to be defined by domestic, civil, criminal and administrative law and depends on the nature and formulation of each civil and political right.

Article 6(1) of the International Covenant on Civil and Political Rights states, for example, that the right to life of every human being 'shall be protected by law'. The inherent right to life basically means that nobody should be arbitrarily killed by a state agent (obligation to respect), by starvation, epidemics, poverty and similar natural or human-made disasters (obligation to ensure) or by ordinary crime (obligation to protect). Of course, murder, homicide and similar crimes occur in every society and states cannot be held responsible for every single assassination, but they have an obligation to protect all human beings under their jurisdiction against such acts by enacting relevant criminal legislation with appropriate penalties and by establishing sufficient police, judicial and other law enforcement organs to prevent such criminal acts and bring the perpetrators to justice.

The same holds true for many other rights, such as the right to personal security. If, in a given country, a high crime rate prevails and a citizen, having received death threats and unsuccessfully having requested police protection, has no other choice than to flee the country, this might amount to a violation of Article 9(1) of the International Covenant on Civil and Political Rights by the state concerned.[11] Under Article 17(2) of the International Covenant on Civil and Political Rights, everyone has the right to the protection of the law against arbitrary interferences with his or her privacy, family, home, correspondence or unlawful attacks on his or her honour and reputation. If states fail to provide adequate legal protection of the right to privacy on the horizontal level, this may lead to a violation of their international obligations.[12] Vulnerable groups, such as children, the elderly, the disabled or minorities, of course need special protection against interferences with the enjoyment of their civil and political rights. On occasion, international law expressly prescribes certain legal measures for the horizontal protection of human rights; for example, the prohibition of slavery and slave trade or the prohibition of any propaganda for war and any incitement to national, racial or religious hatred (Article 20, International Covenant on Civil and Political Rights).

**The Right to Life**

The right to life is the supreme human right from which no derogation is permitted, even in time of war or public emergency. Nevertheless, it is not an absolute right such as, for example, that pertaining to the prohibition of torture. Article 6(1) of the International Covenant on Civil and Political Rights, Article 4(1) of the American Convention on Human Rights and Article 4 of the African Charter of Human and Peoples' Rights only prohibit the arbitrary deprivation of life, without defining which type of killing would be non-arbitrary. Article 2 of the European Convention of Human Rights is more precise, as it only prohibits intentional deprivation of life unless it results from the use of force which is no more than absolutely necessary in defence of any person from unlawful violence, in action lawfully taken for the purpose of quelling a riot or insurrection, and in order to effect a lawful arrest or to prevent the escape of a person lawfully detained. In a case against the United Kingdom, the European Court of Human Rights ruled by a majority of 10:9 that the intentional killing by members of the British security forces of three members of the IRA suspected of involvement in a bombing mission in Gibraltar violated Article 2 of the European Convention of Human Rights.[13] The Court held that, even when dealing with dangerous terrorists, operations to prevent the explosion of a car bomb must be organized in such a manner that the use of lethal force does not become unavoidable.

A typical example of a violation of the right to life is the arrest or abduction, and subsequent arbitrary or summary execution, of a political opponent by members of the army, intelligence or police, as unfortunately happens on a systematic level in many countries of the world, in particular in (military) dictatorships as well as in the context of international and internal armed conflicts.[14] The Inter-American Commission on Human Rights established such violations of the right to life in Article 4 of the American Convention on Human Rights or Article 1 of the American Declaration of the Rights and Duties of Man in a considerable number of cases relating to countries such as Argentina, Bolivia, Chile, Colombia, El Salvador, Guatemala,

Nicaragua, Peru, Surinam and Uruguay.[15] Similarly, the United Nations Human Rights Committee found arbitrary deprivations of life by state organs in a number of cases against Colombia, Surinam, Uruguay and Zaire.[16]

Another, particularly obnoxious, practice of state repression involving the violation of a number of human rights, often including the right to life, is the phenomenon of enforced or involuntary disappearance. Several thousand political opponents were abducted, held incommunicado and finally 'disappeared' during the last 20 years in military dictatorships, such as Argentina, Chile and Iraq, or in the context of internal armed conflicts in countries like Colombia, El Salvador, Guatemala, Peru, Sri Lanka and the former Yugoslavia.[17] Often the abductions are carried out, not directly by government agents, but by 'death squads' consisting of retired police and military officers or other persons closely related to the government. States usually deny that the disappeared person has ever been arrested or detained. The vast majority of these victims of political repression are still missing. Although most of them may have been killed and buried in mass graves a long time ago, their family members continue to hope until their fate and whereabouts are clearly established beyond reasonable doubt. In a famous judgment against Honduras, the Inter-American Court of Human Rights established in 1988 that the phenomenon of enforced disappearances constitutes a violation of the right to life, even if government agents are only indirectly involved and even if the body of the victim has not been found.[18] The Human Rights Committee followed this jurisprudence in cases against Colombia and the Dominican Republic.[19]

Despite a clear trend towards abolition of the death penalty in international law and in the practice of many states, the execution of a person who was sentenced to death for a capital offence after a fair trial by a competent court does not (yet) amount to a violation of the right to life. While Article 2(1) of the European Convention of Human Rights plainly excludes the death penalty from the application of the right to life, the provisions of Article 6 of the International Covenant on Civil and Political Rights and Article 4 of the American Convention on Human Rights took certain developments into account and, therefore, contain a number of limitations: the death penalty may be imposed only for the most serious crimes, it shall not be re-established in states which have abolished it, it shall not be imposed for crimes committed by persons under 18 years of age, it shall not be carried out on pregnant women, and every person sentenced to death shall have the right to apply for amnesty, pardon or commutation of sentence. The campaign for the abolition of the death penalty by Amnesty International and other non-government organizations finally led to the adoption of the sixth Additional Protocol to the European Convention of Human Rights (1983), the Second Optional Protocol to the International Covenant on Civil and Political Rights in 1989 and the Second Additional Protocol to the American Convention on Human Rights in 1990. The States Parties to these protocols are under the legal obligation (at least in time of peace) not to apply the death penalty and not to reintroduce it in the future. Unfortunately, only 40 states, mostly from Europe and Latin America, have ratified these protocols in 1999, whereas in other countries, such as China, Iran, Saudi Arabia and the United States, the death penalty is applied in a huge or even increasing number of cases.[20]

In 1986, the Inter-American Commission on Human Rights concluded that the execution of minors in the United States violated Article 1 of the American Declaration of the Rights and Duties of Man.[21] Nevertheless, upon ratification of the International Covenant on Civil and Political Rights in 1992, the United States government reserved the right to impose capital punishment for crimes committed by minors.[22] However, the Human Rights Committee, in its comments on the initial report of the United States, found this reservation incompatible with the object and purpose of the Covenant and requested the United States government to withdraw it.[23]

Although the United States did not recognize any individual complaints system (apart from the one before the Inter-American Commission under the Organization of American States (OAS) Charter), the question of capital punishment in the United States was the subject of international case law in extradition cases. In 1989, the European Court of Human Rights held that the extradition of a German citizen by the United Kingdom to the United States on charges of capital murder would expose him to the 'death row phenomenon' there and would, therefore, constitute inhuman and degrading treatment by the United Kingdom.[24] Similarly, the Human Rights Committee held that the extradition of a British citizen by Canada to the United States would amount to cruel and inhuman treatment because of the method of execution applied in California (gas asphyxiation).[25]

In a considerable number of capital punishment cases against Jamaica, the Human Rights Committee established its constant jurisprudence that states must observe rigorously all the guarantees of a fair trial laid down in Article 14 of the International Covenant on Civil and Political Rights, and that the imposition of a sentence of death upon conclusion of a trial in which these guarantees have not been fully respected constitutes a violation of the right to life in Article 6 of the International Covenant on Civil and Political Rights.[26]

Another controversial issue related to the right to life is the question of abortion. Article 4(1) of the American Convention on Human Rights protects the right to life, 'in general, from the moment of conception'. However, since Article I of the American Declaration of the Rights and Duties of Man is less explicit on this matter, the Inter-American Commission of Human Rights found in 1981 in the famous 'Baby Boy' case that the decision of the United States Supreme Court legalizing abortion until the end of the first trimester[27] did not constitute a violation of the right to life.[28] Article 6 of the International Covenant on Civil and Political Rights, Article 2 of the European Convention of Human Rights and Article 4 of the African Charter of Human and Peoples' Rights do not expressly determine the point at which the protection of life begins. From the *travaux préparatoires* of the Covenant, however, it becomes clear that the unborn child was not to be protected from the point of conception.[29] Whereas some domestic courts reaffirmed this interpretation, neither the Human Rights Committee nor the Strasbourg organs had to decide on it. Even if the foetus is protected by the right to life, its rights have to be balanced against the rights of the mother. The European Commission of Human Rights held in this respect that certain restrictions on the right to abortion are compatible with the right to privacy of pregnant women under Article 8 of the European Convention of Human Rights.[30]

As has been stated above, the protection of the right to life goes beyond the prohibition of arbitrary killings by state agents and the criminal prohibition of homicide offences. The obligation to ensure the right to life also extends to other threats to human life, either natural or human-made. In two general comments on Article 6 of the International Covenant on Civil and Political Rights, the Human Rights Committee called upon governments 'to take all possible measures to reduce infant mortality and to increase life expectancy, especially in adopting measures to eliminate malnutrition and epidemics',[31] and observed that 'the production, testing, possession, deployment and use of nuclear weapons should be prohibited and recognized as crimes against humanity'.[32]

## Prohibition of Torture

Torture is a particularly barbaric violation of the right to physical and mental integrity, and represents a direct attack on the core of the human personality. It was, therefore, abolished from criminal procedure during the Age of Enlightenment, and is prohibited, without exception even in emergency situations, by present international law, both treaty-based and customary. Nevertheless, it experienced a dubious renaissance during the second half of the twentieth century and is today practised, often systematically, in a great many countries around the world.[33]

Article 1 of the 1984 United Nations Convention against Torture defines torture as acts of public officials which intentionally inflict severe physical or mental pain or suffering in order to fulfil a certain purpose, such as the extortion of information or confessions or the punishment, intimidation or discrimination of the victim. Other forms of ill-treatment lacking one or more of these elements of definition might amount to cruel, inhuman and degrading treatment or punishment, which is equally prohibited by the Convention against Torture, Articles 7 and 10 of the International Covenant on Civil and Political Rights, Article 3 of the European Convention of Human Rights, Article 5 of the American Convention on Human Rights and Article 5 of the African Charter of Human and Peoples' Rights. Most difficult is the delineation of torture as opposed to cruel and inhuman treatment according to the degree of the severity of suffering inflicted. In a highly controversial judgment of 1978, the European Court of Human Rights qualified the five combined deep interrogation techniques used by British security forces in Northern Ireland (hooding detainees, subjecting them to constant and intense noise, depriving them of sleep and sufficient food and drink, and making them stand for long periods on their toes against a wall in a painful posture) 'only' as inhuman treatment.[34]

The Inter-American Commission of Human Rights established in a huge number of individual cases all forms of ill-treatment practised by military regimes in Bolivia, Chile, El Salvador, Guatemala and Haiti.[35] These practices are usually applied during interrogations in the initial period of (often 'incommunicado') detention and range from verbal assaults and beatings to the most brutal forms of torture, including electro-shocks, burns, amputations, drowning, extended hanging and so on. Similar practices have been established by the Human Rights Committee in Uruguay, Zaire and a number of other countries in Latin America and Africa.[36] Under the European Convention, the most systematic forms of torture have been found in the context of inter-state cases against the military regimes in Greece (during the late 1960s) and in Turkey (in the 1980s).[37] In two reports, both the United Nations Committee against Torture and the European Committee for the Prevention of Torture confirmed allegations of systematic torture in Turkey.[38]

Article 3 of the Convention against Torture provides that no state shall expel, return or extradite a person to another state where there are substantial grounds for believing that he or she would be in danger of being subjected to torture. This principle of non-*refoulement* also derives from Article 33 of the Geneva Refugee Convention of 1951 and from the case law of the Strasbourg organs and the Human Rights Committee regarding Article 3 of the European Convention of Human Rights and Article 7 of the International Covenant on Civil

and Political Rights.[39] Consequently, every domestic authority ordering the extradition or expulsion of a person to another country is
under an international legal obligation to evaluate the human rights
situation in that country, in particular the practice of torture and the
application of the death penalty. In two cases against Switzerland
and Canada, the United Nations Committee against Torture found
that the expulsion of the applicants to Zaire and Pakistan, respectively, would constitute a violation of the non-*refoulement* principle.[40]

The eradication of torture can only be achieved through effective
preventive measures ranging from the respective training of law enforcement and prison officials to the prohibition of 'incommunicado
detention', the video or tape recording of every interrogation of a
suspect, the right of detainees to have prompt access to a doctor,
lawyer and family members, the prosecution and punishment of individual torturers and the regular inspection of prisons and other places
of detention by independent bodies. The finding that torture is usually
practised during the initial period of police detention led to the development of a preventive system of regular visits to places of detention
by an independent international body. Such a system has been functioning since 1990 in the framework of the Council of Europe on the
basis of the European Convention for the Prevention of Torture of 1987
and is currently being prepared by the United Nations.[41]

### Prohibition of Slavery

Slavery is the most extreme expression of the power human beings
possess over their fellow human beings, representing the most direct
attack on the essence of the human personality and dignity. Like
torture, slavery was officially abolished during the Age of Enlightenment and is prohibited, without any exception even in emergency
situations, by present international law, both treaty-based and customary. The last country which officially abolished slavery was
Mauritania, in 1983. More subtle forms of slavery-like practices continue, however, to the present day and even increase in the context of
drug trafficking, forced prostitution, trafficking in women, child labour and international sex tourism.

In Article 8 of the International Covenant on Civil and Political
Rights, Article 4 of the European Convention of Human Rights, Article 6 of the American Convention on Human Rights and Article 5 of
the African Charter of Human and Peoples' Rights, slavery is prohibited together with the slave trade, servitude and forced or compulsory
labour. According to Article 1(1) of the 1926 Slavery Convention,
slavery is defined as the 'status or condition of a person over whom
any or all of the powers attaching to the right of ownership are

exercised'. The status of slavery also implies a violation of the right of everyone to recognition as a person before the law, in accordance with Article 16 of the International Covenant on Civil and Political Rights, Article 3 of the American Convention on Human Rights and Article 5 of the African Charter of Human and Peoples' Rights. Servitude not only refers to the traditional forms of serfdom, peonage and debt bondage,[42] but also includes modern slavery-like practices, such as traffic in women and children, bride sales (for example, in India), forced prostitution and modern forms of debt bondage in large agricultural undertakings (for example, in Brazil). However, in the Boy Soldiers case, the European Commission of Human Rights, in 1968, held that it did not constitute servitude when 15 and 16-year-old boys voluntarily, and with the consent of their parents, enlisted in the British Navy for a period of service of eight to twelve years, even though the enlistment could not be terminated.[43]

Forced or compulsory labour has been defined in Article 2 of ILO Convention No. 29 concerning Forced Labour of 1930 as 'all work or service which is exacted from any person under the menace of any penalty and for which the said person has not offered himself voluntarily'. Certain forms of forced labour are, however, explicitly excluded from the prohibition in the ILO Conventions and the respective provisions in general human rights treaties cited above, including military and substitute service, duties in cases of emergency, normal civic duties and other normal work in detention. In a number of cases before the Strasbourg organs, members of various professions (barristers, doctors and so on) argued that the imposition of obligations to provide services of a certain type (for example, free legal aid) or in a given location (for example, in an isolated part of Norway) constituted a violation of Article 4 of the European Convention of Human Rights. In view of the vague formulation of the exceptions cited above, it is not surprising that no violations have been found.[44]

## Liberty and Security of the Person

Personal liberty is one of the oldest human rights already to be found in the British *Magna Carta Libertatum* of 1215. Its meaning must not be confused with that of liberty in a general sense. Liberty of the person relates only to the freedom of bodily movement in the narrowest sense, that is to the freedom from forceful detention of a person at a certain, narrowly bounded location, such as a prison, police detention centre, psychiatric hospital, concentration camp or a detoxification facility for alcoholics or drug addicts.

Article 9 of the International Covenant on Civil and Political Rights and similar provisions in regional treaties (Article 5 of the European

Convention of Human Rights, Article 7 of the American Convention on Human Rights, Article 6 of the African Charter of Human and Peoples' Rights) do not prohibit deprivation of personal liberty as such, but only establish certain procedural guarantees and minimum standards against arbitrary arrest and detention. Article 5(1) of the European Convention of Human Rights is more precise and establishes an exhaustive list of permissible cases of deprivation of liberty. Most important are custody and pre-trial detention of a suspected criminal and the serving of a prison sentence after conviction by a criminal court. In addition, minors may be detained for the purpose of educational supervision, aliens for the purpose of ensuring their expulsion or extradition, 'persons of unsound mind' may be forced to stay in a psychiatric hospital, alcoholics or drug addicts may be held in a detoxification facility, persons with infectious diseases may be put in quarantine, witnesses may be forced to attend a trial, men may be forced to undergo paternity testing, and even vagrants may be detained outside the context of a criminal charge.

Other types of deprivation of liberty, such as preventive detention not related to a criminal charge, are not permissible under Article 5 of the European Convention of Human Rights and will be deemed arbitrary in relation to the other provisions cited above. In particular, detention merely on the ground of inability to fulfil a contractual obligation (detention for debt) is explicitly prohibited by Article 11 of the International Covenant on Civil and Political Rights, Article 7(7) of the American Convention on Human Rights and Article 1 of the Fourth Additional Protocol to the European Convention of Human Rights.

Any deprivation of liberty is only permissible if it is carried out in accordance with a procedure established by domestic law and if it is in conformity with the minimum guarantees laid down in the respective provisions: every detainee shall be informed promptly of the reasons for his or her arrest, shall be entitled to take habeas corpus proceedings before a court (which has to decide without delay and order release if the detention is unlawful) and shall have an enforceable right to compensation if detention was unlawful. In addition, persons held in custody shall be brought promptly, that is within a few days, before a judge who must either release them or authorize pre-trial detention. They are entitled to trial within a reasonable time and to release in exchange for bail or some other guarantee to appear for trial. In other words, pre-trial detention shall not be the general rule and shall be as short as possible depending on the complexity of the case, but never longer than a few years.

The Human Rights Committee, the United Nations Working Group on Arbitrary Detention, the Inter-American and European Commissions and Courts of Human Rights have developed a fairly detailed case law on the various and highly complex issues related to the right to personal liberty.[45] Many terms are extremely vague ('arbitrary', 'promptly', 'speedily', 'without delay', and so on) and their meaning can only be established on a case-by-case basis taking into account all relevant circumstances.

Article 10 of the International Covenant on Civil and Political Rights and Article 5(3) to (6) of the American Convention on Human Rights guarantee to all persons deprived of their liberty a special right to humane treatment and to certain minimum conditions of pre-trial detention and imprisonment, such as segregation of the accused from convicted persons or segregation of juveniles from adults. These provisions go beyond the general prohibition of torture and inhuman treatment by establishing a minimum standard of prison conditions based on the policy that the treatment of prisoners shall aim at their reformation and social rehabilitation. Article 10 of the International Covenant on Civil and Political Rights establishes an obligation to ensure humane prison conditions by means of positive action, regardless of economic difficulties.[46] In a case against Hungary, the Human Rights Committee ruled that the limited time of only five minutes per day for personal hygiene and five minutes for exercise in the open air was not compatible with this provision.[47]

The right to personal security implies an obligation of states to provide some kind of minimum protection to individuals whose life or personal integrity is threatened by private persons. Although the Strasbourg organs do not attribute any independent significance beyond personal liberty to the right to security in Article 5 of the European Convention of Human Rights, since 1990 the Human Rights Committee has established in a number of cases, against Colombia, the Dominican Republic, Equatorial Guinea and Zambia, that, in the case of serious threats to the life of persons under their jurisdiction, states are under an obligation to take reasonable and appropriate measures to protect them.[48] This right may also be violated in cases of enforced disappearances.

### Procedural Guarantees in Civil and Criminal Trials

The right to a fair administration of justice holds such a prominent place in societies based on the rule of law that international human rights law has established very detailed obligations of states to ensure by means of positive action that their domestic court proceedings correspond to minimum international standards. These standards give rise to highly complex questions of interpretation and sometimes force states to carry out far-reaching changes to their domestic legal systems. The majority of judgments delivered by the European

Court of Human Rights relate to Article 6 of the European Convention of Human Rights and related provisions in the Seventh Additional Protocol. As a result of this controversial case law, many continental European states, notably Austria, had to overcome their traditional separation of the administrative and judicial state powers and subject considerable parts of their administrative (penal) law to judicial review.[49] In the present context, only a short survey of the relevant provisions and jurisprudence can be provided.

According to Article 14 of the International Covenant on Civil and Political Rights, Article 6 of the European Convention of Human Rights, Article 8 of the American Convention on Human Rights and Article 7 of the African Charter of Human and Peoples' Rights, everyone is entitled, in the determination of any criminal charge or of his or her (civil) rights and obligations in a suit at law, to a fair and public hearing by a competent, independent and impartial tribunal established by law. In other words, states are under an international obligation to establish a sufficient number of independent tribunals and vest them with the power to decide all criminal charges and civil disputes. This implies the internationalization of the liberal principles of separation of powers (only purely administrative matters may be decided by administrative authorities) and the independence of the judiciary. Most of the legal terms cited above lack a clear meaning in different legal systems and are, therefore, in need of an autonomous interpretation by the competent international organs.[50]

The terms 'suit at law' and 'civil rights and obligations' refer to the classical Roman distinction between public and private law. Disputes under private law need to be decided by an independent tribunal, whereas claims under public law might be decided by an administrative authority. In reality, many decisions of administrative bodies (for example, real-estate approvals in the sale of agricultural property, the granting or revocation of licences, prohibitions on the exercise of a profession and social security claims) are, directly decisive as regards the determination of civil rights and obligations. Consequently, at least a final review by a tribunal is needed. In a case against France, the Human Rights Committee, in contrast to the Strasbourg organs, considered even a procedure concerning dismissal from employment to constitute the determination of rights and obligations in a suit at law.[51]

Similar difficulties arise with respect to the interpretation of the term 'criminal charge'. In the opinion of the European Court of Human Rights, not only the nature and severity of the threatened sanction but also the type of the sanctioned offence are to be drawn upon. If it is directed at the general public, even a small fine for a traffic offence is considered a criminal charge – though not disciplinary measures against soldiers amounting to five days' imprisonment. Similarly, the expulsion of aliens, the dismissal from public employment and the temporary loss of a driving licence were not viewed as punishment in need of review by a tribunal.

The requirement of an 'independent and impartial tribunal' is usually satisfied if a domestic civil or criminal court decides. Special courts, such as military or revolutionary tribunals, often do not meet the required standards of independence and impartiality. On the other hand, administrative authorities might fulfil these criteria if their members are appointed for a period of several years and are not subject to directives from other state organs.

The Human Rights Committee interprets the concept of a fair hearing as requiring a number of conditions, such as equality of arms, respect for the principle of adversary proceedings, preclusion of *ex officio* reformation *in pejus*, and expeditious procedure.[52] Most important is the principle of equality of arms; that is, that the parties in civil or criminal proceedings must have an equal opportunity to present their case, to examine witnesses and to be present at all stages.

'Justice must not only be done, it must be seen to be done.' This famous phrase explains the rationale behind the requirement of a public hearing. This is not only in the interest of the parties. In order to ensure confidence in the administration of justice and a kind of democratic control, the public at large and the media have a right to attend hearings in civil and criminal proceedings: those parts of a trial where the facts are determined by the parties. Appellate proceedings limited to questions of law need not be public. In addition, the public and the media may be excluded for reasons of morals, public order or national security, or in the interest of the parties. As a general rule, however, judgments must be made public; that is, publicly accessible to everyone.

In addition to the basic requirements of a fair trial cited above, which apply equally to civil and to criminal proceedings, the relevant provisions enlist a number of minimum guarantees of the accused in criminal trials only. All persons charged with a criminal offence have the right to be presumed innocent until proved guilty, to be informed promptly of all charges, to have adequate time for the preparation of their defence, to be tried without undue delay, to defend themselves in person or through legal counsel, to receive free legal assistance and the free assistance of an interpreter, to call and examine witnesses, not to be compelled to testify against themselves, to an appeal against their conviction, to compensation for any miscarriage of justice and to the principle of *ne bis in idem*. In addition, Article 15 of the International Covenant on Civil and Political Rights, Article 7 of the European Convention of Human Rights and Article 9 of the American Convention on Human Rights prohibit retroactive criminal laws and the imposition of a heavier penalty than the one applicable at the time when the criminal offence was committed.

## Freedom of Movement and Protection against Arbitrary Expulsion

In view of increasing international mobility, tourism and migration on the one hand, alarming tendencies of xenophobia and restrictive attitudes of many states towards asylum seekers, migrant workers and aliens on the other, the rights relating to freedom of movement have become increasingly important and at the same time controversial. These rights are laid down in Articles 12 and 13 of the International Covenant on Civil and Political Rights, Articles 2 to 4 of the Fourth Additional Protocol and Article 1 of the Seventh Additional Protocol to the European Convention of Human Rights, Article 22 of the American Convention on Human Rights and Article 12 of the African Charter of Human and Peoples' Rights. In addition, the principle of non-*refoulement*,[53] the protection of privacy and family life[54] as well as special treaties relating to refugees, stateless persons or migrant workers have to be taken into account.[55] Some of these rights apply to everyone, some to persons lawfully within the territory of a state, others only to nationals, aliens or stateless persons, others to aliens lawfully in the territory of a state, and others only to specific groups of aliens, such as refugees or migrant workers.

International law does not grant a general right to enter another country and to reside there. Rather, the right to liberty of movement and freedom to choose one's residence is restricted to persons 'lawfully within the territory of a state'. It falls, therefore, in principle within the domain of state sovereignty to decide whom to admit on its territory. Apart from the rare exception of a punishment of exile provided by law, the unrestricted right to enter one's own country in Article 12(4) of the International Covenant on Civil and Political Rights guarantees to all nationals, as well as to those stateless persons and aliens who have set up a permanent home in the territory of another state, a right to entry and an absolute prohibition of expulsion.[56]

Article 3 of the Fourth Additional Protocol to the European Convention of Human Rights and Article 22(5) of the American Convention on Human Rights limit this right, albeit without any exception, to nationals. In addition, Article 4 of the Fourth Additional Protocol, Article 22(9) of the American Convention on Human Rights and Article 12 of the African Charter of Human and Peoples' Rights prohibit, again without any exception, the collective expulsion of aliens. The expulsion of individual aliens 'lawfully in the territory of a state' is, however, only restricted by certain procedural guarantees (right to submit reasons against the expulsion, to have the case reviewed and to be represented) laid down in Article 13 of the International Covenant on Civil and Political Rights and Article 1 of the Seventh Additional Protocol to the European Convention of Human Rights. The principle of non-*refoulement* and the protection of privacy and family life might provide a stronger protection against expulsion, since it also applies to aliens who are illegally in the territory of a state. Article 14 of the Universal Declaration of Human Rights, Article 22(7) of the American Convention on Human Rights and Article 12(3) of the African Charter of Human and Peoples' Rights guarantee to refugees a right to seek and obtain asylum, but this controversial right has not found its way into the Covenant or the European Convention.

Whereas the right to enter a country is generally restricted to nationals of that country, everybody enjoys the right to leave any country. This freedom to emigrate and travel abroad, which was central to the ideological debates of the Cold War is, however, in practice limited by the restrictive immigration and visa policy of other countries. In addition, the right to leave is subject to legal restrictions in the interests of national security, public order, public health, morals or the rights and freedoms of others. For example, the refusal to issue a passport to a citizen or the confiscation of a passport on the ground that he failed to report for military service, or that he or she is accused of having committed a crime may be justified in the interests of national security or public order.[57] However, in the so-called 'passport cases' submitted by nationals of Uruguay living for political reasons in exile, the Human Rights Committee made it clear that states (and their consulates abroad) are under a positive obligation to ensure the effective guarantee of the right to leave a country by issuing travel documents without unreasonable restrictions, such as on political grounds or for the economic well-being of a country.[58]

The same limitations apply to the liberty of movement and residence within a country. There are many reasons why the access to certain areas, such as military zones, hunting grounds, places where toxic waste is disposed, private property, and so on may be prohibited or restricted. For example, in the famous *Lovelace* case, the Human Rights Committee ruled that, in the interests of the protection of minorities, states may create reserves and limit the freedom to reside therein to members of a certain indigenous group.[59] Banishment to a certain area of a state is permissible as a punishment if provided by law and imposed by a court, but not as a purely administrative measure.[60]

### Right to Privacy, Marriage, Family Life and Rights of Children

Manifested in the right to privacy is the core of the liberal concept of freedom centred around the human being as an autonomous subject; that is, the individual who is sovereign over himself or herself and all of his or her actions which do not interfere with others.[61] The right to respect for and protection of one's privacy, as guaranteed in Article 17 of the International Covenant on Civil and Political Rights, Article 8 of the European Convention of Human Rights and Article 11 of the American Convention on Human Rights,[62] is quite a complex human right which, first of all, might be divided into a right to individual existence and to autonomy.

With respect to the area of an individual existence, the right to privacy protects one's identity, integrity and intimacy. Identity includes one's name, gender, appearance, feelings, honour and reputation, style of hair and beard, and so on. Mandatory hairstyle rules, therefore, interfere with privacy as much as the forced changing of a name or 'brainwashing' with psychoactive drugs. Privacy, however, is not an absolute right. Only arbitrary or unlawful interferences are prohibited; in order to know whether a given interference actually violates the right to privacy, we have to balance it with certain domestic interests, such as national security, health, morals, the prevention of crime or the rights and freedoms of others. For example, in a case against the Netherlands, the Human Rights Committee decided that the refusal of the Dutch authorities to change into Hindu names the surnames of Dutch citizens who wanted to study to become Hindu priests in India was an arbitrary interference with their identity and violated their privacy.[63] The same holds true if states prohibit transsexuals from changing sex. Forced medical treatment which interferes with the individual's integrity might, however, be justified in the interests of the rights of others, as is the case with mandatory withdrawal of blood for the purpose of determining paternity. Intimacy is at the very heart of privacy and means that certain private characteristics, actions or data should be kept secret. In view of the threats caused to privacy by electronic data processing, states are under an obligation to adopt data protection laws with effective supervision measures.[64]

States interfere with a person's autonomy if they prohibit or penalize acts that, in principle, only concern himself or herself, such as committing suicide, taking drugs or refusing to wear safety helmets or use seat belts. In highly complex and interdependent modern societies, however, this right to 'individual self-determination' becomes more and more restricted and states increasingly justify their interference with social costs (for example, the public health system) involved or with the protection of the rights of others. A typical example is the anti-smoking laws as adopted in the United States and France. Autonomy also covers the right to communication and to establish emotional relations with others. In the case of divorce, for example, states have a positive obligation to ensure the right of communication and contact between children and the parent without custody.[65] Interferences with sexual life and autonomy cannot be justified merely on the ground of morals or health. Both the European Court of Human Rights and the Human Rights Committee, therefore, found a general prohibition of homosexuality a violation of the right to privacy.[66]

In addition to individual existence and autonomy, the right to privacy also protects specific private institutions, such as the home, correspondence and the family. The term 'home' is to be interpreted in the broad sense and, therefore, also covers business and commercial space.[67] A typical example of permissible interference is the house search ordered by a judge for the purpose of securing evidence in a criminal case. The term 'correspondence' also needs a broad interpretation and covers today, in addition to written letters, all forms of communication over distance, by telephone, telegram, telex, telefax, electronic mail and so on. The most common interferences are secret state surveillance measures (such as opening letters, metering and tapping of telephone calls, monitoring faxes) for the purpose of preventing crime, combating terrorism and so on. Similar to house searches, such interference is permissible only on the basis of a law and strict procedures ensuring the principle of proportionality. In a number of cases concerning secret surveillance, the European Court of Human Rights established certain European minimum standards to be followed by domestic laws.[68] Similar standards have been developed with respect to the control and censorship of the correspondence of prisoners.[69]

In a universal context, the term 'family' also needs to be interpreted in a broad sense, taking into account various cultural and religious traditions ranging from the European nuclear family to the 'extended family' of traditional African societies. In addition to blood relationship and statutory forms of establishing relations (marriage, adoption), other criteria such as life together or economic ties are essential for the existence of a family. In the context of the right to privacy, respect for family life means primarily that the state should not interfere by, for example, arbitrarily separating children from their parents. In practice, this principle has a certain impact on the policy of states regarding the admission or expulsion of aliens, and states must pay attention to family reunification in their immigration policies. The European Court of Human Rights decided, for example, that the Netherlands had no right to expel a Moroccan citizen upon divorce from his Dutch wife because he maintained close contacts with his daughter.[70]

In addition to respect for family life in the context of the right to privacy, the family as 'the natural and fundamental group unit of society' is entitled to special protection under Article 23 of the International Covenant on Civil and Political Rights, Article 17 of the American Convention on Human Rights, Article 18 of the African Charter of Human and Peoples' Rights and other treaties relating to economic, social and cultural rights. This institutional guarantee of the family is closely related to the right to marry and found a family, which is also protected by Article 12 of the European Convention of Human Rights and Article 5 of the Seventh Additional Protocol. States are under an obligation to establish marriage and family as special institutions under their private law systems, to regulate the conditions and limits of marriage and family life according to their own cultural traditions, but at the same time respecting the freedom of spouses to enter voluntarily into a marriage and the equality of rights and responsibilities of spouses. The African Charter attaches particular attention to the states' duty to assist the family, which is defined in Article 18(2) as 'the custodian of morals and traditional values recognized by the community'. An absolute prohibition of divorce based on the religious dogma of the indissolubility of marriage violates the right to marry notwithstanding a 1986 ruling of the European Court of Human Rights to the contrary.[71] States are not allowed to prohibit prisoners from marrying, but this does not grant a right to cohabitation.[72] In the case of divorce, spouses continue to enjoy equal rights, and children have a right to special protection. In particular, they enjoy a right to regular contact with both parents.[73]

Finally, Article 24 of the International Covenant on Civil and Political Rights, Article 19 of the American Convention on Human Rights and the 1989 Convention on the Rights of the Child establish the right of children to such measures of protection by the family, society and the state as are required by their status as minors. In particular, every child shall be registered immediately after birth, shall have a name and the right to acquire a nationality. In a case concerning the disappearance of an Argentinian child during the former military regime, the Human Rights Committee found that the failure of the present government for many years to legally establish her real name and issue identity papers entailed a violation of Article 24 of the International Covenant on Civil and Political Rights.[74] Children also enjoy special protection against any form of discrimination, in particular against children born out of wedlock.[75] Article 1 of the Convention on the Rights of the Child defines childhood as the period up to the age of 18 years, and contains a detailed enumeration of the various civil, political, economic, social and cultural rights of the child; Article 3 establishes the best interest of the child as the primary consideration in all actions concerning children, whether undertaken by public or private social welfare institutions, courts of law, administrative authorities or legislative bodies.[76]

## Political Freedoms

The freedoms of thought, conscience, religion, belief, opinion, expression, media, art, information, association, assembly and trade unions in Articles 18 to 22 of the International Covenant on Civil and Political Rights, Articles 9 to 11 of the European Convention of Human Rights, Articles 12 to 16 of the American Convention on Human Rights and Articles 8 to 11 of the African Charter of Human and Peoples' Rights, all have in common the conviction stemming from the rationalism of the Enlightenment that the individual's spiritual existence, that is one's belief in spiritual ideas and convictions, the communication of spiritual subject matters to fellow citizens, and the freedom to defend one's thoughts and ideas in public, either individually or in community with others, requires special protection by the state.[77] As stressed above, these rights constitute the link between civil and political rights and their underlying concepts of liberal and democratic freedom. They are, therefore, grouped together under the term 'political freedoms', which does not, of course, mean that they are protected only with regard to their political function. However, in addition to their liberal function in warding off interference for a solely private benefit, inherent in these rights is the function of political participation in the democratic (public) interest. The political function is naturally more predominant with freedom of assembly than with freedom of religion.

All provisions cited above contain a similar and fairly far-reaching limitation clause restricting the communicative (public) function of these freedoms. This is an expression of the conviction that the public exercise of political freedoms carries with it special duties and responsibilities, and that an unrestricted or irresponsible exercise might endanger the rights and freedoms of others or legitimate public interests to protect public order, safety, health or morals. Only the interplay between these rights and their restrictions is what truly determines the actual scope of the individual's rights.[78] This delicate balancing of private and public interests is first and foremost the task of domestic authorities. The actual degree of enjoyment of political freedoms is one of the best indicators of the functioning of a democratic society. That is why many of these limitation clauses, above all in the European Convention, permit restrictions only to the extent 'necessary in a democratic society'.[79] The European Court of Human Rights, while according to states a broad 'margin of appreciation' in balancing private and public interests, has nevertheless developed a fairly strict interpretation of these limitation clauses; restrictions must be regulated with sufficient precision in a generally accessible law, must serve one of the purposes explicitly mentioned, and must be necessary (in a democratic society): that is, must be proportional and serve a pressing social need.[80]

The private freedom of thought, conscience, religion, belief and opinion is closely associated with the right to privacy. It is an absolute right which does not permit any limitation.[81] This right of spiritual and moral existence includes the right to adopt a religion, belief or opinion of one's own choice, the right not to be subject to any coercion (indoctrination, 'brainwashing' and similar forms of manipulation) and the private practice of religion, for example, by praying alone. The right to adopt a religion includes the right to leave and change a religion, and states are under an obligation to institute mechanisms to this effect. The terms 'belief' and 'religion' are to be broadly construed, encompassing theistic, non-theistic and atheistic beliefs, as well as the right not to profess any religion or belief.

The public freedom of religion or belief is the right to manifest one's religion or belief in worship, observance, practice and teaching. It may, of course, be restricted in accordance with the relevant limitation clauses. Most controversial are the questions concerning what is meant by the practice of a religion,[82] whether the refusal to fulfil certain legal duties (for example, to pay taxes and social insurance fees, or to serve in the military) can be justified on religious grounds, and which restrictions are permissible. For instance, the refusal of Jehovah's Witnesses to accept a blood transfusion for themselves is a manifestation of their religion which should not be restricted by state action. However, if parents refuse a blood transfusion aimed at saving the life of their child, the state would have a right, and even a duty, to interfere in order to protect the child's right to life. The requirement of the Canadian National Railway Company to wear safety headgear during work did not, in the opinion of the Human Rights Committee, violate the religious freedom of a Sikh who wears a turban in daily life.[83] With respect to the controversial question of conscientious objection to military service, the Committee adopted a modern approach departing from its earlier jurisprudence and stated that such a right can be derived from Article 18 of the International Covenant on Civil and Political Rights.[84]

Freedom of religion also includes the liberty of parents to ensure the religious and moral education of their children in conformity with their own convictions (Article 18(4) of the International Covenant on Civil and Political Rights, Article 2 of the First Additional Protocol to the European Convention of Human Rights, Article 12(4) of the American Convention on Human Rights). This can be achieved by founding private schools, by sending children to an existing private school of their choice, or by exempting children from religious instruction in public schools. If moral or ethical instruction is mandatory in public schools, it must be performed in a neutral and objective way, paying respect to other or non-religious beliefs.[85]

Freedom of expression and information constitutes one of the essential foundations of a democratic society. It includes the freedom to seek, receive and impart information and ideas of all kinds through any media; that is, orally, in writing, through print media, radio and television, commercials, film, electronic media, music, graphic and other arts, and so on. In the '*Little Red Schoolbook*' case, the European Court of Human Rights stressed that freedom of expression is not only applicable to information and ideas 'that are favourably received or regarded as inoffensive or as a matter of indifference, but also to those that offend, shock or disturb the State or any sector of the population. Such are the demands of that pluralism, tolerance and broadmindedness without which there is no democratic society'.[86] In a number of cases, the European Court tried to establish a fair balance between legitimate state interests of interfering and freedom of expression. The level of states' 'margin of appreciation' varies according to the nature of the expression, its subject and object. Because of their role in a democratic society, the media and political speech enjoy greater protection than commercial speech.[87]

While politicians enjoy a higher level of protection, they must also accept stronger criticism by journalists. This is illustrated, for example, by the cases of two Austrian journalists who had been found guilty by Austrian courts of defamation because they were unable to establish the truth of their value-judgments. In both cases, the European Court ruled that the limits of acceptable criticism are wider for politicians than for private individuals and that the truth of value-judgments is not susceptible of proof.[88] In a case against the United Kingdom, the European Court found that the extraordinary amount of libel damages (£1.5 million) awarded by a High Court jury against a historian for publication of a pamphlet in which a former high-ranking British Army officer had been accused of war crimes at the end of the Second World War violated Article 10 of the European Convention of Human Rights.[89]

Although the level of protecting freedom of expression might be lower outside Europe, the Human Rights Committee found, for example, that sentencing a Korean trade union leader to one and a half years' imprisonment for having supported a strike and condemned the government's threat to send in troops violated Article 19 of the International Covenant on Civil and Political Rights.[90] The Inter-American Commission decided that Guatemala had violated Article 14 of the American Convention on Human Rights by denying a Guatemalan bishop re-entry into his country upon returning from

Rome, where he had presented to the Pope a critical report on the situation of the Church in Guatemala.[91] Most violations of freedom of expression found by the Human Rights Committee and the Inter-American Commission, however, concerned serious repressive measures, including torture, against political opponents or trade union leaders by countries such as Colombia, Haiti, Madagascar, Uruguay or Zaire.[92]

Although state licensing of broadcasting, television or cinema enterprises is explicitly permitted by Article 10(1) of the European Convention of Human Rights, the European Court of Human Rights found that the *de facto* broadcasting monopoly in Austria was a restriction of freedom of expression and information, which in the age of satellite and cable television can no longer be deemed necessary in a democratic society.[93]

Under Article 20 of the International Covenant on Civil and Political Rights and Article 13(5) of the American Convention on Human Rights, any propaganda for war as well as incitement to national, racial or religious hatred shall be prohibited by law. A far right-wing political party which was precluded from using Canadian telephone services to disseminate anti-Semitic views inciting racial hatred could not, therefore, invoke the protection of freedom of expression.[94] Similarly, political freedoms must also not be misused for activities aimed at the destruction of human rights of others (Article 5(1) of the International Covenant on Civil and Political Rights, Article 17 of the European Convention of Human Rights). These prohibition of abuse clauses have been applied by the Human Rights Committee and the Strasbourg organs only in exceptional cases concerning, for example, the West German Communist Party, as well as neo-fascist and racist organizations in Italy and the Netherlands.[95]

Freedom of assembly protects all types of intentional, temporal gatherings of several persons for a specific, usually political, purpose, such as public meetings, street processions, demonstrations, religious gatherings and festivals. The protection extends, however, only to peaceful assemblies. An assembly loses its peaceful character when the participants are armed, when persons are physically attacked, displays smashed, furniture destroyed, cars set on fire, rocks or Molotov cocktails thrown, and so on. On the other hand, 'sit-ins', blockades and similar non-violent forms of civil disobedience are peaceful assemblies, so long as their participants do not use force or exercise active opposition.

The contents of the messages, opinions and ideas imparted at an assembly (such as incitement to racial hatred) are, however, subject to restrictions and the possible prohibition of an assembly in accordance with the respective limitation and abuse clauses. The mere fact that a large gathering of individuals advocating unpopular views might lead to clashes or might provoke counter-demonstrations is, however, no reason for state authorities to prohibit an assembly which is duly foreseen. Rather, states are obliged to protect demonstrators and, in particular, those belonging to minorities and other fringe groups of society, against threats or interference by private parties through adequate police and security measures. In the case of an anti-abortion demonstration in Austria threatened by a counter-demonstration, the European Court of Human Rights strongly underlined the following positive state obligation:[96]

> In a democracy the right to counter-demonstrate cannot extend to inhibiting the exercise of the right to demonstrate. Genuine, effective freedom of peaceful assembly cannot, therefore, be reduced to a mere duty on the part of the State not to interfere: a purely negative conception would not be compatible with the object and purpose of Article 11. Like Article 8, Article 11 sometimes requires positive measures to be taken, even in the sphere of relations between individuals, if need be.

Minor private interferences with an assembly, such as raising a banner on the occasion of a meeting of a foreign head of state, criticizing the human rights record of the visiting head of State, must, however, be tolerated in a democratic society.[97] In addition to protecting demonstrators against threats by private individuals, states are also obliged to ensure the right to peaceful assembly through other positive measures, such as making available public thoroughfares, rerouting traffic and making available public buildings in a non-discriminatory manner.

Freedom of association is the right to form and join any type of organization (legal persons under civil or commercial law, *de facto* associations and so on) established voluntarily for any purpose, such as political parties, religious societies, sport clubs, trade unions, commercial undertakings, or cultural or human rights organizations. Not included, however, are public corporations, chambers and similar institutions established by law or administrative act. The freedom of association also protects the negative freedom, the right not to join a certain organization. In the 'Closed Shop' case, the European Court of Human Rights held that an agreement between British Rail and certain trade unions, conditioning employment on membership of one of these unions, violated Article 11 of the European Convention of Human Rights.[98] To what extent freedom of association, and the right to form trade unions in particular, also protects the right of such organizations to perform activities in order to protect the interests of their members is a controversial question. Although one could argue that the right to strike is an important means of exercising trade union rights, the Human Rights Committee held that this right was not covered in Article 22 of the International Covenant on Civil and Political Rights, but only in Article 8(1) of the International Covenant on Economic, Social and Cultural Rights.[99]

In addition to the general limitation and abuse clauses, Article 22(2) of the International Covenant on Civil and Political Rights, Article 11(2) of the European Convention of Human Rights and Article 16(3) of the American Convention on Human Rights contain special restrictions for members of the armed forces and the police and, in the case of the European Convention of Human Rights, even for civil servants in general. In the case of the British signals intelligence organization, the European Commission of Human rights interpreted this provision to the extent that prohibiting employees from being trade union members was compatible with Article 11(2) of the European Convention of Human Rights.[100]

## Political Rights

While political freedoms are a necessary precondition for a democratic society, political rights in the strict sense of Article 25 of the International Covenant on Civil and Political Rights, Article 3 of the First Additional Protocol to the European Convention of Human Rights, Article 23 of the American Convention on Human Rights and Article 13 of the African Charter of Human and Peoples' Rights constitute the very essence of democracy in terms of subjective rights.[101] The right to take part in the conduct of public affairs, directly or through freely chosen representatives, is the most direct expression of political (democratic) freedom, as distinguished from the concepts of liberal or socialist freedom. It encompasses plebiscitarian forms of participation as practised, for example, in Switzerland (referenda and popular initiatives),[102] the right of petition and similar forms of direct participation. Since democracy is, however, usually functioning by means of representative participation, the most important political rights are the right to vote, the right to be elected and the right of equal access to public service.

Although political rights form an essential part of the classical concept of human rights, primarily the Western states objected to their inclusion in a universal bill of rights.[103] This also explains why Article 3 of the First Additional Protocol to the European Convention of Human Rights is the only substantive provision of the European Convention which only contains an obligation of states to hold free elections rather than a subjective right of individuals to vote. In practice, the European Commission and Court of Human Rights, by way of a dynamic interpretation, accepted this provision as a subjective human right entitling individuals to lodge a complaint.[104]

The right to vote and to be elected is a good example to illustrate the interdependence of states' obligations to respect, to ensure and to protect.[105] First of all, states are under an obligation to ensure that elections are held at periodic intervals (for example, every four to six years), at least for parliaments and other bodies exercising legislative functions. The duty to ensure the right to vote includes the obligation to provide, by means of positive state action, for free, fair and secret elections on the basis of universal and equal suffrage. This also means the duty to guarantee that all persons who are entitled to vote, including the elderly, the sick, the disabled and persons deprived of their liberty, actually have an opportunity to exercise this most important political right.

Secondly, states shall refrain from interfering with free and fair elections by, for example, privileging certain political parties in their electoral campaigns (through means of party financing or granting more time at public broadcasting stations), by committing electoral fraud or by arbitrarily excluding voters or political parties. Only reasonable and non-discriminatory restrictions are permissible, such as the exclusion of aliens (political rights are in principle still citizens' rights), minors, the mentally ill or persons convicted in court for certain crimes. Only in exceptional cases may certain (for example, fascist or racist) parties be prohibited from participating in elections. Exclusion is not permitted with regard to illiterate persons, civil servants, pre-trial detainees; nor is exclusion on any discriminatory grounds such as sex, race, religion, property, social origin or political opinion permitted. In a number of decisions, the Human Rights Committee found the statutory deprivation of political rights for Marxists by the former military regime in Uruguay a violation of Article 25 of the International Covenant on Civil and Political Rights.[106] In a case against the Netherlands, certain restrictions of the right of civil servants to be elected to municipal councils were, however, deemed reasonable.[107]

Thirdly, states have a positive duty to protect voters from undue pressure by private individuals or groups. In particular, the principle of free and fair elections means that states must guarantee in times of election campaigns that voters and candidates are not intimidated, harassed and threatened by powerful parties and pressure groups. During elections, the strict observance of a secret ballot is the best guarantee of ensuring free elections.

The right of equal access to public service obliges states to provide for minimum procedural guarantees, such as publicly announcing vacant positions and ensuring a selection procedure which grants all applicants equal chances of access according to objective criteria. In *Stalla Costa* v. *Uruguay*, the Human Rights Committee held that reasonable measures of affirmative action (preferential treatment of persons who had been arbitrarily dismissed during the military regime) did not constitute discrimination.[108] This also holds true for temporary special measures aimed at accelerating *de facto* equality between women and men (Article 4 of the Convention on the Elimination of All Forms of Discrimination against Women) or at securing adequate advancement of minorities and disadvantaged or ethnic groups (Article 1(4) of the Convention on the Elimination of All Forms of Racial Discrimination).

### Equality and Non-discrimination

Along with liberty, equality is the most important principle imbuing and inspiring the concept of human rights. True liberty can only exist on the basis of equality for all. Originally, as one of the major achievements of the bourgeois revolutions of the eighteenth and nineteenth centuries, the right to equality meant equality before the law; that is, the formal claim that laws should be applied by courts and administrative agencies in the same manner to all persons subject to it. In essence, it prohibits arbitrary enforcement of laws. With the emergence of modern democratic and social ideas, this formal principle has gradually been transformed into a principle of substantive equality, the right to the equal protection of the law. In other words, democratically elected legislative bodies were entrusted with the task of creating the legal conditions to ensure substantive, that is social or *de facto* equality.

This democratic ideal that real equality can be achieved by law is, however, extremely vague and subject to different philosophical and political views of equality and justice. Therefore, in the course of the twentieth century, the prohibition of discrimination on grounds of certain personal characteristics, such as class, race, sex or religion, has come to be the most essential element in a substantive structuring of the human right to equality. Practice shows, however, that, in the case of deeply rooted privileges or discriminatory attitudes against certain groups of the population, mere statutory prohibitions of discrimination are often insufficient to guarantee true equality. In cases such as the traditional discrimination of women, Blacks or Jews, states must resort to positive measures of protection against discrimination, such as affirmative action programmes, compulsory integration of artificially segregated groups or quota systems in the access to education or jobs.

These four historical stages of the right to equality and non-discrimination are laid down in Article 26 of the International Covenant on Civil and Political Rights and, to a lesser degree, in Article 24 of the American Convention on Human Rights and Article 3 of the African Charter of Human and Peoples' Rights. The European Convention, on the other hand, only contains an accessory prohibition of discrimination, that is the right to the equal enjoyment of other human rights (Article 14 of the European Convention of Human Rights). The most deeply rooted types of discrimination have also been tackled by means of special human rights treaties of the United Nations and its specialized agencies, above all the Convention on the Elimination of All Forms of Racial Discrimination, the Convention on the Elimination of All Forms of Discrimination against Women and relevant treaties of the International Labour Organisation (ILO) and United Nations Educational, Scientific and Cultural Organization (UNESCO).

In practice, however, it is extremely difficult to establish clear and universal standards for what is meant by equality and discrimination. Domestic courts and international monitoring bodies have developed a variety of formulae, such as 'equals should be treated equally, unequals unequally'. Not every distinction established by law is discriminatory, but only a distinction that is not based on 'reasonable and objective criteria'. It is not surprising that the ultimate answer to whether a given differentiation is reasonable or not depends on subjective value judgments as well as on the respective cultural, religious and social traditions of different societies. This explains why the right to equality is one of the most controversial human rights.

Violations of the right to equality can, therefore, only be established on a case-by-case basis. The European Court of Human Rights found discriminatory certain disadvantages for children born out of wedlock in Belgian law.[109] Gender-specific distinctions in immigration laws were found unreasonable by the European Court and the Human Rights Committee.[110] Most controversial were the Dutch social security cases. Under the Dutch Unemployment Benefits Acts, married women received support only when they could prove that they were 'breadwinners', whereas this proof was not required of married men. Although this distinction concerns economic and social rights and may still have been a reflection of the traditional role of women in many societies, the Human Rights Committee found a violation of Article 26 of the International Covenant on Civil and Political Rights.[111] Other gender-specific discriminations established by the Committee concerned the Peruvian Civil Code and the Austrian Pension Act.[112] Politically motivated dismissals from public service were considered discriminatory on the ground of political opinion,[113] and the privileged treatment of Jehovah's Witnesses with respect to conscientious objection to military service was deemed unreasonable.[114] In a case against the Czech Republic concerning the rehabilitation of persons whose property had been confiscated by the former communist government, the Committee found that the cumulative conditions of citizenship and permanent residence in the restitution act discriminated against those persons who still live abroad.[115]

Affirmative action programmes, that is temporary special measures aimed at accelerating *de facto* equality, have been developed in a number of states, notably the United States, with respect to women, Blacks and other racial or ethnic minorities. Although such measures shall not be considered discrimination in the respective United Nations treaties (Article 4 of the Convention on the Elimination of All Forms of Discrimination against Women, Article 1(4) of the Convention on the Elimination of All Forms of Racial Discrimination), the European Court of Justice ruled in a highly controversial judgment concerning preferential access of women to public office in Germany that such a programme in the state of Bremen violated European Community law.[116]

## Other Rights

It is sometimes difficult to draw a clear distinction between civil and political rights, on the one hand, and other human rights of the so-called second or third generation, on the other.[117] As has been shown, the political freedom of association includes the right to form and join trade unions, whereas the exercise of trade union rights, above all the right to strike, is usually considered as an economic right.[118] Similarly, the right to education is usually regarded as a social or cultural right, although it is listed under Article 2 of the First Additional Protocol to the European Convention of Human Rights.[119] The International Covenant on Civil and Political Rights contains rights that are usually categorized as 'third generation' rights, such as the right of peoples to self-determination (Article 1) and certain rights of persons belonging to ethnic, religious or linguistic minorities (Article 27).[120] In Chapter II of the American Convention on Human Rights, entitled 'Civil and Political Rights', one finds the right to a name (Article 18 of the American Convention on Human Rights) and to a nationality (Article 20 of the American Convention on Human Rights) which are protected in Article 24 of the International Covenant on Civil and Political Rights only as special rights of the child.[121]

One particular controversial right which can be considered as both an economic and a civil right is the right to property. It definitely belongs to the classical concept of human rights as exemplified by John Locke's famous triangular of life, liberty and possessions, as well as by various domestic bills of rights of the eighteenth and nineteenth centuries. On the international level, the right to property is guaranteed in Article 17 of the Universal Declaration of Human Rights, Article 1 of the First Additional Protocol to the European

Convention of Human Rights, Article 21 of the American Convention on Human Rights and Article 14 of the African Charter of Human and Peoples' Rights. During the drafting of the International Covenants, however, the socialist states succeeded in eliminating it from the list of human rights to be guaranteed in a binding universal treaty.

Because of its controversial character, the right to property is subject to particularly far-reaching limitation clauses. States enjoy a wide 'margin of appreciation' to restrict it in the 'public interest' (Article 1 of the First Additional Protocol to the European Convention of Human Rights), in the 'interest of society' (Article 21 of the American Convention on Human Rights) or in the 'general interest of the community' (Article 14 of the African Charter of Human and Peoples' Rights). These restrictions might even entail the total expropriation of private property if the public interest in constructing motorways, railways and so on so demand. Only Article 21(2) of the American Convention on Human Rights explicitly provides for just compensation in case of deprivation of property.

It is therefore not surprising that violations of the right to property have only been found in exceptional cases. One example was a Stockholm City Ordinance which authorized the city to expropriate a property on almost unlimited grounds. The European Court of Human Rights ruled that, notwithstanding the broad limitation clause, states must strike a fair balance between the interests of the community and the rights of the individual, including minimum procedural guarantees against government decisions concerning expropriation, the control of use of private property, or compensation. The court found a violation of Article 1 of the First Additional Protocol to the European Convention of Human Rights and afforded the applicants a considerable amount of compensation in accordance with Article 50 of the European Convention of Human Rights.[122]

## Notes

1  Cf. Manfred Nowak (1988, pp.29ff) with further references.
2  For the concept and the contents of the Universal Declaration of Human Rights, see Eide *et al.* (1992).
3  For the European Convention and its 11 Additional Protocols, as applied in the case law of the European Commission and Court of Human Rights, see for example van Dijk and van Hoof (1990); Council of Europe (1984), and loose-leave edition; Gomien (1991); Matscher and Petzold (1988); MacDonald *et al.* (1993); Pettiti *et al.* (1995).
4  For the American Convention and its two Additional Protocols, as applied in the case law of the Inter-American Commission and Court of Human Rights, see for example Buergenthal and Shelton (1995); Wilson (1994, p.19); Shelton (1994, p.333). For OAS member states which are not parties to the American

Convention on Human Rights, the Charter-based system of monitoring the American Declaration of the Rights and Duties of Man of 1948 applies.

5 Cf. Bloed (1993).
6 For the Covenant and its two Optional Protocols, as applied in the case law of the UN Human Rights Committee, see Nowak (1993); Manfred Nowak, 'The activities of the UN Human Rights Committee: Developments from 1 August 1992 to 31 July 1995', *Human Rights Law Journal*, 16, 1995; McGoldrick, (1991).
7 For the African Charter see for example Benedek (1991, p.43); Umozurike (1991, p.5); Wolfgang Benedek, 'The African Charter and Commission on Human and Peoples' Rights. How to Make it More Effective', *Netherlands Quarterly of Human Rights*, 1993, 25; M'Baye (1992); B.G. Ramcharan, 'The *Travaux Préparatoires* of the African Commission on Human Rights', *Human Rights Law Journal*, 1992, 307; C.E. Welch Jr, 'The African Commission on Human and Peoples' Rights: a five-year report and assessment', *Human Rights Quarterly*, 1992, 43; Ouguergouz (1993); Astrid Danielsen, *The State Reporting Procedure under the African Charter*, Copenhagen, Danish Institute for Human Rights, 1994.
8 For the text and background of the Vienna Declaration, see Nowak (1994).
9 Cf., for the following, Nowak (1993, pp.36ff).
10 Cf. General Comment 24/52 adopted by the Human Rights Committee on 2 November 1994 on issues relating to reservations (UN Doc. CCPR/C/21/Rev. 1/Add. 6) and the observations of Nowak, *supra*, note 6, *Human Rights Law Journal*, 16, 1995.
11 Views of the Human Rights Committee in *Delgado Paéz* v. *Colombia*, Comm. N° 195/1985.
12 Cf. the judgment of the European Court of Human Rights in *X and Y* v. *the Netherlands*, Series A. 91.
13 Judgment of the European Court of Human Rights of 27 September 1995 in *McCann et al.* v. *U.K.*, *Human Rights Law Journal*, 16, 1995, 260.
14 Cf. the annual reports of the UN Special Rapporteur on Summary and Arbitrary Executions; for example, UN-Doc. E/CN.4/1995/61.
15 Cf. Wilson (1994, pp.67ff, 242ff).
16 Cf. Nowak (1993, pp.111ff).
17 Cf. the annual reports of the UN Working Group on Enforced or Involuntary Disappearances; for example UN-Doc. E/CN.4/1995/36.
18 *Velásquez Rodríguez* v. *Honduras*, judgment of 29 July 1988, *Human Rights Law Journal*, 9, 1988, 212.
19 *Sanjuán brothers* v. *Colombia* (Comm. N° 181/1984); *Mojica* v. *Dominican Republic* (Comm. N° 449/1991).
20 Cf. Amnesty International, *Death Penalty News*, June 1995, London, Amnesty International; ibid., *The Death Penalty – List of Abolitionist and Retentionist Countries*, September 1995, London, Amnesty International; ibid., *Abolition of the Death Penalty Worldwide – Developments in 1994*, October 1995, London, Amnesty International.
21 *Roach and Pinkerton* v. *US* (Case 9647).
22 For the text of the reservation, see Nowak (1993, p.770).
23 UN Doc. CCPR/C/79/Add.50. Cf. also general comment 24/52 of 2 November 1994 on issues relating to reservations.
24 *Soering* v. *UK*, judgment of 7 July 1989, Series A. 161.
25 *Ng* v. *Canada* (Comm. N° 469/1991).
26 Cf. Nowak (1993, pp.118ff); Nowak, *supra*, note 10.
27 *Roe* v. *Wade*, 410 U.S. 113, 160, 1973.
28 *White et al.* v. *US* (Case 2141).
29 Cf. Nowak ( 1993, p.123).

30  *Brüggemann and Scheuten* v. *Germany* (Case 6959/75).
31  General comment 6/16 of 27 July 1982, para. 5.
32  General comment 14/23 of 2 November 1984, para. 6.
33  Cf. the relevant reports of non-governmental organizations, such as Amnesty International, or of intergovernmental expert organs, such as the UN Special Rapporteur on Torture (for example, annual report in UN Doc. E/CN.4/ 1995/34) or the European Committee for the Prevention of Torture: latest annual report CE Doc. CPT/INF (95) 10. See also Manfred Nowak, 'States of bondage', *UNESCO Courier*, March 1994, p.28.
34  Judgment of 18 January 1978 in the Northern Ireland case, Series A. 25.
35  Cf. Wilson (1994, pp.114ff, 242ff).
36  Cf. Nowak (1993, pp.131ff, 186ff).
37  See the reports of the European Commission on Human Rights in the Greek case (1969) and the Turkey case (1985).
38  For the Convention against Torture Committee report, see UN Doc. A/48/ 40/Add.1, for the CPT report, cf. CE Doc. CPT/INF (93) 1. See also the most recent case law of the European Court of Human Rights in individual cases against Turkey, for example, *Aksoy* v. *Turkey* (1996).
39  Cf., for example, the *Soering* and *Ng* cases above (notes 24 and 25) as well as the judgments of the European Court of Human Rights in the cases of *Cruz Varas et al.* v. *Sweden*, Series A. 201; *Vilvarajah et al.* v. *UK*, Series A. 215; *Vijayanathan and Pusparajah* v. *France*, Series A. 241-B.
40  Cases of *Mutombo* v. *Switzerland* (UN Doc. CAT/C/12/D/13/1993, 15 (1994), 164) and *Tahir Hussain Khan* v. *Canada* (UN Doc. CAT/C/13/D/15/1994); cf. Walter Suntinger, 'The principle of non-refoulement: looking rather to Geneva than to Strasbourg?', in *Austrian Journal of Public and International Law*, 1995, 203.
41  Cf. Manfred Nowak and Walter Suntinger, 'International mechanisms for the prevention of torture', in Arie Bloed, Liselotte Leicht, Manfred Nowak and Allan Rosas (eds), *Monitoring Human Rights in Europe*, Dordrecht, Martinus Nijhoff Publishers, 1993, p.145.
42  For legal definitions, cf. the UN Supplementary Convention on the Abolition of Slavery, the Slave Trade, and Institutions and Practices similar to Slavery of 1956.
43  *W, X, Y and Z* v. *U.K.* (Cases 3435–3438/67).
44  Cf. Gomien (1991, p.23).
45  Cf. Nowak (1993, pp.167ff); Wilson (1994, pp.145ff, 242ff); Stefan Trechsel, 'Liberty and security of person', in MacDonald *et al.* (1993, pp. 277ff); van Dijk and van Hoof (1990, pp.251ff). Cf. also the annual reports of the UN Working Group on Arbitrary Detention, for example in UN Doc. E/CN.4/1995/31.
46  Cf. general comments 9/16 and 21/44 of the Human Rights Committee.
47  Views of the Human Rights Committee in *Párkányi* v. *Hungary* (Comm. N° 410/1990).
48  Views of the Human Rights Committee in *Delgado Paéz* v. *Colombia* (Comm. N° 195/1985), *Chiiko* v. *Zambia* (Comm. N° 314/1988), *Oló Bahamonde* v. *Equatorial Guinea* (Comm. N° 468/1991) and *Mojica* v. *Dominican Republic* (Comm. N° 449/1991). Cf. Nowak (1993, pp.161ff).
49  Cf., for example, Gomien (1991, pp.34ff); van Dijk and van Hoof (1990, pp.294ff); Georg Ress, 'The effects of judgments and decisions in domestic law', in Macdonald *et al.* (1993, pp.822ff) concerning effects on the Austrian legal system.
50  Cf. Nowak (1993, pp. 241ff); Wilson (1994, pp.194ff).
51  Views of the Human Rights Committee in *Casanovas* v. *France* (Comm. N° 441/1990).

52   Views of the Human Rights Committee in *Morael* v. *France* (Comm. N° 207/ 1986).
53   See *supra*, under chapter 5 (prohibition of torture).
54   See below, 'Right to Privacy, Marriage, Family Life and Rights of Children'.
55   Cf., for example, the Geneva Convention relating to the Status of Refugees 1951 and its Protocol of 1966, the OAU Convention Governing the Specific Aspects of Refugee Problems in Africa 1969, the UN Convention on the Reduction of Statelessness 1961, the UN Convention relating to the Status of Stateless Persons 1954 and the UN Convention on the Protection of the Rights of All Migrant Workers and Members of Their Families 1990.
56   Cf. Nowak (1993, pp.218ff).
57   Cf. the views of the Human Rights Committee in *Peltonen* v. *Finland* (Comm. N° 492/1992).
58   Cf., for example, *Vidal Martins* v. *Uruguay* (Comm. N° 57/1979); also *Bwalya and Kalenga* v. *Zambia* (Comm. N°s 314 and 326/1988) and *Oló Bahamonde* v. *Equatorial Guinea* (Comm. N° 468/1991).
59   *Lovelace* v. *Canada* (Comm. N° 24/1977).
60   Cf. *Mpaka-Nsusu, Birindwa and Tshisekedi* v *Zaire* (Comm. N°s 157/1983, 241 and 242/1987).
61   Cf. Nowak (1993, pp. 287ff).
62   Interestingly enough, the African Charter does not contain a right to privacy.
63   *Coeriel and Auriek* v. *Netherlands* (Comm. N° 453/1991).
64   See the Human Rights Committee's general comment 16/32 of 23 March 1988, para. 10. See also in regard to the European Convention of Human Rights, for example, van Dijk and van Hoof (1990, pp.372, 377).
65   Cf. the views of the Human Rights Committee in *Fei* v. *Colombia* (Comm. N° 514/1992).
66   Judgments of the European Court of Human Rights in *Dudgeon* v. *U.K.*, *Norris* v. *Ireland* and *Modinos* v. *Cyprus*, Series A. 45, 142 and 259; views of the Human Rights Committee in *Toonen* v. *Australia* (Comm. N° 488/1992).
67   General comment 16/32, para. 5.
68   Cf. the judgments of the European Court of Human Rights in *Klass* v. *Germany*, Series A. 28; *Malone* v. *U.K.*, Series A. 82; *Kruslin* v. *France*, Series A. 176-A and *Huvig* v. *France*, Series A. 176-B.
69   Cf., for example, the judgments of the European Court of Human Rights in *Golder* v. *U.K.*, Series A. 18; *Silver* v. *U.K.*, Series A. 61; and the views of the Human Rights Committee in *Pinkney* v. *Canada* (Comm. N° 27/1980) and *Angel Estrella* v. *Uruguay* (Comm. N° 74/1980).
70   *Berrehab* v. *the Netherlands*, Series A. 138.
71   Cf. *Johnston* v. *Ireland*, Series A. 112 and Nowak (1993, pp.411ff).
72   Cf. the rulings of the European Commission on Human Rights in *Hamer and Draper* v. *U.K.* (Cases 7114/75 and 8186/78).
73   Cf. the views of the Human Rights Committee in *Hendriks* v. *the Netherlands* (Comm. N° 201/1985), *Balaguer* v. *Spain* (Comm. N° 417/1990).
74   *Mónaco and Vicario* v. *Argentina* (Comm. N° 400/1990).
75   Cf. the judgment of the European Court of Human Rights in *Marckx* v. *Belgium*, Series A. 31, and Nowak (1993, pp.429ff).
76   For the implementation of the Convention on the Rights of the Child, cf. the annual reports of the UN Committee on the Rights of the Child, UN Doc. A/ 49/41. For the practices of the sale of children, child labour, prostitution, pornography and so on, cf. also the annual reports of the UN Special Rapporteur on the Sale of Children, for example UN Doc. E/CN.4/1994/84 and the provisional report of 20 September 1995, UN Doc. A/50/456.
77   Cf. Nowak (1993, pp.312ff).

78  Cf. general comment 10/19 of the Human Rights Committee, para. 3.
79  Cf. Articles 21 and 22(2) of the International Covenant on Civil and Political Rights, para. 2 of Articles 9 to 11 of the European Convention of Human Rights and Articles 15 and 16(2) of the American Convention on Human Rights.
80  Cf., for example, the judgments of the European Court of Human Rights in *Sunday Times* v. *U.K.*, Series A. 30; *Handyside* v. *U.K.*, Series A. 24; *Malone* v. *U.K.*, Series A. 82; *Lingens* v. *Austria*, Series A. 103; for other cases see *Jersild* v. *Denmark*, Series A. 298 (1994); *Vereniging Weekblad Bluf* v. *the Netherlands*, Series A. 306-A (1995). See also Gomien (1991, pp.52ff); van Dijk and van Hoof (1990, pp.583ff).
81  Cf. general comment 22/48 of the Human Rights Committee, paras 1–3.
82  Cf. the comprehensive list of activities in Article 6 of the 1981 UN Declaration on Religious Intolerance.
83  *Singh Bhinder* v. *Canada* (Comm. N° 208/1986).
84  General comment 22/48; for its earlier jurisprudence, cf. Nowak (1993, pp. 322ff).
85  Cf. the judgment of the European Court of Human Rights in the Danish Sex Education Case (Series A. 23) and the views of the Human Rights Committee in *Hartikainen et al.* v. *Finland* (Comm. N° 40/1978).
86  *Handyside* v. *U.K.*, Series A. 24.
87  Cf., for example, the judgment in the case of *Barthold* v. *Germany* (Series A. 90) and the decision of the European Commission on Human Rights in the case of *Church of Scientology* v. *Sweden* (N° 7805/77). See also the views of the Human Rights Committee in *Ballantyne et al.* v. *Canada* (Comm. N° 359 and 385/1989) and *Singer* v. *Canada* (Comm. N° 455/1991).
88  Judgments in *Lingens and Oberschlick* v. *Austria*, Series A. 103 and 204. Cf. also *Castells* v. *Spain*, Series A. 236 and *Thorgeir Thorgeirson* v. *Iceland*, Series A. 239.
89  *Miloslavsky* v. *U.K.*, Series A. 316-B, *Human Rights Law Journal*, 16, 1995, 295.
90  *Sohn* v. *Korea* (Comm. N° 518/1992).
91  *Bishop Gerardi* v. *Guatemala* (Case 7778).
92  Cf. Nowak (1993, p. 346); Wilson (1994, p.218).
93  *Informationsverein Lentia et al.* v. *Austria*, Series A. 276.
94  Decision of the Human Rights Committee in *Western Guard Party* v. *Canada* (Comm. N° 104/1981).
95  Cases before the European Commission on Human Rights, cf. *K.P.D.* v. *Germany* (Case 250/57), *Glimmerveen and Hagenbeek* v. *the Netherlands* (Cases 8438/78, 8406/78); *M.A.* v. *Italy* (views of the Human Rights Committee in Comm. N° 117/1981).
96  *Plattform 'Ärzte für das Leben'* v. *Austria*, Series A. 139.
97  Views of the Human Rights Committee in *Kivenmaa* v. *Finland* (Comm. N° 412/1990).
98  *Young, James and Webster* v. *U.K.*, Series A. 44.
99  *Alberta Union* v. *Canada* (Comm. N° 118/1982). Cf. the critique of Nowak (1993, pp.391ff).
100  *C.C.S.U.* v. *U.K.* (Case 11603/85).
101  Cf. Nowak (1998).
102  Cf. Markku Suksi, *Bringing in the People: A Comparison of Constitutional Forms and Practices of the Referendum*, Dordrecht, Martinus Nijhoff Publishers, 1993.
103  Cf. Nowak (1993, pp.437ff).
104  Cf. the case of *Mathieu-Mohin and Clerfayt* v. *Belgium*, Series A. 113 and Nowak (1988, pp.208ff) with further references.
105  Cf. *supra*, chapter 3.
106  Cf. Nowak (1993, p.442). See also *Bwalya* v. *Zambia* (Comm. N° 314/1988).

107   *Debreczeny* v. *the Netherlands* (Comm. N° 500/1992).
108   *Stalla Costa* v. *Uruguay* (Comm. N° 198/1985).
109   *Marckx* v. *Belgium*, Series A. 31.
110   *Abdulaziz et al.* v. *U.K.*, Series A. 94; Mauritian Women Case before the Human Rights Committee (Comm. N° 35/1978).
111   *Broeks and Zwaan-de Vries* v. *the Netherlands* (Comm. Nos. 172 and 182/1984).
112   *Ato del Avellanal* v. *Peru* (Comm. N° 202/1986); *Pauger* v. *Austria* (Comm. N° 415/1990).
113   *Bwalya* v. *Zambia* (Comm. N° 314/1988); *Orihuela* v. *Peru* (Comm. N° 309/1988); cf. also *Oló Bahamonde* v. *Equatorial Guinea* (Comm. N° 468/1991).
114   *Brinkhof* v. *the Netherlands* (Comm. N° 402/1990). Since the applicant was not considered a victim, the Committee finally did not find a violation of Article 26.
115   *Simunek et al.* v. *the Czech Republic* (Comm. N° 516/1992).
116   Judgment of 17 October 1995 of the European Court of Justice in the case of *Kalanke* (C-450/93), published in, for example, *Europäische Grundrechte Zeitschrift*, 1995, pp.546ff.
117   Cf. *supra*, under chapter 1 (Introduction).
118   Cf. the views of the Human Rights Committee, in *Alberta Union* v. *Canada* (Comm. N° 118/1982).
119   For the liberty of parents to ensure the education of their children in conformity with their own religious and philosophical convictions, see above, 'Political Freedoms'.
120   For these rights, cf. Chapters 5 and 8 of the present volume.
121   Cf. above, 'Right to Privacy, Marriage, Family Life and Rights of Children'.
122   *Sporrong and Lönnroth* v. *Sweden*, Series A. 52. Cf. also the judgments of the European Court of Human Rights in the cases against Sweden of *Jacobsson*, Series A. 163; *Hakansson and Sturesson*, Series A. 171-A; and *Langborger*, Series A. 155.

# Bibliography

Amnesty International (1994), *'Disappearances' and Political Killings: Human Rights Crisis of the 1990s: A Manual for Action*. London, London, Amnesty International.

Amnesty International (1995), *Abolition of the Death Penalty Worldwide – Developments in 1994*, London, Amnesty International.

Amnesty International (1995), *Death Penalty News*, June, London, Amnesty International.

Amnesty International (1995), *The Death Penalty – List of Abolitionist and Retentionist Countries*, September.

Benedek, Wolfgang (1991), 'The African Human Rights', in C. Krause and A. Rosas (eds), *Development Co-operation and Processes toward Democracy*, Nordic Seminar, Hanasaari, October, Helsinki.

Bloed, Arie (ed.) (1993), *The Conference on Security and Co-operation in Europe: Analysis and Basic Documents, 1972–1993*, Dordrecht, Martinus Nijhoff.

Buergenthal, T. (1995), *International Human Rights in a Nutshell*, 2nd edn, Saint Paul, Minnesota, West Publishing Co.

Buergenthal, Thomas and Dinah Shelton (1995), *Protecting Human Rights in the Americas: Cases and Materials*, 4th ed, Kehl/Strasbourg/Arlington, N.P. Engel.

Council of Europe (1984), *Digest of Strasbourg Case-Law Relating to the European Convention on Human Rights*, Cologne, Carl Heymans Verlag.

Donnelly, Jack (1993), *International Human Rights*, Boulder, CO, Westview Press.

Eide, Asbjørn, Gudmundur Alfredsson, Goran Melander, Lars Adam Rehof and Allan Rosas, with the collaboration of Theresa Swineheart (eds) (1992), *The Universal Declaration of Human Rights: A Commentary*, Oslo, Scandinavian University Press.

Gomien, Donna (1991), *Short Guide to the European Convention on Human Rights*, Strasbourg, Council of Europe.

Hannum, H. (ed.) (1992), *Guide to International Human Rights Practice*, 2nd ed, Philadelphia, University of Pennsylvania Press.

MacDonald, Ronald St.J., Franz Matscher and Herbert Petzold (eds) (1993), *The European System for the Protection of Human Rights*, Dordrecht, Martinus Nijhoff Publishers.

Matscher, Franz and Herbert Petzold (eds) (1988), *Protecting Human Rights: The European Dimension. Studies in honour of Gérard J. Wiarda*, Cologne, Carl Heymanns Verlag.

M'Baye, Kéba (1992), *Les Droits de l'homme en Afrique*, Paris/Geneva, Editions A. Pedone.

McGoldrick, Dominic (1991), *The Human Rights Committee, Its Role in the Development of the International Covenant on Civil and Political Rights*, Oxford, Clarendon Press.

Nowak, Manfred (1988), *Politische Grundrechte*, Vienna, Springer Verlag 1988.

Nowak, Manfred (1993) *U.N. Covenant on Civil and Political Rights – CCPR Commentary*, Kehl/Strasbourg/Arlington, N.P. Engel.

Nowak, Manfred (ed.) (1994), *World Conference on Human Rights – The Contribution of NGOs*, Vienna, Manz Verlag.

Ouguergouz, Fatsah (1993), *La Charte africaine des droits de l'homme. Une approche juridique des droits de l'homme entre tradition et modernité*, Paris, Presses Universitaires de France.

Pettiti, Louis-Edouard, Emmanuel Decaux and Pierre-Henri Imbert (1995), *La Convention européenne des droits de l'homme*, Paris, Economica.

Shelton, Dinah (1994), 'The Jurisprudence of the Inter-American Court of Human Rights', *The American University Journal of International Law and Policy*, **10**, (1).

Umozurike, U.O. (1991), 'The African Charter on Human and Peoples' Rights – An Introduction', *Review of the African Commission on Human and Peoples' Rights*, The Hague, Martinus Nijhoff, 1997.

Van Dijk, Pieter and Fried van Hoof (1990), *Theory and Practice of the European Convention on Human Rights*, 2nd edn, Deventer, Kluwer Publishers.

Wilson, Richard J. (1994), 'Inter-American Commission on Human Rights: individual case resolutions', *The American University Journal of International Law and Policy*, **10**, (1).

# 4 Economic and Social Rights

## ASBJØRN EIDE

## Introduction: Origin, Content and State Obligations

*Introducing Economic and Social Rights*

A normative system of internationally recognized human rights exists. These rights are interdependent and indivisible. Their content is found, in broad outline, in the International Bill of Human Rights, which consists of the Universal Declaration of Human Rights, the International Covenant on Civil and Political Rights, and the International Covenant on Economic, Social and Cultural Rights.

The moral foundation of international human rights is found in Article 1 of the Universal Declaration: 'All human beings are born free and equal in dignity and rights. They are endowed with reason and conscience and shall act towards each other in a spirit of brotherhood.'

When the General Assembly, on 10 December 1948, in its resolution 217A(III) adopted the Universal Declaration of Human Rights, it stated in the Preamble that the Universal Declaration of Human Rights was proclaimed

> to the end that every individual and every organ of society, keeping this Declaration constantly in mind, shall strive by teaching and education to promote respect for these rights and freedoms and by progressive measures, national and international, to secure their universal and effective recognition and observance, both among the peoples of member states themselves and among the peoples of territories under their jurisdiction.

At the time when the Universal Declaration was adopted, the rights were obviously not universally enjoyed. They were not even universally recognized. Now, 50 years later, their enjoyment has increased and their recognition has undoubtedly become more widespread. However, much has still to be done, both in terms of increasing the recognition of the rights and, even more, in obtaining their actual enjoyment. This applies, in particular, to economic and social rights. In many parts of the world they are still not properly recognized: we continue to find both individuals and states which claim that economic and social rights are not proper human rights. Such scepticism, with outright negative attitudes to economic and social rights, derives from cultural traditions. One manifestation of the relativity inherent in cultural traditions is the assumption in some Western societies that human rights shall be construed as natural rights, securing the freedom of the individual from the state. On the basis of this narrow construction of human rights, significant parts of the International Bill of Human Rights can be challenged.

The International Bill of Human Rights was not drafted to codify a particular set of philosophical assumptions prevalent in the eighteenth century, but to develop a comprehensive system of rights which could constitute solutions to important moral and political problems. There is no single philosophical strand which can claim the property of human rights; consequently, the only platform on which a consensus can be built is, indeed, the International Bill of Human Rights, as adopted by the United Nations. It will therefore be taken for granted here that the whole Bill of Human Rights is equally valid.

A practical argument can be added to this. Anyone who wants to pick out some parts of human rights but deny the validity of others cannot refer to the Universal Declaration as the source of validity of the rights they refer to. What is left, therefore, is only a reference to their own particular subjective opinions.

In the next section, however, we shall also show that, even within Western societies, a broadening understanding of human rights took place as a consequence of the evolution of society, and that by the time of the adoption of the Universal Declaration in 1948, economic and social rights had become an important component of the legal and administrative systems of Western states. Indeed, there was solid support from the West for the introduction of economic and social rights in the International Bill of Human Rights, contrary to what has often been argued subsequently.

The International Bill of Human Rights should be seen as a global programme with a number of sub-projects. It is a global programme in the sense expressed in the Preamble to the Universal Declaration quoted above: that by teaching and education the human rights should be promoted, and that by progressive measures their universal and effective observance should be achieved. Only in a very philosophical sense were human rights universal by 1948. What is required is to make them universal by taking part in the programme established in

1948 and to pursue the various projects that can be derived from it. The realization of economic and social rights can be conceived of as one sub-programme within the overall task, and the realization of each of the particular rights could be looked at as projects within the wider task.

Economic and social rights are found as part and parcel of many international instruments, universal and regional. Among the universal instruments adopted by the United Nations are the following: the Universal Declaration of Human Rights; the International Covenant on Economic, Social and Cultural Rights; the Convention on the Rights of the Child; the Convention on the Rights of Migrant Workers and Their Families; the Convention on the Elimination of All Forms of Racial Discrimination; and the Convention on the Elimination of All Forms of Discrimination against Women. At the regional level, the following are of particular relevance: the American Declaration of the Rights and Duties of Man; the American Convention on Human Rights; the Additional Protocol to the American Convention on Human Rights in the area of Economic, Social and Cultural Rights; the African Charter on Human and Peoples' Rights; and the European Social Charter. References to economic and social rights to be applied in particular circumstances are made in numerous other instruments.

Neither in 1948, at the time of the adoption of the Declaration, nor in many of the instruments adopted in more recent years, such as the Convention on the Rights of the Child in 1989, has any division been made between civil and political rights, on the one hand, and economic and social rights, on the other. In contrast to this, within the International Bill of Human Rights, the content of the Universal Declaration was divided in two: one covenant for civil and political rights, and one for economic, social and cultural rights.

The division must in part be explained by the intensification of the ideological controversy during the Cold War between what was then the East and the West in the Northern hemisphere. Notwithstanding their rather bad performance with regard to human rights as a whole, the socialist countries sought to justify their system by claiming that they were giving priority to economic and social rights. In response, some Western societies and their governments overstated their priority given to civil and political rights, to the extent of a near rejection of economic and social rights as part of the human rights system. This was in sharp contrast with their own political and social development within the last century, as we shall see in the next section. Since the ideological quarrel has ended with the disappearance of the communist systems, there should be no reason to continue this rather sterile dichotomy between the two sets of rights.

The division within the International Bill of Human Rights was also pursued within the Council of Europe, where the European

Convention of Human Rights contains mainly civil rights (political rights were added afterwards, in Protocol 1), while most of the economic and social rights are contained in the European Social Charter.

The separation between these instruments has often been used as evidence of inherent differences between the two categories of rights. This has not only led to a widespread philosophical and legalistic tradition to establish a hierarchy where civil rights are put at the top; it has also affected the work of non-governmental human rights organizations which pay much less attention to economic and social rights than to civil and political rights.

The United Nations Committee on Economic, Social and Cultural Rights noted, in an address to the World Conference on Human Rights in 1993, that:

> The international community as a whole continues to tolerate all too often breaches of economic, social and cultural rights which, if they occurred in relation to civil and political rights, would provoke expressions of horror and outrage and would lead to concerted calls for immediate remedial action. In effect, despite the rhetoric, violations of civil and political rights continue to be treated as though they were far more serious, and more patently intolerable, than massive and direct denials of economic, social and cultural rights.[1]

It is a matter of urgency to develop and strengthen the discourse on all aspects of human rights, including economic and social rights. They need to become part of the national debate, to be taken up by individuals and groups in addressing their own governments, pointing out the responsibility that states have undertaken to ensure economic and social rights, and to bring about a dialogue about the ways in which they can be realized, in particular for the most vulnerable members of society.

One argument often used against economic and social rights from a legalistic point of view is that they are not 'justiciable'. This means that they are not suitable for handling by courts or similar institutions. Several arguments can be made against this.

First, many aspects of economic and social rights can be made justiciable, as can be seen in many domestic legal systems. Second, the concept of justiciability is in itself very fluid and reflects differences in legal traditions and in philosophical views about the relationship between courts and the state. Third, human rights can still be human rights even when they are not in all aspects justiciable. Compliance with the corresponding obligations can be monitored nationally and by international bodies, as indeed they are. Furthermore, rights which are not initially justiciable can gradually become so by concretization both through practice and through more detailed standard-setting at the international level and by legislation at the national level. Again, we must revert to the point made above that the adoption of the Universal Declaration was the initiation of a programme by which, as stated in its Preamble: 'every individual and every organ of society' shall by progressive measures 'secure the universal and effective recognition and observance of these human rights'. To do so includes the concretization of the rights to such an extent that more and more components thereof also become justiciable in domestic legal systems. This is a continuing process and will not be solved in all its aspects in the near future.

The task has been set by adopting these rights; what is required is to make use of these rights not only at the international level, but even more at the national level. Individuals and groups should draw on these rights in their discourse with the state, through a dialogue demanding that the rights be implemented, and through a discussion on the ways in which this can be done, including the contributions to be made by individuals in order to secure the actual enjoyment of these rights. Subsequently, this chapter will have this overall task in mind by indicating elements which can be pursued in the discourse, both at the national and international levels, on the basis of the economic and social rights which have been adopted as part of the universal human rights system.

## National Origins of Economic and Social Rights: Experiences of the Early Industrialized Countries

The formulation of economic and social rights in the Universal Declaration is significantly influenced by the experience of industrialization in Western countries. In 1950, the British social historian T.H. Marshall presented a model of the evolution of the rights of citizens in Western societies, using the United Kingdom as an example. It corresponds to the understanding of the historical evolution of modern human rights in these societies. Marshall claimed that three sets of rights have emerged in some European states since the eighteenth century, and in the following order.

1  Civil rights, such as liberty of person, freedom of speech, thought and faith, the right to own property, expanded from the latter part of the seventeenth century and throughout the eighteenth century.
2  Political rights, such as the franchise and the right of access to public office developed in the nineteenth century.
3  Social rights ranging from 'the right to a modicum of economic welfare and security to the right to share to the full the social heritage and to live life as a civilized being according to the

standards prevailing in society', were gradually introduced in the late nineteenth and early twentieth century.[2]

This development took somewhat different paths in different Western countries. On the basis of comprehensive empirical material, Esping-Andersen (1990) has argued that three different systems of welfare capitalism emerged and, consequently, three different approaches to economic and social rights. He argues that the 'welfare state' is a system of social stratification which actively orders social relations. The earliest model, which still has its followers, developed poor laws and provided poor relief, but at extremely low levels. This had the effect of maintaining a social stigma for those who were given relief, with a view to preventing persons from wanting to obtain social assistance. It was based on an extreme reliance on the market and on contractual relations, coinciding with the elimination of the feudal system which pushed large numbers of people off the land where they had previously made their living as serfs and, later, as peasants without property. Having lost their means of livelihood, they became a cheap commodity for the emerging capitalist society. Only those who could not be absorbed, even at the lowest possible wages mainly in mining and in the budding industries, were given a modicum of poor relief in order not to die from starvation. This was an extreme reliance on the market, and any type of action which could interfere with labour as a cheap commodity was ideologically resisted. Remnants of this still exist in means-tested social assistance approaches, in societies where to be 'on welfare' is still considered a stigma.

A second approach was promoted by conservative reformers such as Bismarck in Germany, through the social insurance model. It sought, according to Esping-Andersen:

> to achieve two simultaneous results in terms of stratification. The first was to consolidate divisions among wage-earners by legislating distinct programs for different class and status groups, each with its own conspicuously unique set of rights and privileges which was designed to accentuate the individual's appropriate station in life. The second objective was to tie the loyalties of the individual directly to the monarchy or to the central state authority. This was Bismarck's motive when he promoted a direct state supplement to the pension benefit. This state–corporatist model was pursued mainly in nations such as Germany, Austria, Italy and France, and often resulted in a labyrinth of status-specific insurance funds.[3]

The third approach is the universalistic system. Under this, all citizens are endowed with similar rights, irrespective of class or market position. The system is meant to cultivate cross-class solidarity, a solidarity of the nation. This is the democratic, flat-rate, general revenue-financed model which was first formulated by Lord Beveridge, as Chairman of the Beveridge Commission in 1942.[4] It has subsequently been developed to its fullest extent in the Nordic countries.

From the above, it can be seen how economic and social rights emerged as a consequence of industrialization. Reflecting on the introduction in the United States of the Social Security Act in 1935, which introduced at a very modest level some old-age pension and unemployment benefits, the American economist J.K. Galbraith observed:

> The need for protection of the old and the unemployed is inescapably allied with industrial development and had for long been so recognized. An industrial society has its own built-in system of social security. The farms or peasant holdings are passed on to the offspring, and the latter, often by rigorously enforced custom, look after their elders. A major reason for rural population increase in much of the world is the need to be assured of sons who will do the work in the fields and be responsible for their parents in their old age. As to unemployment compensation, there is the stolid fact that there is no unemployment on a farm. By lowering the effective wage, some or much of which can be earned in kind, some employment can always be provided or invented. It is with urbanization and industrialization that old age pension and unemployment compensation become socially essential. It is then that, with a much loosened family structure, the old have no support, the unemployed have no income.[5]

While this gives a useful description of the historical process within the industrialized north, it does not fully take into account the problems of the landless and dispossessed, of whom there were many in the early industrialization of England (the effect of the 'Enclosure Acts') and are currently in parts of the Third World, partly as a consequence of the 'Green Revolution'.

Since economic and social rights have now been introduced at the universal level, they have had to relate not only to industrial but also to agricultural societies. This makes it necessary to develop different approaches depending on the circumstances of the particular situations.

Generally, however, it can be observed that fewer efforts are made to secure economic and social rights to the rural than to the urban population in many parts of the world. This may in part be due to the different needs mentioned by Galbraith above, but also to the lesser influence of the rural poor on the policy and decision making of their respective governments.

Human rights are therefore all the more important since their application can compensate for political weakness. One illustration in this respect is the provision in Article 14 of the Convention on the Elimination of All Forms of Discrimination Against Women. Not only is the rural population often the weakest part of society, but rural women are doubly weak. The emphasis in Article 14 on the economic and social rights of rural women constitutes one of the most important challenges to the whole edifice. To this we shall return later.

*Origins and Evolution of Economic and Social Rights at the International Level*

The evolution of human rights at the national level was closely related to the expansion of the concept and content of citizenship. However, even when human rights are lifted up to the international level, we have either to separate them from the notion of citizenship or to broaden the content of that concept.

Since trade and investment cross borders, there also emerged in the process of industrialization a concern with labour relations in other countries, and gradually also with social rights applying in other countries. Differences in wages and in social security have an influence on the cost of production. In order to ensure that countries with a relatively high level of social security are not at a disadvantage in competition on the international market, there emerges a concern with equalizing the treatment of labour and of social security. Added to this are the ties of solidarity which to some extent have existed between workers and labour movements in different parts of the industrialized world. International cooperation related to labour laws emerged as a result of the desirability of harmonization in this field.

International cooperation related to economic and social rights preceded cooperation related to civil and political rights. In the area of labour rights, such cooperation emerged as a result of the desirability of harmonizing labour laws among industrialized countries. The first efforts were made as early as the latter part of the nineteenth century, on the urging of personalities such as Robert Owen in England and Daniel Legrand in France.

A conference convened by the German government was held in Berlin in 1890 to consider an international agreement on labour conditions. It adopted resolutions on work in mines, weekly rest and the work of children, young persons and women. However, the resolutions were not followed up. In 1900, a group of scholars and administrators formed the International Association for the Legal Protection of Workers, which set up an office in Basle and which undertook studies and dissemination of labour laws. At its initiative, the Swiss government convened conferences in 1905 and 1906 which led to the adoption of the first international labour conventions, which prohibited nightwork by women in industry and the use of white phosphorous in the production of matches.[6]

At the end of the First World War, this was given impetus by the establishment of the International Labour Organisation, founded in 1919. One of its main activities was, and still is, to adopt conventions and recommendations on labour standards, and to supervise the implementation of these instruments.

Cooperation related to what is now called 'the right to health' has its origin in the efforts to develop conventions to prevent the spread of communicable diseases, in particular the adoption of sanitary conventions on cholera and the plague. A number of these conventions were consolidated into a single text in 1903. In 1907, the Office International d'Hygiène Publique (OIHP) was established. The Health Organization of the League of Nations was established on the basis of Article 23(f) of the Covenant of the League of Nations, which called for joint steps to prevent and control disease. A much more comprehensive approach to international cooperation in the field of health was introduced with the establishment of the World Health Organization[7] in 1946.

International cooperation related to what is now called 'the right to education' has a more limited history. A private organization, the International Bureau of Education, was established in Geneva in 1924 and was transformed into an intergovernmental organization in 1929 as an international coordinating centre for institutions concerned with education. A much broader approach was chosen, however, with the establishment of UNESCO in 1945.

These and various other early international efforts were brought together when the United Nations was founded. The need to develop universal standards in the economic and social field was recognized from the earliest preparations for the United Nations. The main initiatives came from the United States. The 'Four Freedoms' address made in January 1941 by the President of the United States, Franklin D. Roosevelt, called for measures to ensure the enjoyment 'everywhere in the world', of four freedoms, one of which was the freedom from want. The same concern was repeated in the Common Programme of Purposes and Principles, known as the Atlantic Declaration, adopted by the American President and the British Prime Minister, Winston Churchill, in August 1941, which listed eight purposes and principles. Under the fifth of these, they declared that they would endeavour 'to bring about the fullest collaboration between all nations in the economic field with the object of securing, for all, improved labour standards, economic advancement and social security. Less than six months later, on 1 January 1942, at the initiative of the United States, the programme of the Atlantic Charter was subscribed to by 25 states which signed the Declaration of the United Nations.

Against this background, a number of initiatives were taken during the Second World War to draft an international bill of human rights. One of the most successful efforts was undertaken by a United States-based institution, the American Law Institute. In 1942, it convened a group of jurists coming from the United States and 23 other countries, which elaborated a Declaration of Essential Human Rights. The work was completed in 1944, and the Declaration contained nearly the whole range of human rights – civil, political, economic, social and cultural – which later found their way into the Universal Declaration of Human Rights. When the Secretariat of the United Nations made its first draft for the Universal Declaration, this Declaration of Essential Human Rights was one of the main sources of inspiration.[8]

Throughout the evolutionary history of human rights, three aspects of human existence have sought to be safeguarded: human integrity, freedom and equality. Axiomatic is the respect for the dignity of every human being. The way in which these issues have been addressed has matured over time, from initial, idealistic assertions of vague principles to the adoption of the comprehensive, international normative system now in existence. That system contains a wide range of specific rights and, to some extent, also corresponding obligations of states. The latter need to be explored when seeking to link rights with concrete development concerns and approaches.

When the Universal Declaration on Human Rights was finally adopted in 1948, there was thus not much doubt that economic and social rights had to be included. The great contribution of this Declaration is, however, that it extended the human rights platform to embrace the whole field – civil, political, economic, social and cultural – and made the different rights interrelated and mutually reinforcing. The realization, particularly in the West, that the political upheavals and the emergence of totalitarian regimes in the period between the two world wars had been due to widespread unemployment and poverty had contributed to a genuine interest in securing economic and social rights, not only for their own sake but also for the preservation of individual freedom and democracy. This view was based on a conviction that, even in periods of recession, it is necessary to ensure that basic economic and social rights are enjoyed by all.[9]

These concerns are more relevant than ever at the present time, in the light of escalating unemployment, increasing poverty and growing disparities in income, not only in the Third World but also in Central and Eastern Europe and in the West. It is necessary, therefore, to increase the efficiency of international mechanisms in this field and possibly to develop new ones.

## Human Rights and Corresponding Obligations

*Economic, Social and Cultural Rights as Part of the Human Rights Package*

Economic, social and cultural rights constitute three interrelated components of a more comprehensive package, with obvious links to civil and political rights. As human rights and fundamental freedoms are indivisible and interdependent, equal attention should be paid to the implementation, promotion and protection of both civil and political, and economic, social and cultural rights.

At the core of social rights is the right to an adequate standard of living: Universal Declaration of Human Rights – Article 25; International Covenant on Economic, Social and Cultural Rights – Article 11; Convention on the Rights of the Child – Article 27. The enjoyment of these rights requires, at a minimum, that everyone shall enjoy the necessary subsistence rights: adequate food and nutrition, clothing, housing and the necessary conditions of care. Closely related to this right is the right of families to assistance (International Covenant on Economic, Social and Cultural Rights – Article 10; Convention on the Rights of the Child – Article 27). In order to enjoy these social rights, there is also a need to enjoy certain economic rights. These are the right to property (Universal Declaration of Human Rights – Article 17), the right to work (Universal Declaration of Human Rights – Article 23; International Covenant on Economic, Social and Cultural Rights – Article 6) and the right to social security (Universal Declaration of Human Rights – Articles 22 and 25; International Covenant on Economic, Social and Cultural Rights – Article 9; Convention on the Rights of the Child – Article 26).

Economic rights have a dual function, most clearly demonstrated in regard to the right to property. On the one hand, this right serves as a basis for entitlements which can ensure an adequate standard of living while, on the other hand, it is a basis of independence and therefore of freedom. The initial concern in early modern times with the right to individual property, articulated by John Locke in 1689,[10] was directed against the feudal order where control over land and other resources was based on a hierarchical system constituting profound inequality and dependencies. England was still a predominantly agricultural society; Locke's primary concern was that land should belong to the tiller, 'not to the fancy or covetous'. 'As much land as a man tills, plants, improves, cultivates, and can use the product of, so much is his property,' Locke observed.[11]

The right to property became a crucial element in the early quest for freedom and equality, but the right to property in the traditional understanding of the term cannot be enjoyed on an equal basis by

all. The transformation from an agricultural to an urban and industrial society requires a more complex system of rights in order to
ensure livelihood in dignity for all. The right to property therefore
has been supplemented by at least two other rights: the right to work
with a remuneration which ensures an adequate standard of living
for all those who are willing to work and are able to find work, and
the right to social security which is a substitute for work for those
who either cannot find work or are unable to work, and a substitute
for insufficient income derived from property or from work: insufficient, that is, in regard to the enjoyment of an adequate standard of
living.

The right to work functions as a basis of independence, provided
the work is freely chosen by the person concerned, that sufficient
income is obtained from it, and provided the workers can protect
their interests through free trade unions.[12]

The right to social security is essential, particularly when a person
does not have the necessary property available, or is not able to
secure an adequate standard of living through work, owing to unemployment, old age or disability.

*Regional human rights provisions*   Largely based on the Universal Declaration, specific human rights instruments have been adopted by
regional organizations: the Council of Europe, the Organization of
American States and the Organization for African Unity. The main
instruments of the Council of Europe are the European Convention for
the Protection of Human Rights and Fundamental Freedoms, adopted
in 1950, and the European Social Charter, adopted in 1961. The main
instruments of the Organization of American States are the American
Declaration of the Rights and Duties of Man of 1948, the Inter-American
Convention on Human Rights of 1969, and the Additional Protocol of
San Salvador, adopted in 1988, which deals with economic and social
rights. The main African instrument is the African Charter on Human
and Peoples' Rights, adopted in 1981, which includes civil, political,
economic, social and cultural rights within the same text.

Regional instruments may sometimes be more effective than universal ones in terms of implementation, owing to the greater similarity
among the member states of each of the regional organizations. This
has led to more advanced mechanisms of supervision and handling
of complaints in the Council of Europe and in the inter-American
system, though mainly with regard to civil and political rights. The
monitoring mechanism under the African Charter, being more recent
in origin, is as yet less developed.

In the Asian region, it has not proved possible, in spite of various
initiatives, to develop a comparable regional organization and consequently no regional instrument on human rights exists. The

explanation may partly be found in the greater diversity of cultural and political systems within the vast Asian region.

*Subjective rights aspects of human rights*　A distinction must be made between those aspects of human rights which can be treated without difficulty as individual, subjective rights and those which cannot, unless further concretization has been made through legislation or practice.

Most human rights, including economic and social rights, contain some elements which can be dealt with at the national level as subjective rights. For these, individuals can have an effective remedy through competent national tribunals or courts in the case of violations.

Other aspects of the same rights are less amenable to direct transformation into subjective rights. They are, at least initially, elements of a right to a social order in which the particular rights can be realized. The process of realization forms part of state obligations under international law.

If, by subjective legal rights, we refer to rights which will be upheld by a court when an individual brings a claim alleging violations, and if we limit ourselves for the time being to domestic courts (within a given national legal system), several conditions would have to be fulfilled for international human rights to be a legal right in that particular setting: what is the position of international human rights law in domestic law? Is it directly applicable or does it have to be incorporated into national law in one way or another? If international human rights law is directly applicable, the next question is whether the particular right in question is self-executing or whether it has to be given a more specific form and content in domestic legislation in order to become applicable by domestic courts. If the position of international human rights law in domestic law depends on some form of incorporation, the question whether it is a legal right under domestic law depends on the nature and scope of that incorporation and also whether the particular international human right is self-executing.

There is no guarantee for any international human rights that they will be treated as legal rights in domestic law, but some are more easily accepted than others. This, however, also depends on the political and cultural system of the society concerned. The overall purpose of the International Bill of Human Rights is to promote their acceptance within all domestic systems and, as far as possible, also to make them into legal rights within domestic systems. However, not all international human rights lend themselves easily to being made justiciable in domestic systems, nor is it obvious that all aspects should be justiciable.

With regard specifically to economic and social rights, some elements can be made more easily justiciable than others. First, those aspects which deal with freedom from the state are, at least in Western societies, the elements which are most easily made into enforceable legal rights. The right to peaceful possession of property and the right to freedom from forced labour are among the most obvious examples. Of much greater significance is the application of the principle of non-discrimination. It may be uncertain how far a state is obliged to go in developing a system of social security. Where the right to social security is not immediately a subjective legal right, unless appropriate domestic legal legislation has been adopted, it becomes a legal right as soon as a state starts adopting such legislation, since it will then have to respect the principle of non-discrimination. Consequently, for every step a state wants to take, possibly based on purely pragmatic reasons relating to domestic needs, in developing social rights, it will have to apply these rights equally even if the domestic law itself is restrictive. On the basis of international human rights law, a justiciable legal right can emerge for the individual. This has tremendous significance, and is the most formidable platform on which the economic and social rights edifice can be gradually built up at the domestic level. Second, there are certain economic and social rights which can be seen as minimum rights that should be available to everyone and, on that basis, objective individual rights might emerge. The right to primary education free of charge is in the process of becoming such a basic right, and may already be considered a subjective right for every individual, whether this be based on customary international law or on treaty law.

However, beyond these rights, we are very often faced with situations where it is impossible to identify the subjective right of the individual which flows from a particular international human right. In these cases it is better to see international human rights as directive principles for the state concerned, in the sense of principles which should guide domestic legislation and other decision making. This does not make these rights devoid of legal significance. When directive principles are not applied in good faith by a State Party to a convention, such as when available resources are not appropriately used for the particular purpose of that right, the relevant international bodies can draw the conclusion that there has been non-compliance with international obligations. This can have consequences, even though the sanctions available for the international community are limited. It may affect bilateral relations; donor states may make their continued cooperation dependent on better compliance with international obligations. Negative international publicity can also affect the domestic political processes and make the internal civil society more inclined to push for better application of the directive principles.

These directive principles also have another significant legal consequence within the domestic system: they affect the balancing between rights in a way which would not exist without these directive principles. If, to take one example, a state imposes rent control in order to make housing more easily accessible and thereby fulfil the right to housing under Article 11 of the International Covenant on Economic, Social and Cultural Rights, the owners of the house might claim that this is unacceptable interference with their right to property. In such a situation, the state would be entitled to claim that the measures were necessary in order to ensure another human right. This aspect of the legal significance of economic and social rights has not been given sufficient attention, even though particular cases can demonstrate the validity of this observation.

This brings us back to the point that the international human rights system is a package of interrelated rights, and the different rights have to be interpreted in light of each other. This includes the necessity of taking into account economic and social rights, including those aspects which are not in themselves amenable to becoming individual legal rights.

We therefore have to distinguish between minimum obligations of states flowing from international human rights, and the optimal realization of these rights, which go far beyond the minimum. 'Optimal realization' refers to the most suitable balancing between the different rights in order to obtain the best possible results for all individuals. In doing this, of course, no right can be limited to a greater extent than provided for in the specific right itself, and some rights are absolute and can never be limited. In regard to many other rights, however, the necessity of limitation due to other human rights is generally well recognized and has to be taken into account.

This point will be elaborated at greater length in regard to the specific rights discussed below. An illustration could be given here: the right to health includes both the right for individuals to have access to health services, which can easily be transformed at the national level into an individual subjective right, but it also includes the right to a public health order in which epidemic and endemic diseases are prevented or controlled. This aspect of the right to health is more difficult to translate into individual, subjective rights to be pursued by individuals before tribunals or courts, but it is nevertheless an essential part of the normative human rights system. It can be made use of both nationally and internationally by non-governmental organizations (NGOs) and concerned groups, calling upon monitoring bodies at the international level to request the state to adopt more effective measures, and at the national level to demand changes in policies. The neglect of such obligations can have more serious consequences for individuals than the violation of rights which have been transformed into individual, justiciable rights.

*State Obligations*

It is essential to explore the corresponding obligations in order to understand the substance of rights. The Universal Declaration of Human Rights envisaged that the rights contained therein shall be enjoyed by everyone throughout the world. The rights must be absorbed into the legal, administrative and political culture of nations, first by a recognition that they are achievable ideals and then by implementation in national law and administration through relevant political and social reforms. Global institutions had to be set up to monitor the implementation of human rights worldwide and to bring about cooperation in the fields of economic, social and cultural matters to establish conditions for their full enjoyment throughout the world.

The Universal Declaration was initially an expression of ideals to be achieved. The process of transforming these ideals into 'hard law' ('positivization' in legal language) at the international level started with the adoption of the two international covenants adopted in 1966 (the International Covenant on Civil and Political Rights and the International Covenant on Economic, Social and Cultural Rights), followed by numerous specific conventions. While this created obligations for states under international law, the main task was to ensure that the rights were incorporated into national law and administrative practice. This transformation, whether into constitutions or into statutory law, can be fully achieved only when it goes hand-in-hand with the evolution of a human rights culture where individuals as well as politicians, administrators and security forces know and accept, not only their own rights, but also their duties flowing from the rights of the other members of the community on a basis of equality.

Under international law, obligations for human rights are primarily held by states. When states seek to implement these obligations in national law, they are also required to impose duties on persons subject to their jurisdiction. Such duties include the requirement to respect the rights of other persons, such as the duty to respect the property of others which is imposed through criminal law provisions on theft, and other measures. Duties have also to be imposed on all individuals to contribute to the common welfare, including taxation. The compliance with such duties makes it possible for the state to assist and to fulfil (provide) in ways which enable everyone to enjoy his or her economic, social and cultural rights.

The duties of individuals are in most cases not contained in international instruments; they are underlying necessities, but left to the

state for adoption through national legislation. Nor are the obligations of states spelled out in great detail in the main human rights
instruments: they are gradually clarified through additional, more
specific instruments, and through the practice of monitoring bodies.
While these processes are still at an early stage at the international
level, an inventory of the obligations contained in the many specific
international instruments now adopted shows that a wide range of
concrete obligations have already been undertaken, and that the treaty
bodies are also contributing to the clarification of the obligations. At
the national level, many states have comprehensive and detailed
legislation concerning economic, social and cultural rights.

The Universal Declaration of Human Rights imposes above all a
moral obligation on all states to realize social and economic rights.

*The Main Provision on State Obligations: International Covenant on
Economic, Social and Cultural Rights, Article 2*

Under Article 2 of the International Covenant on Economic, Social
and Cultural Rights, States Parties have undertaken legally binding
obligations to take steps, to the maximum of their available resources,
to 'achieve progressively' the full realization of economic and social
rights in that Covenant.

The meaning of these obligations has been examined by a group of
experts who adopted the Limburg Principles.[13] These were adopted
by a group of scholars and experts in Maastricht from 2 to 6 June
1986 to consider the nature and scope of the obligations of States
Parties to the International Covenant on Economic, Social and Cultural Rights. They are not in themselves legally binding, but provide
the best guidance to the understanding of the obligations flowing
from the ratification of that Covenant by a State Party. Since the
Covenant is an international treaty, it must, in accordance with the
Vienna Convention on the Law of Treaties (1969), be interpreted in
good faith, taking into account the object and purpose, the ordinary
meaning, the preparatory work and relevant practice.

The words 'achieve progressively' have often been misinterpreted.
The treaty body for this Covenant, the Committee on Economic,
Social and Cultural Rights, points out that, while the concept of
progressive realization constitutes a recognition of the fact that full
realization of all economic, social and cultural rights will generally
not be able to be achieved in a short period of time, the phrase must
be seen in the light of the overall objective, which is to establish clear
obligations for States Parties to move as expeditiously as possible
towards the realization of these rights. All States Parties have an
obligation to begin immediately to take steps towards full realization
of the rights contained in the Covenant. States Parties shall use all

appropriate means, including legislative, administrative, judicial, economic, social and educational measures, consistent with the nature of the rights in order to fulfil their obligations under the Covenant but legislative measures alone are not sufficient to fulfil them.

The obligation of progressive achievement does not only refer to an increase in resources, but even more to an increasingly effective use of the resources available, which must be optimally prioritized to fulfil the rights listed in the International Covenant on Economic, Social and Cultural Rights, taking into account the need to ensure for everyone the satisfaction of subsistence requirements, as well as the provision of essential services. States Parties are obliged, regardless of the level of economic development, to ensure respect for minimum subsistence rights for all. It is essential to ensure equitable and effective use of and access to the available resources. Its 'available resources' include not only the resources found within a state, but also those available from the international community through international cooperation and assistance. An essential aspect of economic and social rights is the duty of international cooperation and assistance pursuant to the Charter of the United Nations (Articles 55 and 56). International assistance should give full priority to the realization of all human rights and fundamental freedoms, economic, social and cultural as well as civil and political.

In passing, it should be noted that the more recent Convention on the Rights of the Child (1989), which includes many economic and social rights and corresponding state obligations, does not contain the qualifying clause 'progressive realization'. Under this Convention, the obligations arise immediately, but their implementation is still qualified by the phrase 'within their means'.

*The Roles and Levels of State Involvement*

A widespread misunderstanding has been that all economic, social and cultural rights must be provided by the state, and that they are costly and lead to an overgrown state apparatus. This view is the result of a very narrow understanding of the nature of these rights and of the corresponding state obligations; consequently, and given their relevance to development policies, a few words about their nature are required. The availability of resources refers, not only to those which are controlled by or filtered through the state or other public bodies, but also to the social resources which can be mobilized by the widest possible participation in development, as necessary for the realization by everyone of the rights recognized in the Covenant.

A realistic understanding of state obligations must take into account, as laid down in Article 2 of the Declaration on the Right to Development, that the individual is the active subject of all economic and social development.[14] Most human beings strive to take care of their own livelihood by their own efforts and resources, individually or in association with others. Use of his or her own resources, however, requires that the person has resources which can be used – typically, land or other capital, or labour. This could include the shared right to use communal land, and the land rights held by indigenous peoples.

State obligations must be seen in this light. States must, at the primary level, respect the resources owned by the individual, his or her freedom to find a job and the freedom to take the necessary actions and use the necessary resources – alone or in association with others – to satisfy his or her own needs. It is in regard to the latter that collective or group rights become important: the resources belonging to a collectivity of persons, such as indigenous populations, must be respected in order for them to be able to satisfy their needs. Consequently, as part of the obligation to respect these resources, the state should take steps to recognize and register the land rights of indigenous peoples and land tenure of smallholders whose title is uncertain. By doing so, the state will have assisted them in making use of their resources in greater safety in their efforts to maintain an adequate standard of living. Similarly, the rights of peoples to exercise permanent sovereignty over their natural resources may be essential for them to be able, through their own collective efforts, to satisfy the needs of the members of that group.

At a secondary level, state obligations mean to protect the freedom of action and the use of resources against other, more assertive or aggressive subjects – more powerful economic interests, such as protection against fraud, against unethical behaviour in trade and contractual relations, against the marketing and dumping of hazardous or dangerous products. This protective function of the state is the most important aspect of state obligations also with regard to economic, social and cultural rights, and it is similar to the role of the state as protector of civil and political rights. Significant components of the obligation to protect are spelled out in existing law inside most states. Such legislation is subject to judicial review, and therefore belies the argument that economic and social rights are inherently non-justiciable. Legislation of this kind must, of course, be contextual: that is, it must be based on the specific requirements of the country concerned. To take one example: legislation requiring that land can be owned only by the tiller of the land is essential where agriculture is the major basis of income, but may be much less relevant in highly industrialized, technological societies where only a small percentage of the population lives off the land. For groups of people whose culture requires a close link to the use of land, protection of that land is even more important as an obligation to realize the right to food – again, the indigenous peoples serve as the clearest example. Protection against hazardous or undesirable elements in foodstuffs is an important obligation in ensuring a safe food supply as part of realizing the right to adequate food, and countries have established more or less effective surveillance and control mechanisms to ensure this.

At the tertiary level, the state has the obligation to facilitate opportunities by which the rights listed can be enjoyed. This takes many forms, some of which are spelled out in the relevant instruments. For example, with regard to the right to food, the state shall, under Article 11(2) of the International Covenant on Economic, Social and Cultural Rights, take steps to 'improve measures of production, conservation and distribution of food by making full use of technical and scientific knowledge and by developing or reforming agrarian systems'.

At the fourth and final level, the state has the obligation to fulfil the rights of everyone under economic, social and cultural rights. The obligation to fulfil could thus consist of the direct provisions of basic needs, such as food or resources which can be used for food (direct food aid, or social security) when no other possibility exists, for example (1) when unemployment sets in (recession); (2) for the disadvantaged and elderly; (3) during sudden situations of crisis or disaster (see below); and (4) for those who are marginalized (for example, owing to structural transformations in the economy and production).

### Analysing the Separate Rights

*The Right to an Adequate Standard of Living*

*Sources*   According to Article 25(1) of the Universal Declaration of Human Rights, 'everyone has the right to a standard of living adequate for the health and well-being of himself and of his family'. With the wording slightly changed, the term the 'right to an adequate standard of living' appears in Article 11 of the International Covenant on Economic, Social and Cultural Rights: 'the States Parties to the present Covenant recognize the right of everyone to an adequate standard of living for himself and his family'. Under Article 27 of the Convention on the Rights of the Child, 'States Parties recognize the right of every child to a standard of living adequate for the child's physical, mental, spiritual, moral and social development'.

Reference to an 'adequate' or 'decent' living occur in many other provisions, as an element of the work-related rights or as a purpose underlying other rights. In the American Declaration of the Rights and Duties of Man, both the right to education (in Article 12) and the right to fair remuneration for work (in Article 14) are intended to ensure or to raise the standard of living of the person concerned. Similarly, under Part 1, Principle (4) of the European Social Charter, workers have a right to a fair remuneration sufficient for a decent standard of living for themselves and their families. The same is reiterated in Article 4(1) of the International Covenant on Economic, Social and Cultural Rights. Other examples could be mentioned.

*Analysis*   The right to an adequate standard of living will be given extensive treatment here, since it sums up a large part of the concerns underlying all economic and social rights, that is to integrate everyone into a humane society. It is intimately linked to the foundation of the whole human rights system, that everyone is born free and equal in dignity and rights and should act towards each other in a spirit of fraternity (Article 1 of the Universal Declaration of Human Rights).

The rights to property, to work and to social security which have been examined above are all sources of subsistence or income which ideally should make it possible for everyone to enjoy an adequate standard of living. When, nevertheless, a specific right to an adequate standard of living has been included in the international system of human rights, it is to cover the loopholes and to address the most basic needs to which every human being is entitled.

As to the loopholes, the provision serves to address the rights of the most vulnerable members of society. In the developed countries, a large majority already enjoys an adequate standard and sometimes much more than that. In the developing countries, the number of those who are vulnerable is much larger, though it differs substantially in different countries. But, in developing countries, there are also significant sections of the population which have a standard of living far above what is required under the international human rights instruments.

The Committee on Economic, Social and Cultural Rights has noted that the most vulnerable groups are 'landless peasants, marginalized peasants, rural workers, rural unemployed, urban unemployed, urban poor, migrant workers, indigenous peoples, children, elderly people and other especially affected groups'.[15] To this list could be added persons who are temporarily in very difficult positions, such as internally displaced persons, refugees and persons in detention or in psychiatric institutions.[16]

It is essential, therefore, that states identify the vulnerable groups and take measures to improve their conditions. The Committee on Economic, Social and Cultural Rights has drawn up guidelines for state reports under the International Covenant on Economic, Social and Cultural Rights whereby states are required to supply information on the current standard of living of the population, in respect of both the aggregate and different socioeconomic, cultural and other groups within society. The Committee also requires information about the income per capita/GNP for the poorest 40 per cent of the population, and whether there is a 'poverty line' in existence in the country concerned, and its basis. The Committee also calls on the State Parties to indicate the country's position on the Physical Quality of Life Index, and whether there has been any change in the standard of living over time (for example, compared with ten years and five years ago) with regard to the different groups. This makes it possible to assess whether there has been an improvement in living conditions for the entire population or only for some groups; and whether those whose standard has been improved are those who were vulnerable before or those who were already well-off earlier.[17]

*A right to have the basic needs met*    In Article 25 of the Universal Declaration of Human Rights, this term means 'adequate for the health and well-being of himself and of his family, including food, clothing, housing and medical care and necessary social services'; in Article 11 of the International Covenant on Economic, Social and Cultural Rights, it includes 'adequate food, clothing and housing';[18] whereas the right of the child is to 'a standard of living adequate for the child's physical, mental, spiritual, moral and social development'.

The right to an adequate standard of living requires therefore that the basic needs required to live a life in dignity are met, not by charity but by right. It includes, but goes beyond, the basic necessities of food, clothing and housing, under conditions which enable everyone to participate in the everyday life of society.

Everyone shall be able, without shame and without unreasonable obstacles, to be a full participant in ordinary, everyday interaction with other people. This means, *inter alia*, that they shall be able to enjoy their basic needs under conditions of dignity. No one shall have to live under conditions whereby the only way to satisfy their needs is by degrading or depriving themselves of their basic freedoms, such as through begging, prostitution or bonded labour, or to depend on the charity of others.

In purely material terms, 'adequate standard of living' can be understood to imply the maintenance of a level of living which is above the poverty line of the society concerned. The realization of human rights clearly requires the eradication of poverty worldwide, as envisaged in the 'Four Freedoms Address' by President Franklin D. Roosevelt in 1941, and which was among the inspirations underlying the whole edifice of international human rights.

The poverty line can, according to the World Bank, 'be thought of as comprising two elements: the expenditure necessary to buy a minimum standard of nutrition and other basic necessities and a further amount that varies from country to country, reflecting the cost of participating in the everyday life of society'.[19] It should be added, however, that the necessities produced for own consumption, including food and clothing, by the person or family concerned should also be taken into account: since they are often not bought, they escape calculation in monetary terms. The same applies to shelters constructed by self-help.

In the following sections, two of the main components of an adequate standard of living, the right to food and the right to housing, are examined.[20]

*Adequate Food*

The 'minimum standard of nutrition and other basic necessities' must include, *inter alia*, adequate food.[21] States parties to the International Covenant on Economic, Social and Cultural Rights are required to provide information about the current situation, in particular as regards the vulnerable groups. They are called upon to provide a general overview of the extent to which the right to adequate food has been realized in the country. General statements do not satisfy; the state must present nutritional surveys and other monitoring arrangements. They are furthermore expected to provide detailed information (including statistical data broken down in terms of different geographical areas) on the extent to which hunger and/or malnutrition exists in the country, with particular attention to the situation of especially vulnerable or disadvantaged groups, including landless peasants, migrant workers, marginalized peasants, indigenous peoples, rural workers, children, rural unemployed, elderly people, urban unemployed and other urban poor, and other especially affected groups. Information should also indicate whether there are any significant differences in the situation of men and women within each of the above groups.

More importantly, on the basis of this detailed and disaggregated information, states are requested to give information about the changes that have taken place over the past five years with respect to the situation of each of the above groups, and whether changes have been made in national policies, laws and practices negatively affecting the access to adequate food by these groups or sectors or within the most deprived regions.

Finally, the government is required to indicate the measures it considers necessary to guarantee access to adequate food for each of the vulnerable or disadvantaged groups and for the most deprived areas, and for the full implementation of the right to food for both men and women, with details of measures taken and time-related goals set.

Adequate food can be broken down into several elements. *Adequacy of the food supply* means that the types of foodstuffs commonly available (nationally, in local markets and eventually at the household level) should be *culturally acceptable* (fitting the prevailing food or dietary culture);[22] furthermore, the overall supply should cover overall *nutritional needs* in terms of quantity (energy) and quality (providing all essential nutrients, including micronutrients such as vitamins and iodine) and, last but not least, be *safe* (free of toxic factors and contaminants) and of good food quality (for example, taste and texture).

*Stability of the supply and access to food* presupposes *environmental sustainability*, implying that there is a judicious public and community management of natural resources which have a bearing on the food supply, as well as *economic* and *social sustainability* in terms of conditions and mechanisms securing food access. Economic and social sustainability concern a just income distribution and effective markets, together with various public and informal support and safety nets. These supports could be public social security schemes, as well as numerous forms of community transactions, self-help and solidarity networks, the latter becoming particularly important when people need to cope with various crisis situations.[23]

It must be borne in mind that food is not the only need of concern; therefore any form of food procurement is only *viable* when the available resources are sufficient to also cover other basic human needs. This notion is consistent with that of a 'livelihood approach' to food security, rather than a 'food first' approach.[24]

### Adequate Housing

Essential to a life in dignity is adequate housing. The right to housing is recognized in Article 11(2) of the International Covenant on Economic, Social and Cultural Rights and in several other sources. The reality, however, is disturbing. The United Nations estimates that there are over 100 million homeless persons worldwide and over a billion who are inadequately housed.[25] There is no indication that this number is decreasing. The Committee on Economic, Social and Cultural Rights has observed:

> the right to housing should not be interpreted in a narrow or restrictive sense which equates it with, for example, the shelter provided by merely having a roof over one's head or views shelter exclusively as a commodity. Rather it should be seen as the right to live somewhere in

security, peace and dignity. [ ... ] The right to housing is integrally linked to other human rights and to the fundamental principles upon which the Covenant is premised. This 'inherent dignity of the human person' from which the rights in the Covenant are said to derive requires that the term 'housing' be interpreted so as to take account of a variety of other considerations, most importantly that the right to housing should be ensured to all persons irrespective of income or access to economic resources. [ ... ] The Commission on Human Settlements and the Global Strategy for Shelter to the Year 2000 have stated: 'Adequate shelter means [ ... ] adequate privacy, adequate space, adequate security, adequate lighting and ventilation, adequate basic infrastructure and adequate location with regard to work and basic facilities – all at a reasonable cost'.

Basing itself on its examination of a large number of state reports, the Committee on Economic, Social and Cultural Rights has identified the contents of the right to housing to include, *inter alia*:

(a) Legal security of tenure, whether rental (public and private) accommodation, co-operative housing, lease, owner-occupation, emergency housing and informal settlements. All persons should possess a degree of security of tenure which guarantees legal protection against forced eviction, harassment and other threats, and States should take immediate measures to confer legal security of tenure upon those persons and households currently lacking such protection.
(b) Availability of services, materials, facilities and infrastructure. An adequate house must contain certain facilities essential for health, security, comfort and nutrition: Sustainable access to natural and common resources, safe drinking water, energy for cooking, heating and lighting, sanitation and washing facilities, means of food storage, refuse disposal, site drainage and emergency services.
(c) Affordability. Personal or household financial costs associated with housing should be at such a level that the attainment and satisfaction of other basic needs are not threatened or compromised.
(d) Habitability. Inhabitants must have adequate space and protection from cold, damp, heat, rain, wind or other threats to health, structural hazards and disease. The physical safety of occupants must be guaranteed as well.
(e) Accessibility. Disadvantaged groups, including the elderly, children, the physically disabled, the terminally ill, HIV-positive individuals, persons with persistent medical problems, the mentally ill, victims of natural disasters, people living in disaster-prone areas and other groups, must be accorded full and sustainable access to adequate housing resources and should be ensured some degree of priority consideration in the housing sphere.
(f) Location. Adequate housing must be in a location which allows access to employment options, health-care services, schools, childcare centres and other social facilities.

(g) Cultural adequacy. The way housing is constructed, the building materials used and the policies supporting these must appropriately enable the expression of cultural identity and diversity of housing.

The necessity to take the right to housing more seriously has received considerable attention internationally over the last few years. A comprehensive study has been conducted, on behalf of the United Nations Sub-Commission on Prevention of Discrimination and Protection of Minorities, by R. Sachar (India),[26] who recommended that states should seek to fully integrate the contents of General Comment No 4 on the right to adequate housing (Article 11(1) of the International Covenant on Economic, Social and Cultural Rights) into the relevant national legislative and policy domains (para. 161): that they shall clarify and strengthen the human right to adequate housing by paying due attention to including housing rights provisions in constitutions and legislation (paras 162–3). States should, at a minimum, ensure that no violations of the right to adequate housing are allowed and, when they occur, they shall take all necessary measures to halt any further violations and bring to justice any person(s) responsible for such infringements.

Forced evictions will normally constitute gross violations of human rights, in particular the right to adequate housing. Sachar recommends in his study that states should scrupulously avoid sponsoring, tolerating or actively carrying out forced evictions of any type which are not in conformity with international human rights law (para. 166). The same applies to local and municipal governments. Development projects which lead to eviction should not be initiated until a full resettlement policy is in place. Complete rehabilitation, in accordance with international law, must be ensured, taking into account the needs of special groups: women, children and the aged. Rehabilitation policies must ensure, in keeping with the provisions of the right to housing, basic amenities, services and livelihood opportunities (para. 168).

In this connection, it is worth noting that the World Bank has over recent years developed a resettlement policy whose main elements are that involuntary displacement should be avoided or minimized whenever possible; that, when avoidance is impossible, the World Bank's objective is to improve or at least restore former living standards and earning capacity. Displaced persons should be compensated for their losses at replacement costs, be given the opportunity to share in project benefits and be assisted in the transfer and in the transition stage at the relocation site.[27]

*Adequate Care*

It is often overlooked that an adequate standard of living also requires adequate care. Adequate care, necessary for all, is particularly important for children, the elderly and for those who have immediate responsibility for small children. The concept of adequate care encompasses a number of extremely critical factors in the development of nutritional well-being among individuals, especially the most vulnerable groups in society: young children, especially poor young children, and mothers-to-be. Adequate care is also pivotal for other groups and individuals, such as the elderly and the disabled, and normally healthy individuals who are temporarily exposed to health hazards or other crises in their lives which may affect their ability to procure food, their food intake and their nutritional status, and thus their health and productivity. Under international human rights law, these issues have found their clearest expression in Article 24(2) of the Convention on the Rights of the Child,[28] which in part reads:

> States Parties shall [ ... ] take appropriate measures:
> (b) To ensure the provision of necessary medical assistance and health care to all children, with emphasis on the development of primary health care;
> (c) To combat disease and malnutrition, including within the framework of primary health care, through, *inter alia*, the application of readily available technology and through the provision of adequate nutritious foods and clean drinking-water, taking into consideration the dangers and risks of environmental pollution;
> (d) To ensure appropriate pre-natal and post-natal health care for mothers;
> (e) To ensure that all segments of society, in particular parents and children, are informed, have access to education and are supported in the use of basic knowledge of child health and nutrition, the advantages of breast-feeding, hygiene and environmental sanitation and the prevention of accidents;
> (f) To develop preventive health care, guidance for parents, and family planning education and services.

*Levels of Obligation*

*The obligation to respect*   The duties of states to ensure an adequate standard of life for everyone within their jurisdiction are obligations primarily of result, not so much of conduct; the measures mentioned in Article 11 of the International Covenant on Economic, Social and Cultural Rights are indicative and certainly do not cover the entire range of measures which can be taken. The essential issue is whether everyone is provided with a situation whereby he or she can enjoy an adequate standard of living. The ensuring of such a situation is dependent on the specific circumstances in the country concerned, therefore precise obligations of conduct with general applicability cannot easily be drawn up. For example, in agricultural societies the approaches must differ considerably from typical industrialized countries, whereas these again differ from the post-industrial societies where the service sector predominates.

The (often unstated) prerequisite for the realization of an adequate standard of living is that the individual takes all measures within his or her capacity to achieve the conditions which ensure an adequate standard of living. The individual is expected to use his or her own property or working capacity, to the best of his or her judgment, for this purpose. This is not always explicitly stated in the relevant instruments, but is generally assumed to be so. In one case, however, it is explicit: under Article 27(2) of the Convention on the Rights of the Child, the parents responsible for the child 'have the primary responsibility to secure, within their abilities and financial capabilities, the conditions of living necessary for the child's development'.

The obligation for the state to respect the efforts and the achievements of the individuals themselves involves, *inter alia*, the obligation to respect the homes and the land from which the persons concerned make their living or find their shelter. Its most obvious implication is that no one shall be dispossessed, or forcibly removed from their homes and their land.

This is a matter of considerable magnitude. It has been addressed in international human rights law in particular with regard to the right to housing, which forms part of the right to an adequate standard of living. The first part of state obligations is to respect the space available to everyone who is able by their own means to produce their own food or to obtain it through exchange arrangements, normally by purchase on the market. Governments, particularly those which are non-representative, but in some cases even those which are democratically elected, sometimes neglect or violate the rights of the more marginal parts of their population and sometimes deprive that population of its existing resource base. The most obvious illustration of this is the dispossession of large parts of the black population's land in South Africa during the period of apartheid. These dispossessions effectively prevented most of the black population from taking care of their own needs by the use of their own assets. Land reform constitutes a major task in post-apartheid South African society.

While the South African case is extreme, dispossession of vulnerable groups with government participation, or at least acquiescence, has also occurred elsewhere. These actions have particularly affected indigenous peoples. Governments of territories settled by immigrants (the Americas, Australia, New Zealand) have rarely been representative of, or accountable to, their indigenous populations. The lack of recognition of the collective land rights of indigenous peoples has been a major cause of their impoverishment in many parts of the world. Slowly, however, governments are becoming more representative of, or at least more accountable to, their indigenous populations. It is becoming increasingly recognized both at the national and the international level that land rights must be respected and protected.

Dispossession from land or other property has often followed racial or ethnic lines as was the case, for example, in South Africa. Ethnonationalism can lead to similar results. At present, 'ethnic cleansing' in parts of the former Yugoslavia and in some parts of the former Soviet Union constitutes extreme violations on many levels, including the denial of a right to an adequate standard of living by seizing property and deliberately forcing persons of unwanted ethnic or religious groups off their land.

Frequently, the state has contributed to the dispossession of weaker groups in order to promote what the dominant groups consider to be overarching national goals, for example by building huge dams which destroy the established livelihood for persons living in the region. These practices have been described by the former Vice-Rector of the United Nations University, Kinhide Mushakoji, as 'development racism',[29] since they serve the interests of urban elites and tend to harm indigenous and other weaker ethnic groups unable to influence the developmental policies in the national metropolis. The World Bank has started to address these violations by requiring that the removal of populations shall be avoided if at all possible and, where it cannot be avoided, that those affected shall be resettled in other places under equally good conditions: nobody shall be worse off as a consequence of the development project.

*The obligation to protect*   Probably the most important aspect is the obligation to protect. The protection of the access to adequate, safe and nutritious food, or the protection of homes and shelter against dispossession, requires extensive national legislation and forms a normal part of the laws of many societies. The state is also obliged to protect the preservation of existing entitlements or resource bases against third parties. Prevention of encroachment on the land of indigenous peoples or vulnerable groups forms one aspect of this obligation. Another aspect of the protection is to prevent, wherever possible, persons from needing to sell their land in, for example, a situation of crisis where a drought or other difficulties temporarily inhibit their repayment of a debt. There is a need for states to establish a buffer which makes it possible for those on the borderline of poverty to overcome a crisis and to again become capable of ensuring an adequate standard of living through their own means.

The obligation to protect has additional dimensions. One is to ensure that foods on the market are safe and healthy, which requires strict food control within the framework of the *Codex Alimentarius*.[30] Protection can also consist of obligations to ensure food availability, regulation of food prices and subsidies, and rationing of essentials while ensuring that producers receive a fair price.

However, Article 27(3) of the Convention on the Rights of the Child introduces state obligations:

> States Parties, in accordance with national conditions and within their means, shall take appropriate measures to assist parents and others responsible for the child to implement this right and shall in case of need provide material assistance and support programmes, particularly with regard to nutrition, clothing and housing.

State obligations are intended to supplement these personal efforts of achieving an adequate standard of living whenever necessary: for example, if the person concerned does not have the opportunities which are available to others, has a disability, faces special obstacles which makes the endeavour impossible, or if conditions in general are such that an adequate standard cannot be achieved without external assistance.

*The obligation to facilitate*   States must be considered obliged to assess, without delay, the current situation in the country as a whole, and to repeat such assessments at brief intervals. Through such assessments, groups which do not enjoy an adequate standard of living should be identified and, on that basis, the necessary measures to remedy the situation should be taken urgently. Periodically, reassessments are required, both to find out whether the measures adopted have in reality improved the situation for the groups concerned and to determine whether other groups not previously identified have difficulties in enjoying an adequate standard of living.

The assessment requires the use of appropriate indicators. Specific indicators relating to the enjoyment of an adequate standard of living, including food, health conditions and care, include the following: indicators on nutritional outcomes, disaggregated by gender, race or ethnicity, urban/rural groups, by income groups and, in agricultural areas, by the situation of farmers, smallholders and the landless.

Nutritional assessments do not only consist of the mere counting of calories, since that alone does not determine the nutritional outcome. A gradual process towards the development of appropriate indicators of nutrition outcomes has taken place within the Sub-Committee on Nutrition of the United Nations Administrative Committee of Co-ordination.[31]

The purpose of developing adequate indicators is to adopt precise guided measures in order to ensure the enjoyment of an adequate standard of living. This does not necessarily mean that the state should provide direct material support, but it does mean that it should remove the obstacles which make it difficult for the vulnerable groups to enjoy their basic rights. Each particular circumstance determines what efforts a state should make to ensure an adequate standard of living. In the light of these efforts, it is essential that a proper assessment be made and that the most suitable measures be adopted to relieve the situation. This should be combined with a continuing evaluation both of the unfolding situation and of the effectiveness of the measures adopted. States parties to the International Covenant on Economic, Social and Cultural Rights and the Convention on the Rights of the Child are requested to indicate in their reports to the monitoring bodies these assessments, review their choice of indicators and outline the measures taken on the basis of their evaluation of the indicators to remedy the situations where the population is not enjoying an adequate standard of living.

The obligation to facilitate requires assistance, in particular to those who are close to the poverty line or below it, to make better use of their entitlements. This would include services to assist peasants in improving productivity under conditions which do not undermine their security of tenure, and credit arrangements which assist the vulnerable but which do not create dangerous indebtedness. The International Fund for Agricultural Development was created to assist Third World states in this task.[32] In recent years, several non-state credit institutions have emerged which aim to provide access to credit for the most marginal groups under conditions which do not create destructive indebtedness. The most well-known of these institutions is probably the Grameen Bank, in Bangladesh. Other areas of assistance aimed at ensuring full use of existing entitlements in production or exchange relations include the dissemination of nutritional knowledge, and respect for traditional food when it is sufficiently nutritious and cost-effective. Use of traditional food avoids dependence on imports and allows for improvement in the standard of living without changing basic cultural patterns.[33]

The obligation to further assist includes technical and vocational training programmes to improve the capacity of persons to earn their own living,[34] and special training and facilitating programmes for the disabled.[35] At a different level, assistance in securing access to an adequate standard of living can be achieved through price regulation and subsidies.[36]

The obligation to assist may also comprise providing equal opportunities when past developments have caused serious inequalities to arise, such as land hoarding in societies dependent on agriculture.

Agricultural reform is one of the measures provided for among state obligations under Article 11(2) of the International Covenant on Economic, Social and Cultural Rights, and in Article 14(2)(g) (which deals with the situation of rural women).

*Obligation to fulfil or to be the provider*   Obviously, the state cannot ensure an adequate standard of living solely by respecting entitlements, by protecting entitlements against third parties, by assisting the vulnerable to make best possible use of them, and by carrying out the necessary reforms to ensure equal opportunities for everyone. Governments will probably face strong opposition to such wide-ranging reforms, and these, in turn, may be in conflict with the right to property.

In a market-oriented industrializing or industrialized society, where other forms of capital than land play a predominant role, the question of land reform becomes less relevant. While measures such as vocational and technical training, prevention of discrimination in access to employment and affirmative action can be of use to many, there is undoubtedly a need for some entitlements to be directly provided for by the state, which in a market-oriented society can be done through measures of redistribution combined with social security arrangements.[37]

The obligation of the state as provider can range from a minimum safety net along the lines envisaged by the Reagan administration in the United States, from 1981 onwards,[38] to a full comprehensive welfare model, as in the Nordic countries. That the state has obligations in this direction was already established by Article 25 of the Universal Declaration of Human Rights providing for 'the right to security in the event of unemployment, sickness, disability, widowhood, old age or other lack of livelihood in circumstances beyond his control'.

Special measures must be taken by the state to ensure an adequate standard of living for children. Children can never be blamed for not doing their utmost to take care of their own needs, and they cannot be blamed for their choice of parents when they are insufficiently responsible. Consequently, there is an obvious need for society to assist.[39]

Individuals deprived of their freedom (detained persons in prisons and institutions) obviously cannot by their own means ensure their enjoyment of basic needs. Provisions must therefore be made by those who have detained or institutionalized the persons concerned. The Standard Minimum Rules for the Treatment of Prisoners, approved by the Economic and Social Council in 1957 and 1977, contain provisions requiring that the prisoners be provided with adequate nutritious food and drinking water. Similar provisions can be found in regard to other institutionalized persons.

Asylum seekers, refugees and displaced persons do not have the same opportunity as others to achieve an adequate standard of living on the basis of their own efforts. They therefore require, to a larger extent than the ordinary public, direct provisions until conditions are established in which they can obtain their own entitlements. While recognized refugees should have a right to work under certain conditions, this is limited in countries where wage labour is limited and unemployment is very high.

The obligations arising from the right to an adequate standard of living depend therefore on contexts and must be spelled out for greater precision in the different contexts. To some extent this can be done through international standard-setting, but the main burden falls on the state to adopt legislation for different situations and groups in their society, in line with existing conditions, and based on appropriate assessments and indicators. The general international norms contained in Article 11 of the International Covenant on Economic, Social and Cultural Rights and similar provisions in other instruments can only provide a general guideline. The monitoring bodies are responsible not only for developing the interpretation of the obligations in greater specificity but also for encouraging their adoption in national legislation, corresponding to the needs of the vulnerable groups in each society, through their dialogue with government.

## The Right to Work and Work-related Rights

*Sources*

The right to work and related rights were first addressed in Article 23 of the Universal Declaration of Human Rights (right to work, equal pay for equal work, and just and favourable remuneration). Its Article 24 provides for the right for everyone to rest and leisure, including reasonable limitation of working hours and periodic holidays with pay. These rights were further developed in Articles 6 and 7 of the International Covenant on Economic, Social and Cultural Rights. Article 6 deals with the right to work and, under Article 7, States Parties recognize the right of everyone to the enjoyment of just and favourable conditions of work.

Under Part I of the European Social Charter, states recognize that everyone shall have the opportunity to earn their living in an occupation freely entered upon, that all workers shall have the right to just conditions of work, that they shall have the right to safe and healthy working conditions and to a fair remuneration sufficient for a decent standard of living for themselves and their families. In Part

II, which contains the specific commitments of states, Article 1 expresses the commitments to be undertaken by states as follows:

1. to accept as one of their primary aims and responsibilities the achievement and maintenance of as high and stable a level of employment as possible, with a view to the attainment of full employment;
2. to protect effectively the right of the worker to earn his living in an occupation freely entered upon;
3. to establish or maintain free employment services for all workers;
4. to provide or promote appropriate vocational guidance, training and rehabilitation.

Article 2 deals with the undertakings to limit the working hours and ensure as a minimum two weeks of holiday with pay. Article 3 deals with the right to safe and healthy working conditions, and Article 4 addresses the right to a fair remuneration.

In the Additional Protocol to the American Convention on Human Rights in the area of economic, social and cultural rights (American Convention on Human Rights, Protocol 1), the corresponding rights are found in Articles 6 and 7. Article 15 of the African Charter on Human and Peoples' Rights provides that every individual shall have the right to work under equitable and satisfactory conditions and shall receive equal pay for equal work.

Under Article 5(e)(i) of the International Convention on the Elimination of All Forms of Racial Discrimination, States Parties undertake to guarantee the right of everyone, without distinction as to race, colour or national or ethnic origin, to equality before the law in the enjoyment of the rights to work, to free choice of employment, to just and favourable conditions of work, to protection against unemployment, to equal pay for equal work and to just and favourable remuneration. Under Article 11 of the Convention on the Elimination of All Forms of Discrimination against Women, States Parties shall take all appropriate measures to eliminate discrimination against women in the field of employment in order to ensure, on a basis of equality of men and women, the same rights, in particular the right to work as an inalienable right of all human beings, the right to the same employment opportunities, including the application of the same criteria for selection in matters of employment; the right to free choice of profession and employment, the right to promotion, job security and all benefits and conditions of service and the right to receive vocational training and retraining, including apprenticeships, advanced vocational training and recurrent training; the right to equal remuneration, including benefits, and to equal treatment in respect of work of equal value, as well as equality of treatment in the evaluation of the quality of work.

*General Analysis*

The 'right to work' refers to a cluster of provisions entailing many different components of rights and obligations. Drzewicki[40] has suggested the following subcategories:

- employment-related rights;
- employment-derivative rights;
- equality of treatment and non-discrimination rights;
- instrumental rights.

The 'right to work' is normally understood in regard to employment in the service of and paid by others, as distinct from self-employment. In passing, it should be noted that nowhere in the human rights system is there an express reference to a right to self-employment. It must be generally understood to exist, however, as part of the freedom of every individual and, more particularly, as a consequence of the freedom from forced labour.

Rights derived from employment include the right to just conditions of work (working hours, annual paid holiday and other rest periods), the right to safe and healthy working conditions, the right to a fair remuneration, the right to vocational guidance and training, the right of women and young persons to protection in work, and the right to social security. The principles of equality of treatment and non-discrimination relate to both of these and indeed the whole set of social rights.

Instrumental rights include the freedom of association and the right to organize, the right to collective bargaining, the right to strike and the freedom of migration of workers. Drzewicki makes the point that these are instrumental in the sense that they provide indispensable implements and set a favourable framework without which an unimpeded exercise of work-related rights might be seriously affected.

The right to work has at least two significant social functions: it is a source of livelihood and income, and a source of dignity and self-realization. For it to be a source of livelihood, everyone must have access to work, and it must provide a just and favourable remuneration ensuring for them and their family an existence worthy of human dignity (Universal Declaration of Human Rights, Article 25); to be a source dignity and self-realization, it must be work which a person freely chooses or accepts, and he or she must enjoy safe and healthy working conditions and equal opportunity to be promoted to appropriate higher levels, subject to no considerations other than those of seniority and competence (International Covenant on Economic, Social and Cultural Rights, Article 7).

'The right to work' is sometimes construed, both by its adherents and by its detractors, as a *guarantee* of work, that is a subjective right of every person in all circumstances to hold a job with adequate remuneration. No such right exists, however, nor would it be possible to implement such a right, unless other human rights were intolerably restricted. It would, at the extreme, imply forced labour. When states under Article 6 of the International Covenant on Economic, Social and Cultural Rights recognize the right to work, this includes 'the right of everyone to the opportunity to gain his living by work which he freely chooses or accepts'. The steps states have to take 'to achieve the full realization of the right to work shall include technical and vocational guidance and training programmes, policies and techniques to achieve steady economic, social and cultural development and full and productive employment under conditions safeguarding fundamental political and economic freedoms to the individual' (Article 6(2)).

## Levels of Obligation

*The obligation to respect*   The most basic obligation is that concerning freedom from slavery and from forced labour. This is also reflected in Article 8 of the International Covenant on Civil and Political Rights, which prohibits slavery, servitude and forced or compulsory labour. Reference in this connection should also be made to the International Labour Organisation (ILO) conventions on the elimination of forced labour.

Article 6 of the International Covenant on Economic, Social and Cultural Rights refers to the right of everyone to the opportunity to gain their living by work which they freely choose or accept. The American Convention on Human Rights, Protocol 1, Article 6, uses language which includes the opportunity to secure the means for living a dignified and decent existence by performing a freely elected or accepted lawful activity. Article 15 of the African Charter on Human and Peoples' Rights is much more succinct: 'every individual shall have the right to work under equitable and satisfactory conditions'.

One aspect of the obligation to respect is the requirement that the state shall not discriminate in access to public work. Some distinctions are accepted, however: access to public service can be restricted to citizens of the country (this follows implicitly from Article 25(*c*) of the International Covenant on Civil and Political Rights. Whether distinctions can be made between different citizens, apart from the mere question of merit, is more uncertain. The issue of the so-called *Berufverbot*, preventing access to certain sensitive jobs on the basis of the political orientation of the applicant, has been the subject of some controversy.

Distinction in public service cannot be made on the basis of race, colour, ethnic or national origin, or on the basis of gender.

*The obligation to protect*   To a large extent, the right to work and even more the work-related rights imply an obligation for states to protect. First, protection is required against discrimination in access to work and in working conditions, as spelled out in the International Convention on the Elimination of All Forms of Racial Discrimination, the Convention on the Elimination of All Forms of Discrimination against Women and in several ILO conventions. Second, protection against arbitrary dismissals should be enforced, by ensuring legislation on 'job security'. Finally, there should be protection of just conditions of work (ensuring reasonable daily and weekly working hours, providing for public holidays with pay, and annual holidays also with pay; the right to safe and healthy working conditions promoted by the adoption of safety and health regulations and to provisions for the enforcement and supervision of such regulations, and the right to fair remuneration which will give workers and their families a decent standard of living, ensuring equal pay for work of equal value.

*The obligation to facilitate*   Numerous provisions exist within international instruments requiring states to facilitate access to work. The right to vocational guidance is in evolution, including the provision of technical and vocational training, operating systems of apprenticeship and maintaining adequate and readily available training facilities, preferably with few or no fees or charges.

*The obligation to fulfil*   While the relevant instruments do not require that the state guarantee a job to everyone, it does call on states to pursue 'policies and techniques to achieve steady economic, social and cultural development and full and productive employment under conditions safeguarding fundamental political and economic freedoms of the individual' (International Covenant on Economic, Social and Cultural Rights, Article 6(2)). A comparable provision is found in the American Convention on Human Rights, Protocol 1, Article 6(2): 'the States Parties undertake to adopt measures that will make the right to work fully effective, especially with regard to the achievement of full employment'. Under Article 1(1) of the European Social Charter, Contracting Parties undertake 'to accept as one of their primary aims and responsibilities the achievement and maintenance of as high and stable a level of employment as possible, with a view to the attainment of full employment'. One element in this connection is also in the ILO Conventions Nos 2 and 122.

The expert committees within the ILO and under the European Social Charter assess whether states adopt policies for employment, whether they address groups of persons or regions particularly affected by unemployment, and whether they move towards a higher level of employment.

## Social Security

*Sources*

Under Article 25 of the Universal Declaration of Human Rights, everyone shall, 'as a member of society', have the right to social security. Additionally, Article 25(1) refers to the right to security in the event of unemployment, sickness, disability, widowhood, old age or lack of livelihood in circumstances beyond one's control.

Article 9 of the International Covenant on Economic, Social and Cultural Rights provides for the right of everyone to 'social security, including social insurance'. Article 10, which deals with protection of the family, mentions social security benefits[41] during maternity leave.

The brief text of Article 9 of the International Covenant on Economic, Social and Cultural Rights must be seen against the background of the much more developed ILO standards. The principal ILO instrument in the field of social security is the Social Security (Minimum Standards) Convention of 1952 (No. 102).[42] This menu-type Convention is structured around nine specific branches of social security: (1) medical care (Part II), (2) sickness benefit (Part III), (3) unemployment benefit (Part IV), (4) old-age benefit (Part V), (5) employment injury benefit (Part VI), (6) family benefit (Part VII), (7) maternity benefit (Part VIII), (8) invalidity benefit (Part IX), and (9) survivors' benefit (Part X). In its interpretation of the vague and brief Article 9 of the International Covenant on Economic, Social and Cultural Rights, the Committee on Economic, Social and Cultural Rights relies on the branches of social security listed in the ILO convention in the guidelines drawn up for state reporting.[43] Under Article 5(e)(iv) of the International Convention on the Elimination of All Forms of Racial Discrimination, the right to social security and social assistance shall be guaranteed without discrimination on the grounds of race. The Convention on the Elimination of All Forms of Discrimination against Women lists several forms of social security which must be provided for women, taking gender-specific needs and obstacles into consideration.[44] Regarding children, primary responsibility for the material well-being of the child rests mainly with his or her parents but, in the Convention on the Rights of the Child, States Parties have undertaken obligations to provide material assistance and support for the realization of such responsibilities.[45]

Article 27 of the International Convention on the Protection of the Rights of All Migrant Workers and Members of Their Families[46] includes a provision on the right of all migrant workers to social security on the basis of receiving treatment equal to that of the nationals of the country of residence. In addition, migrant workers in a regular situation should enjoy certain complementary rights to social security benefits and services (Articles 45 and 54).

In the European Social Charter, the general provision is found in Article 12, which uses the term 'social security' in the same meaning as the ILO, and Article 12(2) refers to ILO Convention No. 102 as a minimum standard to be used under this Charter. Under Article 12(3), states undertake 'to raise progressively' the system of social security to a higher level. Social and medical assistance for those in need is provided for by Article 13. The European Social Charter guarantees family benefits (Article 16)[47] and services for mothers and children (Article 17).[48] Article 14 protects the right to social welfare services.[49] The 1988 Additional Protocol to the European Social Charter has, in its Article 4, a provision on the right of elderly persons to social protection.

Beyond the Convention on the Rights of the Child, specific instruments have also been adopted on social security by the Council of Europe. The most important is the 1964 European Code of Social Security,[50] revised in 1990. The American Declaration of the Rights and Duties of Man provides in Article 16 for the right to social security, specifying unemployment, old age and mental or physical disability as situations in which the right is actualized. The American Convention on Human Rights has a general clause on economic, social and cultural rights, calling for their progressive realization (Article 26), but the Additional Protocol in the Area of Economic, Social and Cultural Rights of 1988 contains more detailed provisions on the right to social security on the basis of Article 16 of the American Declaration, adding death of a beneficiary, work accidents, occupational diseases and childbirth, to unemployment, old age and mental or physical disabilities – situations in which the right applies (Article 9 of the Protocol).

The African Charter on Human and Peoples' Rights contains no provision on the right to social security, but Article 16 (the right to health), Article 18(4) (the right of the aged and the disabled to special measures of protection) and Article 29 (the individual's duties towards society) have significance for social security.

*General Analysis*

Basically, international human rights recognize three bases to ensure an adequate standard of living: property, work and social security. The organization of social security can take different forms and scope. The minimum approach has evolved from the poor relief of previous centuries and extends therefore only to those who do not manage to obtain a living through the operation of the market. The second approach is to organize social security by way of insurance to be paid by workers and employers, but with more or less extensive obligations established by law to ensure that such insurance arrangements are in fact applied. It may also be more or less extensive in scope, concerning insurance against accidents in work and insurance against disability, or periods of unemployment. It may also extend to obligatory means for old-age pensions. Such arrangements can provide guarantees only for those who actually work. For the jobless and the more or less self-employed and, particularly, those employed in the so-called 'informal sector', such insurance cannot provide security. Consequently, it may have to be combined with the first type of 'poor relief', the so-called 'safety net', to cater for those who fall outside. The more advanced systems of social security extend to everyone, based partly on contributions made obligatory by workers and employers, but supplemented by state funding derived from taxation and other sources of income. Such comprehensive social security may sometimes extend to coverage of disability, unemployment, old age, child allowances and leave with pay during periods of pregnancy and childbirth.

*Levels of Obligation*

*The obligation to respect*   This level is not applicable with regard to the social security obligation.

*The obligation to protect*   This is a significant part of the obligation arising from social security: the obligation to ensure that in contractual labour relationships, provisions are made for social insurance. It is also part of the protective function to ensure that these insurance arrangements are effective, and that guarantees are established so that, even in cases of bankruptcy, the necessary payments are available to beneficiaries.

*The obligation to facilitate*   To the extent that 'social security' is based on social insurance, a state may undertake certain tasks in order to complement the contributions made by the worker and the employer, by way of establishing the institutions administering the insurance and also by adding, through state funding, to the contributions made by the worker and the employer.

*The obligation to fulfil*   The minimum obligation could consist of providing assistance to those who are not covered by social insurance arrangements. This also follows from Article 11 of the International Covenant on Economic, Social and Cultural Rights on the right to an adequate standard of living for everyone, to which we shall return. The optimal fulfilment of obligation would be achieved by organizing a comprehensive social security system which combines social insurance and social assistance into a comprehensive whole. This model, which corresponds to the welfare state model, was first introduced in the Beveridge Commission in the United Kingdom in 1941, and has become the paramount system, particularly in the Nordic countries.

## Conclusions

The right to social security covers three different options: social assistance which is provided only to the needy and which often tends to be of a very minimal scope; social insurance which is based primarily on the more or less obligatory contributions made in working relationships under national laws; and social security in its full sense, which combines social assistance and social insurance into a comprehensive and universalistic approach.

It is obvious that the latter approach is only possible for highly industrialized states, and is impossible to implement in developing countries, particularly those which are still based to a large extent on subsistence agriculture. In the latter case, social security will depend on the ownership of land and on various forms of self-employment, rather than on state assistance. This does not exclude some minimal arrangements being made practically everywhere in order to ensure that at least a threshold level can be made available to everyone. It will be affected, on the other hand, by the way in which primary resources are distributed: the more widely the land is distributed, the less there will be a need for social security operated by the state. On the other hand, should it be considered that it is more cost-effective to accept accumulation of capital and land in order to achieve a higher level of productivity, this should then be complemented by redistributing the part of the income derived from such production in order to ensure the social security of those who otherwise might have been marginalized as a consequence of the processes of accumulation.

## The Right to Health

*Sources*

*Universal instruments*   The right to health was included in the Universal Declaration of Human Rights as part of Article 25: 'Everyone has the right to a standard of living adequate for the health and well-being of himself and of his family.'

In the International Covenant on Economic, Social and Cultural Rights, Article 12, notes: 'The States Parties to the present Covenant recognize the right of everyone to the enjoyment of the highest attainable standard of physical and mental health.'

The steps to be taken by states include those listed in Article 12(2):

(a) the provision for the reduction of the stillbirth rate and of infant mortality and for the healthy development of the child;
(b) the improvement of all aspects of environmental and industrial hygiene;
(c) the prevention, treatment and control of epidemic, endemic, occupational and other diseases;
(d) the creation of conditions which would assure to all medical service and medical attention in the event of sickness.

In Article 24(1) of the Convention on the Rights of the Child, we read: 'States Parties recognize the right of the child to the enjoyment of the highest attainable standard of health and to facilities for the treatment of illness and rehabilitation of health. States Parties shall strive to ensure that no child is deprived of his or her right of access to such health care services'. The relevant steps to be taken include those listed in Article 24(2):

(a) to diminish infant and child mortality;
(b) to ensure the provision of necessary medical assistance and health care to all children, with emphasis on the development of primary health care;
(c) to combat disease and malnutrition, including within the framework of primary health care, through, *inter alia*, the application of readily available technology and through the provision of adequate nutritious foods and clean drinking-water, taking into consideration the dangers and risks of environmental pollution;
(d) to ensure appropriate pre-natal and post-natal health care for mothers;
(e) to ensure that all segments of society, in particular parents and children, are informed, have access to education and are supported in the use of basic knowledge of child health and nutrition, the advantages of breast-feeding, hygiene and environmental sanitation and the prevention of accidents;

(f) to develop preventive health care, guidance for parents and family planning education and services.

In the instruments concerning prevention of discrimination, the right to health is not normally dealt with as an independent right but as a right to ensure that persons are not discriminated against in their access to health services.

Article 5 of the International Convention on the Elimination of All Forms of Racial Discrimination states that: 'The States Parties undertake to [ ... ] guarantee the right of everyone, without distinction as to race, colour, or national or ethnic origin, to equality before the law, notably in the enjoyment of the following rights ... ', and Article 5(*e*) (iv) concerns the right to public health, medical care, social security and social services.

Article 12(1) of the Convention on the Elimination of All Forms of Discrimination against Women notes: 'States Parties shall take all appropriate measures to eliminate discrimination against women in the field of health care in order to ensure, on a basis of equality of men and women, access to health care services, including those related to family planning'. However, this Convention goes further than mere prevention of discrimination to deal with the issues of particular significance to women. Its Article 12(2) provides that, notwithstanding the provisions of paragraph 1 of this Article: 'States Parties shall ensure to women appropriate services in connection with pregnancy, confinement and the post-natal period, granting free services where necessary, as well as adequate nutrition during pregnancy and lactation'. Additional requirements are found in Article 14 of the Convention on the Elimination of All Forms of Discrimination against Women which deals with the situation of rural women. According to its para. 2(b), states shall ensure that rural women have 'access to adequate health care facilities, including information, counselling and services in family planning'.

*Regional instruments*   Article 11 of the American Declaration of the Rights and Duties of Man provides that 'every person has the right to the preservation of his health through sanitary and social measures relating to food, clothing, housing and medical care, to the extent permitted by public and community resources'.

In the American Convention on Human Rights, Protocol 1, Article 10, the text reads: 'Everyone shall have the right to health, understood to mean the enjoyment of the highest level of physical, mental and social well-being.'

In the African Charter on Human and Peoples' Rights, the right to health is found in Article 16(1): 'Every individual shall have the right to enjoy the best attainable state of physical and mental health.'

Article 11 of the European Social Charter states that:

> With a view to ensuring the effective exercise of the right to protection of health, the Contracting Parties undertake, either directly or in co-operation with public or private organizations, to take appropriate measures designed *inter alia*: (1) to remove as far as possible the causes of ill-health; (2) to provide advisory and educational facilities for the promotion of health and the encouragement of individual responsibility in matters of health; (3) to prevent as far as possible epidemic, endemic and other diseases.

## Analysis

The right to health has two major dimensions: first, it is a right to access to health services, spelled out with different degrees of concretization in the different instruments; second, it is a right to a social order which includes obligations of the state to take specific measures for the purpose of safeguarding public health. These measures shall be undertaken so that they provide equal protection to all. Public health measures shall protect as far as possible against epidemic, endemic, occupational and other diseases, and shall include measures of hygiene and sanitation, dissemination of information on health-related matters, shall reduce still-births and infant mortality, and combat malnutrition. The right to health is also closely associated with conditions of living in general, including the establishment and preservation of conditions which can ensure that care can be given to children, disabled persons and the elderly.

In this connection, it is important to remember the interdependence between the different sets of human rights. The enjoyment of an individual's civil rights can sometimes come into conflict with measures adopted to ensure the enjoyment of the right to health. An appropriate balance has to be struck between these concerns. Most civil rights can therefore be subject to some restrictions: a standard clause is the following, taken from Article 13 of the International Covenant on Civil and Political Rights which deals with the freedom of movement:

> Article 13(3). The above-mentioned rights shall not be subject to any restrictions except those which are provided by law, are necessary to protect national security, public order (*ordre public*), public health or morals or the rights and freedoms of others, and are consistent with the other rights recognized in the present Covenant.

The conflict between these different human rights is sometimes unavoidable, but it can be mitigated by careful balancing between the different sets of concerns. Essential in this connection is the need to ensure due process in order to determine with precision where the balance shall be drawn. The issue has received great attention as a consequence of the HIV/AIDS epidemics, where over-zealous public health officials or even decision makers with little understanding of the health issues involved sometimes adopt draconian measures which cause severe discrimination of persons infected or suffering – or suspected of being infected or suffering – from HIV/AIDS.

The treatment of persons suffering from mental illness is another important case in point. In particular, treatment and confinement of such persons without their informed consent has in the past caused considerable violation of human rights. The General Assembly therefore adopted, on 17 December 1991, resolution 46/119: 'Principles for the protection of persons with mental illness and the improvement of mental care.' The general rule is that treatment and admission to a mental health facility shall take place only when voluntary, based on the free and informed consent of the patient (Principles 11 and 15). Where this is not forthcoming and the illness is severe and when the judgment of the patient is impaired, or where there is an imminent likelihood of harm to third persons, confinement and treatment may take place within certain specified limitations provided the decision is made by an independent authority. Continued confinement and treatment shall be subject to review by a judicial or other independent body, and certain procedural guarantees have to be fulfilled (Principles 17 and 18).

The balance between individual civil rights and the rights of protection of health through public health measures has received particular attention as a consequence of the HIV/AIDS epidemic. Tomaševski (1995) has observed that:

> Public health has been affected by the principle that law and not medicine should regulate restrictions of fundamental rights and freedoms. Consequently, international human rights law recognizes that *individual* rights may be limited to protect public health, but such limitations are legitimate only when required on public health grounds, and compatible with the general human rights principles. This has been reaffirmed most recently in the context of the AIDS pandemic. ... The mention of standard-setting relating to AIDS is an example of the progress made in law-making to protect persons whose health is impaired. This is a significant achievement, as discrimination against people with impaired health forms part of our historical heritage.[51]

## Levels of State Obligation

*The obligation to respect* As pointed out above, in ensuring the right to health, state authorities have to respect the other human rights of the persons concerned. This aspect will not be further examined here, since it mainly falls within the scope of civil rights. Readers are referred to the article by Tomaševski referred to above. We shall only examine here the obligations arising from the realization of the right to health itself.

The requirements of public health may tend to make regulations somewhat more restrictive and sometimes more authoritarian than necessary. One issue of some significance has been the freedom of practitioners of so-called 'alternative medicine' which often meet with scepticism from modern, traditional medicine. Authorities have been inclined to be guided by the more professional schools of medicine. In recent years, however, some adaptation has been made. It remains a matter of some dispute to what extent the practice of 'alternative medicine' can be restricted or prohibited by the authorities.

*The obligation to protect*   The major substance of the right to health is the right to enjoy a social order in which protective measures have been taken by or through the encouragement of the state to remove as far as possible the causes of ill-health, and to prevent as far as possible epidemic, endemic and other diseases.

*The obligation to facilitate*   International instruments also require states to provide advisory and educational facilities for the promotion of health and the encouragement of individual responsibility in matters of health.

*The obligation to fulfil*   Under Article 12(2)(d) of the International Covenant on Economic, Social and Cultural Rights, states are required to create 'conditions which would assure to all medical service and medical attention in the event of sickness'. The specific obligations of states in providing access to health care for their populations, however, still remain vague. Special attention has been paid to mother and child care, as reflected in several of the international instruments. The World Health Assembly has also urged states to introduce laws and regulations to provide access to free medical service for pregnant women and during the child's first year, when immunization is crucial for its survival.[52]

In 1978, the World Health Organization adopted its 'Health for All Strategy', proclaiming a global commitment to health for all. The Declaration of Alma-Ata proclaimed in its preamble 'the need for urgent action by the world community to protect and promote the health of all the people of the world'.[53]

If the international instruments containing the right to health are to be optimally implemented, primary health care should be extended to all and be effective, efficient, affordable and acceptable.

This is linked to the issue, examined under the right to social security, whether publicly funded health services should be organized in accordance with the principle of social assistance and therefore extended free of charge or subsidized only to particular groups who are not by themselves able to pay for them, or to everyone as part of a comprehensive social security system including health services. Generally, international instruments do not take a position on this. They are satisfactorily implemented even if based on a principle of social assistance only. As an illustration, Article 13 of the European Social Charter can be quoted which deals with the right to social and medical assistance:

> With a view to ensuring the effective exercise of the right to social and medical assistance, the Contracting Parties undertake: (1) to ensure that any person who is without adequate resources and who is unable to secure such resources either by his own efforts or from other sources, in particular by benefits under a social security scheme, be granted adequate assistance, and, in case of sickness, the care necessitated by his condition; (2) to ensure that persons receiving such assistance shall not, for that reason, suffer from a diminution of their political or social rights; (3) to provide that everyone may receive by appropriate public or private services such advice and personal help as may be required to prevent, to remove, or to alleviate personal or family want.

*Conclusions*

For most of the developed, industrialized countries it would be possible to organize an all-embracing system, which is funded partly by obligatory contributions by all who can pay them (through taxes and in other ways), but extended to all on a basis of near-equality, even to those who have been unable to contribute. There are, however, at least three different sets of practices within these countries, some of which still rely on the social assistance model.

Developing countries have fewer possibilities for direct assistance, though this varies greatly with their level of GNP/per capita and with several other factors such as the urbanization ratio. A focus on primary health care at relatively low cost would be possible, however, and should be encouraged, rather than the establishment of expensive health facilities in the urban centres, a priority which all to often has been pursued.

## Advancing the Implementation of Economic and Social Rights

*Obstacles and Goals to be Pursued*

The preceding chapters have examined the comprehensive normative system of rights and corresponding obligations which states
must take into account in developing their economic and social policies. A presentation has also been made of international institutions
which monitor the compliance with these obligations and pursue a
dialogue with governments on how to advance their implementation, a process in which non-governmental organizations are becoming
increasingly involved. There are, however, formidable obstacles to
the realization of these rights; they appear for some to be so great
that the idea of a global realization of economic, social and cultural
rights seems utopian.

The *UNDP Human Development Report 1994* informs us that 'a fifth
of the developing world's population goes hungry every night, a
quarter lacks access to even a basic necessity like safe drinking water,
and a third lives in abject poverty – at such a margin of human
existence that words simply fail to describe it'.[54] From other sources,
it can be learned that more than a billion people in the world today
live in poverty, and some 550 million go to bed hungry each night.
More than 1.5 billion lack access to clean drinking water and sanitation, some 500 million children do not have access to even primary
education, and approximately one billion adults remain illiterate.

## Changes in Attitudes and in the International Setting

There is an increasing reaction to the prevailing, dominant attitudes
among governments which give uncritical pre-eminence to economic
thinking. The World Social Summit of 1995 was convened against the
background of the present crisis in social development. The deteriorat-
ing conditions of life among growing numbers of people in many
parts of the world give rise to uncertainty concerning how or whether
such problems can be resolved. Neoliberal experiments in worldwide
market operations in recent years have not generally increased social
well-being, deregulation has not limited rent-seeking activities or other
market distortions and the curtailing of state activities has neither
strengthened civil society nor improved the functioning of democracy.

The tendency in recent years to allow economic criteria alone to
dominate the social policy agenda has distorted the way fundamental social questions are addressed.[55]

The *UNDP Human Development Report 1994*, commenting on the
crisis pervading social policy in recent years, notes that only in the

twentieth century did social sciences become increasingly concerned with the economics of wealth rather than with people, giving the economy priority over the society, preoccupied with the 'national treasure' in surplus trade balances, GNP/per capita or with the accumulation of national wealth. 'It is this low road of regarding humanity as an instrument of production – rather than the high road of acknowledging the universality of life claims – that fits well with the reputation of economics as "the dismal science".'[56]

During the last decade there has been a far-reaching change in attitudes towards trade and investment. While, until the late 1970s, there was widespread support for notions of self-reliance, including import substitution, trade regulations and strictly controlled foreign investment, the trend now is generally in favour of open trade relations, and foreign investment is eagerly sought. Trade policies affect fundamentally the lives of people everywhere, and their differential impact on the enjoyment of economic, social and cultural rights has not been paid much attention. The achievements made in the Uruguay Round are likely to give unequal benefits to different states – and to different groups within states. Some of the trade barriers against the products of developing countries in the field of agricultural products and labour-intensive manufactured goods still remain. Social policies require that more attention be given to the consequences of trade policies.

The rapid development of new technologies has irreversibly changed global relations. A worldwide information revolution has taken place during the last decade, with an impact almost as great as the Industrial Revolution of the nineteenth century. While new technologies can improve people's lives, the social consequences depend on access to knowledge and information. Deep-seated and historically produced unequal access to resources, technology and knowledge have intensified socioeconomic inequality within and among nations. For years to come, socioeconomic inequalities will exist; governments and the international community must devise means to ensure welfare and livelihood for those who are unable to have access to or make use of the new possibilities.

There is an accelerating process of globalization in many fields beyond those of technology and communication mentioned above.[57] An increasing proportion of economic activities and transactions are transnational in nature and composition; multinational corporations and international financial institutions have increasing power to make decisions with a global impact. These processes have vastly different consequences for different states and different groups in society. The dominant concern is a search for profit rather than for improvement of living conditions for those in most need.

Many observers have noted the current trends towards the disintegration of national societies and a drift towards anarchy.[58] The number of internal conflicts has risen steeply; the conduct of warfare shows a staggering neglect of minimum humanitarian standards. It has been argued that this process is related to the extreme inequalities which exist in the world today, and to the profound insecurity of the future.

The role of the state is in decline, affected by the processes of globalization, on the one hand, and disintegration and trends towards anarchy on the other. Under the international human rights system, the state is seen to hold the primary responsibility for the realization of human rights; if it is increasingly weakened, it may be unable to perform this role. Controversies exist over the extent to which the institutions of a democratic state should intervene to redress inequalities caused by market forces. Ways can and must be found, however, for the state to ensure respect for and protection of economic, social and cultural rights and environmental protection, while preserving conditions of a relatively free market economy. Government action should promote social equity, overcome social inequalities, compensate imbalances created through the functioning of markets, and ensure a sustainable human development. The relation between government and the market should be complementary. A constructive interaction benefits both, whereas an entirely unregulated market eventually destroys itself through social unrest, soaring criminality and human insecurity.

## The Population Problem

Poverty and social inequality both contribute to and are affected by demographic changes, in particular population growth. When the Universal Declaration of Human Rights was adopted in 1948, there were about 2.5 billion people living on the Earth; the figure in the mid-1990s is estimated to be 5.8 billion, and by 2050 the world is likely to have 10 billion people. The accelerating process of urbanization, together with a push towards international migration, causes considerable difficulties in addressing the economic, social and cultural needs of the people; population pressures combined with environmental degradation also contribute to conflicts which, in turn, cause disintegration and anarchy.

The escalating involuntary movement of peoples, including internally displaced persons, asylum seekers and refugees, poses additional problems for the international agenda. These movements reflect the failure of societies to offer their citizens adequate personal security or acceptable standards of living where they can enjoy their human rights and fundamental freedoms. Throughout known history, people have migrated in order to improve their conditions. Those who seek to move are not the persons to blame. The international community must set itself a double agenda in this field. On the one hand, it should cooperate in ensuring conditions of security and socioeconomic justice inside countries to remove the root causes of unwanted mass migration; on the other hand, it should treat with respect and provide protection to those who do migrate.

*The Problem of Poverty*

The causes of poverty in different societies must be better understood. The *World Development Report 1990*[59] is devoted in its entirety to an examination of poverty worldwide. Poverty is more often than not combined with malnutrition, lack of education, low life expectation and substandard housing. These are factors which also impede efforts to move out of poverty: a malnourished child living in substandard housing has few prospects for success in school, even if one is available. The main cause of poverty, from the perspective of the affected individual, is the accident of being born into poverty. Chronic family poverty affects the child from birth, if not before: he or she experiences severe deficiencies in health, education, cultural skills and social relations. For the individual it is extremely difficult to break out of this vicious circle. Efforts to redress the situation must take into account different forms of poverty. The poverty which arises in situations of crisis, such as famine, requires measures to help individuals and families cope with the crisis and to come out of it with sufficient strength to manage their own needs during more normal conditions. Pockets of poverty in rich countries can be absorbed through appropriate, selective interventions, sometimes by affirmative action if the cause is social discrimination. Endemic mass poverty in poor countries requires entirely different measures.

We should, however, recognize that there have been positive developments in the last three or four decades, even if there has been a slowdown or reversal during the last few years. According to the *UNDP Human Development Report 1994*, nearly 70 per cent of humanity survived in abysmal human conditions in 1960 (below a human development index of 0.4), but only 32 per cent suffered such conditions in 1992. The share of the world population enjoying fairly satisfactory human development levels (above a human development index of 0.6) increased from 25 per cent to 60 per cent in 1992.[60]

While these are encouraging facts, they should not cause complacency, nor should they be taken as proof that the achievements are the result of the most recent trends in the market economy. This does show, however, that poverty can be eliminated: the task is far from hopeless. Efforts to secure for everyone the right to an adequate standard of living must be given top priority in the years to come. It is not only a moral but also a legal obligation under international human rights law to ensure that all human beings enjoy the basic and adequate food, housing and social services necessary for health, dignity and social participation. To achieve this goal, national and international action is required. First, attitudes must be changed in order to make economic and social policies address the problems of those below the poverty line; second, specific policies aimed at the realization of economic, social and cultural rights must be the central concern of development policies.

There is, however, an unfortunate assumption that the realization of economic, social and cultural rights can only be achieved through what is loosely called 'welfare', which is understood by many as the transfer of resources through the state to the poor – and to everyone else. This is a tragic misunderstanding. Most people prefer to take care of most of their own needs, if they have the opportunity to do so, in ways which allow their dignity and self-esteem to be respected. There are areas of concern which are best resolved through common efforts, and situations of risk whereby collective state arrangements are the most rational solution. The basis must be the efforts of the individual human being to ensure for herself or himself an adequate standard of living, and the opportunities for doing so must be available to everyone. Unemployed or underemployed persons represent a productive potential. The structural causes and the immediate manifestations of poverty need to be examined and remedies must be found in all societies. The structures and processes influencing distribution and redistribution of income in a society, including availability of employment, differentials in wages and salaries, tax structures and use of other public revenue sources, must be taken into account, as must the distribution of land, legal structures and processes which determine the ownership and control of productive resources, market and price structures, macroeconomic policies and the availability of and access to public services and social benefits.

### The Implementation of State Obligations

As has been pointed out above, the first level of state obligations is, wherever possible, to respect the freedom and the resources of those at risk, so that they can find solutions to their own problems, if possible.[61] The situations of many indigenous and other peripheral groups in societies, which in the past have been displaced or marginalized as a result of development activities directed from the centre, illustrate this point. Efforts to ensure the enjoyment of economic and social rights for the vulnerable must respect their integrity and dignity, focusing on helping them to identify and implement their own solutions to their problems. Their potential energy and resourcefulness, in situations where they can enjoy the basic necessities of adequate food, shelter and education, can be put to more productive use, rather than recourse to hand-outs, which add to their self-depreciation. Human beings who neither have access to land and other productive resources nor are able to find work which would enable them to earn their livelihood and participate in the life of society, become prey to despair and alienation. Work is essential to self-respect. Long experience of underemployment and unemployment can destroy the mental balance of the individual, ravage the family structure and cause decay in social relations.

Of even greater importance is the second level of state obligations: to protect the space for the vulnerable to find their own solutions from those who in one way or another seek to block them from doing so. There are a multitude of ways in which they are barred by the activities of others, for example usury, bonded labour relations, discrimination based on class, colour, race or gender, encroachment on their unprotected land by treasure hunters and gold diggers, and exploitation of labour due to the weakness or non-existence of trade unions. The agenda for protection is vast and constitutes the most important area in the realization of social, economic and cultural rights.

The above is not to deny that the state and the international community also have to take positive measures and to adopt arrangements to supplement the efforts made by all members of society. Arrangements to secure an adequate livelihood for those who, for reasons beyond their control, are unable to attain it themselves, through some kind of collective, obligatory nationwide insurance arrangements, are not only required under international human rights law, but are also a rational way to secure social harmony.

*Means for Achieving these Goals*

When formulating social, economic and financial policies, the central goal should be to create conditions of self-employment and jobs, and thereby to reduce, and ultimately to prevent, poverty. Investment, credit, taxation, the financing of systems of social protection, and land distribution and planning must all be geared to this goal. It is on these bases that all the other elements – education, health services, social security, family protection, health protection and cultural rights – can be built.

Nation building has in the past all too often been pursued through a process of homogenization, with little tolerance of cultural diversity and cultural innovations. It is increasingly recognized that uniformity is not a desirable goal, nor does it lead to tolerance and solidarity. Cultural development must allow for free artistic creation and access by the greatest possible number to the works of the past and present; it must also allow for the manifestation and evolution of different cultural traditions present on the same soil, the carriers of identity and self-respect for different groups.

The most urgent task is to raise awareness, at the international level, concerning the significance of these issues. Fortunately, a global process of recognition is already taking place. The World Summit for Social Development met in Copenhagen in March 1995 to examine many of these issues.[62] It follows other important events: (1) the World Conference on Education for All in 1990; (2) the Second United Nations Conference on the Least Developed Countries in 1990; (3) the World Summit for Children in 1990; (4) the United Nations Conference on Environment and Development in 1992; (5) the World Conference on Human Rights in 1993; (6) the International Conference on Population and Development in 1994 and (7) the Fourth World Conference on Women in 1995. The United Nations General Assembly has also called for a series of awareness-raising efforts for related concerns: the International Year for the World's Indigenous People, 1993; the International Year of the Family, 1994; the United Nations Year for Tolerance, 1995; and the International Year for the Eradication of Poverty, 1996.

Several requirements have to be fulfilled in order to make constructive headway. One of them is a proper basis for assessing the current situation and measuring progress; for this, we need a system of indicators. This was a major concern in the comprehensive study prepared for the Sub-Commission on Prevention of Discrimination and Protection of Minorities, entitled 'The Realization of Economic, Social and Cultural Rights'.[63] Another concern is to ensure that development agencies, including intergovernmental financial institutions, take the matters examined here into consideration. Finally, since the overall task is to ensure that economic, social and cultural policies are based on the comprehensive system of human rights, it is essential that advisory services and technical assistance in this field be expanded.

## Monitoring and Prospects for Complaint Procedures[64]

An essential component of modern international human rights law is the practice of international monitoring and review of state compliance with universal norms of human rights. At present the monitoring takes three forms: investigative reports, prepared for the Commission on Human Rights by special rapporteurs or working groups; individual complaint procedures by which nationals and other residents of a state can complain to international bodies for alleged violations of their human rights; and reports prepared by states which have ratified international human rights conventions and which therefore, in legal language, are parties to the convention concerned. Such reports are submitted periodically to international expert bodies (treaty bodies) set up in conformity with the convention concerned.

Periodic reporting by states to international bodies about their domestic implementation of human rights, and the examination of these reports in the presence of representatives from the state concerned, are now a routine matter and generally seen to constitute a constructive dialogue. This is the main mechanism available for monitoring the implementation of economic, social and cultural rights.

*Reporting Obligations and Procedures*

The obligation to report has been built into the respective conventions adopted by the United Nations, including the two International Covenants on Human Rights, the Convention on the Rights of the Child, the Convention on the Elimination of All Forms of Racial Discrimination and the Convention on the Elimination of All Forms of Discrimination against Women. Reporting obligations are found in the provisions of the conventions, which have also provided for the establishment of independent expert committees to examine the reports.

The principal instrument for the protection of economic, social and cultural rights within the United Nations human rights system is the International Covenant on Economic, Social and Cultural Rights. The international monitoring of this Covenant rests completely on a reporting procedure established by its Article 16. Since 1987, the consideration of the reports has been entrusted to the Committee on Economic, Social and Cultural Rights, established by the United Nations Economic and Social Council. States Parties are required to present comprehensive periodic reports every five years.

In practice, then, the reporting procedure under the International Covenant on Economic, Social and Cultural Rights is based on a dialogue between the State Party and the Committee on Economic, Social and Cultural Rights. This is achieved through a list of questions prepared by Committee members, on the basis of written reports and public hearings, for discussion between the Committee and a government delegation. Following an oral hearing, the Committee adopts its concluding observations in relation to a specific state report, expressing its positive appreciation where improvements have been made, and its issues of concern where implementation is proceeding too slowly or where there have been regressive lapses. In addition to country-specific observations, the Committee also uses 'general comments' and 'general discussions' for reaching a better understanding of the contents of the treaty obligations.

The Convention on the Elimination of All Forms of Discrimination against Women adopted in 1979 integrates civil, political, economic, social and cultural rights, and is of particular interest in relation to nutrition rights. The reporting obligations are laid down in its Article 18, according to which, after the initial report, periodic reports are to be submitted 'at least' every four years and whenever the Committee on the Elimination of Discrimination against Women requests them. On the basis of its consideration of reports, this Committee adopts suggestions and general recommendations regarding certain articles or specific subjects of the Convention dealing with matters which give rise to particular concerns of the Committee. The Convention on the Rights of the Child, similarly to the Convention on the Elimination of All Forms of Discrimination against Women, covers the traditional categories of human rights and enables an integrated approach to all human rights.

Under Article 44 of the Convention on the Rights of the Child, the States Parties undertake to submit an initial report within two years of the entry into force of the Convention and thereafter periodic reports every five years. It should be noted that the Committee on the Rights of the Child has shown considerable procedural innovation and openness to non-governmental organizations.

Article 5 of the International Convention on the Elimination of All Forms of Racial Discrimination includes an all-encompassing list of human rights and establishes the obligation of States Parties to prohibit and eliminate racial discrimination and to guarantee equal treatment in the enjoyment of these rights. Economic, social and cultural rights are covered extensively by this provision, particularly in Article 5(e), including six sub-paragraphs, each naming one of six specific rights. In its general guidelines for reporting, the Committee on the Elimination of Racial Discrimination has also asked governments to report on 'legislative, judicial, administrative and other measures' which give effect to Article 5(e).

Under the International Convention on the Elimination of All Forms of Racial Discrimination, States Parties are to submit an initial report within one year of the entry into force of the Convention, and periodic reports at two-year intervals. From 1989, the Committee on the Elimination of Racial Discrimination began to nominate one of its members as a country rapporteur for each report. On the basis of its examination of a report, the Committee may ask for further information or an additional report. The Committee also formulates suggestions and general recommendations as part of the reporting process.

The practice of the UN treaty bodies varies in relation to the use of comments or other material submitted by national or international NGOs. So far, only a few among the hundreds of human rights

NGOs have developed a competence in the field of economic, social and cultural rights sufficient to make a strong impact on the process. Labour organizations are an exception to this, as they play a major role in the ILO process.

## The Functions Served by Reporting

In the *Manual on Human Rights Reporting under Six Major International Human Rights Instruments,*[65] prepared by the UN Centre for Human Rights in collaboration with the UN Centre for Training and Research in Geneva, Philip Alston, then Chairman of the Committee on Economic, Social and Cultural Rights, discussed the purposes and functions of the state reporting system. This section draws on his analysis. The primary aim of this activity, Alston emphasizes, is to assist governments in improving their performance, even though this is coupled with a critical assessment of the efforts made. The state reports and their review by the treaty bodies make possible a continuing process to promote and enhance respect for human rights, by which each government confirms its commitment to respecting the human rights of those living within its territory and who are subject to its jurisdiction. In preparing the reports, government agencies take stock of their achievements to date and initiate measures to remedy any shortcomings identified.

Admittedly, the reporting process is taken more or less seriously. A conscientious preparation of state reports takes time and requires human resources, but advances the awareness of shortcomings and the need for domestic policy making. When a state becomes a party to an international treaty, it is expected to review its domestic law and practice to ensure that it is in compliance with the obligations contained in the treaty. Before submitting its initial report to the relevant treaty body, the state party is expected to undertake a comprehensive review of national legislation, administrative rules and procedures and practices in order to ensure the fullest possible conformity with the provisions of the treaty.

Reports shall provide not only the legislative and administrative measures adopted and the situation as it exists in practice; a precondition for effective reporting is an adequate system for monitoring regularly the situation with respect to each of the rights.

## Supervision

Monitoring of the relevant information by an independent, international body of experts is a first step towards identifying and subsequently remedying any human rights problems. Statistical information is expected to accompany the narrative description, serving to disaggregate the available information in order to investigate the situation, not only in the country as a whole, but also in the different regions and groups within the country. The Committee on Economic, Social and Cultural Rights has requested that 'specific attention be given to any worse-off regions or areas and to any specific groups or subgroups which appear to be particularly vulnerable or disadvantaged'.

Many human rights problems can be resolved merely by amending the relevant legislation, by changing administrative practices or by issuing appropriate instructions to the authority concerned. Others, however, are not susceptible of such rapid resolution and require the formulation of a long-term set of policies designed to ensure full and lasting compliance with treaty obligations. For example, efforts to eliminate some aspects of discrimination on the grounds of race or sex might require changes in cultural traditions which cannot be achieved overnight. In such instances the reporting process can act as a catalyst to the formulation of carefully tailored policies designed to respond to the problems identified. The supervisory committees will not expect the impossible to be achieved overnight, but they do expect to see evidence of policies likely to achieve the necessary remedial action within a reasonable period of time.

International supervisory procedures and control mechanisms can never be considered as substitutes for national mechanisms and national measures. The periodic report on the implementation of a treaty should be seen as an important document destined for a domestic as well as an international audience. Human rights treaties seek to promote and enhance not only a government's international accountability but also its accountability to its own citizens. The preparation of the report thus provides an important occasion for consultation of the appropriate social, economic, cultural and other sectors of society.

In this regard a variety of states from different regions of the world have begun to experiment with different forms of consultation. Some have sought inputs from non-governmental groups on particular issues, others have requested such groups to submit comments on the draft reports, and still others have entrusted the preparation of the reports to a group which includes representatives of the non-governmental sector.

The obligation to prepare successive periodic reports at specified intervals provides an ideal opportunity for evaluating progress achieved over time. The supervisory committees themselves tend to stress this element by making comparisons between the problems identified at the time of the examination of an earlier report and those observed when considering a subsequent report. Similarly, states which set themselves targets or benchmarks against which to assess their own progress can use the periodic reporting process as an occasion for measuring progress (or a lack thereof) and re-evaluating the suitability of the relevant benchmarks.

The principal human rights treaties generally request States Parties to report not only on the progress that they have made, but also on any 'factors and difficulties' which have affected the realization of the rights in question. It is sometimes suggested that states cannot realistically be expected to acknowledge that they are having problems in any areas and that reports will therefore inevitably only deal with 'good news', but this approach is clearly misplaced, and the supervisory committees tend to remain unconvinced by reports suggesting that all is well in the world. It must be accepted that no state can expect to have a perfect record in achieving respect for human rights. Even where the situation is generally very positive, there is always room for improvement. The frank acknowledgment of problems, even if they are reckoned to be almost intractable (or at least not readily capable of resolution), helps to establish the good faith of the government in the eyes both of the supervisory committee and of its own citizens. The reality is that a problem must first be diagnosed before a remedy can be found. In that respect, human rights problems can be compared to drug addiction: unless the existence of a problem is acknowledged, it will almost certainly not be solved.

The information on common experiences (both good and bad) makes it possible for states to learn from one another, and has made it possible for the supervisory committees to formulate 'general comments' based on their awareness of the types of issues governments typically encounter when translating the abstract obligations contained in the treaties into practical reality. Alston observes that the committees can then distil the wisdom of that collective experience into advice which is made available to all interested parties.

*Transparency and Public Scrutiny*

Some states have ensured the widespread dissemination of their reports so that the public at large may comment and thus contribute to a continuing national policy debate. This public scrutiny can be further enhanced by ensuring easy access for the public at large to the United Nations Summary Records which document the examination of the state's report by the appropriate treaty body.

## Concluding Remarks

The normative guidance to international relations and global policies must be sought in the Charter of the United Nations, which is binding on all its member states. The purposes set out for the organized international community are found in Article 1 of the Charter, whereas sub-paragraph 3 is of particular relevance:

> to achieve international co-operation in solving international problems of an economic, social, cultural, or humanitarian character, and in promoting and encouraging respect for human rights and fundamental freedoms for all without distinction as to race, sex, language, or religion.

The implementation of United Nations purposes and principles is regulated in other parts of the Charter. Under Article 56, member states pledge to take joint and separate action in cooperation with the United Nations for the achievement of the more detailed purposes set forth in Article 55, intended to 'create conditions of stability and well-being necessary for peaceful and friendly relations among nations based on the respect for the principle of equal rights and self-determination of peoples'. For this purpose, the United Nations and its member states, individually and collectively, shall promote:

- higher standards of living, full employment, and conditions of economic and social progress and development;
- solution of international economic, social, health and related problems, and international cultural and educational cooperation;
- universal respect for, and observance of, human rights and fundamental freedoms for all without distinction as to race, sex, language or religion.

These commitments then constitute the foundation on which human rights and development activities should both be pursued, whether collectively through the United Nations and other organizations or separately by states. However, while human rights have given rise to precise standard-setting and the evolution of implementation procedures, this has not been the case in the field of development.

While the language of the UN Charter gives strong support for a combination of development activities and the promotion of human rights, these have been treated separately in the practice both of the United Nations and of most states. Separate institutions and different procedures have been established for the two concerns. Different professional expertise has come to dominate each of the two, with economists playing a major role in operationalizing 'development', while legal minds tended to prevail in the elaboration of the human rights system.

As a result of 50 years of standard-setting in the field of human rights by the United Nations, it is possible to explain with relative precision not only the concept of human rights but also which human rights exist, in the sense of being universally recognized. In contrast, there has been until recently little or no consensus on what constitutes 'development'. It is a value-loaded concept, referring to something which is 'better' than that which preceded it. 'Development' qualifies primarily processes of social or economic change: if the change is considered positive, it can be described as 'development', otherwise not. Whether it is positive, or better than what preceded it, requires a value judgment. Better in what respect, and better for whom?

'Growth', understood as an increase in GNP, has long since been discarded, since it could in itself give no clue as to whether it was better or worse for different sections of society or even for the average standard of living measured by indicators of quality of life. It has long since been recognized that, as an indicator of development, the measurement of 'growth' should be combined with measurement of distribution of the benefits of growth: equitable income distribution was defined as positive and gross inequalities were seen as negative.

Building on this achievement, the next step was to see poverty eradication as a primary goal of development, and to ensure that women benefited equally from the economic changes taking place. When concerns with the environmental impacts of economic activities reached maturity in the late 1980s, the composite notion of sustainable development was introduced, giving space also for concern with intergenerational justice.

The understanding that the human being had to be treated as the subject, rather than the mere object, of development led, in the early 1990s, to the introduction by the United Nations Development Programme (UNDP) of the notion of human development. Finally, by 1994, the various concerns were merged, again by UNDP, through the concept of sustainable human development.

The international community has only very recently started to link operationally the promotion of human rights and the advancement of development. The concept of development itself has come to be reinterpreted in light of the human rights system. A major event in this process was the adoption, by the United Nations General Assembly in December 1986, of the Declaration on the Right to Development, the embryo of which is found in Article 28 of the Universal Declaration of Human Rights which proclaims that 'everyone is entitled to a social and international order in which the rights and freedoms set forth in this Declaration can be fully realized'.

With regard to social order, the Declaration on the Right to Development provides, in Article 8(1) that:

States shall undertake, at the national level, all necessary measures for the realization of the right to development and shall ensure, *inter alia*, equality of opportunity for all in their access to basic resources, education, health services, food, housing, employment and the fair distribution of income.

As to the requirement for an international order in which human rights for all can be realized, the Declaration on the Right to Development provides, in Article 3(3), that 'States have the duty to co-operate with each other in ensuring development and eliminating obstacles to development', while, under Article 4, 'States have a duty to take steps, individually and collectively, to formulate international development policies with a view to the full realization of the right to development'.

*Relinking Human Rights and Development*

The right to development is, according to Article 1 of the Declaration:

an inalienable human right by virtue of which every human person and all peoples are entitled to participate in, contribute to, and enjoy economic, social, cultural and political development, in which all human rights and fundamental freedoms can be fully realized.

The final document from the World Conference on Human Rights, held in Vienna in 1993 and attended by more than 170 states, declared that democracy, development and human rights are

interdependent and mutually reinforcing. Democracy is based on the freely expressed will of the people to determine their own political, economic, social and cultural systems and their full participation in all aspects of their lives. [ ... ] The international community should support the strengthening and promoting of democracy, development and respect for human rights and fundamental freedoms in the entire world.

The operationalization of the link between human rights and development confronts formidable obstacles, however, including dominant trends in international economic policies and the gradual weakening of the role of the state in ensuring the satisfaction of human needs. A re-examination of the origins and evolution of human rights in economic and social thought and policies might provide a basis for new directions.

## Notes

1   UN Doc. E/1993/22, p.83, para. 5.

2  Marshall (1950, pp.10–74).
3  Esping-Andersen (1990, p.24).
4  *Social Insurance and Allied Services*, London, HMSO, 1942.
5  Galbraith (1994, p.93).
6  Sampson (1983, pp.87–94).
7  Vignes and Schlenzka, 'World Health Organization', *Encyclopedia of International Law*, vol. 5, Amsterdam, Elseviers Science Publishers B.V., 1983, pp.242–5.
8  Humphrey (1984, p.32).
9  A review of US positions on economic and social rights, including the policies during the Second World War, is found in Alston (1990, pp.365–93).
10  J. Locke, *Second Treatise on Government*, Chapter V.
11  Ibid., para. 32.
12  See Article 8 of the International Covenant on Economic, Social and Cultural Rights and several ILO conventions.
13  See UN document E/CN.4/1987/17.
14  General Assembly Resolution 41/128 of 4 December 1986. Article 2 reads, in part: '1. The human being is the central subject of development and should be the active participant and beneficiary of the right to development. 2. All human beings have a responsibility for development, individually and collectively.'
15  These are the groups referred to in the guidelines for states when reporting to the UN Committee on Economic, Social and Cultural Rights. See Revised Guidelines Regarding the Form and Contents of Reports to be Submitted by States Parties under Articles 16 and 17 of the International Covenant on Economic, Social and Cultural Rights (UN doc. E/1991/23). See, also, Alston (1991, pp.39–77).
16  Maxwell and Frankenberger (1992).
17  See ECOSOC, Official Records, 1992, Supplement No. 3 (E/1992/23)].
18  Note that, in the International Covenant on Economic, Social and Cultural Rights, the right to health is contained in Article 12 and the right to social security in Article 9.
19  *World Development Report 1990*, p.26.
20  On the right to housing, see also Leckie (1995).
21  This section draws heavily on Eide *et al.* (1991). See also Oshaug *et al.* (1994).
22  Cultural acceptability of food does, of course, change over time, but this must be a voluntary process, not forced.
23  This may apply also in wealthy countries when a combination of recession and weak public policies generates increasing hunger and poverty, as has been the case in the United States during the 1980s and into the 1990s. See *Hunger 1994: Transforming the Politics of Hunger*.
24  The difference between a 'food first' approach to food security and a 'food security within a sustainable livelihood' approach was elaborated by Maxwell and Frankenberger (1992).
25  The Global Strategy for Shelter to the Year 2000 adopted by the General Assembly in its resolution 42/191 of 11 December 1987, *Official Records of the General Assembly, Forty-third Session, Supplement No. 8*, addendum (A/43/8/Add.1).
26  The final report of the study on the right to adequate housing by Rajindar Sachar is found in UN doc. E/CN.4/Sub.2/1995/12.
27  *World Bank: Resettlement and Development*, The World Bank Environment Department, Washington, April 1994.
28  See also Hammarberg (1995).
29  See Mushakoji (1991).
30  The *Codex Alimentarius* is a code of food quality operated by FAO and WHO.
31  United Nations Administrative Committee of Co-ordination, Sub-Committee on Nutrition, *Second Report on the World Nutrition Situation*, vol. 1 (Global and

Regional Results) and vol. 2 (Country Trends, and Methods and Statistics), Geneva, 1993.

32   For details, see Eide *et al.* (1991).

33   Of particular interest as the first of its kind is the establishment of the Center for Nutrition and the Environment of Indigenous Peoples (CINE) at McGill University, Macdonald Campus, Ste-Anne-de-Bellevue, Quebec, Canada. This is a research, training and information centre on food and nutrition based on the cultural and environmental traditions of indigenous peoples themselves, and directed by a board consisting of indigenous representatives.

34   This is provided for in Article 6(2) of the International Covenant on Economic, Social and Cultural Rights.

35   Special provisions on the right to technical and vocational training can be found both in the Protocol of San Salvador (Article 6(2)) and in the European Social Charter (Article 15).

36   A much wider range of ways in which the obligations can be affected are spelled out in Oshaug *et al.* (1994).

37   See, further, Scheinin (1995).

38   Which hardly can be held to constitute compliance with the obligations arising from economic, social and cultural rights. The US had not then, and has still not, ratified the International Covenant on Economic, Social and Cultural Rights, but is at least morally obliged under Articles 22–7 of the Universal Declaration of Human Rights.

39   Article 27 of the Convention on the Rights of the Child obliges states, 'in case of need, to provide material assistance and support programmes, particularly with regard to nutrition, clothing and housing'.

40   In Eide *et al.* (1995).

41   The reporting guidelines indicate that this clause relates not only to benefits in cash but also to 'medical and other' benefits. See Revised Guidelines Regarding the Form and Contents of Reports to be Submitted by States Parties under Articles 16 and 17 of the International Covenant on Economic, Social and Cultural Rights (UN doc. E/1991/23).

42   The sources of the right to social security are examined by Bård-Anders Andreassen in Eide *et al.* (1991, p.347). See also Scheinin (1995). The present section on sources draws extensively on the two authors mentioned, and in particular on Scheinin. A list of other relevant ILO conventions and recommendations is found in Andreassen (1991, footnote 77, pp.347–8).

43   The guidelines are contained in Alston (1991).

44   See Articles 11(1)(*e*), 11(2)(*b*) and 13(*a*) of the Convention on the Elimination of All Forms of Discrimination against Women.

45   See Article 27 of the Convention on the Rights of the Child.

46   Adopted by the UN General Assembly in 1990 and not yet in force.

47   For a list of some arrangements covered by the clause on family benefits, see Alston (1990, p.132). For example, public kindergarten services are covered by the provision. On the relationship between Articles 12 and 16, see *supra*, note 17, p.130.

48   On the various dimensions of the provision, see Alston (1990, p.134).

49   On the relationship between Articles 13(3) and 14 of the European Social Charter, see Alston (1990, p.116).

50   Mention can also be made of the European Convention on Social and Medical Assistance (1953), which provides for equal treatment for the nationals of the Contracting Parties in the application of legislation providing for social and medical assistance.

51   Tomaševski (1995).

52 WHO Long-Term Programme for Maternal and Child Health, World Health Assembly resolution WHA32.42 of 25 May 1979, para.2
53 *Primary Health Care. Report of the International Conference on Primary Health Care, Alma-Ata, USSR, 6–12 September 1978*, Geneva, WHO, 1978, p.2.
54 *Human Development Report 1994*, p.2
55 *The Crisis of Social Development in the 1990s: Preparing for the World Social Summit*, Geneva, UNRISD, 1994.
56 *Human Development Report 1994*, p. 14.
57 For a comprehensive discussion, see Robertson (1992).
58 See, for example Kaplan (1994, pp.45–76).
59 *World Development Report 1990.*
60 *Human Development Report 1994*, p.1.
61 For a general discussion on state obligations, see *Human Development Report 1994*, Part I, Section IV.3.
62 Several of the issues discussed in this section are dealt with in the Declaration and Programme of Action for the World Summit.
63 D. Türk, 'The Realization of Economic, Social and Cultural Rights', preliminary report, UN doc. E/CN.4/Sub.2/1989/19; first progress report, UN doc. E/CN.4/Sub.2/1990/19; second progress report, UN doc. E/CN.4/Sub.2/1991/17; and the final report, UN doc. E/CN.4/Sub.2/1992/16. The discussion of indicators can be found, in particular, in the 1991 report.
64 The monitoring of states' implementation of economic, social and cultural rights under the various instruments is analysed in greater detail in Alston (1991) and Craven (1995). See Rosas and Scheinin (1995, which also covers the other instruments). The study by Craven is the first comprehensive analysis of the practice of the International Covenant on Economic, Social and Cultural Rights.
65 UN CHR/UNRISD, 1991.

# Bibliography

Alston, Philip (1990), 'U.S. ratification of the Covenant on Economic, Social and Cultural Rights: the need for an entirely new strategy', *American Journal of International Law*, 84, 365–93.
Alston, Philip (1991), 'The International Covenant on Economic, Social and Cultural Rights', *Manual on Human Rights Reporting*, New York, United Nations, pp.39–77.
Craven, Matthew (1995), *The International Covenant on Economic, Social and Cultural Rights*, Oxford, Clarendon Press.
Drzewicki, Krzysztof (1995), 'The right to work and rights in work', in Asbjørn Eide, Katarina Krause and Allan Rosas (eds), *Economic, Social and Cultural Rights*, Dordrecht/Boston/London, Martinus Nijhoff Publishers.
Eide, Asbjørn, Arne Oshaug and Wenche Barth Eide (1991), 'Food security and the right to food in international law and development', *Transnational Law and Contemporary Problems*, University of Iowa, 1, (2).
Esping-Andersen, Gøsta (1990), *The Three Worlds of Welfare Capitalism*, Cambridge, Polity Press.
Galbraith, John Kenneth (1994), *A Journey through Economic Time*, Boston/New York, Houghton Mifflin.
Hammarberg, Thomas (1995), 'Children', in Asbjørn Eide, Katarina Krause and Allan Rosas (eds) *Economic, Social and Cultural Rights*, Dordrecht/Boston/London, Martinus Nijhoff Publishers.

*Human Development Report 1994* (1994), Oxford, Oxford University Press.

Humphrey, John (1984), *Human Rights and the United Nations: A Great Adventure*, New York, Transnational Publishers.

*Hunger 1994: Transforming the Politics of Hunger* (1994), Silver Springs, Bread for the World Institute.

Kaplan, Robert D. (1994), 'The coming of anarchy', *The Atlantic Monthly*, Boston, **273**, (2), 45–76.

Leckie, Scott (1995), 'The right to housing', in Asbjørn Eide, Katarina Krause and Allan Rosas (eds) *Economic, Social and Cultural Rights*, Dordrecht/Boston/London, Martinus Nijhoff Publishers.

Marshall, T.H. (1950), *Citizenship and Social Class*, Cambridge, Cambridge University Press.

Maxwell, Simon and Thomas Frankenberger (1992), *Household Food Security: Concepts, Indicators, Measurement. A Technical Review*, New York/Rome, UNICEF/International Fund for Agricultural Development (IFAD).

Mushakoji, Kinhide (1991), 'Development and racism in Asia and the Pacific', in *IMADR Yearbook 1991*, Tokyo, The International Movement Against All Forms of Discrimination and Racism, pp.15–30.

Oshaug, Arne, Wenche Barth Eide and Asbjørn Eide (1994), 'Human rights: a normative basis for food and nutrition relevant policies', *Food Policy*, **19**, (6).

Robertson, Roland (1992), *Globalization. Social Theory and Global Culture*, London, Sage Publications.

Rosas, Allan and Martin Scheinin (1995), 'Implementation mechanisms and remedies', in Asbjørn Eide, Katarina Krause and Allan Rosas (eds), *Economic, Social and Cultural Rights*, Dordrecht/Boston/London, Martinus Nijhoff Publishers.

Sampson, Klaus (1983), 'International Labour Organization', in Rudolf Bernhardt (ed.), *Encyclopedia of International Law*, Instalment 5, Amsterdam, Elseviers Science Publishers B.V., pp.87–94.

Scheinin, Martin (1995), 'The right to social security', in Asbjørn Eide, Katarina Krause and Allan Rosas (eds), *Economic, Social and Cultural Rights*, Dordrecht/Boston/London, Martinus Nijhoff Publishers.

Tomaševski, Katarina (1995), 'Health rights', in Asbjørn Eide, Katarina Krause and Allan Rosas (eds) *Economic, Social and Cultural Rights*, Dordrecht/Boston/London, Martinus Nijhoff Publishers.

*World Development Report 1990* (1990), Oxford, Oxford University Press.

# 5 Cultural Rights

## JANUSZ SYMONIDES

## Introduction

*Cultural Rights: a Neglected and Forgotten Category of Human Rights*

Cultural rights are often qualified as an 'underdeveloped category' of human rights. This term was chosen as the title of the seminar organized in 1991 at Fribourg University,[1] and was then broadly accepted. It suggests that, in comparison with other categories of human rights – civil, political, economic and social – cultural rights are the least developed as far as their scope, legal content and enforceability are concerned. Indeed, they need further elucidation, classification and strengthening. However, the term 'development' suggests the process of the creation of new rights. This point of view may be challenged as the existing list of cultural rights is relatively exhaustive. Therefore the problem is linked rather to the fact that these rights are neglected, underestimated, missing or forgotten, and that they are treated as 'poor relatives' of other human rights.

This neglect can be seen in the fact that although, in accordance with the International Covenant on Economic, Social and Cultural Rights, cultural rights are usually enumerated together with economic and social rights, they receive much less attention and quite often are completely forgotten. As observed by Eide, although the expression 'economic, social and cultural' is widely used, in most cases concern appears to be limited to economic and social rights.[2] This can be observed not only in the doctrine but in state practice.

Every year the Commission on Human Rights discusses the question of the realization in all countries of the economic, social and cultural rights contained in the Universal Declaration of Human Rights and in the International Covenant on Economic, Social and Cultural Rights. An analysis of statements during the debate on this item once again shows that, though cultural rights are mentioned together with economic and social rights, in fact attention is limited to economic and social rights, with cultural rights not being debated. This neglect can also be found in reports presented by the States Parties to the International Covenant on Economic, Social and Cultural Rights on its implementation. The attention paid to cultural rights formulated in Article 15 is far from satisfactory.

What are the reasons for the reserve demonstrated by the doctrine and state practice in relation to cultural rights? They are manifold. Cultural rights are scattered throughout a great number of instruments, both universal and regional, adopted by the United Nations, by the specialized agencies and by the regional organizations. This, in the absence of any codifying treaty or declaration, opens the way for various classifications and groupings. In some cases cultural rights are presented as an aggregate – as one right, the right to culture. Such a presentation indeed raises doubts about the clear or precise content of cultural rights.[3]

Among important sources of reservation concerning cultural rights, one should mention fears and suspicions of states that the recognition of the right to different cultural identities, the right of identification with vulnerable groups, in particular minorities and indigenous peoples, may encourage the tendency towards secession and may endanger national unity. For this very reason, the introduction of cultural rights in the Charter of the United Nations was blocked during the San Francisco Conference. By the same token, the cultural rights of persons belonging to minorities are not mentioned by the Universal Declaration of Human Rights. They were only recognized by Article 27 of the International Covenant on Civil and Political Rights in 1966.[4]

*Developments Concerning Cultural Rights in the 1990s*

During the last decade of the twentieth century, cultural rights have received increasing attention from international governmental and non-governmental organizations, as well as from human rights specialists. Among the manifold reasons for which they have become a subject of international debates and discussions, there is no doubt an acknowledgment of the fact that the cultural factor can be found among the most important sources of internal conflicts. Violations of cultural rights of various groups, rejection of the right to be different, to have different cultural identities, have become very dangerous pathologies which fuel aggressive ethnonationalism, xenophobia, racism and anti-semitism. Therefore culture and respect for cultural rights have also been recognized as an essential element in the prevention and resolution of conflicts. This has resulted in increased attention being paid to the elaboration and respecting of the cultural rights of persons belonging to minorities, indigenous people and other vulnerable groups.

At the end of the twentieth century there is also a full recognition of the importance of culture not only for development in its economic dimension, but also for 'human development', understood by the World Summit for Social Development (Copenhagen, 1995) as the social and cultural fulfilment of the individual. Without the implementation of cultural rights – the right to education, the right to participate in cultural life – and without the freedom of artistic, scientific and intellectual activities and pursuits, human development is impossible. The observance of cultural rights, in particular the right to cultural identification, is seen now as a constitutive element of the respect for human dignity.

Reflection on the interrelation between culture and development was initiated by a series of initiatives undertaken by the United Nations system. The General Assembly, by its resolution 41/187, proclaimed the World Decade for Cultural Development (1988–97) and asked UNESCO to play the role of lead agency. Among four of the Decade's objectives, three – affirming and enriching cultural identities, broadening participation in culture and promoting international cultural cooperation – are directly linked to the implementation of cultural rights.[5]

In 1992, the Director-General of UNESCO, in accordance with the request formulated by the General Conference and supported by the General Assembly,[6] established the World Commission on Culture and Development chaired by Javier Pérez de Cuéllar. The Commission's mandate obliged it to prepare a World Report on Culture and Development and 'proposals both for urgent and long-term action to meet cultural needs in the context of development'. The World Commission met six times and set in motion a dynamic of international cooperation through the preparation of regional reports, expert contributions, specially commissioned papers and studies, as well as thematic workshops. During the fourth meeting, the World Commission discussed cultural rights and the right to development.[7] The report of the World Commission on Culture and Development, under the title *Our Creative Diversity*, was published in 1995. Among its ten recommendations for international cooperation, Action 7 is entitled 'Protecting cultural rights as human rights'.[8]

In line with Chapter 9 of the report of the World Commission, 'Rethinking cultural policies', UNESCO organized in Stockholm, from 30 March to 2 April 1998, an Intergovernmental Conference on Cultural Policies for Development. The main objective of the conference was the elaboration of strategies and a plan of action for such policies, as well as to review UNESCO's own preparatory contribution in this field.[9] Cultural rights were presented in the preparatory paper for the conference,[10] in a section of its background document, and was referred to in the Action Plan on Cultural Policies for Development adopted by the conference which states, 'Access to and participation in cultural life being a fundamental right of individuals in all communities, governments have a duty to create conditions for the full exercise of this right.'

In the 1990s, cultural rights of persons belonging to minorities became an important part of the general discussion and international regulations concerning these groups. In 1992, the General Assembly adopted the Declaration on the Rights of Persons Belonging to National or Ethnic, Religious and Linguistic Minorities, which contains a number of provisions dealing with the cultural rights of these persons.

The question of how to improve the protection of the cultural rights of minorities was introduced into UNESCO's programmes in 1992.[11] Studies endorsing the implementation of cultural rights for Europe, Africa, Asia and Latin America were prepared. In 1994, the Executive Board put on its agenda a special item, the protection and promotion of the cultural rights of persons belonging to minorities and indigenous people within UNESCO's field of competence.[12]

As the problem of minorities became especially acute in Europe, various initiatives aimed at the preparation of normative instruments were undertaken by European organizations. In October 1993, the summit of heads of state and government of the Council of Europe called for the preparation of a protocol complementing the European Convention on Human Rights in the cultural field with provisions guaranteeing individual rights, in particular for persons belonging to national minorities.

In 1994, the Framework Convention for the Protection of National Minorities was drawn up and opened for signature. The Convention enumerates the cultural rights of persons belonging to minorities and invests the state with the duty to protect them. A few years earlier the Organization on Security and Co-operation in Europe, during its 1990 Copenhagen meeting, adopted the Concluding Document which presented an exhaustive list of the cultural rights of persons belonging to minorities.

Apart from actions aimed at the protection of the rights of minorities and indigenous people,[13] international governmental and non-governmental organizations as well as the academic community have undertaken in recent years a number of efforts aimed at the better understanding, consolidation and recognition of cultural rights. UNESCO, in its Medium Term Programme 1996–2001 states: 'The definition and content of cultural rights must be clarified and measures must be identified which could improve their effective implementation. The recognition of academic freedom is another important aspect of the promotion of cultural rights.'[14]

In line with this aim, together with the Council of Europe and the University of Fribourg, Switzerland, UNESCO organized a number of meetings and prepared publications concerning cultural rights.[15]

To sum up this rather selective presentation of the developments concerning cultural rights in the 1990s, one can say that they raised awareness concerning the importance of cultural rights. Though these rights still remain a neglected category of human rights, perhaps by the end of the century they could at least be considered less 'forgotten'.

## Different Definitions and Meanings of 'Culture'

Although the notion 'culture' is essential for the formulation, understanding and scope of 'cultural rights', it is impossible to find, among dozens if not hundreds of definitions used, one which is universally accepted. Different formulations and meanings of this term are proposed in different contexts. Thus, as suggested by Stavenhagen, culture may be identified with the accumulated material heritage of humankind or may be regarded rather as the process of artistic and scientific creation; or it may be understood as the sum total of the material and spiritual activities and products of a given social group which distinguishes it from other similar groups.[16]

During a meeting on 'Cultural rights as human rights' held at UNESCO Headquarters in July 1968, experts for the first time discussed a definition of culture in the context of cultural rights. The working paper prepared by the secretariat referred to 'mass culture', 'popular culture', 'traditional culture' and 'world culture'.[17] In the discussion, N'Daw stated that the word 'culture' has been used both in a very wide and in a restricted sense. In the widest sense, it really means the very essence of man, including the sum total of human activities; culture is precisely that which makes man different from nature.[18] Boutros-Ghali noted that there are three separate meanings of culture: culture as a way of life, cultures of universal significance and certain forms of culture that are peculiar to certain communities.[19] Thapar referred to international, national and subnational culture.[20] The experts agreed in the final conclusions:

> Culture is a human experience which is difficult to define, but we recognize it as the totality of ways by which men create designs for living. It is a process of communication between men; it is the essence of being human [ ... ] Culture is everything which enables man to be

operative and active in his world, and to use all forms of expression more and more freely to establish communication among men.[21]

As stated by the report of the World Commission on Culture and Development: 'A great deal of confusion arises in both academic and political discourse when "culture" in the humanistic sense is not distinguished from "culture" in its anthropological sense, notably culture as the total and distinctive way of life of a people or society.'[22] In the context of development, the Commission adopted a broader understanding of culture.

It is worth noting that, during the general discussion conducted during the seventh session of the Committee on Economic, Social and Culture Rights (1992), on the right to take part in cultural life as recognized in Article 15 of the International Covenant on Economic, Social and Cultural Rights, it was also stated: 'that culture meant a way of life [ ... ] Culture mirrored and shaped the economic, social and political life of a community'.[23]

Analysis of various UNESCO instruments allows us to discover a tendency towards the acceptance of a broader understanding of 'culture'. Thus the Declaration of the Principles of International Cultural Co-operation of 4 November 1966 states, in Article III: 'International cultural co-operation shall cover all aspects of intellectual and creative activities relating to education, science and culture.' As far as the aims of international cultural cooperation are concerned, Article IV stresses that it should: 'enable everyone to have access to knowledge, to enjoy the arts and literature of all peoples, to share in advances made in science in all parts of the world and in the resulting benefits and to contribute to the enrichment of cultural life'.

The Recommendation on Participation by the People at Large in Cultural Life and Their Contribution to It of 26 November 1976 explains, in its preamble:

> culture is not merely an accumulation of works and knowledge which an élite produces [ ... ] is not limited to access to works of art and the humanities, but is at one and the same time the acquisition of knowledge, the demand for a way of life and the need to communicate.

Similarly, the Final Report of the 1982 World Conference on Cultural Policies states that, without attempting to lay down a scientific or over-rigid definition of culture, delegates were in agreement in understanding the term 'culture', not in the restricted sense of *belles lettres*, the fine arts, literature and philosophy, but as distinctive and specific features and ways of thinking and organizing people's lives. The report states:

Culture therefore covered artistic creation together with the interpretation, execution and dissemination of works of art, physical culture, sports and games and open-air activities, as well as the ways in which a society and its members expressed their feeling for beauty and harmony and their vision of the world, as much as their modes of scientific and technological creation and control of their natural environment.

The broad anthropological definition of culture was accepted by the Council of Europe. The Arc-et-Senans Declaration (1972) on the Future of Cultural Development explains: 'Culture, as experienced by the majority of the population today, means much more than traditional arts and the humanities. Nowadays, culture embraces the education system, the mass media, the cultural industries.'

The Declaration on Culture Objectives (Berlin, 1984) states: 'Considering the determining role of culture, as a whole of values which gives to human beings their reason to be and to act [ ... ] the main aim of all societies is to enable everyone to achieve personal fulfilment.'[24]

As with the term 'culture' itself, which has broader or narrower interpretations and meanings, cultural rights may also be presented in a twofold manner. The broader understanding of cultural rights means that they also embrace the right to education, the right to participate in scientific progress and the right to information.

This approach is based on the assumption that the above-mentioned rights are so closely linked with other cultural rights that, in some cases, a separation is almost impossible. Indeed, creative activity can sometimes hardly be divided into scientific or artistic, as in many cases new forms and methods of artistic expression are determined by scientific and technological progress. The essence of the protection of moral and material interests is identical and independent of the fact that they result from either scientific or literary production. Similarly, one may say that, without the right to information, without the right to seek, receive and impart information and ideas through any media, neither cultural nor scientific and educational cooperation is possible.

## Cultural Rights as Formulated by the United Nations Human Rights Instruments

*The International Bill of Rights*

The concept of cultural rights was born as part of a new approach to human rights, their 'socialization', which was articulated after the Second World War. During the discussion preceding the adoption of the United Nations Charter, several Latin American states proposed the inclusion of cultural rights. Though the notion of cultural rights was not in the end introduced into the Charter, nevertheless the very fact that human rights were included within the competence of the Economic and Social Council is sometimes interpreted as evidence that the Charter departed from the narrowly interpreted conception of human rights.

On 10 December 1948, the General Assembly adopted the Universal Declaration of Human Rights which, in Article 27, states:

> 1. Everyone has the right freely to participate in the cultural life of the community, to enjoy the arts and to share in scientific advancement and its benefits.
> 2. Everyone has the right to the protection of the moral and material interests resulting from any scientific, literary or artistic production of which he is the author.

The Declaration also provides, in Article 22, that everyone is entitled to the realization, through national effort and international cooperation, of the economic, social and cultural rights indispensable for his dignity and the free development of his personality. The right to education is formulated by Article 26.

A step forward in the development of the concept of cultural rights was made in the International Covenant on Economic, Social and Cultural Rights which, in Article 15, provides:

> 1. The States Parties to the present Covenant recognize the right of everyone:
> (a) to take part in cultural life;
> (b) to enjoy the benefits of scientific progress and its applications;
> (c) to benefit from the protection of the moral and material interests resulting from any scientific, literary or artistic production of which he is the author.
> 2. The steps to be taken by the States Parties to the present Covenant to achieve the full realization of this right shall include those necessary for the conservation, the development and the diffusion of science and culture.
> 3. The States Parties to the present Covenant undertake to respect the freedom indispensable for scientific research and creative activity.
> 4. The States Parties to the present Covenant recognize the benefits to be derived from the encouragement and development of international contacts and cooperation in the scientific and cultural fields.

The text of paragraph 1 is slightly different from Article 27 of the Universal Declaration of Human Rights, as it does not include the phrase that identified the cultural life as that 'of the community'. This change was made because, in some cases, the 'cultural life of the community', in the singular, may be interpreted restrictively to exclude the right of minorities or other groups to participate in their own independent cultural life.

As far as paragraph 2 is concerned, there was, in the Commission on Human Rights and in the Third Committee, considerable debate about whether or not certain goals of scientific and cultural development should be set out. It was proposed that states should undertake to ensure the development of science and culture in the interest of progress and democracy and to ensure peace and cooperation among nations. These proposals were rejected as it was felt that a statement of aims might provide states with a pretext for abusive control of science and culture.

During the debate relating to paragraph 3, certain states found the term 'indispensable' which described freedom as too restrictive. A majority of the Third Committee decided to retain the word which affirmed the right of the state to impose upon the exercise of that freedom limitations required in the interests of national security, public order and morality.

Although presented in terms of a single right, Article 15 in fact recognizes four different rights. Paragraph 4, which speaks about international cooperation, is worded, by the inclusion of the phrase 'recognize the benefits to be derived from', in such a way that it is difficult to speak about binding obligations.

Among the United Nations human rights instruments which, apart from the International Bill of Rights, confirm provisions concerning cultural rights, two deserve special attention. The Convention on the Elimination of All Forms of Discrimination against Women (1979) which, in Article 13, paragraph c, formulates states' obligation to ensure for women, on the basis of equality of men and *women*, 'the right to participate in recreational activities, sports and all aspects of cultural rights'. The same right is *mutatis mutandis* guaranteed for the child by Article 31 of the Convention on the Rights of the Child. Articles 28 and 29 also provide the child's right to education, whereas Article 30 speaks about the cultural rights of the child who belongs to a minority or an indigenous group.

*Regional Normative Instruments*

The American Declaration of the Rights and Duties of Man of 1948 is the first inter-state instrument presenting a catalogue of cultural rights. Article XIII provides:

> Every person has the right to take part in the cultural life of the community, to enjoy the arts and to participate in the benefits that result from intellectual progress, especially scientific discoveries.

He likewise has the right to the protection of his moral and material interests as regards his inventions or any literary, scientific or artistic works of which he is the author.

Important provisions concerning cultural rights are also enshrined in the Protocol of San Salvador.

The African Charter on Human and Peoples' Rights of 1981 formulates both the right of every individual to freely take part in the cultural life of his community (Article 17) and the duty of individuals to preserve and strengthen positive African cultural values in their relations with the other members of the society, in the spirit of tolerance, dialogue and consultation and, in general, to contribute to the promotion of the moral well-being of society. The Charter also speaks about collective rights, the rights of all peoples to their cultural development with due regard to their freedom and identity and in the equal enjoyment of the common heritage of mankind.

The European Convention of Human Rights (1950) does not specifically protect cultural rights, though its Article 20 mentions the right to information and Article 2 of the Protocol speaks about the right to education.

Among instruments adopted by the Council of Europe which are relevant to cultural rights one can mention the European Social Charter (1961), the Convention on the Protection of the Cultural Heritage (1985), the Convention on the Protection of the Archaeological Heritage (1992), the European Sports Charter (1992), the European Charter for Regional or Minority Languages (1992) and the Framework Convention for the Protection of National Minorities (1994).

## UNESCO's Instruments

An impressive number of standard-setting instruments concerning cultural rights have been adopted by UNESCO, which, by its Constitution, is obliged to give fresh impetus to the spread of culture, to maintain, increase and diffuse knowledge and to recommend to the nations concerned the necessary international conventions. Furthering this mission, UNESCO has elaborated nearly 30 standard-setting instruments: conventions, declarations and recommendations dealing with various aspects of cultural rights.[25]

The first convention for the protection of cultural rights was prepared by UNESCO under the influence of the Universal Declaration of Human Rights. To guarantee the right of authors to the protection of their moral and material interests, in 1952 UNESCO convened the Intergovernmental Copyright Conference, which adopted the Universal Copyright Convention, revised in 1971.

Other important conventions include the Convention against Discrimination in Education (1960), the Convention on the Means of Prohibiting and Preventing the Illicit Import, Export and Transfer of Ownership of Cultural Property (1970) and the Convention concerning the Protection of the World Cultural and Natural Heritage (1972).

Of nearly 20 declarations and recommendations dealing with various cultural rights, the three best known are the Declaration on the Principles of International Cultural Co-operation (1966), the Recommendation on Participation by the People at Large in Cultural Life and Their Contribution to It (1976) and the Recommendation concerning the Status of the Artist (1980). Conventions, declarations and recommendations adopted by UNESCO protect and develop the rights to education, to cultural identity, to information, to participation in cultural life, to creativity, to benefits from scientific progress, to the protection of material and moral interests of authors, and to international cultural cooperation.

An original contribution of UNESCO to the development of the concept of cultural rights is the proclamation and elaboration in a series of normative instruments of the right to the protection of and access to the cultural heritage.[26]

*National Constitutions*

Are cultural rights recognized and listed by fundamental laws? Does the analysis of constitutions allow us to formulate a positive answer? In general, one may say that there are three ways in which cultural rights are mentioned. They may be recognized as a specific category of human rights when constitutions, for example, presenting the fundamental rights of citizens contain a chapter or a part on economic, social and cultural rights. Such a chapter may be found in the constitutions of Croatia (1990), Macedonia (1991), Poland (1997), Slovakia (1992) and Surinam (1987), among others. The Indian Constitution (1949), in the part dealing with fundamental rights, has one specific article (29) on cultural rights.[27]

Some constitutions recognize cultural rights indirectly when they have the stipulation confirming the binding character of international human rights instruments. The constitution of the Czech Republic (1992) provides, in Article 10, 'The ratified and promulgated international treaties on human rights and fundamental freedoms [ ... ] shall be applicable as directly binding regulations, having priority before the law.' Similarly, the Constitution of Romania (1991) states, in Article 20, 'Constitutional provisions concerning the citizen's rights and liberties shall be interpreted and enforced in conformity with the Universal Declaration of Human Rights, with the Covenants and other treaties Romania is a party to.' These formulations may be interpreted as the recognition of cultural rights which are listed in the International Bill of Rights and other human rights instruments binding these countries.

The majority of constitutions do not utilize the term 'cultural rights' but enumerate concrete rights belonging to this category. In fact, it is almost impossible to find a constitution which does not list at least one cultural right. Among these, the most frequently quoted is the right to education.[28] Many constitutions – for example, Portugal (1976, amended in 1982), the Republic of Korea (1980), Egypt (1980) and Bulgaria (1991) – formulate the right to freedom of artistic, scientific and intellectual activity and creativity and confirm the protection of the moral and material interests of authors. Several constitutions – Panama (1972), Spain (1978), Peru (1993) – recognize the right of the citizen to access to or participation in culture or cultural life. The right of access to information is mentioned, *inter alia*, by the constitutions of Estonia (1988) and Romania (1991).

The right to cultural identity, and linguistic and educational rights are relatively broadly presented in the constitutions of countries in which there are indigenous people and minorities. The cultural rights of indigenous peoples (communities) are formulated in the constitutions of Latin American countries: Argentina, Bolivia, Brazil, Colombia, Ecuador, Guatemala, Honduras, Panama, Paraguay, Peru, Mexico and Nicaragua. The cultural rights of persons belonging to minorities are presented in the constitutions of several Central and Eastern European countries: Bulgaria, Estonia, Hungary, Lithuania, Moldova, Romania, Slovakia and Slovenia. These constitutions recognize the right of members of minorities to their cultural (ethnic, national) identity and the right to participate in decision making concerning their cultural affairs.

An analysis of constitutional provisions allows us to conclude that cultural rights are recognized by national constitutions, though none of them contains an exhaustive list of these rights. One may also observe that a longer list of cultural rights may be found in constitutions which were adopted relatively recently, in the 1990s.

## Debate Concerning the List of Cultural Rights

Despite the fact that international human rights instruments analysed earlier in this chapter formulate concrete cultural rights, their general enumeration or a full list is far from being agreed upon. For this very reason, the World Commission proposed the establishment of an inventory of cultural rights. As none of the human rights instruments gives in full an enumeration of cultural rights, a call for the preparation of a comprehensive, codifying instrument was formulated by UNESCO. Thus the Programme and Budget for 1994–95 mentioned the need to draft a standard-setting instrument on cultural rights. The continuation of international reflection aimed at the better definition and understanding of cultural rights was also foreseen by the Programme and Budget for 1998–99.

What are the causes or sources of misunderstanding and differences concerning the presentation of a comprehensive list of cultural rights? There are many. First, there is, or rather was, a tendency to replace the whole category of cultural rights with 'the right to culture'. Although the International Bill of Rights does not use this term, it was referred to by specialists and appeared in documentation, programmes and publications of the United Nations and UNESCO.[29] This right was mentioned frequently during the seminar on cultural rights organized by UNESCO in 1968 and during conferences on cultural policies held in the 1970s. Still, in the publication *United Nations Action in the Field of Human Rights* (1992), the paragraph dealing with cultural rights is entitled 'The right to culture'.[30] Fortunately, in the 1990s, the references to this right are less frequent. Probably, 'the right to culture' appeared in human rights vocabulary by misinterpretation. Article 27 of the International Covenant on Civil and Political Rights speaks about the right of persons belonging to minorities to enjoy *their own culture*.[31] The term 'their own culture' should be interpreted as the right to cultural identity for persons belonging to minorities and not as the general right of everybody to culture. In a situation where there is no accepted definition of culture and where at the same time there is an agreement to understand culture in a very broad anthropological sense, the right to culture is too general to have any precise legal meaning. Therefore it may only be understood as the right to a cultural identity, to a cultural heritage.[32]

Differences among various proposed lists of cultural rights are often linked with the tendency to incorporate and to present as cultural rights numerous human rights with cultural dimensions. Thus Article 1 of the Declaration on the Right to Development (1986) provides that every human person is entitled to participate in, contribute to and enjoy economic, social, cultural and political development. There is no need to formulate a separate right to cultural development. This may mean that the holistic, comprehensive right to development will be divided into four independent rights. Many freedoms, such as the freedom of thought, conscience and religion, the freedom of opinion and expression, the freedom of peaceful assembly and association, are indisputable for the implementation of cultural rights. They are intimately linked with the right to cultural identity or the right to creativity, but there is no need to add them to the list of cultural rights.

This tendency to incorporate human rights with cultural dimensions may be observed in the preliminary list of cultural rights established by Leander.[33] This impressive inventory based on a detailed analysis of existing legal instruments, contains 50 rights grouped under 11 titles: the rights to physical and cultural survival; the rights to association and identification with the cultural community; the rights to and respect for cultural identity; the rights to physical and intangible heritages; the rights to religious belief and practice; the rights to freedom of opinion, expression and information; the rights to choice of education and training; the rights to participation in the elaboration of cultural policies; the rights to participation in cultural life and rights to create; the rights to choice of endogenous development; and the rights to people's own physical and cultural environment.

Catalogues of cultural rights may serve various purposes. They may be elaborated for use either as a basis for codification or for progressive development. They may present binding standards or formulate suggestions and proposals. In some cases, confusion concerning cultural rights is caused by putting on the same level conventions, declarations and recommendations adopted by intergovernmental organizations, and drafts or resolutions and proposals formulated by non-governmental organizations or experts. For example, the list of cultural rights proposed by the Secretariat of the Council of Europe was based on texts of conventions and recommendations of the Committee of Ministers; resolutions of the Parliamentary Assembly, resolutions of the Congress of Local and Regional Authorities of Europe; resolutions or recommendations of European Conferences of Specialized Ministers; and of charters and declarations adopted by seminars or conferences. Obviously the legal character of these texts varies substantially.[34]

Work to prepare a draft declaration on cultural rights in order to present it to the UNESCO General Conference for evaluation and adoption was conducted over several years by the so-called 'Fribourg Group'.[35] In 1998, the draft prepared by the group was published.[36] It enumerates six rights: to cultural identity and heritage; to identification with the cultural community; to participation in cultural life; to education and training; to information; and to participate in cultural policies and cooperation. The draft declaration, which also contains definitions of 'culture', 'cultural identity' and 'cultural community', presents fundamental principles and speaks about responsibilities for its implementation. No doubt this is a contribution to efforts aimed at the recognition of cultural rights as an integral and important part of human rights. However, the need to elaborate a short text has led to a very 'aggregated', combined presentation of some cultural rights.

Analysis of international human rights instruments allows us to propose the following list of cultural rights.

## The Right to Cultural Identity

This right, indirectly formulated by Article 27 of the International Covenant on Economic, Social and Cultural Rights stipulating that persons belonging to minorities have the right *to enjoy their own culture*, may be seen as an articulation of the right provided by Article 1 of UNESCO's Declaration on Race and Racial Prejudice (1978): 'All individuals and groups have the right to be different, to consider themselves as different and to be regarded as such.'

During the World Conference on Cultural Policies (Mexico City, 1982), delegates emphasized people's growing awareness of their cultural identity, of the pluralism stemming from it, of their right to be different and of the respect of one culture for another, including that of minorities. They observed that the affirmation of cultural identity had become a permanent requirement, both for individuals and for groups and nations.

In the Recommendation on Cultural Identity, the Conference called upon member states (1) to respect and work to preserve the cultural identity of all countries, regions and peoples and oppose any discrimination with regard to the cultural identity of other countries, regions and peoples, and (2) to promote the development of cultural identity through all appropriate means.

At present, the right to cultural identity is recognized by human rights instruments and constitutions, in particular those concerning the rights of minorities adopted in recent years. Article 29 of the International Convention on the Rights of the Child provides that the education of the child shall be directed to: '(c) The development of respect for the child's parents, his or her own cultural identity, language and values'.

The right to respect for cultural identity means that everyone, alone or in a community with others, may freely choose his or her cultural identity in its various aspects such as language, religion, heritage and traditions; that everyone may have one or several cultural identities and may freely decide whether or not to identify with one or more cultural communities. Nobody can be subjected against his or her will to forced assimilation.

## The Right to Participate in Cultural Life

This right is mentioned by nearly all universal and regional human rights instruments dealing with cultural rights, though its legal content is open to broader or narrower interpretations. It has two aspects, passive and active. Both of them are mentioned by the Recommendation on Participation by the People at Large in Cultural Life of 26 November 1976, which explains:

> By access to culture is meant the concrete opportunities available to everyone, in particular through the creation of the appropriate socio-economic conditions, for freely obtaining information, training, knowledge and understanding and for enjoying cultural values and cultural property.

The Recommendation also adds an active dimension of participation which embraces:

> The concrete opportunities guaranteed for all – groups and individuals – to express themselves freely, to communicate, act and engage in creative activities with a view to the full development of their personalities, a harmonious life and cultural progress of society.

The Recommendation deals with measures to be undertaken by member states to democratize the means and instruments of cultural activity. Participation in cultural life presupposes involvement of the different social partners in decision making related to cultural policy as well as in the conduct and evaluation of these activities. The broadening of access to and participation in cultural life has to be seen as one of the main objectives of cultural policies.

*The Right to Education*

During the general discussion by the Committee on Economic, Social and Cultural Rights on the right to education (1998),[37] an agreement was reached that four elements define its core content:

1   no one shall be denied a right to education;
2   everyone is entitled to basic (primary) education in one form or another, this includes basic education for adults. Primary education must be compulsory and free. No one may withhold a child from primary education. A state has an obligation to protect this right from encroachment by third persons;
3   there is a free choice of education, without interference by the state or a third person;
4   the minorities have the right to be taught in the language of their choice, in institutions outside the official system of public education.

International instruments also establish state duty concerning human rights education.[38] Education should constitute the free and full development of cultural identity/identities in respect of cultural diversity, plurality and tolerance.

In accordance with its mandate, UNESCO has adopted a number of normative documents, conventions and recommendations ensuring the enjoyment of the right to education for everyone. The best known among these is the Convention Against Discrimination in Education, which was adopted on 14 December 1960 by the General Conference and which entered into force in 1962.

The right to education is intimately linked to the right to teach. In 1966, an intergovernmental conference convened by UNESCO, with the participation of the International Labour Organisation, adopted the Recommendation Concerning the Status of Teachers. In its preamble it underlines that the right to education is a fundamental human right and recognizes the essential role of teachers in educational advancement and the importance of their contribution to the development of man and modern society.

UNESCO's activities for the implementation of the right to education are by no means limited to the preparation of normative documents. The organization also undertakes operational programmes assuring access to education of refugees, migrants, minorities, indigenous people, women and the handicapped. The fight against illiteracy is an absolute priority among the organization's current activities, since collective development proceeds from the education given to each individual human being.[39] At present, the right to education has been placed on the agenda of the Commission on Human Rights. K. Tomaševski has been nominated as the special rapporteur on this right and has presented a preliminary report.[40]

*The Right to Creativity and to Benefit from the Protection of the Moral and Material Interest Resulting from any Scientific, Literary or Artistic Production*

The right to creativity is formulated by human rights instruments and constitutions in the context of freedom from limitation and external interventions. The Recommendation Concerning the Status of the Artist of 27 October 1980 calls upon member states to encourage all measures tending to strengthen respect for artistic creation. It emphasized that governments should help to create and sustain not only a climate encouraging freedom of artistic expression but also the material conditions facilitating the release of creative talents. It stipulates: 'Since freedom of expression and communication is the essential perquisite for all artistic activities, Member States should see that artists are unequivocally accorded the protection provided for in this respect by international and national legislation concerning human rights.'

A number of normative instruments adopted by UNESCO are of direct relevance in promoting the right of everyone to benefit from the protection of interests resulting from intellectual property. Most important amongst them is the Universal Copyright Convention of 1952, as revised in 1971. Both conventions require that each contracting state protect the rights of authors and other copyright holders. Article I, identical in both conventions, stipulates:

> Each Contracting State undertakes to provide for the adequate and effective protection of the rights of authors and other copyright proprietors in literary, scientific and artistic works, including writings, musical, dramatic and cinematographic works, and paintings, engravings and sculpture.

UNESCO has also sponsored the International Convention for the Protection of Performers and Producers of Phonograms and Broadcasting Organizations, adopted in Rome in 1961, and the Convention for the Protection of Producers of Phonographs Against Unauthorized Duplication of Their Phonograms, adopted in Geneva in 1971.

New information and communication technology requires protection against electronic piracy and the violation of the interests of copyright holders. New intellectual property rights like those concerning databases also need regulation.

### The Right to Information

In accordance with the formulation of this right in the United Nations standard-setting instruments, everyone is entitled to seek and receive information, and to participate in its production and dissemination, as well as to obtain the correction of false or distorted information. Freedom of information is rightly regarded as one of the prerequisites for the exercise of human rights and constitutes a very potent confidence-building measure. Accordingly, Article I, paragraph 2(a) of the UNESCO Constitution stipulates that the organization will: 'collaborate in the work of advancing the mutual knowledge and understanding of peoples, through all means of mass communication and to that end recommend such international agreements as may be necessary to promote the free flow of ideas by word and image'. In implementing the right to information, UNESCO strives to eliminate various barriers to the free movement of books, publications and other printed materials. Four agreements have been prepared for this purpose.

The end of ideological rivalry between East and West allowed the organization to adopt a clear-cut strategy concerning freedom of information and free flow of ideas. The organization took an unequivocal position on this subject, foreseeing the encouragement of the free flow of information and promotion of its wider and better balanced dissemination, *without any obstacle to the freedom of expression*. The Major Programme on Communication, Information and Informatics[41] is inspired by the principle of freedom of expression and its corollary: freedom for all to choose their information. This is reflected in action aimed at promoting press freedom, pluralism and media independence, and at supporting efforts in member states to set up independent, pluralist media. The ultimate aim of this strategy is to provide practical responses to the challenges arising from the process of democratization going on in many countries and the demands of sustainable development.

*The Right to Benefit from Scientific Progress and its Application*

This right is recognized, though in a general form, by the International Bill of Rights and regional instruments. Few of the standard-setting documents adopted by UNESCO are relevant to the promotion of this right. The Recommendation on the Status of Scientific Researchers adopted in 1974 underlines that each member state should use scientific and technological knowledge for the enhancement of the cultural and natural well-being of its citizens and to further the ideals and objectives of the United Nations.

Over the last decade, UNESCO has done work on the human and cultural implications of scientific and technological progress and, at a conference in Brasilia in 1985, participants urged the use of science and technology for peaceful ends, and rejected 'any application that places the survival of humanity in jeopardy'. Despite the limited number of standard-setting instruments dealing with the right to benefit from scientific progress, it is reflected in UNESCO's programmes.[42]

In its activities concerning bioethics, UNESCO has attached special attention to the human genome. On 10 November 1997, the General Conference adopted by consensus a Universal Declaration on the Human Genome and Human Rights, the result of four years of deliberations and work of the UNESCO International Bioethics Committee.

*The Right to Cultural Heritage*

This right embraces the enjoyment and protection against destruction and illegal appropriation of cultural heritage both national and international (global). The largest group of UNESCO instruments dealing with cultural rights are those devoted to the protection of cultural property in time both of peace and of war. In 1954, UNESCO convened in The Hague an Intergovernmental Conference which adopted the Convention for the Protection of Cultural Property in the Event of Armed Conflict. The Convention contains provisions for the safeguarding of movable or immovable property of great importance to the cultural heritage of peoples, irrespective of its origin or ownership, and makes respect for such property obligatory. The safeguarding of such property implies that the state within the territories of which it is situated will take all necessary protective measures in time of peace. Respect for protected property is an obligation both on the territorial state and on its enemies in time of armed conflict.

The Convention on the Means of Prohibiting and Preventing the Illicit Import, Export and Transfer of Ownership of Cultural Property of 14 November 1970 defines cultural property qualifying for protection not only on historical, archaeological or artistic grounds but also in the interest of science.

The Convention concerning the Protection of the World Cultural and Natural Heritage adopted by the General Conference on 16 November 1972 defines international protection of the world cultural and natural heritage as: 'The establishment of a system of international cooperation and assistance designed to support States Parties to the Convention in their efforts to conserve and identify that heritage.' The items protected by the Convention are those of outstanding universal value from the point of view of history, art, science or aesthetics. The Convention lays down two basic principles: that each state party recognizes the duty of ensuring the conservation of elements of the world heritage situated on its territory, and that it is the duty of the international community as a whole to cooperate in ensuring the conservation of the heritage which is of a universal character. The World Heritage Committee designates the items which, being regarded as forming a part of the world heritage, fall under protective measures provided for by the Convention.

*The Right to International Cultural Cooperation*

As foreseen by Article 15 of the International Covenant on Economic, Social and Cultural Rights, the States Parties recognize the benefits accruing from the encouragement and development of international contacts and cooperation. The right to international as well as internal cultural cooperation is provided, *expressis verbis*, by normative instruments concerning the rights of minorities.

The Declaration of the Principles of International Cultural Cooperation adopted by UNESCO on 4 November 1966 states, in its Article I, that every people has the right and duty to develop its culture. It explains in Article VI that cultural cooperation is a right and duty for all peoples and all nations, which should share with one another their knowledge and skills.

The aims of international cultural cooperation, bilateral or multilateral, regional or universal, are, *inter alia*, to spread knowledge, to stimulate talent, to enrich cultures, to develop peaceful relations and friendship among the peoples, and to raise the level of the spiritual and material life of man in all parts of the world.

## Academic Freedom

*The Need of an International Human Rights Instrument on Academic Freedom*

The concept of academic freedom, known since the Middle Ages and recognized in its modern form in European universities in the seventeenth century, became a subject of intensive debate by international non-governmental as well as governmental organizations and human rights activists by the end of the 1980s and into the 1990s.

The sources of this renewed interest and the revival of this concept have been manifold. They are linked with the process of democratization, with the fall of many totalitarian communist regimes, and with the realization of the negative consequences for the development of societies brought about by the lack of full academic discussion and the absence of university autonomy. The end of ideological confrontation removed one of the main obstacles blocking the discussion on academic freedom in international fora.

The other reason why the debate on this subject became so important and acute is linked to the fact that academic freedom is threatened and violated in many countries. Academics are persecuted because of their involvement in the process of democratization and in the promotion and defence of human rights and civil society. A thesis that the main functions of higher education include not only 'reproduction', consolidation of the status quo, but also the search for new solutions, change and reform of existing structures, political, economic and social, is far from being accepted in many countries. Governments in some countries use intimidation, physical abuse and imprisonment to silence academics and students and censor teaching, research and publications.

In 1990, the World University Service published its first *Human Rights Report on Academic Freedom*,[43] which presented the whole spectrum of methods and the violations of academic freedom in several countries. A year later Human Rights Watch established a Committee for International Academic Freedom,[44] which is based on the assumption that violations of academic freedom are receiving too little attention in the international human rights community. Therefore the Committee seeks to address this deficiency through casework on behalf of embattled academics and students.

To strengthen the protection of academic freedom, non-governmental organizations worked out several declarations relating to academic freedom: the Declaration on Rights and Duties Inherent in Academic Freedom, adopted by the International Association of University Professors and Lecturers (IAUP) in Sienna (1982); the Lima Declaration on Academic Freedom and Autonomy of Institutions of Higher Education, adopted by the World University Service (WUS) (1988); the Magna Carta of European Universities, adopted by the Standing Conference of Rectors, Presidents and Vice-Chancellors (CRE) in Bologna (1998); the Dar es Salaam Declaration on Academic Freedom and Social Responsibility, adopted by the symposium held for that purpose by members of the African intellectual community (1990); and the Kampala Declaration on Intellectual Freedom and Social Responsibilities, adopted by the symposium on this subject (1990).[45]

The question of academic freedom has been discussed by UNESCO mainly from the point of view of the professional status of various groups. In 1966, a special intergovernmental conference convened by UNESCO, in close collaboration with the ILO, adopted the Recommendation concerning the Status of Teachers which contains a stipulation that 'the teaching profession should enjoy academic freedom in the discharge of professional duties'. However, the Recommendation does not give any clarifications as to how the term 'academic freedom' should be understood and interpreted. In 1974, the General Conference of UNESCO adopted the Recommendation on the Status of Scientific Researchers, which contains several provisions relating to the freedom of research and freedom to disseminate research findings. In paragraph 14 of this Recommendation, member states undertook obligations to encourage conditions in which scientific researchers have the responsibility and right '(a) to work in a spirit of intellectual freedom to pursue, expound and defend the scientific truth as they see it'.[46]

In 1989, UNESCO, in cooperation with the World University Service, organized an international Seminar on Factors and Conditions Conducive to Academic Freedom. The meeting agreed that, although there were extensive international instruments and guidance in the field of human rights in general, there was a lack of these in the field of higher education which covered academic freedom and autonomy. In conclusion, it recommended that UNESCO undertake initiatives aimed at the preparation of an international human rights instrument on this subject.

Reflection continued at a seminar on academic freedom co-organized by UNESCO and the Raoul Wallenberg Institute in Lund, Sweden, in

March 1992. It supported actions aimed at the elaboration and adoption of an international instrument relating to academic freedom. An identical proposition was also tabled by an International Conference on Academic Freedom and University Autonomy, organized by UNESCO in Sinaia, Romania, in May 1992. In the Sinaia Statement, participants urged UNESCO 'to give the matter of academic freedom and university autonomy its utmost attention and to prepare an international instrument for the protection and promotion of these values'.

*Contribution to the Preparation of a Draft Declaration on Academic Freedom of the Montreal Congress on Education for Human Rights and Democracy (1993)*

*Montreal Declaration* In order to advance the work on the elaboration of a draft declaration on academic freedom which could be presented to the General Conference, UNESCO co-organized with the Human Rights Centre of Poznan University in December 1992 a seminar which elaborated a preliminary draft. The document adopted at Poznan was submitted to the International Congress on Education for Human Rights and Democracy, which took place in Montreal in March 1993.[47]

The Congress decided to bring to the attention of the Director-General of UNESCO the document entitled 'Contributions to the preparation of a declaration on academic freedom'. The Montreal Declaration in its preamble states that academic freedom is an essential precondition for those educational, administrative and service functions with which universities and other institutions of higher education are entrusted, that every state is obliged to guarantee academic freedom without discrimination on any grounds. It further underlines that, by pursuing and further developing scientific knowledge and teaching, members of the academic community – persons working or studying in institutions of higher education – carry a special responsibility towards society in conformity with human rights.

Academic freedom is composed of the following rights:

- the right to become, on the basis of ability and competence without discrimination of any kind, a member of the academic community;
- the right of members of the academic community with research functions to freely determine the subject and methods of research;
- the right of members of the academic community with teaching functions to fully determine the content and methods of research;

- the right of students to study, to choose their field of study, to participate in the organization of the educational process and to receive official recognition of the knowledge and experience acquired;
- the right of all members of the academic community to seek, receive, obtain and impart information and ideas of all kinds and in all forms; in the case of restrictions, special facilities and protection shall be granted to members of the academic community carrying out research functions;
- the right of all members of the academic community to cooperate freely with their counterparts in any part of the world.

Academic freedom has its limits. None of the members of the academic community may engage in any activities or perform any act aimed at the destruction of the human rights of others. Research, teaching, and collection and exchange of information shall be conducted in accordance with ethical and professional standards consistent with human rights norms.

As far as autonomy is concerned, the document does not contain developed provisions on this subject and limits itself only to a general statement that the full enjoyment of academic freedom demands the autonomy of institutions of higher education which shall be exercised with the participation of all members of the academic community, including students.

In the second half of 1990, the question of the preparation of a special instrument on academic freedom was undertaken by several non-governmental organizations. Thus the International Association of Universities, following a debate at its Tenth General Assembly (New Delhi, February 1995), decided to set up an Experts' Group on Academic Freedom and University Autonomy, with the task of elaborating further studies and organizing debates in various parts of the world. Similarly, the International Association of Universities associated itself with the international efforts which might lead to the preparation of an international instrument which should be recognized, accepted and approved in all parts of the world.

In line with these initiatives, UNESCO's Division of Human Rights, Democracy and Peace, in cooperation with the International Institute for Human Rights Studies in Trieste, convened an international colloquium on academic freedom in Trieste, Italy, in February 1996. The participants endorsed the Montreal Declaration and proposed ten amendments[48] aimed at the reinforcement of human rights aspects. In particular, it was proposed to add a paragraph stipulating that 'Members of the academic community enjoy, as human beings, all the rights recognized in the existing international human rights instruments. Specifically they enjoy the human rights required for the exercise of their academic functions as spelled out in the present declaration.'

For this very reason, the meeting proposed the inclusion on the agenda of the envisaged World Conference on Higher Education, to be held in 1998, of an item concerning action to be taken, at national and international level, with a view to setting out, in an explicit, comprehensive and efficient way, the concepts, principles and practices for protecting and promoting academic freedom and university autonomy.

*Academic Freedom in the Recommendation concerning the Status of Higher-Education Teaching Personnel*

Though the efforts to adopt a special international normative instrument dealing in a comprehensive way with all aspects of academic freedom have until now not been crowned with success, an important step in this direction was taken in 1997, with the adoption by the General Conference at its 29th session of the Recommendation concerning the Status of Higher-Education Personnel.[49] In fact, this is the first intergovernmental instrument presenting academic freedom in a developed form.

The Recommendation declares that, apart from the rights enjoyed by all human beings, higher-education teaching personnel are entitled to the maintaining of academic freedom. Academic freedom is defined as the right to freedom of teaching and discussion, freedom in carrying out research and disseminating and publishing the results thereof, freedom to express freely their opinion about the institution or system in which they work, freedom from institutional censorship and freedom to participate in professional or representative bodies.

Higher-education teaching personnel have the right to teach without any interference, subject to accepted professional principles. Research work should be free from any interference, or any suppression, and should be in accordance with professional responsibility and subject to nationally and internationally recognized professional principles of intellectual rigour, scientific inquiry and research ethics. Research work is linked with the right to publish the results.

The proper enjoyment of academic freedom requires the autonomy of institutions of higher education, that is, that degree of self-governance which is necessary for effective decision making regarding academic work, standards, management and related activities. Teaching personnel, as stressed by the Recommendation, have not only rights but also duties inherent in academic freedom.[50] It is worth noting that, in the part concerning its implementation, the Recommendation provides that the Director-General of UNESCO will prepare a comprehensive report on the world situation with regard to academic freedom on the basis of the information supplied by member states, or any other information supported by reliable evidence.

*The Question of Academic Freedom at the World Conference on Higher Education*

To set down the guiding principles for the renewal of higher education in the twenty-first century, UNESCO convened the World Conference which took place in Paris from 5 to 9 October 1998. The question of academic freedom was put on its agenda which foresaw a special thematic debate on university autonomy, social responsibility and academic freedom. The debate was based on a working document and a statement prepared by the International Association of Universities (IAU).[51]

The statement emphasized that neither academic freedom which encompasses the freedom to enquire and to teach as well as the freedom of students to learn, nor university autonomy are privileges but are the basic and inalienable conditions which enable universities and their individual members to meet, fully to assume and optimally to fulfil the responsibilities society entrusts to them. The principles of academic freedom have been defined as 'the freedom of members of the academic community – that is scholars, teachers and students – to follow their scholarly activities within a framework determined by that community in respect of ethical rules and international standards, and without outside pressure'.[52] The obligation to transmit and advance knowledge is the basic purpose for which academic freedom is required and recognized.

This point of view was confirmed by other documents prepared for the Conference. Thus the working document, 'Towards an Agenda 21 for Higher Education',[53] stresses that the academic freedoms of higher education institutions and their wide autonomy are essential if these institutions are to carry out their mission. Autonomy presupposes accountability to society. It further clarifies the point that academic freedoms, which serve as a justification and basis for the critical function of higher education, presuppose the observance of certain principles and norms, while laying upon higher education institutions the duty of objectivity, impartiality and intellectual rigour.

During the thematic debate, participants expressed the view that, despite the fact that the Recommendation concerning the Status of Higher-Education Teaching Personnel comprises processes dealing with academic freedom, there is a need for a special normative instrument dealing with this question. This opinion is reflected in the final documents of the World Conference: the 'World Declaration on

Higher Education for the Twenty-First Century' and the 'Framework for Priority Action for Change and Development of Higher Education'. The Declaration states that higher-education institutions and their personnel and students should enjoy full academic freedom and autonomy, conceived as a set of rights and duties, while being fully responsible and accountable to society. The Framework for Priority Action stresses that UNESCO should 'take the initiative to draw up an international instrument on academic freedom, autonomy and social responsibility in connection with the Recommendation concerning the Status of Higher-Education Teaching Personnel'.[54]

The position taken by the World Conference is a compromise. The Recommendation deals with only one category of members of the academic community – teaching personnel – and does not cover the situation of students and researchers without teaching functions. Therefore it cannot be seen as a fully comprehensive instrument. Moreover, academic freedom can be seen as a 'cover' for a number of cultural rights: the right to education on the basis of merit and the right of access to higher education without discrimination on any ground; the freedom of scientific research; the right to benefit from scientific progress; the right to creativity; the right to the protection of the moral and material interests of authors; the right to information; and the right to participate in cultural and scientific cooperation. Academic freedom is also seen as a human right by various constitutions which make reference to it.[55] In the light of these arguments, one can say that academic freedom and university autonomy can be further promoted and protected against violations by the adoption of a special international human rights instrument. The work towards its adoption by UNESCO should be continued. In fact, a basis for the preparation of a declaration has already been prepared.

## Collective Dimensions of Cultural Rights

Cultural rights are individual rights to which every human being is entitled. However, they can often be implemented mainly, if not exclusively, in association with others. This is particularly true with regard to persons belonging to minorities and indigenous people. This fact has been observed by Article 27 of the International Covenant on Civil and Political Rights which provides:

> In those States in which ethnic, religious or linguistic minorities exist, persons belonging to such minorities shall not be denied the right, *in community with the other members of their group* [my emphasis], to enjoy their own culture, to profess and practise their own religion, or to use their own language.

Another important collective dimension of cultural rights of persons belonging to vulnerable groups is linked to the fact that these rights can be fully guaranteed and observed only if the identity and very existence of such groups are protected. For this very reason cultural rights are also collective rights. As declared by the World Commission on Culture and Development:

> Cultural freedom, unlike individual freedom, is a collective freedom. It refers to the right of a group of people to follow a way of life of its choice. Cultural freedom guarantees freedom as a whole. It protects not only the group but also the rights of every individual within it.[56]

Controversy concerning collective rights is linked to the fear that they may be used to subordinate individual to group interests, which may lead to violations of individual rights. To eliminate such a danger, there is a necessity not only to declare but to create guarantees through national and international procedures so that, in case of such contradiction or clash, individual rights will prevail.

Although the Charter of the United Nations and the Universal Declaration of Human Rights do not mention the protection of minorities, the question has not been completely taken off the agenda of the United Nations, as the Economic and Social Council authorized the Commission on Human Rights to make a recommendation on this subject and approved the establishment in 1947 of the Sub-Commission on Prevention of Discrimination and Protection of Minorities.

*Individual Rights of Persons belonging to and Collective Rights of Minorities*

On 18 December 1992, the General Assembly by its resolution 47/135 adopted the Declaration on the Rights of Persons Belonging to National or Ethnic, Religious and Linguistic Minorities. The Declaration formulates the *obligation of states to protect the existence and identity of minorities within their respective territories.*[57] Among rights of persons belonging to minorities, it lists the right to enjoy their own culture; to profess and practise their own religion: to use their own language; to participate effectively in cultural, religious, social, economic and public life, as well as in the decision-making process concerning the minority to which they belong; to establish and monitor their own associations; to establish and maintain, without any discrimination, free and peaceful contacts with other members of their group or other citizens or other states to whom they are related by national ethnic, religious or linguistic ties.

The protection of the cultural identity of minorities, together with the rights of persons belonging to them, has been formulated in a number of human rights instruments adopted by the Organization of Security and Co-operation in Europe and the Council of Europe. Thus the Vienna Concluding Document, adopted in 1989 by the OSCE, imposed on Participating States the duty of creating conditions for the promotion of the ethnic, cultural, linguistic and religious identity of national minorities within their territory.

The Concluding Document of the OSCE 1990 Copenhagen meeting of the Conference on the Human Dimension confirming the principle of non-discrimination and equality, listed specific cultural rights of persons belonging to national minorities: to preserve and develop their ethnic, cultural, linguistic or religious identity; to use freely their national language; to create and maintain their own educational, cultural or religious institutions, organizations and associations; to profess and practise their religion; to establish and maintain contacts with persons of common ethnic, national, cultural or religious origin within and outside their countries; and to take part in public affairs and the activities of international non-governmental organizations. Participating States also agreed, not only to protect the ethnic, cultural, linguistic and religious identity of national minorities, but also to create conditions for their protection. Among means to promote identity, the organization of local administration or autonomy corresponding to the historical and territorial specificity of minorities was mentioned.[58]

The Charter of Paris adopted by the OSCE Summit Meeting on 21 November 1990 declared once again that the ethnic, cultural, linguistic and religious identity of national minorities should be protected and conditions for the promotion of that identity should be created. These principles have also been repeated in a number of bilateral treaties concluded by Central and Eastern European states.

In 1992, the Council of Europe adopted the European Charter for Regional or Minority Languages. The Charter is based on the assumption that the protection and promotion of regional or minority languages in the different countries and regions of Europe represent an important contribution to the building of a Europe based on the principles of democracy and cultural diversity within the framework of national sovereignty and territorial integrity.[59]

The Council of Europe's Framework Convention for the Protection of National Minorities of 1994 invests the state with the duty to respect a number of cultural rights of persons belonging to minorities. They include, *inter alia*, the right to preserve essential elements of their national cultural identity; the right to use freely in private and in public their language; the right to establish their own private instructions; the right to learn their language; and the right to establish and keep contacts with others having the same ethnic, cultural, linguistic or religious identity. Article 1 states: 'The protection of national minorities and of the rights and freedoms of persons belonging to those minorities forms an integral part of the international protection of human rights, and as such falls within the scope of international co-operation.'[60]

## Individual and Collective Cultural Rights of Indigenous People

The International Labour Organisation was the first to undertake initiatives for the protection of the rights of indigenous populations which led to the adoption in 1957 of the Convention (No. 107) concerning the Protection and Integration of Indigenous and other Tribal and Semi-Tribal Populations in Independent Countries. In 1989, the ILO revised this convention and adopted Convention No. 169 concerning Indigenous and Tribal Peoples in Independent Countries, which formulates, *inter alia*, the collective and individual land rights and ownership of natural resources in indigenous people's traditional habitats and promotes consultations between governments and indigenous people.

In 1982, the Economic and Social Council established the Working Group on Indigenous Populations with a mandate to 'give special attention to the evaluation of standards concerning the rights of indigenous people, taking account of both the similarities and the differences in the situations and aspirations of indigenous people throughout the world'.

The draft declaration, as agreed upon by the members of the Working Group at its eleventh session in 1992 and adopted by the Sub-Commission for Prevention of Discrimination and Protection of Minorities in 1994, is composed of a preamble and 45 articles. It pays special attention to cultural rights of indigenous peoples which may be grouped under three headings: the right to practise cultural traditions, religion and language; the right to education and to establish their own media; the right to cultural and intellectual property. Cultural rights are presented as individual and/or collective rights. Thus Article 7 of the draft states: 'Indigenous peoples have the collective and individual right not to be subjected to ethnocide and cultural genocide.' Article 8 provides:'Indigenous people have the collective and individual rights to maintain and develop their distinct identities and characteristics.' Despite the proclamation of the International Decade of the World's Indigenous People (1995–2004), the progress in the work aimed at the adoption of the draft declaration is rather slow.

In order to elaborate measures which should be adopted by the international community to strengthen respect for the cultural property of indigenous peoples, the Sub-Commission decided in 1991 to entrust Erica-Irene A. Daes, as special rapporteur, with the task of preparing a study on the protection of the cultural and intellectual property of indigenous people. During its eleventh session (1993), the Sub-Commission for Prevention of Discrimination and Protection of Minorities endorsed the conclusions and recommendations contained in the study and, in particular, affirmed that the heritage of indigenous people is their own property, collective and inalienable.

The collective cultural rights of indigenous people are, as already mentioned, recognized by constitutions and laws of Latin American countries.[61] In 1993, the Vienna conference, despite strong protests by non-governmental organizations, changed the term 'indigenous peoples' to the singular, 'indigenous people', which is sometimes interpreted as a challenge to their collective rights. It is worth noting that, in constitutions and domestic laws, there is a tendency to replace the terms 'people' and 'minorities' with 'community'.

## Obligations of States to Implement Cultural Rights

The concept of human rights assumes the existence of parallel duties of states to implement them; without these obligations, human rights are meaningless. What is the character of states' obligations in the case of cultural rights? Are they different from those concerning other categories of human rights?

Doubts and contradictory opinions on this subject are due to the fact that the International Covenant on Economic, Social and Cultural Rights, in Article 2, provides:

> 1. Each State Party to the present Covenant undertakes to take steps … to the maximum of its available resources, with a view to achieving progressively the full realization of the rights recognized in the present Covenant by all appropriate means, including particularly the adoption of legislative measures.

Does the phrase about the progressive achievement of the full realization of cultural rights conditioned by the availability of resources mean that states have only the obligation of conduct, not the obligation of result? What is the legal character of obligations formulated by Article 2?

These questions have been tackled and answered by the Committee on Economic, Social and Cultural Rights which, in the General Comment No. 3 (1990), on the nature of States Parties' obligations,[62] stated that obligations formulated by Article 2 include both obligations of conduct and obligations of results. The concept of progressive realization acknowledges the fact that full realization of all economic, social and cultural rights cannot be achieved in a short period of time. In this sense, the obligation differs from that contained in the International Covenant on Civil and Political Rights, which imposes an immediate obligation to respect and ensure all of the relevant rights. Nevertheless, the formulation 'progressive realization' should not be misinterpreted as depriving the obligation formulated in Article 2 of all meaningful content.[63]

Speaking about all appropriate means to be undertaken by states, this article covers, apart from legislative, also administrative, financial, educational, social and other measures. In these contexts, it is important to note that Article 15, paragraph 2 of the International Covenant on Economic, Social and Cultural Rights formulates the concrete obligation of the States Parties to take steps 'necessary for the conservation, the development and the diffusion of science and culture'.

State obligations with respect to Article 15 may be divided into three categories: (a) states should refrain from activities which prevent or obstruct the individual from participating in cultural life, benefiting from scientific progress, the protection of moral and material interests and from undertaking scientific research or creative activity; (b) states should ensure that the enjoyment of the rights foreseen in Article 15 is not disrupted or undermined by the activities of other individuals or states; (c) states are under an obligation to achieve progressively the full realization of the right of access to cultural life, including an obligation to identify and take specific measures to improve the position of the most vulnerable and disadvantaged groups in society.

Among measures which are crucial for the implementation of cultural rights, in addition to legislation, the existence of judicial remedies, the justiciability of these rights, should be mentioned. Though the justiciability of cultural rights is often challenged, the Committee stressed that at least some of them, such as the right to education and the right to benefit from the protection of the moral and material interest resulting from any scientific, literary or artistic production, are justiciable and can be guaranteed by judicial remedy.

In the debate concerning the specificity of states' obligations to ensure the realization of cultural rights, one element seems to be forgotten. Article 2 of the International Covenant on Economic, Social and Cultural Rights refers only to rights mentioned by this Covenant. It cannot be applied to cultural rights listed by the International Covenant on Civil and Political Rights, such as Article 27 (cultural rights of persons belonging to minorities) or Article 19 (right to information) or other relevant human rights instruments adopted by the United Nations, the specialized agencies or regional organizations. This means that in the majority of cases states are obliged to take immediate steps not conditioned by 'availability of resources' to ensure their full realization.

Recognizing that states should first of all create conditions and provide guarantees for the implementation of cultural rights, UNESCO's normative instruments also stress that this responsibility should be shared with other social actors. Thus the Recommendation concerning the Status of the Artist (1980) provides:

> 1. Member States should strive to extend and supplement their own action by co-operating with all the national or international organizations whose activities are related to the objectives of this Recommendation, in particular with National Commissions for UNESCO, national and international artists' organizations, the International Labour Office and the World Intellectual Property Organization.

Similarly, the Declaration of the Principles of International Cultural Co-operation (1966) lists, among those to be guided by its principles, governments, authorities, organizations, associations and institutions responsible for cultural activity. The Recommendation on Participation by the People at Large in Cultural Life (1976) addresses 'Member States or other appropriate authorities'.

The Convention concerning the Protection of the World Cultural Heritage (1972) declares in its Article 6: 'Whilst fully respecting the sovereignty of the States on whose territory the cultural and natural heritage [ ... ] is situated [ ... ] the States Parties to this Convention recognize that such heritage constitutes a world heritage for whose protection it is the duty of the international community as a whole to co-operate.'

## Monitoring and Verification of the Implementation of Cultural Rights

### Periodic Reports

*Reports concerning the International Covenant on Economic, Social and Cultural Rights*   The States Parties to this Covenant are obliged, as foreseen by Article 16, to present reports on measures which they have adopted and on the progress made by them in achieving the observance of the economic, social and cultural rights recognized by the Covenant. A new simplified system adopted by ECOSOC in 1988 requests an initial report covering the whole Covenant within two years of its entry into force for the state concerned and a single comprehensive report every five years thereafter. The reports should be prepared in accordance with general guidelines which were established shortly after the Covenant's entry into force in 1976.

As far as Article 15 of the International Covenant on Economic, Social and Cultural Rights is concerned, guidelines formulate a number of detailed questions concerning the right of everyone to take part in cultural life, to enjoy the benefits of scientific progress and to benefit from the protection of the moral and material interests resulting from any scientific, literary or artistic production. The States Parties in the context of the implementation of the right to participate in cultural life are requested to provide information on availability of funds for the promotion of cultural development and popular participation; the institutional infrastructure established for the implementation of policies to provide popular participation in cultural promotion of cultural identity as a factor of mutual appreciation among individuals, groups, nations or regions; promotion of awareness and enjoyment of the cultural heritage of national ethnic groups and minorities and of indigenous peoples; the role of the mass media and communications media in promoting participation in cultural life; preservation and transmission of mankind's cultural heritage; legislation protecting the freedom of artistic creation and performance; professional education in the field of culture and art; and any other measures taken for the conservation, development and diffusion of culture.

The Committee on Economic, Social and Cultural Rights carries out functions relating to the implementation of the Covenant. It examines reports submitted to it by States Parties. The debate on the report of each state party takes place in an open or public session of the Committee (normally in November/December each year in Geneva) and in the presence of one or more representatives of the state concerned. The discussion which takes place between the members of the Committee and the representative(s) of the state is designed to achieve a constructive dialogue. At the end of each session, the Committee adopts a report for transmission to the Economic and Social Council. The report presents a summary of the consideration of each state's report which indicates the issues raised by members of the Committee.

*Examination of reports by the Human Rights Committee*  Reports presented by States Parties to the International Covenant on Civil and Political Rights give to the Human Rights Committee the possibility of examining and evaluating the implementation of rights to their own culture of persons belonging to ethnic, religious or linguistic minorities, to profess and practise their religion and to use their own language. In line with Article 40, States Parties on whose territory such minorities exist should report on measures they have adopted to give effect to these rights and on the progress made in their enjoyment.

In its general comment on Article 27,[64] adopted during its 50th session in 1994, the Committee underlined that the protection of the rights recognized in this article is directed towards ensuring the survival and continued development of the cultural, religious and social identity of the minorities concerned. These rights must be protected as such and should not be confused with other personal rights conferred on one and all under the Covenant. States Parties have an obligation to ensure that the exercise of these rights is fully protected, and they should indicate in their reports the measures they have adopted to this end.

The Committee, after examination of state reports, in its concluding observations on principal subjects of concern and suggestions and recommendations, quite often presents value judgments of state practice concerning Article 27. Thus, for example, after consideration in 1997 of Germany's report, the Committee expressed its concern that the delimitation of minorities as 'ethnic or linguistic groups which have a traditional area of settlement in particular regions', in paragraph 224 of the country report, is far too restrictive. In its opinion, Article 27 applies also to those who are not concentrated or settled in a particular area or region and those who are immigrants or have been given asylum in Germany.[65]

In the case of Bolivia, the Committee recommended that further measures be taken to ensure that members of indigenous groups are protected from violence within the country and enjoy fully their rights under Article 27 of the Covenant, particularly with regard to the preservation of their culture, language and religion. Legislation on indigenous communities should be enacted without delay.[66] Similarly, in relation to Colombia, the Committee recommended that further measures be adopted to ensure that the rights of indigenous populations and the black minorities, as foreseen by Article 27, be protected. In particular, it stressed the importance of education and urged the government to take appropriate measures to reduce the illiteracy rate among these groups.[67]

Sometimes the Committee, in relation to Article 27, may even raise the question of the very existence of minorities in a given country. Taking note of the avowed commitment of France to respect and ensure to all individuals equal rights irrespective of their origin, the Committee disagreed with the thesis that France is a country in which there are no ethnic, religious or linguistic minorities. The mere fact that equal rights are granted to all individuals and all individuals are equal before the law does not exclude the existence in fact of minorities in a country and their entitlement to the enjoyment of their culture, the practice of their religion and the use of their language in community with other members of their groups.[68]

The position taken by the Committee in the consideration of Article 27 in state reports may no doubt contribute to further progress in the implementation of cultural rights of persons belonging to minorities and indigenous populations. However, even in the case of other report systems, by no means all countries fulfil their obligation to present the required reports.

*Examination of reports by the Committee on the Rights of the Child*   The Convention on the Rights of the Child provides, in Article 44, that States Parties will present reports on the measures they have adopted which give effect to the rights recognized therein and on the progress made for the enjoyment of those rights. The reports are examined by the Committee on the Rights of the Child.[69]

Among the provisions of the Convention, as already mentioned, four deal with cultural rights: Article 28 on education; Article 29 on aims of education; Article 30 on the rights of children of minorities or of indigenous origin to enjoy their own culture and to practise their own religion and language; and Article 31 on the right of the child to leisure, play, to recreational activities and to participate freely in cultural life and the arts.

States Parties to the Convention in their reports present information concerning the implementation of these articles. However, one can observe different degrees of attention paid to each of them in states' reports. Thus the implementation of the right to education is usually presented in an elaborated way, whereas the right to participate freely in cultural life and the arts is mentioned rather sporadically. As to the cultural rights of children belonging to minorities or indigenous populations, obviously there are comments only in reports of countries recognizing the existence of such groups on their territories.[70]

Reports are considered by the Committee during sessions with the participation of the reporting states, representatives of specialized agencies and United Nations bodies and non-governmental organisations. After consideration of a report, the Committee adopts concluding observations which are divided into introduction, positive aspects and principal subjects of concern, and the Committee's recommendations.

As far as Articles 28 and 29 are concerned, the Committee encourages States Parties to include specific information on the provisions of the Convention in their school curricula.[71] It also emphasizes that, as well as undertaking greater efforts to train and sensitize professional groups working for and with children, budgetary austerity measures should be examined carefully with regard to their impact on the progressive implementation of the child's right to education and leisure activities, in accordance with Articles 28, 29 and 31 of the Convention and, in particular, so as to limit their impact on the most vulnerable and disadvantaged groups.

*UNESCO's reporting system*  In accordance with Article IV, paragraph 6 of the UNESCO Constitution, the General Conference receives and considers reports sent to the organization by member states on actions taken upon its recommendations and conventions. Member states submit their reports to the organization 'at such times and in such a manner as shall be determined by the General Conference'.

In addition to the UNESCO Constitution, several conventions and recommendations also contain provisions concerning reports. Thus, for example, Article 16 of the Convention on the Means of Prohibiting and Preventing Illicit Import, Export and Transfer of Ownership of Cultural Property of 14 November 1970 (3) provides that the States Parties shall, in their periodic reports submitted to the General Conference of UNESCO, give information on the legislative and administrative provisions which they have adopted and other actions which they have taken for the application of the Convention, together with details of the experience acquired in this field. Reports received from member states concerning this Convention were examined for the first time by the Committee on Conventions and Recommendations and the General Conference in 1978.

*Reporting system linked with the Convention and Recommendation against Discrimination in Education (1960)*  As foreseen by Article 7 of this Convention, the States Parties shall, in their periodic reports submitted to the UNESCO General Conference on dates and in a manner to be determined by it, give information on the legislative and administrative priorities which they have adopted and other actions they have taken for its appreciation. Since the Convention's entry into force in 1962, the secretariat has organized six periodic consultations of member States Party to the Convention and of all member states with regard to the Recommendation against Discrimination in Education. Consultations ended with the preparation of the final report to the Executive Board's Commission on Conventions and Recommendations considered thereon by the General Conference. They enabled the organization to measure the progress achieved and the obstacles still to be overcome with a view to ensuring equal opportunities and treatment in the sphere of education for all and, thus, fully to take into account in its action the needs and problems which exist in the field of education.

The last of the six consultations was initiated by resolution of the General Conference in 1993.[72] It was decided to focus the consultation process and final report on the basic education of four population groups: (a) women and girls, (b) persons belonging to minorities, (c) refugees, and (d) indigenous people.

In 1995, the Director-General sent out a circular letter and guidelines comprising five questions, concerning general measures taken in favour of the four population groups; specific measures; evaluation of results with statistical data; assessment of the most effective specific educational measures concerning these four groups in the light of Article 5 of the Convention and Recommendation; and measures planned in the above areas.

In response to the circular letter, 56 member states presented reports. Supplemented for the first time by the comments of non-governmental organizations and information sent by member states to the International Bureau of Education (IBE), these reports, together with the analytical reports of the secretariat, were submitted to the Executive Board for examination prior to submitting them with the Executive Board's comments to the General Conference at its 30th session. During the examination of the reports and responses received at the sixth consultation, the members of the Committee on Conventions and Recommendations unanimously emphasized that the struggle against discrimination in education is particularly important in the light of UNESCO's Constitution and of the organization's role in the United Nations system regarding the right to education for all.[73]

To be adequately tackled, this problem demands that new measures and monitoring mechanisms be devised and applied by UNESCO. The present system, which is based only on periodic reporting by member states, is rather weak and very far from comprehensive. Reports should reflect the situation critically, and the relevant reports submitted to the United Nations should be taken into account. UNESCO should not only report on reports received from member states but also organize dialogue with individual member states. Information provided by member states should be evaluated on the basis of agreed criteria. It was recommended that the Committee on Conventions and Recommendations strengthen its original monitoring role.

The Executive Board invited member states which have not yet done so to become parties to the Convention and recalled that the submission of periodic reports concerning the implementation of conventions and recommendations adopted by the General Conference is a constitutional obligation.

The Director-General has also been invited to strengthen UNESCO's action against discrimination and to study, in view of the seventh consultation and in cooperation with the United Nations: 'the possibility of creating a coherent mechanism of reporting on and monitoring of the right to education as set down in various United Nations conventions on human rights, and to inform the Executive Board about measures undertaken to this end'. This decision opens the way for a profound, far-reaching change in the reporting system linked with the Convention and Recommendation against Discrimination in Education.

*The Permanent System of Reporting on education for peace, human rights, democracy, international understanding and tolerance*   In 1985, the UNESCO General Conference at its 23rd session decided that the Permanent System of Reporting on steps taken by member states should also apply to the 1974 Recommendation concerning Education for International Understanding, Co-operation and Peace and Education relating to Human Rights and Fundamental Freedoms. Accordingly, the first synthesis of national reports was submitted to the General Conference at its 25th session in 1989. It covered the achievements and problems identified by member states in promoting education, as foreseen by the 1974 Recommendation.

In 1995, during its 28th session, the General Conference decided to update the Permanent System of Reporting in the context of a number of new UNESCO and United Nations instruments and action plans regarding education for peace, human rights, democracy, international understanding and tolerance. The draft questionnaire for the Permanent System of Reporting was examined by the Advisory Committee on Education for Peace, Human Rights, Democracy, International Understanding and Tolerance.[74]

The Committee on Conventions and Recommendations in its debate on this subject underlined the necessity of sending the questionnaire not only to governments but also to parliaments and non-governmental organizations maintaining official relations with UNESCO, and to take into account data existing in the United Nations system when preparing the third sexennial report within the framework of the Permanent System of Reporting, to be submitted to the General Conference at its 31st session (2001).

The Executive Board adopted the proposed questionnaire, which is unique within the United Nations system, as it applies not only to instruments concerning education for peace, human rights, democracy, international understanding and tolerance adopted by UNESCO but also to those adopted by the United Nations. It is also unique because it requests from member states' comprehensive reports on a totality of actions aimed at the building of a culture of peace through education. In its decision, the Executive Board urged member states, their governments and parliaments, as well as non-governmental organizations, UNESCO chairs, clubs and associated schools and all sectors and actors of society to renew efforts to publicize and implement the 1974 Recommendation, the Declaration and Integrated Framework of Action on Education for Peace, Human Rights and Democracy, and other UNESCO and United Nations instruments and action plans related to the field of education, in particular on the occasion of the International Year for the Culture of Peace (2000) and preparations for the International Decade for the Culture of Peace and Non-Violence for the Children of the World (2001–10).

## Communication Procedures

*Communication procedure foreseen by the Optional Protocol to the International Covenant on Civil and Political Rights*   In accordance with the Option Protocol, the Human Rights Committee may receive and consider communications from individuals claiming to be victims of violations of any rights set forth in the Covenant. This means that persons belonging to ethnic, religious or linguistic minorities in the state party to the Optional Protocol[75] who claim that their cultural rights, provided for by Article 22, have been violated, after exhaustion of all available domestic remedies, may submit a written communication to the Committee for consideration.

In its general comment on Article 27,[76] the Human Rights Committee stated that, in some communications submitted under the Optional Protocol, the right protected under Article 27 had been confused with the right of peoples to self-determination proclaimed in Article 1 of the Covenant. It further clarified the fact that self-determination, a right belonging to peoples, is not a right cognizable under the Optional Protocol, whereas Article 27 relates to rights conferred on individuals and as such is cognizable.

One of the problems presented relatively often in communications linked with Article 27 concerns the question of whether certain economic activities or private companies violate a particular way of life associated with the use of land resources, especially by indigenous peoples. This is the case of *Länsman et al.* v. *Finland*, where the Committee was requested to decide whether logging in an area which the petitioners used for reindeer husbandry violated their rights under Article 27. The Committee reaffirmed that economic activities may come with the ambit of Article 27, if they are an essential denial of the culture of a minority. Though the Committee concluded that the impact of logging in this particular case would not be such as to amount to a denial of the rights under Article 27, nevertheless it pointed out that 'the State Party must bear in mind, when taking steps affecting the rights under Article 27, that although different activities in themselves may not constitute a violation of this article, such activities, taken together, may erode the rights of Sami people to enjoy their own culture.'[77]

In the earlier case of *Bernard Ominayak, Chief of the Lubicon Lake Band* v. *Canada*, the Committee dismissed the allegation of a violation of the right to self-determination but recognized that oil and gas exploration by private companies as well as large-scale expropriation of the land of the Cree Indian Band undertaken by the provincial authorities threatened the way of life and culture of this indigenous group and constituted a violation of Article 27 of the Covenant. Canada was recognized responsible for 'historical iniquities'.[78]

In the case *Kitok* v. *Sweden*,[79] the Committee stated that to enjoy a particular culture may consist of a way of life which is closely associated with territory and use of its resources. The consideration of this and other communications concerning the rights foreseen by Article 27 led the Committee to the general conclusion that 'culture manifests itself in many forms', that this right 'may include such traditional activities as fishing or hunting and the right to live in reserves protected by law'.

*UNESCO's communication procedure*    In 1978, the Executive Board of UNESCO, by its decision 104 EX/3.3, instituted a special procedure for the examination of cases and questions submitted to UNESCO concerning the exercise of human rights in its sphere of competence. In the exercise of its competence, UNESCO is called upon to examine *cases* concerning violations of human rights which are individual and specific and *questions* of massive, systematic or flagrant violations of human rights and fundamental freedoms which result either from a policy contrary to human rights applied *de jure* or *de facto* by a state or from an accumulation of individual cases forming a consistent pattern.

To be considered admissible, a communication has to meet ten conditions set out in paragraph 14 of the decision 104 EX/3.3. Thus it must not be anonymous, must originate from a person or a group of persons who can be reasonably presumed to be victims, or a person or group of persons or organization having reliable knowledge of an alleged violation of human rights falling within UNESCO's fields of competence. It must be compatible with the principles of the organization, the Charter of the United Nations and other instruments in the field of human rights. Communications which are manifestly ill-founded, offensive, based exclusively on information disseminated through mass media, presented beyond a reasonable time limit and which have not exhausted available domestic remedies shall not be considered.

The Executive Board decision did not specify which human rights fall within UNESCO's fields of competence. In practice, it has been accepted that the following belong to this category:

- the right to education,
- the right to share in scientific advancement and enjoy its benefits,
- the right to participate freely in cultural life, and
- the right to information, including freedom of opinion and expression.

These rights may imply the exercise of others, in particular:

- the right to freedom of thought, conscience and religion,
- the right to seek, receive and impart information and ideas through any medium and regardless of frontiers,
- the right to protection of the moral and material interests resulting from any scientific, literary or artistic production, and
- the right to freedom of assembly and association for the purposes of activities connected with education, science, culture and information.

The procedure laid down in decision 104 EX/3.3 of the Executive Board of UNESCO has specific characteristics in comparison with similar procedures in other organizations of the United Nations System. In accordance with decision 104 EX/3.3, a complaint may be directed at any member state, for the very reason that it is a member of UNESCO. The right to present communications does not result from any specific human rights instruments adopted by the organization.

The Committee's competence to examine individual communications concerning alleged violations of human rights in UNESCO's fields of competence has been gradually recognized by practically all UNESCO's member states, and an increasing number of the governments concerned by the communications send representatives to the Committee and cooperate with it although they are under no legal obligation to do so. While the other procedures seem most often to take a conflictual and accusatory form, the UNESCO procedure — although it is largely similar — has from the very beginning been deliberately applied exclusively with a view to seeking a solution with the state concerned. The desire shown by the Committee to take its decisions solely by consensus is no doubt a reflection of the same concern. However, what is perhaps the overriding characteristic of the UNESCO procedure is the emphasis, or indeed the insistence, on its strictly confidential nature, even after cases have been settled.

At its 154th session (1998) the UNESCO Executive Board invited the Director-General to seek views and comments of member states concerning the examination of the methods of work of the Committee on Conventions and Recommendations.

In order to draw up proposals for improving the communications procedure and the working methods of the Committee, which would lead to an improvement in the situation of alleged victims of human rights violations, a working group comprising six members was created.[80] The working group examined 21 proposals in the light of decision 104 EX/3.3. Taking into account the working group's recommendations, the Committee on Conventions and Recommendations agreed on five points[81] concerning the communications procedures.

1   As to the admissibility of communications, the Committee stressed that the recognition of a communication's admissibility does not imply any condemnation of the government concerned. In order to speed up decisions concerning the admissibility of communications, only the governments concerned are requested to make their position known within a time limit of three months from the transmission of the communication by the Secretariat.

2   When a communication submitted to the Committee is being examined or has already been examined by another body in the United Nations system, the Secretariat will check with this other body whether there is any unnecessary duplication or incompatibility. If there is any doubt, the Secretariat will submit the question to the Committee.

3   When the government concerned fails to cooperate, the Committee may, in its report to the Executive Board, draw the board's attention to such a case and suggest a debate in the Executive Board in private meeting.

4   Confronted with the fact that the very existence of the Committee and the communication procedure are not very well known, the Committee underlined the need to continue efforts by the secretariat and the member states to make the procedure better known.

5   On the question of the publication of its annual report, the Committee did not adopt any general rule but decided that it will determine under what circumstances each of its annual reports may be made public.

Decisions taken by the Committee and notes by the Executive Board do not change the basic principles on which the communications procedure is based; nonetheless, they may improve its effectiveness and the speed with which alleged violations of cultural rights are dealt with.

## Concluding Remarks

Answering the question on how to assure the better protection of cultural rights, and how to eliminate their violation, the World Commission on Culture and Development, in its report entitled *Our Creative Diversity*, proposed a whole range of steps from the establishment of an inventory of cultural rights, the preparation of an International Code of Conduct and the setting up of an International Office of the Ombudsman for Cultural Rights, to the establishment of an international court to hear cases brought before it by individuals and groups prosecuted over matters involving cultural rights.[82]

Indeed, though a fair number of standard-setting instruments adopted by the United Nations, UNESCO and regional organizations formulate states' obligation to implement cultural rights, the necessity for their 'inventory' or, in other words, 'codification' cannot be questioned. The adoption of a special normative instrument could not only contribute to the further elucidation of cultural rights but also help to make them better known. However, such a perspective seems to be rather remote.

There is a need to reinforce international protection and monitoring. The international procedures for the implementation of cultural rights based on states' reports can hardly be recognized as very advanced. The communication procedure established by UNESCO, which gives to individuals the possibility of presenting complaints concerning alleged violations of cultural rights is not well known and, in consequence, is used in a rather limited number of cases.[83] This situation may be changed with the adoption of the Optional Protocol to the International Covenant on Economic, Social and Cultural Rights and the establishment of a new procedure for communications.[84]

In the implementation of cultural rights, an important role can be played by indicators. They could provide a means for measuring the progressive realization of these rights and a method for determining difficulties or problems encountered by states. Indicators could also help to reveal the extent to which certain rights were or were not enjoyed in practice and to provide a means to measure and compare the performance of individual countries.

What are the other forms of action leading to further recognition, better understanding and knowledge of cultural rights? Various ways and means may be applied. An important role can be played by the dissemination of existing instruments through human rights education by the mass media and non-governmental organizations. No doubt the involvement of the latter in the promotion and protection of cultural rights, with the exception of Rights and Humanity and Human Rights Watch, can hardly be seen at present as fully satisfactory. A step forward can also be made by the elucidation of various terms and concepts used by the standard-setting instruments, for example, regarding the still undefined term, 'cultural identity'. An important role may be played by the United Nations and UNESCO in providing expertise and consultation for interested states. At the national level, many states can 'recognize' cultural rights by introducing relevant provisions in their legislation and constitutions.

The strengthening of cultural rights and their consolidation may also be seen as a part of an overall action, as a function of a general reinforcement of economic, social and cultural rights.[85] The Vienna Declaration and Programme of Action (1993) stressed the necessity of 'a concerted effort to ensure recognition of economic, social and cultural rights at the national, regional and international levels'. At the same time, it emphasized the *unity and indivisibility of all human rights*, symbolically demonstrated by the change in the traditional enumeration of human rights by categories to an alphabetical order: *civil, cultural, economic, political and social*. This new approach means, in fact, a return to the position taken by the Universal Declaration, which did not separate different categories of human rights but presented them together, thereby underlining their unity.

The experience of the 1990s shows that the recognition of cultural rights of persons belonging to minorities is not a danger and a source of conflict, but rather an important factor for peace and stability. Many internal conflicts are linked to the crisis of existing identities and the creation of new ones; they are generated by the denial or rejection of the right to a different cultural identity, and by the refusal to respect cultural rights of minorities. The existence of cultural differences cannot lead to the rejection of any part of universal human rights. They cannot justify the rejection or non-observance of such fundamental principles as the principle of equality between women and men.

By the end of the twentieth century, cultural rights formulated by the Universal Declaration of Human Rights, developed by the International Covenants and other human rights instruments, are gaining new importance. They are today 'empowering rights'. Without their recognition and observance, without implementation of the right to cultural identity, to education or to information, neither may human dignity and human development be guaranteed nor may other human rights be fully implemented. Without the recognition of cultural rights, cultural plurality and diversity cannot be respected, and democratic societies cannot function properly.

## Notes

1 Actes du VIIIème Colloque interdisciplinaire sur les droits de l'homme, *Les Droits culturels. Actes du VIIIe Colloque interdisciplinaire sur les droits de l'homme*, ed. P. Meyer-Bisch, Fribourg, Editions Universitaires, 1993.

2 See Eide (1995), page 229 of which presents a list of textbooks which analyse the International Covenant on Economic, Social and Cultural Rights, but either does not mention cultural rights at all or presents them in a fragmentary manner.

3 The draft list of cultural rights prepared by the Council of Europe, Strasbourg, 24 August 1994, CDDC Misc. 9413. Nine groups of cultural rights concern heritage, education, schooling, higher education, identity, language, culture, the media and sport.

4 In fact, the first convention which referred to cultural rights of persons belonging to minorities is the UNESCO Convention against Discrimination in Education (1960). In Article 5, para. 1(*c*), it states: 'It is essential to recognize the rights of members of national minorities to carry on their own educational activities.' This article also contains an important explanation providing that 'this right is not exercised in a manner which prevents the members of these minorities from understanding the culture and language of the community as a whole [ ... ] or which prejudices national sovereignty'.

5 During the period 1988–97 more than 1200 projects launched by 166 states, 23 international governmental organizations and 66 non-governmental organizations were recognized as official activities for the World Decade for Cultural Development. Many of them deal with various aspects of cultural rights.

6 Resolution 3.4 adopted in 1991 by the 26th session of the UNESCO General Conference and resolution 46/158 (1992) of the United Nations General Assembly.

7 The meeting took place in June 1994 in Yamoussoukro, Côte d'Ivoire, and discussed the paper by J. Symonides, 'Cultural rights and the right to development', CCD-IV/94/SEC.4.

8 Report of the World Commission on Culture and Development, *Our Creative Diversity* (1996, pp.281–3). The recommendations of the World Commission concerning cultural rights are discussed later.

9 It is worth noting that UNESCO organized a series of conferences on cultural policies starting with the Conference on the Administrative and Financial Aspects of Cultural Policies held in Venice in 1970, followed by Helsinki in 1972, Jogjakarta in 1973, Accra in 1975 and San José in 1978. The series culminated in 1982 with Mondiacult, the World Conference on Cultural Policies in Mexico in 1982. After a period of hesitation linked to neoliberal beliefs, which emerged after the end of the Cold War, that governmental policies for culture have little place in the new dispensation, UNESCO adhered strongly to the position of the World Commission that the question is no longer whether governments should adopt cultural policies, but how they can do so more effectively.

10 H. Niec, 'Cultural rights: At the end of the World Decade for Cultural Development', CLT-98/CONF.210/CLD.6.

11 See UNESCO, Approved Programme and Budget for 1992–1993, Paris, January 1992, p.176.

12 The debate was based on the document prepared by the Secretariat, Executive Board, 144th session, doc. 144EX/15.

13 The United Nations are conducting activities aimed at the elaboration of a standard-setting instrument on the rights of indigenous people. A draft of a declaration on this subject was adopted by the Sub-Commission for Prevention of Discrimination and Protection of Minorities.

14  UNESCO Medium Term Programme, 1996–2001, 28C/4 Approved.
15  These meetings, publications and initiatives are presented in a more detailed manner in other parts of this chapter.
16  R. Stavenhagen (1998, pp.9–10).
17  United Nations Educational, Scientific and Cultural Organization; *Cultural Rights as Human Rights*, Paris, UNESCO, 1970, pp.9–12.
18  Ibid., p.15.
19  Ibid., p.16.
20  Ibid., p.19.
21  Ibid., pp.105–6.
22  World Commission on Culture and Development (1996, p.21).
23  Committee on Economic, Social and Cultural Rights (1993).
24  Council for Cultural Co-operation (1995, p.13).
25  These are analysed by Janusz Symonides. See 'The history of the paradox of cultural rights and the state of the discussions within UNESCO', in *Les Droits culturels. Actes du VIIIe Colloque interdisciplinaire sur les droits de l'homme*, (1993), pp.47–72.
26  See *Conventions and Recommendations of UNESCO concerning the Protection of the Cultural Heritage*, Paris, UNESCO, 1983.
27  Texts of these constitutions can be found in Blaustein and Flanz, Council of Europe (1995). An excellent analysis of cultural rights in Latin American constitutions is presented by Harvey (1992, 1993).
28  Constitutional provisions concerning university autonomy, freedom of scientific research and academic freedom are presented later in this chapter, in the section dealing with academic freedom.
29  On this subject, see H. Niec, 'The concept of culture in the context of human rights' in *Human Rights and Cultural Policies in a Changing Europe. The Right to Participate in Cultural Rights'*, Round Table organized by Circle, Circle Publication No. 6, published by the Arts Council, Finland, Helsinki, 1994, pp.177–81.
30  *Activités de l'ONU dans le domaine des droits de l'homme*, New York, Nations Unies, 1992, pp.186–9.
31  This article is probably the source of other unclear formulations used alternatively by the United Nations, for example in United Nations (1993, p.III), 'Right to enjoy culture'. Once again a specific right of persons belonging to minorities with the omission of 'their own' is presented as a cultural right of all and as a specific common denomination of all cultural rights.
32  During the UNESCO meeting on cultural rights in 1968, Boutros Boutros-Ghali expressed the view that 'By the right of an individual to culture, it is to be understood that every man has the right of access to knowledge, to the arts and literature of all peoples, to take part in scientific advancement and to enjoy its benefits, to make his contribution towards the enrichment of cultural life.'
33  Birgitta Leander, 'Preliminary list of cultural rights', Manuscript, Paris, UNESCO, 1996, established this list to prepare the ground for an inventory of cultural rights suggested by the Commission on Culture and Development.
34  Council of Europe (1994, p.1).
35  A group working in close cooperation with UNESCO and the Council of Europe comprised the following experts: Denise Bindschedler-Robert, Sylvie Boiton Pierre, Marco Borghi, Pascale Bouccaud, Jacqueline Costa-Lascoux, Emmanuel Decaux, Etienne Grosjean, Pierre Imbert, Denis Huber, Maté Kovacs, Jean-Bernard Marie, Janusz Symonides and Raymond Weber. The work was coordinated by Patrice Meyer-Bisch.
36  Groupe de Fribourg (1998).
37  Committee on Economic, Social and Cultural Rights, Report on the Eighteenth and Nineteenth Sessions, Economic and Social Council, Official Records, 1999,

United Nations, New York and Geneva, 1999, p.79.

38   See J. Symonides, 'The state duty to promote human rights education', in Sia Spiliopoulou Åkermak (ed.), *Human Rights Education: Achievements and Challenges;* Turku/Åbo, published by the Institute for Human Rights, Åbo Akademi University, in collaboration with the Finnish National Commission for UNESCO and UNESCO, 1998, pp.11–30; also 'United Nations and Human Rights Education', in D. Bourantonis and M. Evrivades (eds), *A United Nations for the Twenty-First Century,* The Hague, Kluwer, 1996, pp.361–74.

39   The UNESCO Medium-Term Strategy (1996–2001) contains provisions concerning the promotion of lifelong education for all. The Approved Programme and Budget for 1998–1999, in its Major Programme I, 'Education for all throughout life', foresees a number of actions to support a more integrated implementation by UNESCO of the Plan of Action for the Eradication of Illiteracy by the Year 2000 and the Framework of Action which was adopted by the Jomtien World Conference on Education for All (1990). The programme is designed to give further impetus to the renewal of educational systems and thus make education for all, throughout life, a reality.

40   Commission on Human Rights, E/CN.4/1999/49, 13 January 1999.

41   See Approved Programme and Budget for 1998–1999, Major Programme Area IV, pp.91–110.

42   The right to benefit from and to participate in scientific progress and its applications is closely linked to academic freedom, which is discussed later in this chapter.

43   World University Service (1990).

44   At present the Human Rights Watch Academic Freedom Committee is composed of 28 university presidents and scholars. When teachers, researchers and students are harassed or imprisoned for exercising their rights of expression, free association or inquiry, when their work or research is censored, when access to educational institutions is restricted on discriminatory grounds, or when universities are closed for political reasons, the Committee publicizes the abuses, sends protest letters to appropriate government officials and organizes coordinated international action.

45   Texts of these Declarations are annexed to two publications: Raoul Wallenberg Institute for Human Rights and Humanitarian Law (1992); and the European Centre for Higher Education, *Academic Freedom and University Autonomy: Two Perspectives,* Bucharest, European Centre for Higher Education, UNESCO, 1995.

46   See the text of this Recommendation in *UNESCO and Human Rights Standard-Setting Instruments, Major Publications,* Janusz Symonides and Vladimir Volodin (eds), 2nd edn, Paris, UNESCO, 1999, p.226.

47   The Montreal Congress on Education for Human Rights and Democracy was organized by UNESCO in cooperation with the United Nations Centre for Human Rights and the Canadian Commission for UNESCO. It was attended by more than 250 specialists from more than 60 countries, as well as by representatives of intergovernmental and non-governmental organizations. The Congress adopted the World Plan of Action on Education for Human Rights and Democracy, which was then presented to the Vienna World Conference on Human Rights in June 1993, and noted contributions to the preparation of a declaration on academic freedom.

48   See the Final Report of the International Colloquium on Academic Freedom, Trieste, 23–25 February 1996, International Institute for Human Rights Studies, manuscript. Other amendments to the Montreal Declaration on Academic Freedom provide, *inter alia,* that 'All those employed by institutions of higher education have the right to treatment according to fair labour standards' and

'autonomy should not be used to justify violations of human rights or to deny the academic freedom of those within institutions of higher education'.

49 The decision to elaborate this Recommendation was adopted by the General Conference at its 27th session in 1993. A preliminary draft was prepared by Donald Savach, Executive Director of the Canadian Association of University Professors. The ILO and non-governmental organizations specializing in higher education were consulted. The second draft was adopted by the Governmental Experts' Meeting which took place in UNESCO on 8–9 October 1996. See *New Papers on Higher Education. Meeting Documents*, 12, Governmental Experts' Meeting to Examine the Draft Recommendation concerning the Status of Higher-Education Teaching Personnel, UNESCO, Paris, Final Report, ED-96/45.41.

50 Paragraph 34 of the Recommendation concerning Higher-Education Teaching Personnel enumerates these duties very comprehensively in 12 points. They embrace, *inter alia*, the obligation to achieve the highest possible standards in professional work; to teach students effectively and without any discrimination; to conduct scholarly research based on an honest search for truth and to disseminate its results; to observe the ethics and to respect and acknowledge the scholarly work of academic colleagues and students; to ensure that research is conducted according to the laws and regulations of the state concerned and that it does not violate international standards of human rights.

51 Document ED-98/CONF.202/7.12. Paris, August 1998.

52 Statement on Academic Freedom, University Autonomy and Social Responsibility proposed by the International Association of Universities; paper distributed during the panel discussion.

53 Document ED-98/CONF.202/6, Paris, July 1998.

54 The Framework for Priority Action for Change and Development of Higher-Education, para. 14(*e*), adopted 9 October 1998.

55 See, for example, the Constitution of Croatia (1990), Bulgaria (1991), Slovenia (1991) or Estonia (1992). The Constitution of Greece (1975), in Article 16.1, declares: 'Arts and science, research and teaching shall be free [...] Academic freedom and freedom of teaching shall not exempt anyone from his duty of allegiance to the Constitution.' Similarly, the Constitution of Nicaragua (1987), Article 125, states: 'Academic freedom is recognized. The State provides the free creation, research and dissemination of the sciences, arts and letters.' The Constitution of Thailand (1991) provides in Section 40: 'Every person shall enjoy an equal right to receive the fundamental education under the law on compulsory education [...] Academic freedom is protected, provided that it is not contrary to civil duties.' Academic freedom is among the rights recognized and protected by the Spanish Constitution (1978) in Article 20(*c*). The Constitution of South Africa (1993) states in Article 14.1: 'Every person has the right of freedom of conscience, religion, thought, belief and opinion, which shall include academic freedom in institutions of higher learning.' The Constitution of Malawi (1994), in Article 33, states: 'Every person has the right to freedom of conscience, religion, belief and thought and to academic freedom.' The Constitution of Uganda (1995), in Article 29, stipulates: 'Every person shall have the right to [...] (b) Freedom of thought, conscience and belief, which shall include academic freedom in institutions of learning.' Several other constitutions also contain provisions concerning autonomy of universities or higher-education institutions which is as a rule formulated in the context of the right to education.

56 *Our Creative Diversity* (1996, p.15).

57 Article 1 declares: 'States shall protect the existence and the national or ethnic, cultural, religious and linguistic identity of minorities within their respective

territories and shall encourage conditions for the promotion of that identity.'
58  *Documents on Autonomy and Minority Rights*, ed. Hurst Hannum, Dordrecht/ Boston/London, Martinus Nijhoff Publishers, 1993, pp.62–5.
59  Ibid., pp.86–101.
60  *Human Rights. A Compilation of International Instruments, Vol. II, Regional Instruments*, New York/Geneva, United Nations, 1997, p.287.
61  For a full presentation of the texts concerning indigenous peoples, see Vitoria-Gasteiz (ed.) *Derechos de los Pueblos Indigenas*, Bizhaia, Servicio Central de Publicacions del Gobierno Vasco, 1998.
62  Official Records of the Economic and Social Council, 1991, Supplement No. 3 (E/1991/23 and Corr.1), Annex III.
63  'The Limburg Principles on the Implementation of the International Covenant on Economic, Social and Cultural Rights', *Human Rights Quarterly*, 9, (2), May 1987, 122–35, formulated by the groups of experts expressed an opinion that all states must begin immediately to take steps for the implementation of the Covenant using all appropriate means necessary and regardless of the level of their economic development. Some obligations, such as the prohibition of discrimination, require immediate full implementation. They enumerated situations in which states could be held responsible for the failure to comply with the obligations foreseen by the International Covenant on Economic, Social and Cultural Rights.
64  United Nations, 'Compilation of General Comments and General Recommendations adopted by the Human Rights Treaty Bodies, General Comments adopted by the Human Rights Committee', HRI/GEN/1/Rev.2, 29 March 1996, p.41.
65  United Nations (1997, p.33).
66  Ibid., p.39.
67  Ibid., p.49.
68  Ibid., p.65.
69  See Kolosov, Chapter 7 of the present volume.
70  Countries recognizing the existence of minorities and/or indigenous people on their territory present rather comprehensive information concerning Article 30. For example, Slovakia, in its report (document CRC/C/11/Add.17 of 17 August 1998, pp.49–55), speaks about minority laws, education in minority languages (Hungarian, Ukrainian, German and Ruthenian) curricula, textbooks and so on.
71  See, for example, concluding observations: Austria, Guinea, Yemen. Committee on the Rights of the Child, Report on the 20th session, Geneva, 11–29 January 1999.
72  Resolution 27C/1.9 adopted by the 27th session of the General Conference in 1993.
73  See Executive Board, Examination of the reports and responses received in the sixth consultation of Member States on the implementation of the convention and Recommendation against Discrimination in Education, document 156EX/21, Paris, 17 March 1999.
74  Document ED-98/CONF.501, Paris 7 October 1998. Advisory Committee on Education for Peace, Human Rights, Democracy, International Understanding and Tolerance, Fourth session, Paris, 21–23 September 1998.
75  In 1999, of 144 States Parties to the International Covenant on Civil and Political Rights, 95 were parties to the Optional Protocol and thus recognized the right of individuals subject to their jurisdiction to submit communications.
76  *Supra*, no.64, pp.38–41.
77  United Nations Report of the Human Rights Committee, Vol. I, General

Assembly, Official Records, 52nd session, Supplement No. 40 (A/52/40) Case No. 671/1995, p.87.

78  United Nations , Report of the Human Rights Committee, Vol. II, General Assembly, Official Records, 45th session, Supplement No. 40 (A/45/40) Case No. 167/1984. Discussed in Raija Hanskii and Markku Suksi (eds), *An Introduction to the International Protection of Human Rights*, Turku/Åbo, Institute for Human Rights, Åbo Akademi University, 1997, pp.57, 81, 82.

79  United Nations , Report of the Human Rights Committee, General Assembly, Official Records, 43rd session, Supplement No. 40 (A/43/40) Case No. 197/1985.

80  The working group comprised members representing six electoral groups: Belgium, Russian Federation, Brazil, India, Senegal and Libyan Arab Jamahiriya.

81  Report of the Committee on Conventions and Recommendations, 156 EX/52, Paris, 7 June 1999.

82  World Commission on Culture and Development (1996, pp.281–4).

83  See Janusz Symonides, 'International implementation of cultural rights', *Gazette*, **60**, (1), March 1998, 8–24.

84  The Committee for Economic, Social and Cultural Rights decided to present to the United Nations Conference on Human Rights in Vienna (June 1993) a document suggesting the need to reflect on the possibility of elaborating and adopting an optional protocol to the International Covenant on Economic, Social and Cultural Rights which would allow individuals to present petitions concerning alleged violations of their economic, social and cultural rights. Such procedures should be entirely facultative and generally recognized limitations concerning the admissibility of individual communications should be approved. Among arguments for the adoption of this procedure, one can list the following:
(a)   the very principle of indivisibility of human rights leads to a logical conclusion that both categories of human rights, civil and political as well as economic, social and cultural, should have the same guarantees;
(b)   the acceptance of this quasi-judicial procedure will automatically upgrade economic, social and cultural rights;
(c)   the adoption of the right to petition on an international level will encourage governments to introduce more effective internal ways and means of recourse;
(d)   the adoption of such a protocol will force both individuals and governments to interpret and exercise the Covenant in a more precise way.
The World Conference on Human Rights encouraged the Commission on Human Rights, in cooperation with the Committee on Economic, Social and Cultural Rights, to continue the examination of Optional Protocol to the International Covenant on Economic, Social and Cultural Rights. During its fifteenth session (1997), the Committee adopted a report on a draft optional protocol which is now under consideration by the Commission on Human Rights.

85  See Eide, Chapter 4 of the present volume.

# Bibliography

*Academic Freedom and University Autonomy: Two Perspectives* (1995), Bucharest, European Centre for Higher Education.
Blaustein, Albert P. and Gilbert H. Flanz (eds), *Constitutions of the Countries of the World*, (various issues), Dobbs Ferry, New York, Oceana Publications.

Committee on Economic, Social and Cultural Rights, Report on the Seventh Session, Economic and Social Council, Official Records, 1993, Supplement No. 2, p.58.

Committee on Economic, Social and Cultural Rights, Reports, 1990–98, New York, United Nations.

*Conventions and Recommendations of UNESCO Concerning the Protection of the Cultural Heritage* (1983), Paris, UNESCO.

Council for Cultural Co-operation (1995), *Reflections on Cultural Rights*, Synthesis Report, Council of Europe, Strasbourg, 24–26 January.

Council of Europe (1994) 'List of Cultural Rights', draft, CDDC Misc/94/3, Strasbourg, 24 August.

Council of Europe (1995) *The Rebirth of Democracy, 12 Constitutions of Central and Eastern Europe*, edited by the International Institute for Democracy, Strasbourg, Council of Europe Press.

*Cultural Rights of Peoples in Europe* (1991) Report of a meeting in Girona, Spain, 5-8 February, Barcelona, UNESCO Catalunya Centre.

Eide, A. (1995), 'Cultural rights as individual rights', in A. Eide, C. Krause and A. Rosas (eds), *Economic and Cultural Rights, A Textbook*, Dordrecht/Boston/London, Martinus Nijhoff Publishers.

Groupe de Fribourg (1998) *Les Droits culturels, Projet de déclaration*, Paris/Fribourg, Editions UNESCO/Editions universitaires.

Harvey, Edwin R. (1992) *Derecho Cultural Latinoamericano – Sudaméricá y Panamá*, Buenos Aires, Ediciones Depalma.

Harvey, Edwin R. (1993) *Derecho Cultural Latinaamericano – Centroaméricá, México y Caribe*, Buenos Aires, Ediciones Depalma.

Hausermann, J. (1993), 'The Right to Participate in Cultural Life', European Round Table, Helsinki, Finland, 30 April–2 May 1993.

Johnson, G. and J. Symonides (1991), *La Déclaration universelle des droits de l'homme*, Paris, UNESCO.

Marks, S. (1977), 'UNESCO and Human Rights: The implementation of rights relating to education, science, culture and communication', *International Law Journal*, XIII, (1).

McKeon, R. (1953), *Philosophy and the Diversity of Cultures*, Paris, UNESCO, Interrelations of Cultures.

Meyer-Bisch, Patrice (ed.) (1993), *Les Droits culturels: une catégorie sous-développée de droits de l'homme*, Actes du VIIIe Colloque interdisciplinaire sur les droits de l'homme. Fribourg, Editions universitaires.

Niec, H. (ed.) (1998), *Cultural Rights and Wrongs, Institute of Art and Law*, Paris, UNESCO Publishing.

Raoul Wallenberg Institute for Human Rights and Humanitarian Law (1992), *Academic Freedom. Report from a Seminar on Academic Freedom, Lund, 9–11 March 1992*, Lund, Raoul Wallenberg Institute for Human Rights and Humanitarian Law.

Robertson, A.H. (1978), 'The right to culture', *Cultures*, V, (1), Paris, UNESCO.

Schafer, D.P. (1980), 'Culture and cosmos: the role of culture in the world of the future', *Cultures*, VII, No. (2), Paris, UNESCO.

Stavenhagen, R. (1998), 'Cultural rights: a social science perspective', in H. Niec (ed.), *Cultural Rights and Wrongs, Institute of Art and Law*, Paris, UNESCO Publishing.

Symonides, J. (1991), 'Collective rights of minorities in Europe', in R. Lefeber, H. Fitzmaurice and E.N. Vierdag (eds), *The Changing Political Structure of Europe. Aspects of International Law*, Dordrecht/Boston/London, Martinus Nijhoff Publishers.

Symonides, J. and V. Volodin (eds) (1996), *UNESCO and Human Rights*, Paris, UNESCO.

Szabo, I. (1974), *Cultural Rights*, Budapest, Akademiai Kiadç.

UNESCO, *Cultural Rights as Human Rights* (1970), Paris, UNESCO.

United Nations (1984) *Report of the Human Rights Committee*, Vol. II, General Assembly, Official Records, 45th session, Supplement No. 40 (A/45/40) Case No. 167/1984.

United Nations (1985), *Report of the Human Rights Committee*, General Assembly, Official Records, 43rd session, Supplement No. 40 (A/43/40) Case No. 197/1985.

United Nations (1992), *Activités de l'ONU dans le domaine des droits de l'homme*, New York, United Nations.

United Nations (1993), *A Compilation of International Instruments, Vol. I, Universal Instruments*, New York, United Nations.

United Nations (1995), *Report of the Human Rights Committee*, Vol. I, General Assembly, Official Records, 52nd session, Supplement No. 40 (A/52/40) Case No. 671/1995.

United Nations (1997), *Report of the Human Rights Committee*, Vol. I, New York, United Nations.

World Commission on Culture and Development (1995), *Our Creative Diversity*, Paris, UNESCO Publishing.

World Commission on Culture and Development (1996), *Our Creative Diversity*, 2nd edn, Paris, UNESCO.

*World Conference on Cultural Policies, Mexico City, 26 July–6 August 1982* (1982), Final Report, Paris, UNESCO.

World University Service (1990), *Academic Freedom 1990. A Human Rights Report*, eds L. Fernando, N. Hartley, M. Novak and T. Swinehart, London, Zed Books.

# PART III
# HUMAN RIGHTS OF
# VULNERABLE PERSONS
# AND GROUPS

# 6 Women's Rights

## KATARINA TOMAŠEVSKI

### Introduction

The global commitment to equal human rights for women has progressed rapidly during the last 50 years. This has necessitated a radical departure from the previous practice, embodied in national and international law, of taking lesser rights for women for granted. Suffice to recall the following examples: when the United Nations was established, political rights of women were an exception rather than a rule; when the Universal Declaration of Human Rights was being drafted, it was proposed that its first article should read 'All men are brothers'; and protection of maternity in international labour law implicitly discriminated against women by protecting their child-bearing role at the expense of their equal right to work and equal rights in work. With the benefit of hindsight, it is all too easy to criticize such examples, and many more could easily be added. This, however, tells us how much progress has been achieved during the past half-century.

Evolving human rights norms were only recently merged with the parallel process of 'advancement of women', improvement of the 'status of women', or 'women-in-development'. The series of United Nations awareness-raising activities in the 1970s was a catalyst for introducing gender into international and national policy making by giving women visibility in all areas: political, economic, social, cultural, environmental and humanitarian. Gender has today become an integral part of global policies, not only in human rights, but also in development, environment and housing, or with regard to combating violence or refugee protection. Towards the end of the 1980s, human rights were integrated into evolving global policies, and thus opened the way towards merging the previously dissociated 'women's' and 'human rights' approaches. No global conference is nowadays likely just to mention women, as was customary during past decades, when women were added somewhere at the bottom of the agenda, along with children and the disabled.

The series of global conferences in the early 1990s included the Fourth World Conference on Women, which was 'the largest international meeting ever convened under United Nations auspices'.[1] From the human rights viewpoint, the Beijing conference, as it is commonly called, opened questions which were deemed to have already been settled, perhaps wrongly so. Most importantly, the final document of the conference devotes one section to human rights of women, thus creating an impression that education for the girl child falls outside the realm of human rights, or that human rights have no contribution to make relating to the elimination of poverty.[2] Moreover, that final document reflects how much dissent accompanied its adoption, because 65 participating states submitted reservations.[3] The preparations of the Beijing conference also revealed misunderstandings relating to the term 'gender'. In human rights, that term denotes the fact that discrimination on the ground of sex can victimize both men and women, while gender discrimination victimizes women on a range of grounds alongside sex. This is discussed in detail below.

### Evolving Prohibition of Discrimination

The United Nations Charter affirmed explicitly 'the equal rights of men and women'[4] in its Preamble, and included sex among the prohibited grounds of discrimination, alongside race, language and religion. The explicitness of the Charter regarding equal rights for women was thereafter reaffirmed and strengthened in a multitude of international human rights treaties. This process has had to overcome many different obstacles; it was neither rapid nor easy. The Universal Declaration of Human Rights in its final text reaffirmed and reinforced the Charter's postulate of equal rights for women. An early draft of the Universal Declaration, as mentioned above, had proposed that its first article should begin by stating: 'All men are brothers.' This was indicative of the relative lack of gender sensitivity at the time within the Commission on Human Rights, which was drafting the Declaration, although it was chaired by Eleanor Roosevelt, and despite the efforts made by some of its members. The exclusion of the female part of humanity in the wording of a future Declaration was effectively opposed by the Commission on the Status of Women.[5] As a result, the Universal Declaration was in its final text genuinely universal. Keeping in mind that it was drafted in the late 1940s, the careful use of the terms 'everyone' and 'no one' throughout its text appears even more impressive.

The progress in tackling many different obstacles to equal human rights of women during the past five decades can be illustrated by pointing to the principal issues which were singled out by the Commission on the Status of Women. Political rights of women had been recognized in few countries 50 years ago and were therefore tackled first. *The World's Women* reported that, in 1987–8, women had no ministerial positions in 93 countries of the world, while their representation in national parliaments exceeded 20 per cent only in the former Eastern Europe and USSR.[6] This situation has deteriorated since: 'From an average 33 per cent representation in pre-1989 state socialist parliaments, women now hold an average 10 per cent of parliamentary seats.'[7] Such data show the enormity of the task once equality in political representation of women is accepted as a yardstick. The availability of such data, however, has resulted from the initial commitment to equal political rights of women: the fact that inequality has become an object of monitoring in itself indicates commitment.

The initial focus on political rights was followed by a focus on gender discrimination in the private sphere, within the family, neighbourhood and community, which necessitated refocusing human rights standards from the conventionally dominant public sphere, namely relations between the government and the individual, to the private sphere.[8]

Perhaps the most important accomplishment of the past decades has been the realization that women are not discriminated against because of their sex alone, and hence the change from 'sex' to 'gender' in standard-setting instruments aimed at the eradication of discrimination against women. Six different grounds of discrimination may deprive women of the recognition or exercise of their equal human rights: (1) sex, (2) pregnancy and child bearing, (3) maternity, (4) marital status, (5) family status, and (6) family and/or household duties and responsibilities.

Women can be denied property rights, or equal access to citizenship, because they are female. An unregulated labour market can, however, lead to discrimination against pregnant women and mothers with dependent children, not affecting all women, but institutionalizing inequality between men (who cannot bear children) and women (who can), based on the inability of women to compete with men on the labour market, owing to pregnancy and child bearing. Looking further at the role of maternity, one can easily see that legal protections assumed that the parental role pertained to women alone. Women's marital status constitutes an illustrative example of a loss of rights which marriage may entail: single women may enjoy a wider scope of rights than those who are married, such as freedom of movement and residence, access to bank loans or to employment, or even access to health care and/or family planning services. Law has for centuries embodied the notion of the 'head of family' or 'breadwinner' and this role still pertains to men. Women's marital and family status thus determines the scope of rights and freedoms. Their traditional role within the family and/or household further limits their ability to exercise rights and freedoms, even if they are formally granted them. The evolving human rights standards have had to address each of these different forms of discrimination in turn.

Evolving global policies and standards do not automatically translate into effective measures for the elimination of gender discrimination. Even in the part of the world which calls itself 'developed', the translation of norms against gender discrimination into enforceable equal rights for women remains a task for the future. It is no coincidence that the motto of the UN activities was – and remains – *Equality, Development and Peace*. It is the first term, equality, which defines the approach to every and any pertinent issue.

## Defining Global Minimum Standards

The Convention on the Elimination of All Forms of Discrimination against Women (the Women's Convention), as much as any other human rights treaty, lays down human rights norms which are necessarily worded in abstract terms. Human rights treaties are negotiated during protracted and sometimes conflictual intergovernmental meetings. In the case of the Women's Convention, the drafters 'had to face the difficult task of preparing a text applicable to societies of different cultural characteristics and traditions. The ways in which discrimination against women manifested itself varied from one culture to another. The Convention therefore represents a constructive compromise'.[9] Specificity and clarity are thus attained through the interpretation and application of the Convention. It is through the reporting process that the Convention is translated from abstract requirements into a yardstick to monitor the realization of the human rights of women. At least, this should be so in theory. The Committee on the Elimination of Discrimination against Women (CEDAW) has been established on the basis of the Convention, with the main task of monitoring progress made in its implementation.

Governmental reports are rarely self-critical. In most cases, they reproduce the existing constitutional and legal provisions relating to non-discrimination and do not venture into analysing their application, or, indeed, obstacles to the enjoyment of equal rights by all women. Not only is there often a wide gap between formal legal status and reality, but the Convention itself also requires the eradication of *de facto* discrimination. Without data on the actual position of women regarding all their human rights and fundamental freedoms, *de facto* discrimination remains invisible, and policies for its eradication are difficult to elaborate. CEDAW has adopted, following the practice of other human rights treaty bodies, a 'constructive dialogue' for the examination of reports by States Parties. These reports are discussed during public sessions in the presence of representatives of the State Party, who introduce the report prepared by their government and respond to questions and comments by the members of CEDAW. Quite often these questions relate to issues which have not been addressed in the report, but they frequently venture into examining whether a specific law, policy or practice is consistent with the requirements of the Convention. CEDAW has been criticized for failing to move one step further and declare when and where a national law, governmental policy or country's practice constitutes a breach of the Convention: 'CEDAW has never formally pronounced a State Party to be in violation of the Convention, even though the members have clearly felt that some states have failed to carry out their obligations.'[10]

The definition of the nature and scope of governmental obligations under the Convention, however, cannot be assumed but requires an assessment of the impact which many reservations have made, both for the human rights of women in the countries concerned, and also for the entire Women's Convention. The problem of reservations to the Women's Convention was brought to the attention of the World Conference by CEDAW and numerous other bodies. CEDAW noted that this problem was global and therefore should be placed on the agenda, added that the Women's Convention had the highest number of reservations of all human rights treaties, and stressed that 'most reservations were worded so generally' and therefore necessitate the determination of 'the impact the reservations have on the obligation to eliminate discrimination against women'.[11] The following table lists the reservations to the Women's Convention.

In order to facilitate the process of undertaking human rights obligations, governments can reserve the right not to apply a specific part of a treaty and have to declare so when ratifying a treaty by submitting a reservation. This procedure, in the area of human rights, is designed to enhance the realization of human rights by providing for exceptions to those guarantees which governments cannot immediately and fully undertake at the time of ratification. It is not intended to enable governments to behave in a self-contradictory manner: to ratify a human rights treaty and thus express their commitment to it, but to reserve their right not to apply the crucial human rights safeguards which such a treaty requires. Much controversy has been created regarding the Women's Convention, because reservations in many cases appear to be contrary to the very aim of the Convention.

## Reservations to the Women's Convention

| Substantive Provision | Country |
| --- | --- |
| Definition of discrimination (Article 1) | United Kingdom |
| Commitment to eradicate discrimination (Article 2) | Bangladesh, Cook Islands, Egypt, Iraq, [Libya], Malawi, Tunisia, United Kingdom |
| Measures to accelerate *de facto* equality (Article 4) | [Malawi] |
| Measures to eliminate prejudices and stereotyping (Article 5) | Cook Islands, France, [India] |
| Elimination of discrimination in political and public life (Article 7) | Austria, Belgium, Germany, Luxembourg, Spain, Thailand |
| Equal citizenship rights (Article 9) | Cyprus, Egypt, France, Iraq, Jamaica, Jordan, Korea, Thailand, Tunisia, [Turkey], United Kingdom |
| Elimination of discrimination in education (Article 10) | Thailand, United Kingdom |
| Elimination of discrimination in employment (Article 11) | Malta, Mauritius, New Zealand, Thailand, United Kingdom |
| Equal labour rights (Article 11) | Australia, Austria, Ireland, New Zealand, Thailand, United Kingdom |
| Equal access to financial credits (Article 13) | Bangladesh, Ireland, Malta, United Kingdom |
| Full legal capacity (Article 15) | Austria, Brazil, Ireland, [Libya], Jordan, Malta, Thailand, Tunisia, Turkey, United Kingdom |
| Elimination of discrimination in marriage and family (Article 16) | Bangladesh, Brazil, Egypt, France, [India], Iraq, Ireland, Jordan, [Libya], Luxembourg, Malta, Mauritius, Korea, Thailand, Tunisia, Turkey, United Kingdom |

*Note*:   Countries in brackets submitted their reservations upon signature.

*Source*:   *Discrimination against Women: The Convention and the Committee*, Human Rights Fact Sheet No. 22, United Nations, November 1994, pp.63–72.

Reservations are presented in this table as they relate to specific provisions of the Convention, starting from the general principle of non-discrimination. These are important because they indicate the unwillingness of governments to undertake a commitment to eradicate discrimination against women in all its forms, which is the aim of the Convention. The purpose of the table is to review the contents of the Convention in order to show the degree of agreement and disagreement with respect to specific provisions. As can be seen, most reservations have been entered with respect to non-discrimination in family law and citizenship, and with respect to the legal capacity of women. Countries which apply *Shari'a* law submitted reservations concerning the very obligation to eliminate gender discrimination. To illustrate how far-reaching some reservations are, that of Libya states that accession 'is subject to the general reservation that such accession cannot conflict with the laws on personal status derived from the Islamic *Shari'a*'. The reservation of Malawi, subsequently withdrawn, said: 'Owing to the deep-rooted nature of some traditional customs and practices of Malawians, the Government of the Republic of Malawi shall not, for the time being, consider itself bound by such of the provisions of the Convention as require immediate eradication of such traditional customs and practices.'[12]

Some reservations reflect the exclusively male heritage in the exercise of royal powers (Belgium, Luxembourg, Spain), others exclude women from employment in the armed forces or from access to combat duties (Germany, New Zealand, Thailand); yet others restrict employment of women in nightwork or at jobs deemed hazardous to their health (Malta, United Kingdom). Most, however, retain restrictions on equal rights regarding personal status: as to marriage, family, citizenship and legal capacity of women.

The practical implications of reservations can be described by taking Bangladesh as an example. In 1984, at the time of ratification, the government submitted its reservations on a number of articles of the Convention, including the key article on the obligation to eliminate gender discrimination, and also equal rights of spouses and equal rights and responsibilities of parents with regard to their children 'as they conflict with *Shari'a* law based on Holy Koran and Sunna'.[13] Numerous objections were raised to this reservation, both by other States Parties to the Convention and by CEDAW. Mexico and Germany objected to Bangladeshi reservations, alleging their incompatibility with the object and purpose of the Convention. Sweden explained its objections at greater length. It said that the reservations in question, if put into practice, would inevitably result in discrimination against women on the basis of their sex, which was against everything the Convention stood for. It concluded by saying that, if tolerated, such reservations would make human rights obligations meaningless.[14] During the consideration of the initial report of Bangladesh on the implementation of the Convention, CEDAW raised the issue of reservations as a problem and hoped that the government would soon withdraw its reservations.[15]

While reservations made possible the ratification of the Women's Convention by virtually all countries because they can opt out of some of its requirements, they also jeopardized the integral and effective application of the Convention as a whole. In other words, the problem is that formal adherence to the Women's Convention is not accompanied by full commitment to the Convention. This problem led to repeated calls upon the United Nations to secure an authoritative determination of the permissibility of reservations which apparently undermine the commitment to the core human rights obligations towards women. The UN Sub-Commission for Prevention of Discrimination and Protection of Minorities noted in 1993 its concern:

> that certain reservations to the Convention, in particular those in relation to the adoption of policies and institutional measures to implement the terms of the Convention (Article 2), political and public life (Article 7), discrimination in the field of employment (Article 11), equality of men and women before the law (Article 15), and marriage and family relations (Article 16), might diminish the international legal norm and legitimize its violation.[16]

## Human Rights Obligations of Governments

The multitude of human rights standard-setting efforts which the United Nations have undertaken has led to the realization that human rights standards relating to women have to encompass three levels:

1. formal affirmation that human rights and fundamental freedoms apply to women as they do to men;
2. prohibition of discrimination based on sex; that is, safeguards for equal treatment and equal opportunities for women;
3. identification and elimination of obstacles to equal exercise of human rights and freedoms by women, which are gender-specific and derive from child bearing and child rearing or woman's marital or family status.

It is obvious that elimination of gender discrimination necessitates unequal rather than equal treatment: obstacles to equality cannot be eliminated unless they are recognized and, because they hinder women's (but not men's) exercise of human rights, special measures in favour of women are necessary so as to enable them to overcome such obstacles. Because such measures are structural and accord preferential treatment to women as a category, they often appear to be discriminating against individual men, and remain controversial. Governmental obligations aimed at eliminating discrimination, which were useful as a precedent in the drafting of the Women's Convention, had first been laid down for racial discrimination.[17] It was realized that a formal prohibition of discrimination is an indispensable first step, but insufficient to eliminate racial or gender discrimination: it does not provide sufficient grounds for redressing the inherited consequences of decades, even centuries, of discrimination. Categories victimized by discrimination have to be assisted in order to attain a status comparable to that of the rest of the population so as to exercise their nominally equal rights on equal terms with others.

Human rights entail two types of governmental obligations: to prevent abuses of power and to create conditions for the realization of human rights and fundamental freedoms. Prohibitions have been defined quite well, but norms which require governments to undertake specific measures, rather than to refrain from a prohibited action, were and are more difficult to elaborate and monitor. Elimination of gender discrimination involves both types of obligations. The challenge to inequality is inherent in the very notion of human rights; thus the core principle is that all human beings have equal rights, which are properties inherent to human beings. Thus not only should women be accorded rights equal to those of men, but they should be equally able to enjoy all these formally accorded rights. This requires that other than legal obstacles be identified and eliminated. Eliminating *de facto* discrimination is much more difficult than enacting laws which recognize equal rights for all.

The move beyond a formal recognition of equal rights to the identification of problems which specific categories of women face in trying to exercise their rights is evidenced in changed global policies; they evolved towards recognizing that 'women' do not constitute a homogeneous group. Some categories are often deprived of their basic rights (for example, rural women or refugee women) and others are particularly susceptible to human rights violations (for example, imprisoned women or prostitutes). Others may be able, in theory, to enjoy all human rights and freedoms, but their family and household duties prevent them from even knowing about their rights; yet others may be legally denied specific rights and freedoms because they are daughters and wives (rather than husbands and fathers), and whatever their family status may be in practice, in law they are not deemed to be 'heads of the family'. This is particularly important in access to land: many national laws, as well as land reforms, have prevented women from owning land. The UN

Rapporteur on Property Rights found that 'the lack of appropriate information from States and other materials on the legal status of women in all geographical regions and their status in possessing property rights did not permit [him] to elucidate this question completely. This issue is still awaiting more profound and wider study'; and he added: 'The Committee on the Elimination of Discrimination against Women should consider adopting a concise statement or assessment concerning the discrimination faced by women in many countries concerning the exercise of their right to own property. Special attention should be paid to methods aimed at eradicating such discrimination.'[18]

When women's concerns first became articulated in international development policy and practice, the prevalent approach was to identify specific 'women's issues' and design 'women's projects' to address them.[19] The postulate of equality for women in development slowly moved to a formal recognition of equal rights and then beyond to the identification and elimination of multilayered gender discrimination: legal and factual, public and private, direct and indirect, visible and invisible, intentional and unintended. It also necessitates the understanding of the multiplication of the grounds for discrimination affecting women: a woman may be subjected to discrimination because she is an asylum seeker, disabled (and a woman), because she is imprisoned, black, a foreigner (and a woman); a woman migrant worker can be victimized as a migrant worker and, in addition, as a woman. Thus the General Assembly adopted in December 1993 a resolution on violence against women migrant workers[20] in addition to its Declaration on Violence against Women.[21]

## Overcoming the Distinction between 'Public' and 'Private'

Untypical human rights issues, those emerging in the private rather than public sphere, have attained prominence in standard-setting with regard to women. While human rights are generally perceived as protection of the individual against abuses by public authorities, with regard to women marriage and family often represent the focal point for change because denials of equal rights to women and girls are the most noticeable, but also the most difficult to change at that level. A married woman, compared to an unmarried woman, can be discriminated against because of the inherited attitude that the man, the husband, is the head of the family, the breadwinner. The Human Rights Committee therefore affirmed in 1989 that governments are required to ensure equality of rights and responsibilities of spouses as to marriage, during marriage and at its dissolution, and added that 'it is a positive duty of States to make certain that spouses have equal rights'.[22] Because gender discrimination jeopardizes all human rights, persistence of unequal rights in marriage are addressed as a breach of governmental human rights obligations. Decisions on eliminating discrimination against married women, such as access to unemployment and social security benefits, were adopted under the International Covenant on Civil and Political Rights.[23] These cases illustrated another facet of untypical human rights issues: although 'violations' are commonly perceived as abuses, equal rights of married women were violated by governments' failures to change their national legislation; although violations of economic and social rights generally remain outside the mandate of international human rights bodies, those denying equal rights to women have been accepted as breaches of the right to protection against discrimination.

A case concerning the national legislation of Peru illuminates typical obstacles which women may have to overcome to acquire equal rights in the private sphere. According to the Peruvian Civil Code, when a woman is married, only the husband is entitled to represent matrimonial property before the court. The Peruvian Supreme Court affirmed this approach in a case involving a married woman who sought access to justice so as to protect her own property rights. She submitted a communication to the Human Rights Committee, stating that she was denied access to courts because she was a woman, and Peru thus breached the principle of equal rights. The Committee found Peru in breach of the International Covenant on Civil and Political Rights, stating that the application of the Peruvian Civil Code resulted in denying the woman equality before the courts and constituted discrimination, and urged the government to initiate necessary legislative changes.[24]

This case illustrates persisting obstacles to equal rights for women embodied in national legislation which in many countries preclude women from exercising all rights which they should, but do not yet, have. Thus married women may still be required to have the permission of their husbands to enter employment in some countries. Married women are not considered independent or equal (either to men or even to unmarried women) in migration or citizenship. The concept of the 'head of the family' in land ownership, or in loans and credits, constitutes an obstacle for women, who may be responsible for the family in practice, but are considered dependent family members in law.

The cases which were brought before the Human Rights Committee show that women, whether in Africa or Latin America, are determined to seek redress – when they are given access to remedies and when they know both their rights and remedies for cases of their violation. It may have come as a surprise that the denial of equal rights concerning citizenship figures prominently in national and international case law. One could assume, wrongly, that such basic issues as citizenship were solved for all a long time ago. Such false assumptions have to be dispelled to open the way for increased use by women of international complaints procedures.

The UN human rights bodies only addressed the human rights of women in the 1990s. An overview of violations of the human rights of women, however, still necessitates sifting through mountains of documents produced by various human rights bodies. There is no separate agenda item specifically on women which would make such an overview easy and comprehensive. Reasons for this are many. One, often voiced by women's organizations, is the traditional disregard of women in human rights as much as in other areas. Another reason is that it is often difficult to determine whether a specific human rights violation is gender-specific, or whether women are victimized for reasons unrelated to their sex. However, because such an analysis is rare, even those violations which are gender-specific are often not dealt with as human rights issues.

## Balancing the Reproductive Role and Equal Rights

Human rights norms do not treat people as if they were equal because they are not. They demand that people be recognized as having equal rights. Thus disabled persons are accorded a specific set of rights to compensate for their disability and to prevent this from amounting to a handicap. Similarly, pregnant women and mothers with small children enjoy special protection, not because they are women, but because child bearing and child rearing necessitate social and economic support. The main aim of human rights is to accord everyone equal opportunities for free and full development; hence methods of eliminating discrimination include redressing factual inequalities in the enjoyment of human rights.

Human rights require that women do not have to earn societal recognition and protection through motherhood; that women are, as much as men, entitled to full protection of their rights and freedoms because they are human beings. The implications of motherhood for equal rights of women emanate from the biological fact that women bear children and men do not. Societal and legal protection aim to compensate for this biological difference. This protection derives from the acknowledgment that child bearing and child rearing are a societal function; hence compensation is earned by women who perform it: it is not granted them for the mere fact that they are women.

Women's biological role of child bearing, rather than being compensated by society as equal rights require, can be used to perpetuate inequality. Where women are considered to be the property of their husbands and instruments for child bearing (of sons), unequal rights for women remain sanctioned by law. In many countries, women remain minors throughout their lives; national law denies them a full legal personality. They are considered the property of their fathers, husbands and sons. Denial of their full legal personality entails the authorization or consent (of their father or husband) for their access to health services, including family planning. Women's access to family planning continues to be a criminal offence in some countries, while in others it may be conditional upon the husband's written authorization, which denies women full and equal legal personality. Significantly, the Earth Summit urged governments to strengthen the legal capacity of women through constitutional, legal and administrative procedures in order to enable women to enforce their equal rights.[25]

Literature on the effectiveness of population policies regularly singles out the status of women as the principal obstacle to their effectiveness. Moreover, the mere availability of family planning services is often expected to produce significant effects in terms of decreased fertility, but may prove to have a limited effect on human reproductive behaviour: 'Family planning, as a health measure, is partly one of practical containment, and it can be defeated by more primary influences.'[26] These 'primary influences', particularly the status of women, require a broadening of population policies to factors which influence or even determine their reproductive behaviour. They regularly derive from discriminatory heritage. Much has been written about their manifestations, be it women's preference for large families or for sons. Such attitudes are, however, analysed as a cause of reproductive behaviour but not as a consequence of discriminatory heritage, namely a manifestation of gender discrimination.

The identification of causes is obviously crucial for designing remedies. This has yet to be introduced into international policies which originate from 'women's' or 'women-in-development' departments. For example, the 1990 *SIDA Guidelines for Activities within the Area of Population* include a pledge to ensure that 'an increased number of girls/women participate in primary education'.[27] The low participation of girls in primary education is a consequence of a discriminatory heritage, thus its elimination, namely equalizing educational participation for girls, should be the aim and also a yardstick against which progress is measured. When the objective is equal, rather than increased but still unequal, educational participation, an increase of educational enrolment of girls from 10 to 20 per cent is not seen as success, but as persisting discrimination. When human rights standards replace those conventionally adopted to improve the status of women, a different yardstick for measuring progress – departures from the posited equality – sheds a different light on past accomplishments.

Neither legal norms nor development policies can provide more than just a starting point, a catalyst, for change. The emergence of gender discrimination on the human rights agenda broadened the reach of human rights from 'vertical' relations, between individuals and governments, to 'horizontal' relations, between private individuals, within families and communities, and ultimately within couples. The human rights argument is that women should not be left unprotected from abuses from which they may suffer, and that governments have to take the lead in eradicating such abuses even when they occur within families and may be justified by tradition or religion. Rights of individual women thus take precedence over respect for family autonomy.

Moreover, women's participation in decision making underlines the importance of the indivisibility of human rights: women may be denied access to decision making when population policies are being formulated and adopted. These policies affect women – many refer only to women – while decisions may be made by men. Research has shown that 'the most forceful opposition to family planning comes from older males, especially from the devout among them'.[28] Because of their biological role of child bearing, women can be transformed into instruments for the attainment of fertility objectives if they are denied equal rights and fundamental freedoms.

International population policies therefore posit that women's empowerment represents the crucial, but most difficult, area for governmental intervention, and define education as the main path towards it: 'Education is one of the most important means of empowering women with the knowledge, skills and self-confidence necessary to participate fully in the development process.'[29] The Social Summit has gone further and listed a whole range of requirements for women's empowerment, such as 'effective measures, including through the enactment and enforcement of laws, and implement policies to combat and eliminate all forms of discrimination, exploitation, abuse and violence against women and girl children', and removing 'the remaining restrictions on women's rights to own land, inherit property or borrow money, and ensure women's equal right to work'.[30]

## Balancing Individual and Family Rights

International human rights law defines basic rights and freedoms and also their limitations. If limitations do not form part of analysis, human rights appear as a catalogue of rights which may be mutually conflicting, and whose conflicts jeopardize their consistent application. For example, public health is explicitly envisaged as grounds on which individual rights and freedoms may be limited. Another important limitation is embodied in the protection of the rights of others; nobody is allowed to abuse individual rights or freedoms if this negates the equal rights and freedoms of others.

Freedom of religion is often counterpoised to access to family planning, but also to the postulate of equal rights for women and girls, particularly within the family. Much controversy has been generated with regard to family planning. The fact that many countries have submitted reservations to the specific provisions of international human rights treaties on family planning, most recently also to the final document of the International Conference on Population and Development (ICPD), Cairo, September 1994, accepting internationally mandated or recommended policies only to the extent to which they conform to their domestic, religious or customary law, has created many objections and much criticism, but not as yet decisive action to uphold international human rights law. The 1993 World Conference on Human Rights, held in Vienna, called for the 'eradication of any conflicts which may arise between the rights of women and the harmful effects of certain traditional or customary practices, cultural prejudices and religious extremism',[31] thus reinforcing demands for full application of international human rights law.

The human rights documents emanating from Islamic organizations illustrate an approach which indicates that human rights standards are not defined uniformly in all parts of the world. Thus the Cairo Declaration, adopted by the 1990 Islamic Conference of Foreign Ministers, postulates that 'the husband is responsible for the support and welfare of the family', expressing the *Shari'a* principle of men's guardianship over and superiority to women. A woman is deemed equal to a man in dignity, but does not have equal rights: a woman 'has rights to enjoy as well as duties to perform; she has her own civil entity and financial independence, and the right to retain her name and lineage'. The notion of the family is based on marriage and 'both the foetus and the mother must be protected and accorded special care'.[32] Such approaches point to the fact that international human rights instruments were adopted during earlier decades with an assumption that all countries would be governed by secular rather than religious law. An important reason for difficulties in the application of human rights is therefore the fact that quite a few countries have adopted religious law to govern both the public and the private sphere.

This was not anticipated by the drafters of human rights instruments, who had assumed that freedom of religion would constitute one out of many human rights and that national laws would be secular rather than religious. Ensuring compatibility of religious and human rights law has become one of the main controversies today, when the geopolitical map of the world has changed. It is sufficient to recall that, at the time of the Universal Declaration of Human Rights, UN membership was less than one-third of today's. There are, however, two distinct visions of what human rights are: the focus on state sovereignty is increasingly being replaced by an emphasis on state responsibility. Regarding women, it has been stressed, for example, that 'in the Asia–Pacific region, women's rights are violated by increasingly militant assertions of religious and ethnic identity; the fact that these violations often take place through private actors is used by States as a pretext for failing to counter them as transgressions of human rights'.[33]

Besides differences in the approach to the status of women within the family originating in religious or other societal norms, the role of the family as an entity has yet to be defined in international human rights law. The International Year of the Family (1994), proclaimed by the United Nations, drew international attention to the insufficient emphasis that the family had obtained in human rights, in development, or even in population policies. The focus of human rights on the individual vested each member of the family with a set of rights, while the rights of the family as a unit remain undefined. Moreover, the earlier tendency of governments to replace traditional family functions with social provision further undermined the rights of the family as a unit. The detrimental impact of this process has become obvious in many countries where the dominant development pattern has caused the disintegration of extended families, while their functions have not been taken over by public bodies. The International Year of the Family proposed the reversal of this orientation, and implicitly a departure from the excessive individualism typical of Western Europe and North America, suggesting that 'programmes should support families in the discharge of their functions, rather than provide substitutes for such functions'.[34]

Extensive research has been carried out into factors influencing decision making on family size, and results have often pointed to old-age support in the motivation to have large families. It is significant that regional human rights instruments, those originating in Africa and in the Middle East for example, include the obligation of children to provide for their aged parents, thus incorporating into human rights family solidarity between generations. Such provisions seem alien to the Western notion of human rights, but are common in other regions. The obvious implication for the design of population policy is a broadening of the coverage of national social security systems as an indirect method of influencing decisions on family size. However, such indirect measures rarely form part of population policies, recently even less so, owing to financial stringency affecting the entire social sector in both developing and industrialized countries.

The human rights definition of an adequate living standard postulates the family, not the individual, as the bearer of this right and thus the 'unit of measurement' in defining the standard of living. The standard of living encompasses food, clothing, housing, medical care and social services. This right, as much as other economic and social rights, has been relatively disregarded in international human rights standards in terms of definitions of its nature and scope, and corresponding governmental obligations.

The right to social security is included in many international human rights instruments and, although formulations vary, the essence of this right is to secure a minimum livelihood for everybody in circumstances beyond the person's control which jeopardize his or her survival. Old-age pensions are part of most social security schemes and thus eliminate, in theory at least, the necessity of parents to rely on their children to provide for their security in old age. In practice, particularly in Africa and Asia, the coverage of social security schemes is limited to the civil service, industry and commerce, thus leaving beyond their reach the bulk of the population. The gap between governmental willingness and ability to exercise traditional family functions constitutes an important factor in family planning; failure to recognize this leads easily to ineffective population policies, which necessarily affect women because of their reproductive role.[35]

## Recognizing Equal Rights for Female Children

The low worth of the female child, evidenced in the extreme practice of 'femicide', has been made one of the principal targets in international efforts to overcome the continuing prejudice against the female part of humanity. Gender discrimination may start before birth. A girl child is considered a liability, not an asset, to the family into which she is to be born. She becomes an asset to the family into which she is married if she can bear male children. The emergence of traditional practices on the human rights agenda in the 1970s, and the subsequent broadening and deepening of the understanding of what traditional practices are, and what effects they have on women, provide a significant contribution to the design of population policies. At first, traditional practices harmful to women's health and lives had been confined to genital mutilation, but it was soon realized that they reach much further and sometimes lead to death.

The preference given to sons is a reflection of patriarchal society and is worldwide. This constitutes a fact that many would not associate with human rights. Parents who prefer a son to a daughter are not breaching any law, nor could law ever attempt to outlaw people's wishes. The preference for sons becomes an important human rights issue when it results in discrimination against female children, ultimately in femicide. Perhaps the strongest incentive to address 'son' preference within population policies comes from the World Bank, which has argued that it jeopardizes the lowering of fertility rates:

> In China the one-child policy has been challenged by an apparent preference for sons. The same bias in favour of sons exists in Korea, and has been partly responsible for keeping the total fertility from declining to replacement level. To counteract this bias, governments need public information campaigns and legal reforms of inheritance, property rights, and employment. Incentives might also be offered to one-child families with girls, such as lower educational and medical costs.[36]

The human rights movement in India placed 'son' preference in the human rights context. Indian human rights organizations addressed the use of amniocentesis (originally designed to detect genetic abnormalities of a foetus, but widely applied to determine its sex),[37] and prompted the adoption of legislation to outlaw this practice which, in fact, amounted to femicide: data revealed that female, not male, foetuses were aborted.[38] Statistical evidence of gender discrimination was gathered and became a publicly debated issue. The 1991 Indian Census revealed the effects of gender discrimination: the sex ratio decreased from 934 women per 1000 men in 1981 to 929 in 1991.[39] This relatively small decrease in the sex ratio, translated into absolute numbers, becomes alarming: estimates of 'vanished women' have reached one hundred million for Asia.[40] A study into health implications of sex discrimination suggested that causes of 'son' preference be addressed:

> Long-term measures to deal with the phenomenon of 'son' preference would include enactment and implementation of legislation against discrimination on the grounds of sex; provision of adequate social security for older people so that a son is no longer a must for security in old age; abolition of practices such as dowry and bride price; and changing laws to enable women to maintain their maiden name and pass it on to their children so that continuation of the family name is not threatened by non-birth of a son.[41]

Protection of girls from early marriage represents a good example of the need to counter a widespread and historically prevalent practice. The right of everyone to marry and to found a family is conditional upon free consent, while such consent cannot be validly given by children. Knowledge of the widespread practice of child marriages prompted the adoption of the 1962 Convention on

Consent to Marriage, Minimum Age for Marriage and Registration of Marriages.[42] This Convention has had a minuscule number of ratifications: only 49 as of 31 December 1999, too few industrialized as well as developing countries. The small number of countries bound by this Convention reflects the fact that marriages of young girls are not only widespread, but also all too rarely challenged as a human rights issue. Data reported to the United Nations, although incomplete and sometimes outdated, are illustrative of the problem: Gambia does not have any minimum age for marriage; in Kenya the minimum age is 9; eight countries keep the minimum age for girls at 12 (Chile, Ecuador, Ethiopia, Honduras, Lebanon, Sri Lanka, Trinidad and Tobago, and United Arab Emirates); in Iran it is 13; and 12 countries have the minimum age of 14 (Argentina, Bolivia, Colombia, El Salvador, Guatemala, Guyana, Madagascar, Malta, Mexico, Nicaragua, Peru and Spain). All these countries implicitly recognize that girls of compulsory school age can be married. It is indicative that Asian countries, such as China and Korea, have raised the minimum age for marriage to above 20 for girls.[43]

Law generally prescribes younger ages for marriage for women than for men, for girls than for boys. Statistics on women's age at marriage, where these are available, tend to reflect officially registered marriages in urban centres and thus report the average age at marriage of 20, or even higher. Official statistics can therefore be misleading rather than revealing. Child marriages remain regularly unrecorded and unreported, even in those countries which have enacted laws prohibiting them. Such laws often remain unenforced. *World's Women* reported: 'In Mauritania, 39% of girls are married by age 15 and 15% have already given birth. In Bangladesh, 73% of girls are married by the age 15, and 21% have at least one child.'[44] In Nigeria, which has no statutory minimum age for marriage, the fertility survey of 1981/1982 found that 25 per cent of women were married by the age of 14, 50 per cent by the age of 16, and 75 per cent by the age of 18.[45] The majority of girls thus married while they were still, according to the Convention on the Rights of the Child, children.

### Mainstreaming Women's Human Rights

The World Conference on Human Rights (Vienna, June 1993) created a precedent by including equal rights of women in the main body of its final document(s), and thus created a platform for the translation of this commitment into holding governments accountable for safeguarding women's equal rights. The Vienna Declaration and Programme of Action achieved a veritable precedent by incorporating women's human rights into the mainstream of reaffirmed human rights principles and also into the agreed programme of action for their implementation. This happened, much as with other improvements, following worldwide mobilization around equal rights for women. The sheer number of non-governmental organizations' initiatives and proposals aimed at placing women's human rights on the agenda of the 1993 World Conference was impressive. Specific proposals to redress the neglect of women's rights on the global human rights agenda came from all corners of the world. In the words of the NGO Forum which took place during the Conference: 'in all regions it has been found that the United Nations and Governments have by and large failed to promote and protect women's human rights, whether civil and political or economic, social and cultural'.[46]

The many and varied proposals also testified to the fact that demands to respect and protect women's equal rights are universal. Proposals addressed all levels, from global to individual; all actors, governmental and non-governmental, public and private; all sectors, from education and health to employment or international development cooperation, and to international migration or environmental protection; all methods of action, from legislative reform to legal literacy; last but not least, they pertained to all areas of human activity. This also demonstrated the growing awareness that:

> any strategy aimed at raising the status of women by using or confronting the law should include not only formal legal remedies and methods, but also political ones as well. Effecting desired changes in legislation requires an organized, conscious constituency, able to articulate grievances and exert influence. Drafting new legislation and building persuasive arguments to justify it are technical tasks and require legal skills and methods. Most strategies will require a combination of legal and political methods.[47]

The fact that equal rights of women are not recognized in all countries, and thus women remain victimized by *de jure* discrimination, not only unequal possibilities for the exercise of nominally equal rights, received an implicit mention in the final document of the Vienna Conference in one important aspect, namely the conflict between equal human rights and religious or customary laws which deny them. The general affirmation of the universality of human rights opened the way for its specification relating to equal rights of women in the Vienna Declaration and Programme of Action. Nevertheless, the 'escape clause' that accompanied this general reaffirmation of universality of human rights – the need to bear in mind national and regional particularities – was repeated with respect to women in the Programme of Action. It calls on states to take measures to counter practices of discrimination against women, embodied in 'intolerance and related violence based on religion or belief [...] in compliance with their international obligations and with due regard to their respective legal systems'.[48] This was followed by a reference to the rights of the child, where states were urged to 'repeal existing laws and regulations and remove customs and practices which discriminate against and cause harm to the girl-child',[49] and also relating to violence against women, where the Programme of Action calls for the 'eradication of any conflicts which may arise between the rights of women and the harmful effects of certain traditional or customary practices, cultural prejudices and religious extremism'.[50]

During the preparations for the Vienna Conference, the Commission on Human Rights adopted on 8 March 1993 its first resolution on 'integrating the rights of women into the human rights mechanisms of the United Nations', which stressed its wish 'to ensure that information concerning violations of the rights of women is integrated regularly and systematically into all United Nations mechanisms for the promotion, protection and implementation of human rights'. The Commission reminded the UN Centre for Human Rights that it had been requested to utilize gender-disaggregated data in preparing studies for the World Conference and further instructed it 'to ensure that special rapporteurs, experts and working groups are fully apprised of the particular ways in which the rights of women are violated'. The Sub-Commission on Prevention of Discrimination and Protection of Minorities recommended:

> that information on the equality and empowerment of women, and their access to equality in education, work, health and literacy, be included in States' reports to all human rights monitoring bodies and not only to the Committee on the Elimination of Discrimination against Women.[51]

Moreover, the conceptual abyss between 'women' and 'human rights' is being slowly overcome. Efforts to redress the damage caused by genderless development policies were hampered by the invisibility of gender distinctions in the data used in conventional development research and planning. Thus women's participation in the labour force was underreported, women's work ignored, women's ownership of land or access to agricultural loans unknown and wage differentials by sex impossible to document. Genderless categories such as 'peasants', 'the rural poor' or 'the landless' prevailed. Only after the gathering of gender-specific data have inequalities become visible and gender discrimination been documented. The *1989 World Survey on the Role of Women in Development* noted 'a dramatic increase of research on economic variables taking the factor of sex into account'.[52]

The search for causes of harm to women identified institutionalized discrimination against women in virtually every aspect of development: political, economic, social, cultural, and – last but not least – legal. Gender inequalities are often reflected in, and strengthened by, discriminatory laws. These legalize the denial of equal rights to women. Law has not conventionally constituted an area of primary concern in development, which has recently been redressed through increasing insistence on the recognition and protection of human rights in development. Participation in development includes taking part in decision making, not only in carrying out development projects. The recognition of women's rights therefore encompasses all aspects and all levels of development. Moreover, it spans the full range of the rights of women: civil, cultural, economic, political and social. The *Jakarta Declaration for the Advancement of Women in Asia and the Pacific* is a good example.[53] Its strategy towards participation and empowerment is based on full protection of all women's human rights as its necessary prerequisite.

> Within the [Economic and Social Commission for Asia and the Pacific] region, gender inequality remains embedded in legislation on marriage and the family legislation that defines household obligations and the intra-household distribution of authority. Inequality also persists in matters pertaining to nationality, inheritance, land tenure, ownership and control of property, agricultural co-operatives, and access to credit.[54]

The sequence of UN-organized global conferences in the 1990s makes possible a review of increasing difficulties in affirming adherence to universally applicable norms. The World Conference on Human Rights can be seen, with the benefit of hindsight, as having opened the way towards preference for regional and national standard-setting. The International Conference on Population and Development (ICPD) in Cairo, affirmed universally recognized rights, but posited national sovereignty as the ultimate guide to the implementation of all recommendations. Moreover, the Cairo document was adopted with reservations.[55] It stated that:

> the implementation of the recommendations contained in the Programme of Action is the sovereign right of each country, consistent with national laws and development priorities, with full respect for the various religious and ethical values and cultural backgrounds of its people, and in conformity with universally recognized international human rights.

The Preamble noted that, 'while the International Conference on Population and Development does not create any new international human rights, it affirms the application of universally recognized human rights standards to all aspects of population programmes', but added immediately that 'the Programme of Action will require the establishment of common ground, with full respect for the various religious and ethical values and cultural backgrounds.'[56]

The Beijing Conference conformed to the practice established at ICPD one year earlier, and included at the beginning of the Platform for Action a clause which emphasizes sovereignty in implementing recommended approaches and actions, which is accompanied by a list of potentially self-contradictory values which should guide states in translating words into deeds:

> The implementation of this Platform, including through national laws and the formulation of strategies, policies, programmes and development priorities, is the sovereign responsibility of each State, in conformity with all human rights and fundamental freedoms, and the significance of and full respect for various religious and ethical values, cultural backgrounds and philosophical convictions of individuals and their communities should contribute to the full enjoyment by women of their human rights in order to achieve equality, development and peace.[57]

The fact that intergovernmental consensus seems more difficult to reach with every subsequent global conference should not overshadow the fact that much has been accomplished in international standard-setting. The progress in tackling human rights of women during the past four decades is noticeable. While the early efforts in standard-setting were aimed against the discriminatory heritage of humanity, the 1970s marked an orientation towards 'modernity'. It was realized that development might harm women rather than benefiting them: when introduced into an unequal society, development tended to reinforce the pre-existing inequalities. The particular feature of human rights is that respect for them does not occur spontaneously; improvements in human rights are not a necessary corollary of development. Therefore human rights constitute governmental obligations.

The Fourth World Conference on Women, held in Beijing in 1995, included as its first priority area 'increasing awareness among men and women of women's rights under international conventions and national law'.[58] The range of important issues which have yet to be addressed include guarantees for equal political representation of women, attention to human rights of women in the administration of justice, and the need to abolish gender-specific criminal offences.[59] They show how far standard-setting should go in the future so as to fully address *all* gender-specific issues throughout the global human rights agenda.

The Beijing Conference gave women's human rights less prominence than had been expected, or perhaps hoped for. The most important reason for this is that human rights norms are set in treaties rather than by intergovernmental meetings, which are preceded by a lengthy process of agreeing and disagreeing, which is carried out within the framework of the existing human rights law.

## Notes

1   United Nations, Fourth World Conference on Women, Beijing, 4–15 September 1995. Press Release WOM/BEI/40 of 15 September 1995.
2   The final document consists of the Beijing Declaration and Platform for Action. The latter is divided into 12 critical areas of concern (poverty, education, health, violence, armed conflicts, economy, power sharing, mechanisms for the advancement of women, human rights, media and communications, environment and the girl child) and strategic objectives and actions outlined for each of them. United Nations (1995).
3   The final document comprises 135 pages which were adopted by consensus, and which are followed by 20 pages of reservations. Most reservations refer to those parts of the document which lay down preferred approaches to sexuality, foundation of the family and family relations, as well as sex education, and the largest number rejects interruption of pregnancy, especially abortion. Some are, however, all-encompassing, especially those which opt for religious rather than secular law relating to the entire contents covered by the Beijing Declaration and Platform for Action. A careful analysis is therefore necessary before one can identify agreement and disagreement in the final document, and such an analysis goes beyond the purpose and scope of this text.
4   All quoted provisions of international human rights instruments, including their chronological listing and a comprehensive index, can be found in Alfredsson and Tomaševski (1995).
5   Morsink (1991, pp.229–56).
6   United Nations (1991, pp.31–3).
7   Einhorn (1992, p.63).
8   The Commission placed on its agenda in 1947 a review of national legislation on the status of women, in 1952 political rights of women, and in 1954 legal rights of married women, specifically with regard to their employment and matrimonial property, which was followed in 1955 by their right to an independent domicile and exercise of parental authority. In 1957, the Commission addressed married women's access to citizenship, and in 1962 the equal right to marry. The adoption of the Declaration on the Elimination of All Forms of Discrimination against Women in 1967 provided a set of minimum standards aimed at remedying the persistence of unequal rights for women. Cf. K. Tomaševski (1993, pp.104–6).
9   Division for the Advancement of Women, The origins and institutional context of the Convention, U.N. Doc. RS/CEDAW/1992/WP.1 of 24 March 1992, p.8.
10   Byrnes (1989, p.21).
11   Letter from the Chairperson of CEDAW, U.N. Doc. A/CONF.157/PC/53 of 17 September 1992.
12   Tomaševski (1993, p.117).
13   U.N. Doc A/40/623 of 6 November 1984.
14   Objection by Mexico to a reservation made by Bangladesh upon accession,

U.N. Doc. A/40/623 of 11 January 1985; Objections by Sweden to reservations made by Bangladesh, Brazil, Egypt, Jamaica, Mauritius, New Zealand, Republic of Korea, Thailand and Tunisia, U.N. Doc. A/41/608 of 17 March 1986.

15 U.N. Doc. CEDAW/C/SR.96 of 8 April 1987, paras 61–97.

16 Report of the Sub-Commission on Prevention of Discrimination and Protection of Minorities on its forty-third session, Geneva, 5–30 August 1991, U.N. Doc. E/CN.4/Sub.2/1991/65 of 24 October 1991, pp.145–6.

17 The International Convention on the Elimination of All Forms of Racial Discrimination, adopted in 1965, had defined discrimination in a similar way to that done later in the Women's Convention. Moreover, the former Convention had introduced in its Article 1(4) the concept of 'special measures' to enable groups or individuals to ensure 'equal enjoyment or exercise of human rights and fundamental freedoms'.

18 United Nations, 'The right of everyone to own property alone as well as in association with others'. Final report submitted by Luis Valencia Rodríguez, independent expert, U.N. Doc. E/CN.4/1993/15 of 18 December 1992, paras 497 and 498.

19 The evolving international development policies are described in Tomaševski (1993, pp.189–209).

20 Violence against women migrant workers, resolution 48/110 of 20 December 1993.

21 Declaration on the elimination of violence against women, resolution 48/104 of 20 December 1993.

22 Human Rights Committee, General Comment 18 (37) non-discrimination, U.N. Doc. CCPR/C/21/Rev.1/Add.1 of 21 November 1989, para. 5.

23 These cases are discussed in Tomaševski (1995, pp.273–87).

24 Human Rights Committee. Views concerning communication N° 202/1986, *Ato del Avellanal* v. *Peru*, U.N. Doc. CCPR/C/34/D/202/1986 of 31 October 1988.

25 United Nations (1992).

26 International Labour Office (1991, p.168).

27 SIDA, *Guidelines for Activities within the Area of Population*, Stockholm, November 1990, p.3.

28 McDonough and DeSouza (1986, p.117).

29 Empowerment and status of women, Part IV (A) of the Programme of Action of the ICPD, Report of the International Conference on Population and Development, U.N. Doc. A/CONF.171/13 of 18 October 1994, p.25, para. 4.2.

30 Commitment 5, paragraphs (e) and (f), Copenhagen Declaration and Programme of Action, adopted by the World Summit for Social Development, Copenhagen, 6–12 March 1995, Advance unedited text, United Nations Information Centre for the Nordic Countries, 20 March 1995.

31 United Nations, Vienna Declaration and Programme of Action, U.N. Doc. A/CONF.157/23, p.16.

32 U.N. Doc. A/CONF.157/PC/35 of 9 April 1992, paras 5–7.

33 The Bangkok NGO Declaration on Human Rights of 27 March 1993, *Liberty: Special Issue on the UN World Conference on Human Rights*, Spring 1993, 7, para. 3(4).

34 United Nations, *1994 International Year of the Family*, Vienna, United Nations, 1991, p.8.

35 This has been discussed in more detail in Tomaševski (1994, pp.14–22, 84–88).

36 The World Bank (1984, p.178).

37 V. Patel, 'Science in the service of mass murder of female babies in India', *Women in Action*, 3, 1988, 27–8.

38  N. Dutta, 'Law relating to pre-natal diagnosis', *The Lawyers*, Bombay, August 1988, 35–7.

39  'Unwelcome sex: Census highlights effect of bias against females', *Far Eastern Economic Review*, 26 December 1991, pp.18–19.

40  N.D. Kristof (n.d.) 'Asia, vanishing point for as many as 100 million women', *International Herald Tribune*, 6 November 1991, pp.1, 7.

41  Ravindran (1986, p.15).

42  The Convention on Consent to Marriage, Minimum Age for Marriage and Registration of Marriages was adopted on 10 December 1962 and entered into force on 9 December 1964; *United Nations Treaty Series*, vol. 521, p.231.

43  United Nations, *World Population Policies*, Population Studies No. 102, and Add.1–2, New York, United Nations 1989–90, vols 1–3.

44  United Nations (1991, p.59).

45  National Population Bureau, *The Nigeria Fertility Survey 1981/82, Principal Report*, 1984.

46  NGO Forum Final Report. 'All Human Rights for All: Recommendations adopted by the Forum of Non-Governmental Organizations', *Human Rights. The New Consensus*, London, Regency Press in association with the United Nations High Commissioner for Refugees, 1994, p.234.

47  Division for the Advancement of Women of the United Nations – Women's Legal Literacy: Obstacles and Measures, U.N. Doc. EGM/IAWR/1992/WP.1 of 12 May 1992, para. 72, p.17.

48  United Nations, Vienna Declaration and Programme of Action, U.N. Doc. A/CONF.157/23, p.16.

49  Ibid., p.21.

50  Ibid., p.19.

51  Discrimination against women, resolution 1992/4 of 14 August 1992.

52  United Nations, *1989 World Survey on the Role of Women in Development*, Centre for Social Development and Humanitarian Affairs, U.N. Doc. ST/CSDHA/6, New York, 1989, p.7.

53  The mission statement of the Jakarta Declaration lays down three commitments: '(1) To promote and ensure the human rights of women at all stages of their life-cycle; (2) To create or reorient political, economic and social processes and institutions to enable women to participate fully and actively in decision-making in the family and community and at the national, regional and international levels, and (3) To empower women and men to work together as equal partners and to inspire a new generation of women and men to work together for equality, sustainable development, and peace' (Jakarta Declaration for the Advancement of Women in Asia and the Pacific, Second Asian and Pacific Ministerial Conference on Women in Development, Jakarta, 7–14 June 1994, U.N. Doc. ST/ESCAP/1411, p.5).

54  Economic and Social Commission for Asia and the Pacific, Human rights-related concerns in the Asian and Pacific region. Contribution to the World Conference on Human Rights, U.N. Doc. A/CONF.157/PC/61/Add. 7 of 22 February 1993, pp.15–16.

55  Afghanistan, Argentina, Brunei Darussalam, Dominican Republic, Ecuador, Egypt, El Salvador, Guatemala, Holy See, Honduras, Iran, Jordan, Kuwait, Libya, Malta, Nicaragua, Paraguay, Peru, Philippines, Syria, United Arab Emirates and Yemen submitted reservations.

56  Programme of Action of the International Conference on Population and Development, Report of the International Conference on Population and Development, Cairo, 5–13 September 1994, U.N. Doc. A/CONF.171/13 of 18 October 1994, pp.13–14.

57  United Nations (1995, para. 9).

58 Commission on the Status of Women, Preparations for the World Conference on Women in 1995, resolution 35/4 of 8 March 1992.
59 Report of the Ninth Nordic Seminar on Human Rights held by the Nordic Institutes of Human Rights at Lund, Sweden, 18–20 January 1993, U.N. Doc. A/CONF.157/PC/78 of 16 April 1993.

## Bibliography

Alfredsson, G. and K. Tomaševski (eds) (1995), *Thematic Guide to Human Rights of Women*, The Raoul Wallenberg Institute Human Rights Index, Volume 1, Dordrecht, Martinus Nijhoff Publishers.

Amnesty International (1995), *Human Rights are Women's Rights*, London, Amnesty International.

Broadbent, Ed. (1996), 'Women's Rights as Human Rights', Occasional Paper No. 8, January. Montreal, International Centre for Human Rights and Democratic Development.

Byrnes, A.C. (1989) 'The "other" human rights treaty body: The work of the Committee on the Elimination of Discrimination against Women', *Yale Journal of International Law*, **14**, (1).

Cook, R. (1994), *Human Rights of Women: National and International Perspectives*, Philadelphia, University of Pennsylvania Press.

Dallmeyer, G.D. (1993), *Reconceiving Reality: Women and International Law*, Washington, DC, The American Society of International Law.

Einhorn, B. (1992), 'Concepts of women's rights', in V.M. Moghadam (ed.), *Privatization and Democratization in Central and Eastern Europe and the Soviet Union: The Gender Dimension*, Helsinki, Wider, p.63.

Human Rights Watch (1995), *Global Report on Women's Human Rights*, New York, Human Rights Watch.

International Labour Office (1991), *Gender and Population in the Adjustment of African Economies: Planning for Change*, Geneva, ILO.

Interparliamentary Union (1997), *Men and Women in Politics: Democracy Still in the Making*, series 'Reports and Documents' No. 28, in English and French, Geneva, Inter-Parliamentary Union.

Kerr, J. (1993), *Ours by Right: Women's as Human Rights*, London, Zed Books.

McDonough, P. and A. DeSouza (1986), *The Politics of Population in Brazil. Elite Ambivalence and Public Demand*, Austin, University of Texas Press.

Morsink, J. (1991), 'Women's rights in the Universal Declaration', *Human Rights Quarterly*, **13**, (2), May.

Nasir, Jamil J. (1994), *The Status of Women under Islamic Law and Under Modern Islamic Legislation*, 2nd edn, The Hague, Graham and Trotman.

Ravindran, S. (1986), 'Health implications of sex discrimination in childhood. A review paper and an annotated bibliography', Doc. WHO/UNICEF/FHE 86.2.

Schuler, M.A. (ed.) (1995), *From Basic Needs to Basic Rights: Women's Claim to Human Rights*, Washington, DC, Women, Law and Development International.

Tomaševski , K. (1993), *Development Aid and Human Rights Revisited*, London, Pinter Publishers.

Tomaševski , K. (1993), *Women and Human Rights*, Women and World Development Series, London, Zed Books.

Tomaševski , K. (1994), *Human Rights in Population Policies. A Study for SIDA*, Stockholm, SIDA (Swedish International Development Authority).

Tomaševski , K. (1995), 'Women', in A. Eide, K. Krause and A. Rosas (eds) *Economic, Social and Cultural Rights. A Textbook*, Dordrecht, Martinus Nijhoff Publishers.

United Nations (1991), *The World's Women 1970–1990. Trends and Statistics*, Social Statistics and Indicators, Series K, No. 8, New York, United Nations.

United Nations (1992), *Agenda 21*, Report of the United Nations Conference on Environment and Development, Rio de Janeiro, 3–14 June, U.N. Doc. A/CONF.151/26/ Rev.1, Vol. 1, para. 24.4, p.376.

United Nations (1995), Report of the Fourth World Conference on Women, Beijing (4–15 September), UN Doc. A/CONF.177/20 of 17 October.

Wolper, A. and J. Peters (1955) *Women's Rights, Human Rights: International Feminist Perspectives*, New York, Routledge.

World Bank (1984) *World Development Report 1984*, Oxford: Oxford University Press.

# 7 The Rights of the Child

## YURI KOLOSOV

### The Child

What is a child? In most cases, the answer is that the child is an infant, a minor or an adolescent. A child is regarded as belonging to or even being the property of the family in many societies. During babyhood the family usually feels it has the duty to feed the child and care for him, to instruct him to a certain extent and to discipline him. Later the child is understood to have various duties, including going to school or assisting adults in the home. In some societies, adolescents are already treated as adults and are expected to work or even to serve in the army. Nevertheless, they are not self-supporting until they become full members of society on reaching their majority or through 'emancipation' by the family.

In rare cases, the child has rights; not only moral rights, but also legal ones. It is not always perceived that the child is not only an object of his family's rights and duties but a subject of his own rights, like every human being.

### The Child in National Laws

Until recently, national laws did not always contain a legal definition of the notion of the 'child'. Usually, all persons who do not have full legal capacity until a certain age are regarded as children. The age of full legal capacity varies from state to state. Many national legal systems recognize the limited legal capacity of children relating to various activities.[1]

Today, an increasing number of states adopt special codes or laws on the legal status of the child. It is noteworthy that they have many common features reflecting the contents of the UN Convention on the Rights of the Child.

## The Convention on the Rights of the Child

The Convention on the Rights of the Child was adopted on 20 November 1989 by the United Nations General Assembly resolution 44/25. There are 191 States Parties to the Convention, as of 31 May 1999. A number of important considerations enabled this set of human rights to be codified and recognized by states in the form of an international instrument.

Childhood is the most sensitive part of life of every human being. It is in this period of life that every individual is brought up, educated and adjusted to realities of life. The identity of the individual is formed during childhood. Children comprise about 50 per cent of the Earth's population and are its most vulnerable component. They are in practice fully dependent on adults, can be easily manipulated and are particularly susceptible to all kinds of influence, both physical and mental.

At the same time, today's children are the foundation of every society of tomorrow. The quality of forthcoming generations will reflect the conditions of their respective childhood. In the interdependent community of nations, states cannot be uninterested in the quality of societies with which they will have to coexist.

The concept of the equality of all human beings, as embodied in the Universal Declaration of Human Rights of 1948, presupposes a certain minimum of generally recognized standards in the field of the treatment of the child. The Convention on the Rights of the Child stemmed from the League of Nations Declaration of the Rights of the Child of 1924, the United Nations Declaration of the Rights of the Child of 1959, and from a whole set of international legal instruments dealing with the promotion and protection of human rights. Yet its provisions are not a mere compilation of human rights and freedoms adjusted to children; the Convention has a value of its own.

It is not by chance that it entered into force on 2 September 1990, after its ratification by 20 states within a year of its adoption by the United Nations General Assembly, and that today, ten years later, there are 191 States Parties to it. The Vienna World Conference on Human Rights of 1993, in its Declaration and Programme of Action,[2] recognized the need for universal ratification of the Convention by 1995.

Hence it is important that the Convention is known and understood by adults as well as by children themselves.[3] This goal may be achieved through various means, including the mass media. Since children will always exist as a component of society, though its composition is ever-changing (every day, new children are born and other children attain adulthood), the teaching of the rights to the child must be continual. That is why this subject must be an integral part of the university and school curricula.

## Special Characteristics of the Convention

The Convention recognizes that every human being below the age of 18 years can be called a child. This means that every such individual is entitled to enjoy all the rights covered by the Convention. There are two exceptions to this rule: in cases where national laws recognize the age of majority to be less than 18 years, the Convention is applicable to persons under such age; certain rights may be enjoyed only in a manner consistent with the evolving capacities of the child and therefore, in such cases, parents or other persons legally responsible for the child should provide appropriate direction and guidance in the exercise of their rights.

Full legal capacity is attained at majority. Under that age the child enjoys only partial legal capacities in respect to certain rights (derogation of the right). The Convention itself does not regulate this issue by establishing certain minimal ages relating to this or that right of the child. The ages for the attainment of partial legal capacity may differ in various countries. For example, the marriageable age in Austria is 16 for women and 19 for men; in Malta it is 16 for both sexes; in Romania 18 for men and 16 for women; and so on. Nevertheless, most of the rights of the child covered by the Convention are non-derogable.

The Convention on the Rights of the Child is to be understood, interpreted and implemented in the context of all existing international norms in the field of human rights, including customary, contractual, universal or regional norms. Article 41 of the Convention stipulates that its provisions shall not preclude the applicability of the norms which are more conducive to the realization of the rights of the child and which may be contained in national laws or international instruments. For example, Article 32(2) prescribes adoption of national laws establishing a minimum age or ages for admissions to employment. It should be taken into account by states that the International Labour Organisation's Convention No. 138 sets the working age at 15 years for most purposes.

As another example, Article 38 establishes that States Parties to the Convention shall refrain from recruiting any person who has not attained the age of 15 years into their armed forces. In many countries, this age is set at 18 years, or even higher.

All the rights of the child are of equal importance. The right to rest and leisure, to engage in play and recreational activities (Article 31) is no less significant than the right to life, survival and development

(Article 6) because rest and leisure, recreation and cultural activities are necessary for survival and development.

All the rights of the child are interrelated. The right to freedom of expression (Article 13) may not be fully enjoyed if the right to education (Article 28) is not implemented. The right to health and health services (Article 24) is closely linked to the right to social security, including social insurance (Article 26). Therefore the Convention should be interpreted and implemented holistically.

The Convention covers various sets of rights: civil and political; social, economic and cultural; and specific rights of children in difficult circumstances (children separated from their parents, abused and neglected children, adopted children, refugee children, disabled children, exploited children, children in armed conflicts, children in conflict with law, and so on).

The cardinal concept of the Convention is the recognition of the child as an active subject of rights rather than as the property of the family or the object of the rights of adults. Children are recognized as full members of the human family. By constituting the natural environment for the growth and well-being of children, the family is recognized as a fundamental group of society which should be afforded all necessary protection and assistance.

The Convention makes no mention of the child's duties. This does not mean that such duties are non-existent, but that the authors of the Convention presumed that the duties are normally hardly forgotten or neglected by society, and this is not the case in relation to the rights of the child. Unlike adults, children have few possibilities of protecting their rights and therefore they need special protection by law.

### The Natural Rights to be Protected

Every child has the inherent right to life (Article 6) of any human being. The difference is that the child has fewer possibilities of struggling for life and can be easily deprived of it. To live does not only mean to exist physically. The child is entitled to develop properly as an individual in society. Therefore the same article of the Convention requires that States Parties ensure, to the maximum extent possible, the survival and development of the child.

The child has the right to a name (Article 7) and therefore must be registered immediately after birth. There exist various systems of birth registration: medical, which is done immediately after birth by the hospital or maternity home officials indicating the family name; ecclesiastical, following baptism and the registration of the given name in the church records; and civil registration by authorized local municipal authorities of the given name and family name. In some countries the system of birth registration is not efficient and many children remain without birth certificates. This causes such unregistered children to be deprived of many of their human rights, since they are allegedly 'non-existent' and cannot claim these rights because of the lack of legal personality. Non-governmental organizations take care of such children in some states and arrange their registration. Elsewhere the authorities alleviate the procedure of birth registration by establishing registration centres convenient for families, for example at post offices.

The right to acquire a nationality (Article 7) is an important prerequisite for every citizen. Stateless persons are not entitled to diplomatic protection. They are normally treated as aliens in the country of their residence or domicile. The Convention relating to the Status of Stateless Persons was adopted in 1954. It entered into force on 6 June 1960, but there were only 45 States Parties to it as of 31 May 1999, which means that about 146 of the States Parties to the Convention on the Rights of the Child had no obligations *vis-à-vis* stateless persons in accordance with that Convention. The status of children without a nationality in many countries is therefore not properly regulated and they may be easily deprived of fundamental rights and freedoms.

Children may be considered as stateless in those countries where mothers are married to aliens and the child can only acquire the father's nationality in accordance with the national laws of the country of birth. At the same time, in the country of the father's nationality, legislation provides for acquiring the nationality only by those persons who were born in that country (*lex soli*). This situation can only be improved by introducing the *lex soli* principle into the legislation of all States Parties to the Convention on the Rights of the Child.

The child has the right to know his or her parents (Article 7). The problem mainly arises when the child is abandoned by the parents, or when the child is born out of wedlock, or when the parents divorce. This provision is closely interrelated with Article 8 of the Convention, which contains the obligation of states to protect basic aspects of the child's identity, that is nationality, name and family relations. States have the duty to preserve the child's identity both by law and in practice.

The right to maintain family relations with both parents in case of separation from one or both of the parents is envisaged in Article 9. The states must ensure the respect of this right unless it is contrary to the child's best interests.

## Civil, Political and Cultural Rights

The child has the right to freedom of expression, which includes freedom to seek, receive and impart information and ideas of all kinds, regardless of frontiers (Article 13), as well as the right to have access to appropriate information (Article 17). This right and possible restrictions of its exercise by law are exactly the same as those recognized with respect to adults (see Article 19 of the International Covenant on Civil and Political Rights of 1966).

The child has the right to freedom of thought, conscience and religion (Article 14). The difference from Article 18 of the International Covenant on Civil and Political Rights is that parents or legal guardians have the right and duty to provide assistance to the child in the exercise of this right in a manner consistent with the evolving capacities of the child. As with adults, children have freedom of association and peaceful assembly, and the right to protection from interference with privacy, as well as from attacks on their honour and reputation (Articles 15 and 16).

Education is one of the most important elements of a child's life. Education is the way to develop the child's personality, talents, and mental and physical abilities. Through education, the child learns about human rights and fundamental freedoms. Education is necessary to make the child aware of his or her cultural and linguistic environment, as well as about other civilizations.

Thus States Parties to the Convention recognize the right of every child to education. Education should seek to prepare the child for a responsible life in a free society; it should be realized in the spirit of understanding, peace, tolerance, equality of sexes, friendship among all peoples and respect for the natural environment.

All these values have universal importance and therefore no child should be deprived of education. The Convention stipulates that primary education should be compulsory and free to all. Different forms of secondary education should be developed with a view to making it available and accessible to every child. Vocational education and guidance should also be accessible. The disciplining of children in schools should be administered in a manner consistent with the child's human dignity, excluding corporal punishment. Where necessary, States Parties agree to promote international cooperation in matters relating to education.

Although Articles 28 and 29, dealing with the issue of education, are vital for the child's development, there are other means through which the child learns to be a member of modern society. The Convention therefore stipulates the dissemination through the mass media of proper information which is beneficial for the child, and the production and dissemination of children's books, as well as the protection of the child from information injurious to his or her well-being (Article 17).

As indicated above, the child develops at moments of leisure, through play and recreational activities, through participation in cultural life and access to the arts. This side of the child's life is a part of the educational process. States Parties have therefore agreed to respect and promote the right of the child to leisure, play and participation in cultural and artistic activities.

The child has the right to express his or her opinion freely in all matters affecting him or her. Such views must be taken into account in accordance with the age and maturity of the child (Article 12). This means, *inter alia*, that the child should be given the opportunity to be heard in judicial and administrative proceedings affecting his or her interests. However, this right should not be interpreted in a narrow sense. The child's views should be given due weight in schools, within the family and in any other circumstances where adults may take decisions affecting the child.

### Social and Economic Rights

Implementation of social and economic rights usually requires material investments. The economic situation in many countries limits the promotion of social and economic rights of the child. The Convention on the Rights of the Child contains a very important provision to that end: 'With regard to economic, social and cultural rights, States Parties shall undertake' [measures for their implementation] 'to the maximum extent of their available resources and, where needed, within the framework of international co-operation' (Article 4).

The obligation to use the available resources to the maximum extent possible requires in certain cases budgetary reallocations. Another possible source of assistance is international cooperation. Such cooperation has been arranged within the framework of the United Nations Children's Fund (UNICEF), the World Health Organization (WHO), the International Labour Organisation (ILO), United Nations Educational, Scientific and Cultural Organization (UNESCO), the United Nations High Commissioner for Refugees (UNHCR) and other United Nations organs and specialized agencies. Within this context, the role of international non-governmental organizations is not the least, and bilateral cooperation between various states should be also mentioned.

Social and economic rights of children depend on their families' well-being. Article 18 of the Convention recognizes that parents have the primary responsibility for the upbringing and development of the child. On the other hand, States Parties have the obligation to render appropriate assistance to parents in the performance of their child-rearing responsibilities and to ensure the development of institutions, facilities and services for the care of children.

The child has the right to the enjoyment of the highest attainable standard of health and to facilities for the treatment of illness and rehabilitation of health (Article 24). In accordance with this obligation, States Parties to the Convention must take measures to diminish infant and child mortality, to combat disease and malnutrition, and to ensure pre-natal and post-natal health care for mothers.

Every child is entitled to benefit from social security, including social insurance (Article 26). Every child has the right to a standard of living adequate for his or her development (Article 27). The child has the right to be protected from economic exploitation (Article 32). Children should not perform any work which may be hazardous or which interferes with education, as well as any work which may be harmful to their health or development. States have an obligation to ensure the implementation of this right through the establishment of a minimum age for admission to employment, adoption of regulations regarding conditions of employment, and imposing sanctions to ensure effective enforcement of the above-mentioned conditions.

## Fundamental General Principles

The respect and promotion of any right of the child must be implemented on the basis of four general principles underlying all the goals and objectives of the Convention on the Rights of the Child. These general principles concern non-discrimination, the best interests of the child, the right to life, survival and development, and respect for the views of the child.

All the rights of the child set forth in the Convention should be respected and ensured by states for each child within their jurisdiction (irrespective of citizenship) without discrimination of any kind on the grounds of race, colour, sex, language, religion, political or other opinion, national, ethnic or social origin, property, disability, birth or other status. The list is merely indicative and no other grounds may justify any sort of discrimination.

The differences listed in Article 2 of the Convention refer not only to children but also to their parents or legal guardians. Furthermore, the child must be protected by states against all forms of discrimination or punishment on the basis of the status, activities, expressed opinions or beliefs of the child's parents, legal guardians or family members (Article 2(2)).

Article 3 of the Convention deals with the principle of the best interests of the child. These must be a primary consideration in all actions concerning children. States Parties have the duty to ensure that the child has such protection and care as is necessary for his or her well-being.

The right to life, survival and development is reflected in Article 6 but, in fact, nearly every other provision of the Convention is closely linked to this cornerstone principle. Perhaps Article 24 is closest to the principle dealing with the inherent right to life, survival and development. This article confirms that the child has the right to the highest standard of health and medical care. No child may be deprived of access to effective health services.

The principle of respect for the views of the child is reflected in Article 12. When the child is capable of forming his or her own views, the right to express those views should be assured. The child has the right to express his or her views freely in all matters affecting him or her, and such views should be given due weight in accordance with the age and maturity of the child. In practical terms, the implementation of this right is very often affected by subjectivity. In certain circumstances the child has the ability to express views but refrains for fear of not being understood correctly or of being punished. The role of social workers and psychologists may be very important in such circumstances, in particular whenever the child is given the opportunity to be heard in any judicial and administrative proceedings.

### Protection of Children's Rights in Difficult Circumstances

Many children encounter various difficult circumstances, among which the Convention covers such cases as separation from parents (Article 9), illicit transfer and non-return (Article 11), abuse and neglect (Article 19), refugee children (Article 22), disabled children (Article 23), children of minorities or indigenous populations (Article 30), sale, trafficking and abduction (Article 35), deprivation of liberty (Article 37) and children in armed conflicts (Article 38).

Parental care and guidance are indeed vital for the child. Therefore separation of a child from the parents is admissible as the last resort only (in cases of the detention, imprisonment, exile or deportation of one or both parents). Such separation may be undertaken for the best interests of the child. The child has the right to maintain personal relations and direct contact with both parents on a regular basis. When a child and his or her parents happen to be in different countries, States Parties to the Convention should deal with applications by the child or his or her parents for family reunification in a positive, humane and expeditious manner (Article 10). To this end, the child has the right to leave any country, including his or her own, and to enter it. A child deprived of his or her family environment shall be entitled to special protection and assistance on the part of the state (Article 20). Such children should be granted alternative care, including adoption.

States Parties must take measures to combat illicit transfer and non-return of children to other countries. Besides legal, administrative and practical steps, States Parties are urged by the Convention to conclude appropriate bilateral or multilateral international agreements.

The child has the right to be protected by law from all forms of physical or mental violence, injury or abuse, neglect or negligent treatment, maltreatment or exploitation, including sexual abuse. Such protection should cover the relationship of a child with his or her parents, legal guardians or any other person who has the care of the child, for example school teachers. Preventive social programmes and judicial protection of the child should be undertaken to this end whenever necessary. Furthermore, there are many abandoned children in various parts of the world, which makes the problem of so-called 'street children' most acute.

A child seeking refugee status, or who is already a refugee, should receive appropriate protection and humanitarian assistance. A refugee child is entitled to enjoy all rights set forth in the Convention. He or she is under the protection of the special international instruments relating to refugees, including the mechanism of the United Nations High Commissioner for Refugees.

Mentally or physically disabled children deserve special protection to enable them to enjoy a full and decent life, including their active participation in the community. States must provide special care and assistance for disabled children and for those responsible for their care. Such assistance should be aimed at the fullest possible social integration and individual development of a disabled child.

Children belonging to ethnic, religious, or linguistic minorities, as well as children of indigenous origin, shall enjoy the right to their own culture, to profess their own religion, or to use their own language. This right can also be exercised in the community with other members of the same population group.

As regards the abduction or the sale of, or traffic in, children for any purpose or in any form, States Parties to the Convention agreed to prevent this criminal activity by taking all appropriate measures at national, bilateral and multilateral levels.

The problem of juvenile criminality is acute. Most often adults corrupt children and involve them in criminal activities. Sometimes the poor living conditions of families encourage juvenile criminal behaviour, which is why juvenile offenders should be primarily treated as victims in criminal cases. Nonetheless, states are facing the need to combat crimes committed by children. In accordance with the Convention, the deprivation of liberty should be regarded as the last resort. No child may be deprived of his or her liberty unlawfully or arbitrarily. The arrest, detention or imprisonment of a child should cover the shortest possible period of time. Every child deprived of liberty must be treated in a manner which takes into account the needs of persons of his or her age. Every child deprived of liberty should be separated from adults and should have the right to maintain contacts with the family, except in exceptional circumstances. These children have the right to prompt access to legal assistance. States Parties to the Convention recognize the right of children infringing penal law to be treated consistently with the children's sense of dignity. The primary goal should be the promotion of the child's reintegration into society.

The Convention urges the States Parties to establish special institutions to deal with juvenile offenders. Many states have special juvenile courts or special judges trained to deal with accused youngsters. The Convention requires the establishment of a minimum age below which children shall be presumed not to have the capacity to infringe penal law. Many states establish such ages at 14 or 15 years. Neither capital punishment nor life imprisonment without possibility of release shall be imposed for offences committed by persons below 18 years of age. It is desirable to avoid judicial proceedings and to resort to other measures for dealing with juvenile offenders.

Institutional care for children must exist in various forms, such as care, guidance and supervision orders, counselling, probation, foster care, education and vocational training, and so on.

One of the most important articles is Article 38, dealing with the issue of children in armed conflicts. Unfortunately, the modern world is not safe from military conflicts, both international and internal. In order to protect children from the effects of armed conflicts to the maximum extent possible, the Convention provides for States Parties to take all feasible measures to ensure that persons who have not attained the age of 15 years do not participate directly in hostilities. They should refrain from recruiting such persons into the armed forces. Many states believe that such an age limit should be raised to 18 years. An appropriate additional protocol to the Convention is currently under consideration.

Since children are unavoidably present in areas of military operations, the Convention requires states to respect and ensure respect for rules of international humanitarian law applicable in armed conflicts relevant to the child.[4]

Article 39 of the Convention relates to various cases of children in difficult circumstances. It reads as follows:

States Parties shall take all appropriate measures to promote physical and psychological recovery and social reintegration of a child victim of: any form of neglect, exploitation, or abuse; torture or any other form of cruel, inhuman or degrading treatment or punishment; or armed conflicts. Such recovery and reintegration shall take place in an environment which fosters the health, self-respect and dignity of the child.

## Who is Responsible for Children's Rights?

The answer to this question is hardly simple. The Convention establishes that: 'States Parties shall undertake all appropriate legislative, administrative, and other measures for the implementation of the rights recognized in the [...] Convention' (Article 4). This means that such responsibility is vested in heads of state and governments, national parliaments, local governments, various ministries and administrations (health, social security, interior, defence, education, culture and many other governmental structures). In many states, coordinating committees have been established within either the parliamentary or the governmental systems. In some countries special commissioners (or ombudsmen) monitor respect for children's rights. National and international non-governmental organizations also play a significant role in promoting the rights of the child and often establish special funds to support the implementation of children's rights.

Parents or legal guardians have the primary responsibility for the upbringing and development of the child and therefore States Parties to the Convention agree to: 'render appropriate assistance to parents and legal guardians in the performance of their child-rearing responsibilities' (Article 18).

Children themselves should feel responsible for the promotion of their rights. There are various known forms of active children's participation in protecting their own rights: committees of school children, children's parliaments, children's local governments and so on. To achieve these goals, every member of society must be aware of children's rights. Article 42 of the Convention states: 'States Parties undertake to make the principles and provisions of the Convention widely known, by appropriate and active means, to adults and children alike.' The role of the mass media should not be underestimated in this connection. The rights of the child should also be included in curricula in schools and pedagogical institutions.

Humanity as a whole is responsible for the implementation of the rights of the child. The adoption by the United Nations of the Convention on the Rights of the Child is only the first step on this endless road. The actual implementation of these rights on a daily basis in every corner of the Earth is the noble goal of the international community.

## The Committee on the Rights of the Child

The Committee on the Rights of the Child was established in accordance with Articles 43 to 45 of the Convention in order to examine the progress made by States Parties in achieving the realization of obligations under the Convention.

The Committee comprises ten experts competent in the field covered by the Convention. Elected from the list of candidates nominated by States Parties, the members of the Committee serve in their personal capacity. They are fully independent and impartial. The first Committee was elected at the first conference of States Parties on 28 February 1991 for a term of four years. The first ten members were nationals of Barbados, Brazil, Burkina Faso, Egypt, Peru, Philippines, Portugal, Sweden, the USSR and Zimbabwe. After two years, five of them were re-elected (their term expired after two years as a result of the chairman of the Committee choosing by lots).[5] A further five members stood for re-election in February 1995, when nationals of Israel and the Russian Federation became members of the Committee, replacing the nationals of Peru and the USSR.[6]

The composition of the Committee is multidisciplinary, including experts in such fields as law, medicine, economy, sociology, education and international law. Their principal task is to consider national reports of States Parties on the measures adopted to give effect to the rights of children and on the progress made in the enjoyment of such rights. The reports are submitted by the State Party concerned, initially after two years from the entry into force of the Convention, and thereafter every five years.

The Committee meets three times a year in Geneva and considers six to eight reports at each session. The performance of the functions of the Committee is supported by the staff of the Office of the High Commissioner for Human Rights (OHCHR) in Geneva. The Committee elects its chairperson, three vice-chairpersons and its rapporteur every two years.

The Committee has adopted rules of procedure and general guidelines for drafting national reports. National reports indicate existing factors and difficulties affecting the fulfilment of obligations under the Convention. They must contain sufficient information to enable the Committee to understand the situation concerning children's rights in a given country.

The reports are presented to the Committee by competent national delegations, after a constructive dialogue between the delegation and the members of the Committee, who adopt concluding observations and recommendations to the State Party concerned.

The United Nations specialized agencies, UNICEF and other United Nations organs, as well as national and international non-governmental organizations, are represented at the meetings of the Committee. Every two years the Committee submits its report to the United Nations General Assembly, which adopts resolutions relating to its activities.

The Committee has the right to request additional information relating to the implementation of the Convention from States Parties, to invite competent international organizations to provide expert advice on the implementation of the Convention, to suggest to competent international bodies that they provide interested states with technical advice and assistance, to recommend to the United Nations General Assembly that the Secretary-General undertake special studies on specific issues relating to the rights of the child, and to make general comments on various issues covered by the Convention.

The Committee convenes annually informal regional meetings with the support of UNICEF. Such regional meetings have been held in Latin America, South-East Asia, Africa and South Asia. These meetings have enabled the Committee to become familiar with the realities of children's lives in a number of countries, to meet local non-governmental organizations working in this field, and to have fruitful dialogues with central and local authorities of receiving states.

## The World Summit for Children (1991)

The World Summit for Children was convened in New York in 1991. It adopted the *World Declaration on the Survival, Protection and Development of Children and Plan of Action*. This important document contains concrete goals to be achieved before the end of the twentieth century in various fields of children's lives.

On the basis of the World Summit Plan of Action, adopted and signed by many heads of states and governments, national action plans for 1991–2000 were adopted. These plans aimed at reducing infant and maternal mortality rates, reducing malnutrition and illiteracy, providing access to safe drinking water and to basic education, combating devastating emergencies resulting from natural disasters and armed conflicts, and solving the problem of children in extreme poverty.

## The World Conference on Human Rights

The World Conference on Human Rights (Vienna, 14–25 June, 1993) paid great attention to children's rights in the Vienna Declaration and Programme of Action adopted on 25 June 1993,[7] Section B.4 of which deals with the rights of the child.

The World Conference urged universal ratification of the Convention on the Rights of the Child by 1995 and its effective implementation by States Parties through the adoption of all the necessary legislative, administrative and other measures, and the allocation to the maximum extent of available resources (paragraph 21 of the Vienna Declaration).[8]

The Conference recognized the need to strengthen national and international mechanisms and programmes for the defence and protection of children. International cooperation and solidarity should be promoted to support the implementation of the Convention on the Rights of the Child. It also agreed that the rights of the child should be a priority in the United Nations system-wide action on human rights.

The World Conference urged all states to address the acute problem of children under especially difficult circumstances: exploited and abused children, female infanticide, harmful child labour, sale of children and organs, child prostitution, child pornography and other forms of sexual abuse. The Conference recommended that the situation of children and their human rights be regularly reviewed and monitored by all relevant organs and mechanisms of the United Nations system.

## Conclusions

The Convention on the Rights of the Child sets up universally recognized principles and norms as minimal standards for children's rights. It should be emphasized that, in accordance with the Convention, every child, without any exception whatsoever, has the right to benefit from these standards. By implementing children's rights, society proves its commitment to future generations.

The effectiveness of the Convention will depend, to a great extent, on a widespread knowledge of the Convention by adults and children alike, as well as on the support by all of the implementation of its provisions. It is of crucial importance that mass media, local and central authorities, and national and international non-governmental organizations contribute to the dissemination of information on the Convention. Everybody has a role to play in ensuring that the letter and spirit of the Convention become reality.

The World Conference on Human Rights emphasized the importance of incorporating human rights into educational programmes.[9] This is essential with regard to the right of the child.

The Committee is the main focal point for international efforts to translate the provisions of the Convention into everyday practice in every state. It identifies problems inhibiting the fullest possible realization of the rights of the child, points out possible solutions and encourages the mobilization of resources to respond to the needs of children.

The States Parties to the Convention have the duty to translate its provisions into national laws, plans of action and actual everyday practices. The rights of the child must be the priority of modern civilization.

## Notes

1  Ages at which children are legally entitled to carry out a series of acts in Council of Europe Member States; Strasbourg, 7 November 1994, Doc. CDPS III.8 (94) 1 REV.
2  UN Doc. A/CONF.157/23, 12 July 1993.
3  See Article 42 of the Convention on the Rights of the Child.
4  See the Geneva Convention relative to the Protection of Civilian Persons in Time of War of 14 August 1949 and the Additional Protocols thereto of 1977.
5  To ensure the succession in the deliberations of the Committee it is important that as a result of the second and subsequent elections not all members become new ones. To avoid such probability Art. 43, para. 6 of the Convention establishes that the term of five of the members elected at the first election shall expire at the end of two years. Those five were chosen by lot by the Chairman of the meeting of States Parties immediately after the first election.
6  After the elections in 1999 the following States Parties are represented by the experts: Brazil, Burkina Faso, Egypt, Finland, Indonesia, Israel, Italy, Lebanon, the Netherlands and South Africa.
7  UN Doc. A/CONF. 157/23, 12 July 1993.
8  As of November 1999 there are 191 States Parties to the Convention (only Somalia and the USA have not yet ratified it).
9  Ibid., para. 33.

## Bibliography

Alston, Ph. (ed.) (1994), *The Best Interests of the Child – Reconciling Culture and Human Rights*, Oxford, Clarendon Press.
*Bulletin of Human Rights* (1992), 'The rights of the child', New York, United Nations Centre for Human Rights, p.82.
Children's Rights Centre, University of Ghent (1996), *Monitoring Children's Rights*, ed. Eugeen Verhellen, The Hague/Boston/London, Martinus Nijhoff Publishers.
Hammarberg, Thomas (1994), 'Making Reality of the Rights of the Child', Rädda Barnan (Swedish Save the Children), p.26. Includes the text of the Convention on the Rights of the Child.

Van Bueren, Geraldine (1995), *The International Law on the Rights of the Child*, Dordrecht, Martinus Nijhoff Publishers/Kluwer Academic Publishers.

Veerman, P. (1992) *The Rights of the Child and the Changing Image of Childhood*, The Hague/Boston/London, Martinus Nijhoff Publishers.

Verhellen, Eugeen (1994), *Convention on the Rights of the Child*, Louvain/Apeldoorn, Garant.

*Vienna Declaration and Programme of Action* (1993), World Conference on Human Rights, UN Doc. A/CONF.157/23, 12 July 1993.

# 8 The Rights of Persons Belonging to Minorities

## HURST HANNUM

## Introduction

The somewhat awkward title of this chapter reflects the difficulties which individual governments and the world community have had in defining the rights of a particular class of people; that is, those who belong to groups which are distinguished from the rest of society by characteristics such as language, religion, ethnicity and culture. Unlike human rights, which belong to all individuals, or inherently collective rights (such as the right of peoples to self-determination or of states to diplomatic immunity or freedom of the high seas), the rights of minorities[1] apply only to some individuals who happen to belong to a particular kind of group known as a 'minority'.

Many vulnerable categories of people have been singled out for protection by the international community in the past 50 years, as more specific norms have been developed to complement the general norms found in the Universal Declaration of Human Rights. Among these categories are workers, refugees, women, prisoners, indigenous peoples, children, disabled persons and migrant workers; measures against discrimination on the basis of race and religion have also been adopted.

Although ethnic and other minorities have suffered historically from discrimination and repression, they were not among the vulnerable groups with whose rights the international community was concerned until very recently. In light of the attention paid to minorities in the period from 1919 until the outbreak of the Second World War, as well as the proliferation of human rights norms since 1945, this failure to develop international norms to protect minorities seems incongruous. Why has the world been reluctant to address this particular issue?

First, the concept of 'minorities' does not fit easily within the theoretical paradigm of the state, at least as the state has been defined in the individual social-contract theory of Western democracies or the class-based precepts of Marxism. Under these two views, the state is seen as a collection of shifting coalitions founded either on individual self-interest or on the economic interests of classes; neither takes account of ethnic, religious or linguistic ties.

Similarly, the heterogeneity of states in the modern world runs counter to the theory of the nation-state as it developed in the nineteenth century. Both older and more recently independent states have largely accepted the rhetoric of 'one people-one state', with little concern for the strong national or cultural ties which exist below the level of the often artificial 'sovereign' state and its people. As a result, 'nation building' in the 1960s and 1970s (more accurately described as state-building) rarely included respect for diversity among its goals, and few states adopted constitutional or other provisions which recognized that minorities might need special protection.

Third, there is a fundamental fear on the part of all countries, and especially newer states, that the recognition of minority rights may encourage fragmentation or separatism, thus undermining national unity and the requirements of national development. Despite the fact that international law has insisted that minorities have no right of self-determination and has never defined a legal right to secession, states fear that recognizing differences among ethnic communities or any form of 'group' rights might make it impossible to forge a larger, multicultural unity which encompasses all of the state's citizens.

Finally, one must recognize the unpleasant fact that widespread discrimination and intolerance based on religion and ethnicity continue to exist, and minority rights are unlikely to be taken seriously in such an environment. This intolerance exists in all regions of the world and in states at all stages of economic development. It may be fanned by dictators and democrats alike to serve narrow political interests or to identify convenient scapegoats. Without entering into a discussion of whether intolerance is inherent in the human species, it seems clear that prejudice and fear of 'the other' often are present, even prior to the violent exploitation of those fears by 'ethnic entrepreneurs' who can arise from within both majority and minority populations.

## Historical Developments

The reluctance to consider minorities as worthy of particular attention is only a phenomenon of the second half of the twentieth century, which has recently begun to change. For example, most early empires considered at least religious minorities worthy of recognition.[2] The 'millet' system which developed under the Ottoman Empire allowed religious communities a degree of personal and cultural autonomy, although it has been observed that the millets were 'the solution devised by a government that did not know what nationality meant and, therefore, was unfamiliar with the majority–minority concept'.[3] The development of autonomous, religious-based communities was also consistent with Koranic injunctions of tolerance for other religions, and large non-Muslim communities continued to flourish throughout the Ottoman Empire.[4]

In Europe, international protection of minorities can be traced back to the Treaty of Westphalia in 1648, under the terms of which the parties agreed to respect the rights of certain religious minorities within their jurisdiction. However, given the historical congruence of religious and secular authority prior to this period, such agreements could just as easily be seen as recognizing the power of certain political groups, rather than guaranteeing religious rights *per se*.

In the nineteenth century, the development of nationalism in Europe was based on the theory that political power was best exercised by groups which shared ethnic or linguistic ties.[5] 'Nations' sought to establish a separate political identity, whether by incorporating peoples spread over many countries (Germany, Italy) or by demanding greater political power for groups which had formerly been considered as minorities within existing empires (Greece, Hungary, Serbia, Poland, the Baltic States, and others).

The overriding concern in the nineteenth century with nationalism and the protection of cultural, linguistic and ethnic minorities led to a conscious and comprehensive attempt to protect minorities in the early twentieth century, with the adoption of the so-called 'minority treaties' at the end of the First World War and their monitoring by the League of Nations.[6] These treaties, adopted in 1919 or soon thereafter, fell into three categories, although the substantive protections included in each were similar.[7] The first group of treaties included those imposed upon the defeated states of Austria, Hungary, Bulgaria and Turkey. The second included either new states created out of the dissolution of the Ottoman Empire or states whose boundaries were altered, at least in part, to respond to the demands of ethnic or linguistic groups; in this category were Czechoslovakia, Greece, Poland, Romania and Yugoslavia. Finally, special provisions relating to minorities were included in the international regimes established in the Åland Islands, Danzig, the Memel Territory and Upper Silesia.

Among the protections commonly included in the first two categories of treaties were the right to equality of treatment and non-discrimination; the right to citizenship (although a minority group member could opt to retain another citizenship if desired); the right to use one's own language; the right of minorities to establish and control their own charitable, religious and social institutions; a state obligation to provide 'equitable' financial support to minority schools (in which primary school instruction would be in the minority language) and other institutions; and recognition of the supremacy of laws protecting minority rights over other statutes.[8]

A major advance of this period was the legitimization of international interest in protecting minority rights, evidenced by the supervisory role of the League of Nations in monitoring the treaties.[9] The rather cumbersome mechanism established by the League to fulfil this role began with the filing of a petition with the League's secretariat, which was forwarded to the government concerned for comment. The petition was next considered by a 'Committee of Three', which consisted of the President of the League Council and two other Council members. The procedure was confidential, but minority complaints could ultimately be raised publicly before the Council of the League itself.

There have been extensive critiques of the minority treaties which need not be repeated here, and there can be little doubt about their ultimate failure.[10] Neither the Committee nor the Council had any power of enforcement, and it appears that there was a general bias in favour of governments – although such weaknesses are no more debilitating than those from which many present-day human rights monitoring bodies also suffer.

> The fate of the League minority system was largely determined by its international political context. The problem of minorities was not a technical matter which could be handled in routine fashion by an agency isolated from the vicissitudes of political conflicts; it was a political problem of great moment, and it could be solved only in conjunction with other political problems. When the League failed to cope with the factors making for the disintegration of the world order, the collapse of the minority system was inevitable; it was an integral part of the League, and its destiny could not be divorced from that of the League.[11]

Nevertheless, the result of the Versailles Treaty was a map of Europe which did more closely approach the theoretical goal of a collection of true nation-states than did pre-war Europe. While approximately half of the population of Europe were 'minorities' in 1914, only one-quarter were minorities in 1919. Albania, Bulgaria, Estonia, Hungary, Latvia, Lithuania, Poland and Romania had ethnic majorities, while Czechoslovakia and Yugoslavia had dominant, if not majority, ethnic groups.[12]

Outside Europe, formal concern with minority issues was less common, although indigenous federations or empires continued to grant varying degrees of autonomy to many nations or ethnic groups within them. Colonial empires, on the other hand, were notorious for ignoring ethnic, linguistic, and other 'national' considerations, leaving such complexities to be dealt with by the independent states which emerged from decolonization. While ethnic groups in Africa and Asia were often set against one another by colonial powers, there seems to have been no concern for the protection of 'minorities' *per se* – unless it was the consolidation and protection of the privileges of the white colonist.[13]

One of the few examples of non-European legal provisions relating to minorities is the 1926 Lebanese Constitution, which provided for proportional legislative representation for seven religious groups, including one labelled 'minorities'; in some ways, this might be considered a natural extension of the Ottoman millet system. In contrast, the traditional immigrant destinations of North and South America and Australia had an individualistic orientation which left little room for concern with the rights of minority groups; the United States concept of the 'melting pot' was perhaps typical in assuming that assimilation would be the desired and inevitable fate of new immigrant groups.

The existence of German-speaking minorities outside Germany had provided one excuse for Hitler's aggression in the 1930s, and there was thus little concern for the rights of 'national minorities' on the part of the victorious Allies after the Second World War. The Charter of the United Nations does not specifically mention minority rights. Instead, emphasis was placed on the importance of respect for (individual) human rights 'for all without distinction as to race, sex, language, or religion'[14] and the principle of (collective) 'self-determination of peoples'.[15]

The drafters of the UN Charter seemed to assume (1) that European and other minorities would be satisfied if their individual rights, particularly those of equality and non-discrimination, were respected; and (2) that the principle of self-determination would be adequate to resolve the larger problem of colonial territories. Despite the disastrous consequences for the individual victims of, for example, the Greek–Turkish population 'exchange' of 1920–22, migration became the preferred solution for post-1945 European minorities; it was largely the people (especially Germans) who moved, not the boundaries.[16] Unfortunately, there is thus ample historical precedent for the solution of 'ethnic cleansing' which re-emerged in the former Yugoslavia in the 1990s.

There were occasional exceptions to this general refusal to consider minority problems *per se*, although such ad hoc initiatives lacked the regular international supervision offered by the League of Nations. The German-speaking minority in the Italian South Tyrol, for example, was the subject of a 1946 agreement between Italy and Austria. The Austrian State Treaty, which re-established Austria within its pre-1938 borders, contains specific provisions for the protection of the Slovene and Croat minorities. The UN proposal for a Free Territory of Trieste and the UN-approved establishment of an autonomous Eritrea federated with Ethiopia were also designed to address minority situations, although each envisaged a greater degree of political autonomy than would traditionally have been reserved to a minority group.

Another important post-war example of the recognition of the vulnerability of minority groups was the adoption of the International Convention on the Prevention and Punishment of the Crime of Genocide in 1948.[17] The Genocide Convention is directed specifically against the destruction of national, racial, ethnic and religious minorities *per se*, as opposed to addressing even mass violations of the rights of individuals.

The 1948 Universal Declaration of Human Rights makes no specific mention of minority rights, and a separate part of the same resolution (ominously titled 'fate of minorities') noted accurately, if somewhat disingenuously, that 'it was difficult to adopt a uniform solution for this complex and delicate question [of minorities], which had special aspects in each State in which it arose'.[18] The UN Commission on Human Rights did establish a Sub-Commission on Prevention of Discrimination and Protection of Minorities, but early attempts by the Sub-Commission to address minority issues were essentially rebuffed by the Commission.[19]

In 1960, UNESCO adopted the Convention Against Discrimination in Education, which recognizes the right of members of national minorities to carry on their own educational activities, including the maintenance of schools and the use or teaching of their own language.[20] However, the latter right is dependent upon 'the educational policy of each State' and the general right to minority education is not to prevent minority group members 'from understanding the culture and language of the community as a whole and from participating in its activities, or [to be exercised in a manner] which prejudices national sovereignty'.[21]

Drafting of binding international agreements to implement the Universal Declaration began soon after the Declaration's adoption, and Article 27 of the International Covenant on Civil and Political Rights does specifically address the issue of minority rights. It provides, in full:

> In those States in which ethnic, religious or linguistic minorities exist, persons belonging to such minorities shall not be denied the right, in community with the other members of their group, to enjoy their own culture, to profess and practise their own religion, or to use their own language.

The Covenant addresses only minimal, traditional minority rights, that is, cultural, religious and linguistic rights. The fact that rights are granted to 'persons belonging to such minorities' rather than to minority groups themselves is an indication of the individualistic orientation of the Covenant, as well as its reluctance to recognize the rights of groups which had yet to be satisfactorily defined.[22]

Often forgotten in discussions of minority rights is the International Convention on the Elimination of All Forms of Racial Discrimination, which entered into force in 1969 and has been ratified by approximately 150 states.[23] 'Racial discrimination' under the Convention is defined in Article 1 as any distinction 'based on race, colour, descent, or national or ethnic origin' which impairs the exercise of human rights. Article 2 of the Convention requires, *inter alia*, that parties take, in appropriate circumstances, 'special and concrete measures to ensure the adequate development and protection of certain racial groups or individuals belonging to them, for the purpose of guaranteeing them the full and equal enjoyment of human rights and fundamental freedoms'.[24] An analogous provision is found in the UNESCO Declaration on Race and Racial Prejudice.[25]

The UN Sub-Commission on Prevention of Discrimination and Protection of Minorities was finally able to address the issue of minorities in greater depth in the mid-1970s. Its special rapporteur, Francesco Capotorti, completed in 1978 what has remained the leading study on discrimination against minorities.[26] The Sub-Commission subsequently suggested the preparation of a Declaration on the Rights of Minorities, and a draft declaration was submitted to the Commission on Human Rights by Yugoslavia in 1979. A revised Yugoslav draft was put forward in 1981, and the Commission considered the draft declaration throughout the succeeding decade.

The Declaration on the Rights of Persons belonging to National or Ethnic, Religious or Linguistic Minorities was finally completed and adopted by the General Assembly in 1992.[27] There is little doubt that progress on the Declaration was greatly aided by the end of East–West rivalry, although it is ironic that it was completed after the disintegration of its original sponsoring state, Yugoslavia. While it continues the individualistic orientation of Article 27 of the International Covenant on Civil and Political Rights by referring to 'the rights of persons' belonging to minorities, the Declaration does expand on existing provisions and contains progressive language related to minority participation in the political and economic life of the state. In addition, the Preamble recognizes that protecting minority rights will 'contribute to the political and social stability of States in which they live' and, in turn, 'contribute to the strengthening of friendship and co-operation among peoples and States'.

Among the more noteworthy provisions of this relatively short declaration are the following:

### Article 1

1.  States shall protect the existence and the national or ethnic, cultural, religious and linguistic identity of minorities within their respective territories, and shall encourage conditions for the promotion of the identity. [...]

### Article 2

2.  Persons belonging to minorities have the right to participate effectively in cultural, religious, social, economic and public life.

3. Persons belonging to minorities have the right to participate effectively in decisions on the national and, where appropriate, regional level concerning the minority to which they belong or the regions in which they live, in a manner not incompatible with national legislation.

### Article 4

2.  States shall take measures to create favourable conditions to enable persons belonging to minorities to express their characteristics and to develop their culture, language, religion, traditions and customs, except where specific practices are in violation of national law and contrary to international standards.

It was not until 1995 that the Commission on Human Rights created a mechanism to monitor observance of the Declaration, when it authorized the Sub-Commission to establish a five-member working group to 'review the promotion and practical realization' of the Declaration, 'examine possible solutions to problems involving minorities [and recommend] further measures, as appropriate, for the promotion and protection of the rights of persons belonging to national or ethnic, religious and linguistic minorities'.[28]

Other UN initiatives which have contributed to developing standards for the protection of minorities include the adoption of the 1981 Declaration on the Elimination of All Forms of Intolerance and Discrimination Based on Religion or Belief;[29] the appointment of special rapporteurs by the Commission on Human Rights and its Sub-Commission in the 1980s to consider specific aspects of religious intolerance and discrimination; and a 1993 report by the Sub-Commission on 'the possible ways and means of facilitating the peaceful and constructive solution of problems involving minorities'.[30]

Just as Europe was the centre of concern with minority rights from the mid-nineteenth century until the Second World War, it is Europe which has devoted the most attention to the issue of minority rights since the end of the Cold War in the late 1980s. Perhaps spurred by renewed concerns over 'ethnic' conflicts in both Eastern and Western

Europe, European governments have attempted to set new standards for minority rights and have at least begun to devise new means of monitoring those standards.

The first indication that agreement on an expanded definition of minority rights was possible came in 1990, when a Final Document was adopted by consensus at the Copenhagen meeting of the Conference on the Human Dimension of the Conference on Security and Co-operation in Europe (CSCE).[31] This remarkable document (which also contains detailed provisions relating to democracy, the rule of law and other human rights) was drafted and agreed to in only six weeks, and it represented the first detailed articulation of minority rights by governments since the post-First World War minorities treaties. It addressed, in particular, minority rights in the areas of language use, education and political participation, each of which is discussed further in the next section.

Two years later, the CSCE (known since 1995 as the Organization on Security and Co-operation in Europe (OSCE)) created the position of High Commissioner on National Minorities, in order to provide '"early warning" and, as appropriate, "early action" at the earliest possible stage in regard to tensions involving national minority issues that have the potential to develop into a conflict within the CSCE area, affecting peace, stability, or relations between participating States'.[32] Although the High Commissioner's mandate is to prevent conflict rather than protect minority rights *per se*, his interventions thus far appear to have contributed to both goals.[33]

In recent years, it has almost appeared as though the Council of Europe was competing with the CSCE to see which organization could most quickly define rights to protect minorities and establish procedures to implement those rights. In 1992, the Council of Europe adopted and opened for ratification a Charter on the Protection of Minority and Regional Languages.[34] Modelled on the European Social Charter, its provisions offer a wide range of guarantees from among which states may choose the level of obligations they are willing to accept. The following year, the Parliamentary Assembly recommended that a protocol on minority rights be added to the European Convention of Human Rights.[35] A more ambitious Framework Convention for the Protection of National Minorities was adopted in 1994,[36] and entered into force in February 1998.

Of course, most minority issues continue to be dealt with through domestic legislation or on a bilateral basis, when national or other minorities inhabit a territory which straddles recognized international boundaries.[37]

### The Current Content of Minority Rights

Most recent instruments concerning minority rights have taken the form of 'soft law', that is, declarations or resolutions which constitute solemn political commitments but which do not create binding legal obligations. However, as readily demonstrated by the political impact of the CSCE since 1975 and many other international human rights instruments, political commitments can sometimes be as influential as legally binding treaties. What is significant is that these documents, whether universal or regional, provide evidence that there is an emerging consensus over at least the minimum content of internationally recognized minority rights. This section outlines the substance of those rights.

Two preliminary questions must be addressed before the content of the current rights of minorities can be identified. The first issue is that of defining a 'minority' or its members; the second is whether states' obligations with respect to minorities are limited to non-interference and non-discrimination, or whether states may be under a more demanding obligation to take affirmative measures to promote minority cultures.

The difficulties in arriving at an agreed definition of 'minority' have frequently prevented substantive consideration of minority rights, and the adoption of the Minorities Declaration only became possible after a decision was taken to proceed with the Declaration without defining the persons to whom it would apply. Even if there were agreement on a general definition of 'minority', the various instruments speak of different kinds of minorities, including national, ethnic, religious and linguistic minorities.[38] A final related issue is the distinction between protecting 'minorities' *per se* and protecting 'persons belonging to' minority groups.

It should first be recognized that definitional questions are important only if they carry with them legal or political consequences. In the case of minorities, emerging international norms would obviously benefit groups which fall within their scope, while they would be unavailable to groups considered to be only political, regional or social groups. However, there are also some potentially negative consequences to being classified as a minority; for example, 'minorities' do not enjoy any right to self-determination, while 'peoples' do enjoy that right.[39]

The most widely cited definition of 'minority' is probably that proposed by Francesco Capotorti. In his seminal 1979 report, he defined a minority as a group:

> numerically inferior to the rest of the population of a State, in a non-dominant position, whose members – being nationals of the State

– possess ethnic, religious or linguistic characteristics differing from those of the rest of the population and show, if only implicitly, a sense of solidarity, directed towards preserving their culture, traditions, religion, or language.[40]

In 1984, during the course of the deliberations which would eventually lead to adoption of the Minorities Declaration, the Commission on Human Rights requested the Sub-Commission to explore again the issue of defining 'minority'. After surveying various national and international precedents, Sub-Commission member Jules Deschenes submitted the following definition, which did not differ substantially from that suggested in the earlier Francesco Capotorti report:

A group of citizens of a State, constituting a numerical minority and in non-dominant position in that State, endowed with ethnic, religious or linguistic characteristics which differ from those of the majority of the population, having a sense of solidarity with one another, motivated, if only implicitly, by a collective will to survive and whose aim is to achieve equality with the majority in fact and in law.[41]

The Jules Deschenes proposal was simply forwarded to the Commission without having been approved by the Sub-Commission, and the Commission's working group eventually decided to postpone further consideration of definitional questions and to proceed to elaborate the substantive articles of the draft declaration. At the very least, however, Capotorti and Deschenes reflect the consensus that any definition of minority must include both objective factors (the existence of shared ethnicity, language, religion or similar cultural traits) and subjective factors (individuals must identify themselves as members of a minority group).[42] Whether or not a minority exists is a question of fact and does not depend on a formal determination by the state.[43]

Article 27 of the International Covenant on Civil and Political Rights refers only to 'ethnic, religious or linguistic' minorities. Instruments adopted by the Conference on Security and Co-operation in Europe and the Council of Europe, on the other hand, refer only to 'national' minorities. The Minorities Declaration has the broadest scope, encompassing persons belonging to 'national or ethnic, religious and linguistic minorities'; the Declaration also refers to protecting 'cultural' identity. However, there has been no consistent attempt to claim that different types of minorities possess different rights.

The Human Rights Committee's General Comment on Article 27 addresses definitional issues only indirectly. It observes in a cursory manner that 'it is not relevant to determine the degree of permanence that the term "exist" connotes', and then goes on to adopt the expansive view that Article 27 applies to everyone belonging to one of the named categories of minorities and present within a country, including 'migrant workers or even visitors'.[44]

The Committee's comments include no reference to relevant *travaux préparatoires* of the Covenant to support its conclusions, and there is no further attempt to clarify which groups fall within or outside the scope of Article 27. The General Comment appears to represent the personal views of Committee members as much as an authoritative interpretation of the actual text of the Covenant.[45]

As noted above, only 'national' minorities are specifically protected under the various European instruments, with the exception of the Charter for Regional or Minority Languages. The only definition of 'national minority' included in any of the texts is that proposed by the Parliamentary Assembly of the Council of Europe, and it, too, includes both objective and subjective criteria:

> the expression 'national minority' refers to a group of persons in a State who:
> (a) reside on the territory of that State and are citizens thereof;
> (b) maintain long-standing, firm and lasting ties with that State;
> (c) display distinctive ethnic, cultural, religious or linguistic characteristics;
> (d) are sufficiently representative, although smaller in number than the rest of the population of that State or of a region of that State;
> (e) are motivated by a concern to preserve together that which constitutes their common identity, including their culture, their traditions, their religion or their languages.[46]

The question of whether 'minority rights' are essentially group rights or individual rights may be of theoretical interest, but the practical implications of the debate are more difficult to discern. For example, Article 27 of the Covenant and all other intergovernmental instruments relating to minorities apply formally only to 'persons belonging to' minorities, but Article 1 of the Minorities Declaration does oblige states to protect 'the existence and [...] identity of minorities within respective territories', not just individual members of minorities.

The very concept of a 'minority' implies a community or group, and the reference in international instruments to the rights of 'persons' should be understood primarily as a jurisdictional rather than a substantive limitation. For example, if rights were accorded only to minority groups *qua* groups, difficult questions might arise as to who was entitled to represent the minority and what persons should be considered to be members of the minority. In general, it is easier (and more supportive of the underlying rights) to adopt the individually oriented approach of the Covenant and other documents, under which any aggrieved member of a minority may complain about alleged violations of his or her rights.[47]

Similar observations apply to distinctions among the various categories of minorities mentioned above: national, ethnic, religious, linguistic and cultural minorities. These terms should be seen as essentially descriptive rather than as defining precise categories of groups for the purpose of recognizing rights for some and denying them to others.[48]

The second preliminary issue which is relevant to all minority rights is the extent to which states are under a positive obligation to promote such rights, as opposed to a merely negative obligation not to interfere with or impede development of a minority's culture. Article 27 of the International Covenant on Civil and Political Rights is phrased in the negative, that is, minorities 'shall not be denied' rights by the state. However, after noting that the rights set forth in Article 27 'depend in turn on the ability of the minority group to maintain its culture, language or religion', the Human Rights Committee has stated that 'positive measures by States may [...] be necessary to protect the identity of a minority'.[49] If minority rights are threatened, 'positive measures of protection are [...] required not only against the acts of the State Party itself, [...] but also against the acts of other persons within the State Party'.[50]

A similar approach is found in other instruments. Under the European Framework Convention, state parties 'undertake to promote the conditions necessary for persons belonging to national minorities to maintain and develop their culture'.[51] The Minorities Declaration calls upon States to 'encourage conditions for the promotion of [minority] identity' and 'adopt appropriate legislative and other measures' to achieve that and other goals.[52] The Copenhagen Document mandates states to 'create conditions for the promotion of that [ethnic, cultural, linguistic and religious] identity [of national minorities ... and] take the necessary measures to that effect after due consultations, including contracts with organizations or associations of such minorities, in accordance with the decision-making procedures of each State'.[53]

As the number of instruments on minority rights proliferates, it becomes easier to conclude that some state action to promote the rights of persons belonging to minorities may be required.[54] Nonetheless, the scope of such positive obligations on states to promote minority culture remains unclear, and it is perhaps best analysed by referring to specific provisions concerning, for example, language, access to the media and education. Of course, states remain free to promote minority cultures even if their actions are not mandated by international law, and governments should consider providing appropriate support for minority schools, publications and similar activities whenever such support would benefit a significant proportion of the state's citizens.

Turning to the substantive content of specific rights, the most basic obligation on states is *to protect the existence and identity* of minorities and their members.[55] In many instances, this may mean simply guaranteeing the most basic human rights – to life and physical integrity, freedom from arrest and torture, due process, property and freedom of expression. It also implies a prohibition against forced assimilation, a prohibition made explicit in several instruments.[56]

Of particular concern to many minorities is the problem of population transfers of members of the dominant majority community to regions inhabited primarily by minorities, in order to alter the demographics and dilute the cohesiveness of the latter.[57] The most recent European instruments specifically prohibit such practices,[58] although it may be difficult in some cases to distinguish between non-permissible population transfers and the legitimate exercise by others of their right to freedom of movement within the territory of the state.

The principles of *equality before the law and non-discrimination* are equally fundamental in all statements of minority rights, and they have by now acquired the status of customary international law binding on all states.[59] The wide ratification of the Convention on the Elimination of All Forms of Racial Discrimination also supports the view that discrimination on the basis of 'national or ethnic origin' is prohibited under international law.

Linked to the principle of equality is the notion that members of minorities are to be equal to members of the majority in fact as well as in law. This concept, borrowed from the decision of the Permanent Court of International Justice in the 'Minority Schools in Albania' case,[60] implies not only that minorities must enjoy formal legal equality, but that they have the right to effective equality of opportunity or result *vis-à-vis* the majority community. This may necessitate that special measures, sometimes known as 'positive discrimination' or 'affirmative action', be taken to ensure that the minority has the same rights in practice as the majority.[61]

The reference in Article 27 of the International Covenant on Civil and Political Rights to the *right of minorities 'to profess and practise their own religion'* has probably been subsumed for all practical purposes under the guarantees of religious freedom included in the Covenant itself and other human rights instruments. However, it could be argued that the identification of religious minorities (or minority religious beliefs) as particularly worthy of protection implies that religious practices which form a significant element of a minority group's identity should receive greater protection than practices which are based simply on personal beliefs. Thus religious practices closely tied to a particular culture (as opposed to a situation in which an ethnic or linguistic minority simply shares widespread religious beliefs common to many other groups) should prima facie be protected, unless they run counter to other universally accepted human rights norms.

The right *to enjoy one's own culture* also seems to be well accepted, although its meaning is less clear. The Minorities Declaration, for example, obliges states to 'create favourable conditions' for the development of minority cultures 'except where specific practices are in violation of national law and contrary to international standards'.[62] While societies vary greatly in their degree of cultural tolerance, most do forbid cultural and/or religious practices which offend fundamental community beliefs (for example, polygamy, divorce, abortion, use of alcohol) or which are deemed to be outweighed by health or safety concerns (for example, restrictions on Sikhs carrying the short dagger known as the *kirpan* or the provision of medical treatment for minors despite the religious objections of their parents).[63]

This potential clash of values between majority and minority presents one of the most difficult issues to resolve, as both communities have the right to promote their own moral and social beliefs. As is the case with most other human rights, minority rights are not absolute. However, they can only be limited under certain circumstances, such as in order to protect the rights of others or if they are being asserted in order to promote activities contrary to international law or the purposes and principles of the United Nations, 'including sovereign equality, territorial integrity and political independence of States'.[64] A state cannot limit minority rights in such a way as to effectively deny the right in question.

It is essential that members of minorities be allowed *to maintain contact with other members of the group*, even (or perhaps particularly) when the group is divided among the territories of different states. Each of the recently adopted instruments guarantees the right of members of minorities to maintain peaceful contacts with other persons, even those in other states, particularly when they are related to such persons by national, ethnic, religious or linguistic ties.

*Use of language* is one of the most divisive issues in minority–majority relations, although the right to use one's own language 'in public and in private' is perhaps the most widely guaranteed minority right in international law.[65] Restrictions on speaking a particular language are clearly unjustified, as would be any blanket or discriminatory prohibition against using a minority language in print, radio, television or other media. The Human Rights Committee notes that the 'right of individuals belonging to a linguistic minority to use their language among themselves [...] is distinct from other language rights protected under the Covenant', although it offers no guidance as to the content of this 'distinct' right.[66]

Recent European instruments specify linguistic rights in greater detail, although most are couched in terms which leave a great deal of discretion to states. The specific rights guaranteed under various instruments include access to the media (which states should facilitate),[67] official recognition of names and surnames chosen by members of minorities,[68] and, where the minority is sufficiently concentrated territorially, the right to use the minority language in contacts with government authorities[69] and to have local names and signs in the minority language.[70] Provisions for the use of one's own language before the courts are found in many human rights instruments, as well as those devoted specifically to minority rights.

*Education* is a primary concern of both minority and majority communities, and current formulations of minority rights attempt to achieve a balance between the legitimate interests of the two groups. At a minimum, minorities clearly have the right to establish their own private educational institutions, although Article 13 of the Framework Convention provides that this does not imply any financial obligation on the part of the state to support such institutions. In areas in which a significant proportion of the population speaks a minority language, children should have the opportunity to be taught in their mother tongue or, at least, to learn their own language.[71] However, none of these rights limits the authority of the state to require that the official language also be taught or that certain minimum educational requirements be met. States also should ensure that the state educational system fosters learning about minority history, customs and culture.[72]

Perhaps the most controversial set of rights concerns the ability of minorities *to participate effectively in decisions* which affect them, a right which was not generally recognized in the treaties supervised by the League of Nations. The earliest formulation of this right was by the CSCE in 1990, when the participating CSCE states agreed to 'respect the right of persons belonging to national minorities to effective participation in public affairs, including participation in the affairs relating to the protection and promotion of the identity of such minorities'.[73] The Declaration adopted by the UN General Assembly two years later expands the right of participation to include 'cultural, religious, social, economic and public life', although the right to participate in decision making is limited to 'a manner not incompatible with national legislation'. Although the text is formulated rather weakly, Article 4(5) of the Minorities Declaration also provides that 'states should consider appropriate measures so that persons belonging to minorities may participate fully in the economic progress and development in their country'.

The CSCE Copenhagen Document 'notes', as one way of achieving the aim of effective participation, the establishment of 'appropriate local or autonomous administrations corresponding to the specific historical and territorial circumstances of such minorities and in accordance with the policies of the state concerned'. The protocol recommended by the Parliamentary Assembly of the Council of Europe is even more specific, providing that 'in regions where they are in a majority the persons belonging to a national minority shall have the right to have at their disposal appropriate local or autonomous authorities or to have a special status'.[74]

Such provisions obviously reach far beyond the scope of 'ordinary' human rights, insofar as they mandate that states adopt forms of government which make 'effective participation' of minorities possible. Even though no particular constitutional or legislative structure is required, this is a much more delicate task than simply prohibiting torture or providing social security. Of course, 'participation' does not necessarily mean 'control', and the precise balance between minority and majority rights will need to be determined on a case-by-case basis. At the same time, however, a purely formal democracy in which members of minorities are consistently denied any share in power might well violate the emerging international norms of minority rights.

## Concluding Observations

Members of minorities have suffered discrimination, land seizures, forced assimilation, deportation and even death at the hand of intolerant majorities and territorially ambitious governments. Despite such pressures, however, minorities will always exist within state boundaries: it is impossible (and perhaps not even desirable) for every state to be ethnically, linguistically and religiously pure. While one must be careful not to undermine the legitimate rights of the majority, upon which democracy is based, the challenge for the twenty-first century is to do a better job of protecting the more vulnerable, often minority, members of society than was evidenced in the twentieth century.

Minority rights can only be understood within the broader context of international human rights law. In the nineteenth and early twentieth centuries, members of minorities required special protection, because otherwise the groups and individuals concerned would fall within the domestic jurisdiction of the state and be left wholly to the mercy of the majority. Today, however, members of minorities are protected by the same umbrella of human rights which protects all other persons within a state's jurisdiction. Indeed, one could argue that respect for 'ordinary' individual human rights would adequately respond to many, if not most, of the complaints raised today by minorities.

But even where human rights are generally respected, members of minorities continue to fear that their cultures and way of life are under attack. These fears are partly a reaction to the refusal of many governments to discuss minority rights seriously until the past few years, as assimilation was thought to be inevitable and minority rights were sacrificed to the demands of political and economic state building.

These fears of active repression are reinforced by minority concerns that they will lose their identity as an inevitable result of the social pressures of modern society. These pressures towards greater global homogenization may only reflect the timeless tension between change and the status quo, but they have contributed to a cultural resurgence among ethnic and linguistic groups around the world. At the same time, economically weaker regions inhabited largely by minorities may feel increasingly isolated from centralized decision makers, and minorities may view economic and political marginalization as resulting from discrimination rather than simply reflecting inevitable regional disparities.

As a result of this tension between the growing assertion of rights by minorities and the reluctance of many states to promote meaningful pluralism, minorities today often seek broader political and economic power over their own lives than the limited cultural and linguistic rights which were traditionally accorded to them. Unfortunately, states may themselves contribute to this escalation of minority demands, if they refuse to recognize even such widely accepted rights as the ability of minorities to speak their own languages and establish their own schools.

Of course, not all assertions of 'minority' rights are based on true concern for the protection of language, religion or culture. The turbulence of the post-Cold War era, which has seen the dissolution of Yugoslavia and the Soviet Union as well as the division of Ethiopia and Czechoslovakia, has encouraged some minorities (or at least their leaders) whose primary goal is to create their own state or aggrandize their own political power. Responding to such demands is not properly the subject of international human rights norms, except insofar as respect for human rights can contribute to the peaceful resolution of conflicts.

Ultimately, the challenge of protecting the rights of persons belonging to minorities is to balance the legitimate concerns of majority and minority communities, so that broader political and economic decisions may be reached in an atmosphere of full equality and respect for human rights. The international community has made significant strides in articulating this balance in only a few years. As with other human rights, the task now is to ensure that the political and legal commitments accepted by states are monitored and implemented in good faith.

## Notes

1 This chapter will normally utilize the shorter phrase 'rights of minorities' to refer both to group and to individual rights, unless the context makes it clear that a distinction is intended.

2 An excellent historical survey of minority rights is J.B. Muldoon, 'The development of group rights' in Sigler (1983, pp.31–66).

3 P.F. Sugar, *South-Eastern Europe Under Ottoman Rule, 1354–1804*, Seattle, University of Washington Press, 1977, p.274.

4 Cf., for example, F. Hassan, *The Concept of State and Law in Islam*, Lanham, Md./London, University Press of America, 1981. Christians and Jews, as monotheistic 'People of the Book', occupy a special position in an Islamic state, and it is on this basis that the millets were allowed to develop their own culture and civil administration. Ibid., p.45.

5 Among the many works which trace the development of nationalism, see B. Anderson, *Imagined Communities*, London, Verso, 1983; J. Breuilly, *Nationalism and the State*, Chicago, University of Chicago Press, 2nd edn, 1993; P. Chatterjee, *Nationalist Thought and the Colonial World*, London, Zed Books, 1986; W. Connor, *Ethnonationalism. The Quest for Understanding*, Princeton, Princeton University Press, 1993; T.H. Eriksen, *Ethnicity and Nationalism, Anthropological Perspectives*, London, Pluto Press, 1993; E. Gellner, *Nations and Nationalism*, Ithaca, Cornell University Press, 1983; E.J. Hobsbawm, *Nations and Nationalism Since 1780*, 2nd edn, Cambridge, Cambridge University Press, 1992; H.R. Isaacs, *Idols of the Tribe*, Cambridge, Mass., Harvard University Press, 1975; E. Kedourie, *Nationalism*, 4th edn, London, Blackwell, 1993; A.D. Smith, *The Ethnic Origins of Nations*, London, Blackwell, 1988.

6 Perhaps the best and most detailed treatment of the adoption and implementation of the treaties is Macartney (1934, pp.212–23); also see United Nations (1979, pp.16–26); Thornberry (1991, pp.38–52).

7 The unilateral declarations to guarantee minority rights made by states before the League of Nations might be considered as a fourth category. See Capotorti study, *supra*, note 6, United Nations (1979, p.18).

8 See generally Claude (1955, pp.17–28); Janowsky (1945, pp.112–15); Macartney, *supra*, note 6, pp.273–94, 502–6 (text of the Polish Minorities Treaty); Capotorti Study, *supra*, note 6, United Nations (1979, pp.18–19); United Nations Sub-Commission on Prevention of Discrimination and Protection of Minorities (1951).

9 See generally Macartney, *supra*, note 6, pp.308–69; Capotorti Study, *supra*, note 6, United Nations (1979, pp.20–24); L.B. Sohn and T. Buergenthal, *International Protection of Human Rights*, Indianapolis, Bobbs-Merrill, 1973, pp.213–306.

10 See, for example, Claude, *supra*, note 8, pp.31–50; Pearson (1983, pp.142–6); Capotorti study, *supra*, note 6, United Nations (1979, pp.25–6).

11 Claude, *supra*, note 8, pp.49–50.

12 Pearson, *supra*, note 10, pp.148–9.

13 There were occasional exceptions to this rule, as exemplified by British attempts, under quite different circumstances, to protect the cultures of the southern Sudan and native Fijians from certain outside influences.

14 UN Charter, Articles 1(3) and 55.

15 Ibid., Articles 1(2) and 55.

16 See generally Alfred M. de Zayas, *Nemesis at Potsdam*, London/Boston, Routledge and Kegan Paul, 1977.

17 Opened for signature 9 December 1948, entered into force 12 January 1951, 78 UNTS 277.

18 G.A. Res. 217A (III) and 217C (III) of 10 December 1948.

19 It required only 2½ pages of a recent 359-page report on the UN's human rights activities to describe the UN's work in the area of minority rights (apart from questions of discrimination). See United Nations, *United Nations Action in the Field of Human Rights*, UN Sales No. ST/HR/2/Rev.3, 1988, pp.245–7; see also Capotorti study, *supra*, note 6, United Nations (1979, paras 141–8); J. Humphrey, 'The United Nations Sub-Commission on Prevention of Discrimination and Protection of Minorities', *American Journal of International Law*, **62**, 1968, 869.

20 Adopted 14 December 1960, entered into force 22 May 1962, 429 UNTS 93, Article 6.

21 Ibid.

22 Neither the American nor the European Convention on Human Rights refers to minority rights; the African Charter on Human and Peoples' Rights contains several references to 'peoples', but none to minorities or groups.

23 Adopted 21 December 1965, entered into force 4 January 1969, 660 UNTS 195.

24 States are required under Article 9 to submit periodic reports on their implementation of the convention to the Committee on the Elimination of Racial Discrimination (CERD). Although most state reports to CERD are concerned with issues such as legal measures to promote equality and non-discrimination or prohibitions against racist propaganda, some discuss issues related to minorities in greater detail. A brief survey of these country reports may be found in Hannum (1996, pp.64–9); also cf. T. Meron, *Human Rights Law-Making in the United Nations*, Oxford, Clarendon Press, 1986, pp.36–44.

25 Adopted by the UNESCO General Conference on 27 November 1978, Article 9(2).

26 *Supra*, note 6, United Nations.

27 General Assembly resolution 47/135 of 18 December 1992 (hereinafter cited as the Minorities Declaration).

28 Commission on Human Rights resolution 1995/24, para. 9, 3 March 1995.

29 General Assembly resolution 36/55 of 25 November 1981. Cf. D.J. Sullivan, 'Advancing the freedom of religion or belief through the UN Declaration on the Elimination of Religious Intolerance and Discrimination', *American Journal of International Law*, **82**, 1988, 487.

30 The final report, by Sub-Commission member Asbjørn Eide, is found in UN Doc. E/CN.4/Sub.2/1993/34 and Adds 1–4, 1993.

31 Document of the Copenhagen Meeting of the Conference on the Human Dimension of the CSCE, adopted on 29 June 1990, reprinted in *International Legal Materials*, **29**, 1990, 1305 (hereinafter cited as Copenhagen Document).

32 Conference on Security and Co-operation in Europe, Helsinki Document 1992, Decisions, Section I, para. 23, 1992.

33 The work of the High Commissioner is theoretically confidential, but the OSCE has authorized publication of most of his formal communications with governments. These are available from the OSCE, and many are reprinted in the journal, *Helsinki Monitor*.

34 European Charter for Regional or Minority Languages, signed 5 November 1992, European TS No. 148.

35 Parliamentary Assembly of the Council of Europe, Recommendation 1201, 1993, 44th session, 22nd Sitting, 1 February 1993 (Text of the proposal for an additional protocol to the Convention for the Protection of Human Rights and Fundamental Freedoms, concerning persons belonging to national minorities) (hereinafter cited as Parliamentary Assembly).

36 Framework Convention for the Protection of National Minorities, signed 1 February 1995, Europe. TS No. 157, reprinted in *International Legal Materials*, **34**, 1995, 351 (hereinafter cited as Framework Convention). See generally A.

Rönquist, 'The Council of Europe Framework Convention for the Protection of National Minorities', *Helsinki Monitor* 6, (1), 1995, 38.

37  Many such texts may be found in Hannum (1993); also see Eide, *supra*, note 30.

38  A list of UN studies and discussions which address the question of a definition of 'minority' may be found in UN Sub-Commission on Prevention of Discrimination and Protection of Minorities, Note by the Secretary-General, UN Doc. E/CN.4/Sub.2/1984/31, 1984.

39  See, for example, General Comment No. 23(50), adopted by the Human Rights Committee under Article 40(4) of the International Covenant on Civil and Political Rights, UN Doc. CCPR/C/21/Rev.1/Add.5, 1994, para. 3.1: 'The Covenant draws a distinction between the right to self-determination and the rights protected under Article 27. The former is expressed to be a right belonging to peoples [...]. Article 27, on the other hand, relates to rights conferred on individuals as such.'

40  Capotorti study, *supra*, note 6, United Nations (1979, p.96).

41  UN Doc. E/CN.4/Sub.2/1985/31 and Corr. 1, 1985, p.30.

42  The Permanent Court of International Justice (PCIJ) offered a similar definition of the word 'community' as used in a Greco-Bulgarian Convention encouraging emigration and population exchange between the two countries: 'The "community" is a group of persons living in a given country or locality, having a race, religion, language and traditions of their own and united by this identity of race, religion, language and traditions in a sentiment of solidarity, with a view to preserving their traditions, maintaining their form of worship, ensuring the instruction and upbringing of their children in accordance with the spirit and traditions of their race and rendering mutual assistance to each other' (Greco-Bulgarian 'Communities', Advisory Opinion, 1930, PCIJ, Series B, No. 17, p.21). However, despite the fact that the PCIJ issued several judgments and advisory opinions dealing with minority issues, it never formally defined the word 'minority'.

43  This point is supported by the Human Rights Committee's General Comment, *supra*, note 39, para. 5.2.

44  General Comment, *supra*, Note 39, para.5.2.

45  Compare, for example, the annotations on the text of the draft International Covenants on Human Rights, prepared by the Secretary-General for the General Assembly in 1955: 'It was agreed that the article should cover only separate or distinct groups, well-defined and long-established on the territory of a State' (UN Doc. A/2929, 1955, para. 184). Other references may be found in M. Bossuyt, *Guide to the 'Travaux Préparatoires' of International Covenant on Civil and Political Rights*, Dordrecht, Martinus Nijhoff, 1987, pp.493–9. Citing, *inter alia*, the Capotorti study, *supra*, note 6, United Nations (1979), a more recent commentator concludes that 'aliens are prima facie excluded' from the scope of Article 27 (Thornberry, 1991, p.171).

46  Parliamentary Assembly, Article 1.

47  Of course, there may be certain rights which are inherently collective, for example communal ownership of property or restrictions on land alienation to non-group members. In such cases, minority rights should be interpreted as belonging to the group and not merely to a disparate collection of individuals.

48  Domestic legislation may draw distinctions among, for example, groups labelled as nations, nationalities or national minorities, but such distinctions have not been carried over into international norms. Under international law, no particular rights or status attach to being a 'nation' which, in most cases, would probably be deemed to be equivalent to a 'national minority'. Cf. the Human Rights Committee's General Comment on Article 27 of the Covenant, *supra*, note 39.

49  General Comment, *supra*, note 39, para. 6.2. The Capotorti study, *supra*, note 6, United Nations (1979, pp.36–7), adopts a similar approach.

50  General Comment, *supra*, note 39, para. 6.1.

51  Framework Convention, Article 5(1).

52  Minorities Declaration, Article 1.

53  Copenhagen Document, para. 33.

54  See, for example, Thornberry (1991, pp.178–86).

55  See Minorities Declaration, Article 1; Framework Convention, Article 5(1); Parliamentary Assembly, Article 3; Copenhagen Document, Article 33.

56  Framework Convention, Article 5(2); Parliamentary Assembly, Article 3; Copenhagen Document, Article 32.

57  See, for example, UN Sub-Commission on Prevention of Discrimination and Protection of Minorities resolution 1994/42, on the human rights dimensions of population transfer, and the progress report on the same topic by the Sub-Commission's rapporteur, A.S. Al-Khasawneh, UN Doc.E/CN.4/Sub.2/1994/18 and Coor.1, 1994.

58  See Framework Convention, Article 16; Parliamentary Assembly, Article 5.

59  See, for example, The Namibia Case, 1971 I.C.J. 16, 76 (Ammoun, J, separate opinion): 'One right which must certainly be considered a pre-existing binding customary norm […] is the right to equality, which by common consent has ever since the remotest times been deemed inherent in human nature'; H. Hannum, 'The status of the Universal Declaration of Human Rights in national and international law', *Georgia Journal of International and Comparative Law*, **25**, (1 & 2), 1995, 56–7 and notes cited therein.

60  Advisory Opinion, 1935, PCIJ, Series A/B, No. 64.

61  Article 1(4) of the Convention on the Elimination of All Forms of Racial Discrimination provides, for example, that 'special measures taken for the sole purpose of securing adequate advancement of certain racial or ethnic groups or individuals requiring such protection as may be necessary in order to ensure such groups or individuals equal enjoyment or exercise of human rights and fundamental freedoms shall not be deemed racial discrimination, provided, however, that such measures do not, as a consequence, lead to the maintenance of separate rights for different racial groups and that they shall not be continued after the objectives for which they were taken have been achieved'. Similar provisions are found in the Copenhagen Document, para. 31, and the Framework Convention, Article 4(2).

62  Minorities Declaration, Article 4(2).

63  See generally T.M. Franck, *Human Rights in Third World Perspective*, Vol. 1, New York, Oceana, 1982, pp.455–510; S.M. Poulter, *English Law and Ethnic Minority Customs*, London, Butterworths, 1986; P. Sieghart, *The International Law of Human Rights*, Oxford, Clarendon Press, 1983, pp.321–6.

64  Minorities Declaration, Article 8(4).

65  See the list of 'special protective measures of an international character' dealing with language, in United Nations, *Protection of Minorities*, 1967, pp.50–55, UN Sales No.67.XIV.3; a compilation of constitutional provisions relating to linguistic rights may be found in A.P. Blaustein and D. Blaustein Epstein, *Resolving Language Conflicts: A Study of the World's Constitutions*, Washington, DC, U.S. English, 1986.

66  General Comment, *supra, note* 39, para. 5(3).

67  Framework Convention, Article 9.

68  Framework Convention, Article 11(1); Parliamentary Assembly, Article 7(2).

69  Framework Convention, Article 19(2); Parliamentary Assembly, Article 7(3).

70  Framework Convention, Article 11(3); Parliamentary Assembly, Article 7(4).

71  See Minorities Declaration, Article 4(3); Framework Convention, Article 14(2); Parliamentary Assembly, Article 8; Copenhagen Document, Article 34.
72  See Minorities Declaration, Article 4(4); Framework Convention, Article 12; Copenhagen Document, Article 34.
73  Copenhagen Document, para. 35.
74  Parliamentary Assembly, Article 11. Cf. Hannum, *supra*, note 24; Y. Dinstein, *Models of Autonomy*, New Brunswick, NJ/London, Transaction Books, 1981.

## Bibliography

Brölmann, C., René Lefeber and Marjoleine Zieck (eds) (1993), *Peoples and Minorities in International Law*, Dordrecht, Martinus Nijhoff Publishers.

Caratini, R. (1987), *La Force des faibles*, Paris, Larousse.

Chaliand, G. (ed.) (1985), *Les Minorités à l'âge de l'état-nation*, Paris, Fayard/Minority Rights Group.

Claude, Jr. I.L. (1955), *National Minorities*, Cambridge, Mass., Harvard University Press.

Ermacora, F. (1964), *Der Minderheitenschutz in der Arbeit der Vereinten Nationen*, Vienna, W. Brumuller.

Ermacora, F. (1984), 'The protection of minorities before the United Nations', *Recueil des Cours*, **182**.

Fenet, A. (ed.) (1989), *Les Minorités et leurs droits depuis 1789*, Paris, L'Harmattan.

Frowein, J.A., R. Hoffmann and S. Oeter (eds) (1993), *Das Minderheitenrecht europaischer Staten*, Berlin, Springer-Verlag, 2 vols.

Giordan, H. (ed.) (1992), *Les Minorités en Europe: droits linguistiques et droits de l'homme*, Paris, Editions Kime.

Gurr, T.R. (1993), *Minorities at Risk*, Washington, DC, U.S. Institute of Peace.

Hannum, H. (1993), *Documents on Autonomy and Minority Rights*, Dordrecht, Martinus Nijhoff Publishers.

Hannum, H. (1996), *Autonomy, Sovereignty and Self-Determination: The Accommodation of Conflicting Rights*, rev. edn, Philadelphia, University of Pennsylvania Press.

Heraclides, A. (1991), *The Self-determination of Minorities in International Politics*, London, Frank Cass.

Janowsky, O.I. (1945), *Nationalities and National Minorities*, New York, Macmillan.

Lerner,N. (1991), *Group Rights and Discrimination in International Law*, Dordrecht, Martinus Nijhoff Publishers.

Macartney, C.A. (1934), *National States and National Minorities*, London, Oxford University Press.

McKean, W. (1993), *Equality and Discrimination under International Law*, Oxford, Clarendon Press.

Minority Rights Group (1990), *World Directory of Minorities*, Chicago, St. James Press.

Muller, K. (1993), *Minderheiten im Konflikt: Fakten, Erfahrungen, Losungkonzepte*, Zurich, Verlag Neue Zurche Zeitung.

Pearson, R. (1983), *National Minorities in Eastern Europe 1848–1945*, London, Macmillan.

Rousso-Lenoir, F. (1994), *Minorités et droits de l'homme: l'Europe et son double*, Brussels, Bruylant.

Sanguin, A.L. (1993), *Les Minorités ethniques en Europe*, Paris, L'Harmattan.

Sigler, J.A. (ed.) (1983), *Minority Rights. A Comparative Analysis*, Westport/London, Greenwood Press.

Thornberry, P. (1991), *International Law and the Rights of Minorities*, Oxford, Clarendon Press.

United Nations (1979), *Study on the Rights of Persons Belonging to Ethnic, Religious and Linguistic Minorities*, F. Capotorti, Special Rapporteur, UN Sales No. E.78.XIV.1.

United Nations Sub-Commission on Prevention of Discrimination and Protection of Minorities (1951), *Treaties and International Instruments Concerning the Protection of Minorities 1919–1951*, UN Doc. E/CN.4/Sub.2/133.

# 9 Protection of the World's Indigenous Peoples and Human Rights

## ERICA-IRENE A. DAES

Over the past 20 years, the international movement of indigenous peoples has grown with extraordinary speed. In 1977, when the non-governmental organization (NGO) conference on this issue was convened at the United Nations Office in Geneva, governments generally assumed that the term 'indigenous' referred to the original inhabitants of North and South America. Today, grassroots organizations in more than 40 countries participate in United Nations activities in this field, and estimates of the number of indigenous peoples worldwide have been revised upwards from 40 million to nearly 350 million.

During this same period of time, diplomats and jurists have completely revised their perceptions of the relationship between the protection of indigenous peoples and other major concerns in the broad field of human rights. In 1977, indigenous peoples were mainly viewed as a small, and particularly vulnerable, category of ethnic minorities; indeed, it was very commonplace to hear them referred to as 'indigenous minorities'. Most governments viewed the problem as discrimination in the enjoyment of these people's individual human rights. Today, indigenous peoples have emerged as a distinct category in international human rights, and it has been universally recognized that they enjoy collective rights to land and to some (still disputed) degree of autonomy.

Indigenous peoples have therefore emerged as a distinct and unique preoccupation of international law. They have collective economic and political rights, but have not been recognized as a sub-set of 'non-self-governing territories'[1] under the Charter. We assign their protection to the human rights domain of the United Nations, rather than to that of decolonization. Yet their rights are quite different from those with which the Commission on Human Rights is accustomed to dealing. They do not fit neatly into any familiar legal or administrative categories at the United Nations. Nonetheless, there is no longer the slightest doubt that they form a large portion of humanity which is threatened with extinction.

At the ceremony on 10 December 1992 in the the General Assembly of the United Nations in New York, which officially launched the International Year of the World's Indigenous People, the Secretary-General, Boutros Boutros-Ghali, stated that the future protection of indigenous peoples would be a critical test of the integrity and effectiveness of the entire United Nations human rights system.[2] I might humbly suggest that, just as the first 50 years of the United Nations brought an end to overseas colonialism, the next 50 years must succeed in emancipating indigenous people from internal colonialism.

A chapter of this length can only hope to identify key issues and arguments. Other scholars have traced the development of the international movement of indigenous peoples, and the negotiation of new instruments and legal standards over the past 20 years. This chapter will not attempt to retrace this complex and interesting history. Instead, the aim will be to offer an intellectual framework for an understanding of the special character of the legal status sought by indigenous peoples, and for an evaluation of the implications of accommodating the claims of these peoples. The first two parts of this therefore consider the nature of the rights sought, and explore a number of apparent contradictions among the rights claimed. The third and final part will present an argument as to why states and the United Nations should, in furthering the aims of the Charter, recognize these rights.

## Substantive Rights

Indigenous peoples seek the right to self-determination and the subsidiary (or subsumed) rights of self-government, autonomy, territorial integrity and exclusive enjoyment of their own lands and resources. This central demand has been the focus, at least since 1990, of the continual political collisions between states and indigenous peoples at international conferences and meetings, as exemplified by the uproar created by some governments at the World Conference on Human Rights in 1993,[3] when they insisted upon referring to indigenous 'people' in the final document. The use of the term 'peoples', these governments feared, would vindicate claims to the rights of 'peoples' under the Charter of the United Nations and the two International Covenants on Human Rights.

Putting aside this terminological dispute, three points are absolutely clear. For indigenous peoples everywhere in the world today, self-determination is the central tenet and main symbol of their movements. They demand that it be addressed squarely, and insist that it is not negotiable. They regard themselves as the last remaining colonized peoples, and contend that any failure to accord them the same rights and status as other colonized peoples in the world represents systemic racism and discrimination by the international community. On objective, ethnological or historical grounds, their position is strong: they were and continue to be culturally and linguistically distinct; they were organized into complex autonomous societies for millennia, and were recognized as such by other nations through treaties and diplomatic relations; they have not willingly surrendered control of their territories to the peoples and states which rule them today. Unfortunately, the application of international law is not always as scientific as we might wish it to be.

In any event, it seems clear that indigenous peoples assign a special meaning to the term, 'self-determination'. They do not usually assume that the right to self-determination is exercised by the creation of new nation-states. Indeed, indigenous peoples tend to be suspicious of the very concept of the nation-state as it has evolved in the modern era. Their ideal of social order is based upon cultural integrity and kinship – including the kinship which they conceive between humans, animals, plants and landforms. Indigenous leaders condemn nation-states as insufferably elitist, authoritarian and materialistic, and they are not particularly anxious to reproduce this structure in their own societies. Thus the creation of new nation-states is actually antithetical to the liberation goals of most indigenous peoples, even though we might someday force them, by our national and international policies, to seek liberation by this familiar means. In my understanding, what indigenous peoples themselves mean when they speak of 'self-determination' is freedom to live the way the Creator made them and taught them. The emphasis is upon freedom, not the reproduction of new centres of state power.

If this claim is subversive to existing nation-states, it is, at the level of philosophy, not a struggle for competing physical power. A growing number of member states have realized this and reassessed their position on the issue of self-determination. At the World Conference on Human Rights and afterwards, notably, the government of Australia has supported indigenous peoples on this issue. Australian diplomats have repeatedly defended their views by explaining the special context in which indigenous peoples use the principle of self-determination.

In my capacity as the chairperson/rapporteur of the Working Group on Indigenous Populations, for nearly 12 years now, I have argued that the right to self-determination for indigenous peoples should be understood as a demand for 'belated nation building'.[4] I believe indigenous peoples are claiming the opportunity to choose their own place in the states within which they live, an opportunity which has been denied to them in the past. Even within states which are proud of their ethnic diversity, and reflect that diversity in their state institutions, indigenous peoples are generally either missing or have been assigned a role that is subordinate to other ethnic and regional populations.

We will return to this theme later. First, however, it is important to emphasize the fact that indigenous peoples are asserting a much broader range of rights and concerns than simply the right to self-determination. All of these other rights could be realized if, perhaps, indigenous peoples eventually achieved independent statehood. However, the fact that indigenous movements have been careful to assert these subsidiary rights in detail is consistent with my understanding that most indigenous peoples expect to remain integrated, to a limited extent, within existing states.

## Identity and Equality

In one important respect, indigenous peoples and minorities[5] assert similar, seemingly contradictory, claims. Both groups seek equality with other citizens of the state, while at the same time they demand state respect and state support for the development of their own cultural, religious and linguistic identities.

The foundation of the liberal theory of the nation-state is the equality of citizens, both in terms of individual rights and with respect to individual responsibilities. Individual or group differences among citizens have traditionally been regarded as a strictly private affair. In principle, everyone remains free to pursue their individual desires and collective activities, so long as they faithfully perform their duties as citizens, and ask no more from the state than other citizens.

Few, if any, modern states have attained this philosophical ideal. Sometimes this has been a result of intolerance directed against particular groups, depriving them of the same rights and freedoms as other constituent groups in national society. Often the problem has been the cost of accommodation within an otherwise tolerant and pluralistic state. How many languages, for example, can realistically be granted official status, so that they can be used freely in education, government and legal proceedings? What number of citizens must speak a language before it is given equal status with other national languages? This problem is a function of diversity. In New Zealand, there is one indigenous language – Maori – and it has official status. In Canada, there are at least ten major indigenous languages, as well as two dominant European languages. Only one indigenous language (Inuktitut) has official status, and that only in Canada's Northwest Territory.

There is still a third important reason why liberal theories of equality fail to respond adequately to the situation of modern states. Different groups may have fundamentally different ideas about the nature of society, economy and the state itself. They may find it impossible to agree on any formula for the rights and duties of national citizenship. There are three possible results in such a case. A national formula of citizenship may be imposed on smaller, more culturally distinct groups on the grounds that limitations on these groups' cultural freedom is justified by the demands of public order. Exceptions to equality may be agreed to by the parties, resulting in a federation of ethnically distinct and legally distinct societies within one state. Alternatively, the existing state may dissolve, as we have seen with such tragic results in the former Yugoslavia.

Legal scholars trained within the liberal Western tradition have difficulty imagining nation-states which represent what the great philosopher Aristotle described as 'geometric equality'. The Western model of the state demands that each citizen be, for the purposes of the law, exactly the same. Geometric equality refers to a state composed of two or more groups of citizens, who differ in mutually agreed ways. The pieces differ in shape, but all fit together according to a shared vision of the picture as a whole – a mosaic. Individual freedom is assured by providing for rights of membership and mobility: no one may be forced to belong to or remain a member of any particular group. It is important to stress this point about geometric equality and the structure of states because indigenous peoples tend to be more different from their neighbours than minorities. States cannot satisfy the aspirations of indigenous peoples using the approaches which may have worked successfully in dealings with national or ethnic minorities. At the same time, indigenous peoples themselves are likely to demand accommodation rather than independence.

Religious freedom provides a clear example of this problem. Religious minorities require freedom to erect and maintain their own places of worship, and freedom to teach and conduct their own religious rites within those places. They may choose to maintain distinct forms of dress or establish separate schools for their children. None of these choices require costly accommodations by other citizens. Indeed, other citizens may scarcely be aware of the existence or beliefs of most religious minorities. However, the religious beliefs of indigenous peoples cannot be confined to a church or school building. Indigenous peoples believe in their personal connections with and personal responsibility for every living creature and landform in their traditional territory. The places of greatest power and religious significance can be large, such as lakes and mountains, but numerous smaller ceremonial and healing sites are scattered throughout their ancestral lands.

Nearly every ecological change has some religious and cultural significance for indigenous peoples. Respect for their religions and cultures requires major changes in national laws controlling the use of land and natural resources, as well as the possibility that a larger part of the national territory will remain, for the foreseeable future, relatively 'underdeveloped'. This does not mean that indigenous peoples are strictly opposed to industrialization or the commercial use of natural resources. If given the choice, however, they are likely to be cautious about ecological changes, and to assign ecological and cultural continuity very high weight in any trade-off against the financial benefits of a project.

Awareness of this fact is already reflected in the decisions of the United Nations Conference on Environment and Development – the 1992 'Earth Summit' – in Rio de Janeiro. There are references throughout the final document to the role of indigenous peoples as partners in the management of natural resources. There is also a significant recognition of the right of indigenous peoples to be protected from any activities which are environmentally unsound, or which indigenous peoples themselves consider to be culturally inappropriate.[6] This supports the wish of indigenous peoples to determine the use of their traditional territories.

Similarly, Article 7 of the ILO Convention on Indigenous and Tribal Peoples, 1989 (No. 169),[7] guarantees to indigenous peoples the right to 'control, as far as possible', their own development and the development of the lands which they traditionally occupy or otherwise use. Articles 5 and 17 of the Convention recognize the right of indigenous peoples to maintain their own systems and institutions of law and land tenure. Furthermore, Articles 4 and 6 require States Parties to seek the consent of indigenous peoples before enacting any measures which will affect them directly, and to obtain their consent to any proposed measures that would treat them differently from other citizens. Articles 2 and 3 guarantee the right of indigenous peoples to enjoy, to whatever extent they choose, the same rights and privileges as other citizens.

These principles are most clearly and completely set out in the United Nations Draft Declaration on the Rights of Indigenous Peoples, which is currently under review by the Commission on Human Rights.[8] The Draft Declaration reaffirms the right of indigenous peoples, both individually and collectively, to demand complete equality before the law, while recognizing their right to exercise whatever level of autonomy or self-determination they choose.

*Autonomy and Integration*

Thus indigenous peoples have already won limited recognition of their right to enjoy both equality as citizens and continuing legal distinctiveness, including rights which go beyond what other citizens may legitimately claim. This apparent paradox of 'equal but different' extends not only to religious, linguistic, social and cultural activities – which are also, to a much lesser extent, a field of protection for minorities – but also to territorial and administrative matters.

It may be recalled that, in the course of negotiations over the text of the United Nations Declaration on the Rights of Persons Belonging to National or Ethnic, Religious and Linguistic Minorities,[9] there were proposals to insert an article on the status of territorial or geographically distinct minorities. It was suggested that the circumstances of such groups justified their enjoying a degree of regional autonomy, and a distinctive voice in decisions affecting their section of the country. States were strenuously opposed to this idea, and it was abandoned. As adopted, the Declaration only calls on states to enable minorities to participate fully in the governance of their countries, at both the national and regional levels. This reaffirms the traditional view that minorities must be content to remain equal to other citizens for the purposes of voting and office holding. It may be instructive to refer to the 1995 decision of the United States Supreme Court, which declared that laws requiring the drawing of electoral boundaries to enable minorities to obtain some seats in Congress was an unlawful form of racial discrimination against the majority.

In the case of indigenous peoples, however, there has been a more favourable international climate for assertions of autonomy. Although few governments are yet prepared to concede the right to self-determination to indigenous peoples, most have accepted the subsidiary or subsumed right of internal self-government since it was first discussed by the Working Group ten years ago. There is an assumption, perhaps, that indigenous peoples are concentrated in small areas, and their control of internal affairs need not be of major inconvenience to the country as a whole. There is also a growing awareness that indigenous peoples can do a more effective and cost-efficient job of solving social, economic, health, environmental and sustainable development problems for themselves, as long as they are provided with adequate resources and freedom to develop their own methods. This is only consistent, after all, with the wider reorientation of thinking about development strategy in the United Nations system since the 1970s. A number of countries, including Denmark (Greenland), the United States and Canada, Nicaragua and Panama have experimented with autonomy for indigenous peoples, and the results have almost uniformly been assessed as positive.

The main difficulty, then, is not the idea of autonomy, but, rather, the integration of local autonomous institutions into the state as a whole. It seems probable that many governments would be content if indigenous peoples agreed to manage their own affairs within their own small territories, and leave the matter there. As long as these autonomous territories remain subject to some degree of national jurisdiction and authority, however, indigenous peoples have a legitimate interest in participating in decision making at the national level. Indigenous peoples, moreover, demand that this participation be effective. They argue that it must involve more than the right to vote, as individual citizens. It must include arrangements to guarantee that their distinct voices are heard at all levels of government, even if they are a small proportion of the total national population. This may be achieved by reserving a certain number of special seats in the national legislature, as provided now by New Zealand, or through a special minister in the national cabinet, as in Nicaragua.

The non-indigenous population may feel that arrangements of this kind give indigenous peoples too much power. The difference between sharing autonomy within indigenous peoples' territories, and sharing responsibility for governing the entire country, is a considerable one. Where there has been a long history of racism, intolerance or the marginalization of indigenous peoples, there can be strong opposition to giving indigenous peoples a decisive voice in decisions affecting their non-indigenous neighbours. However, there are at least two important reasons for taking this step. One reason is to ensure respect for the local autonomy of indigenous peoples. The enforcement of national laws and policies will inevitably continue to be a source of potential conflict between national-level officials and indigenous peoples' own local authorities. Frictions can be minimized if indigenous peoples participate at both levels of law making. Furthermore, a partnership on national issues will tend to emphasize the shared concerns and aspirations of indigenous and non-indigenous people in the country. It will help build mutual understanding and, in the long term, a more stable and cooperative working relationship between national leaders and indigenous leaders.

In the United States, for example, where indigenous peoples have enjoyed some degree of local autonomy since 1934, the growth of national environmental regulations in the 1970s threatened to create new conflicts over the management of water, wildlife and industrial pollution. Indigenous authorities developed their own local conservation programmes, but were often frustrated by lack of coordination with national government agencies, and with the risk of being overruled where they disagreed with national policies or plans. The solution was to revise major US environmental laws. National agencies must now consult indigenous authorities in advance of adopting new policies or plans and, in some cases, must defer to indigenous peoples' own local plans.

I believe that this is what partnership means in the context of the political declarations made in Rio de Janeiro and at the official ceremonies for the International Year and International Decade of the World's Indigenous Peoples in New York. The goal is neither the complete independence of indigenous peoples nor the kind of local autonomy which would lead to social or political isolation and continuing vulnerability of indigenous peoples. What most indigenous peoples seek, and the United Nations has so far endorsed, is a hybrid of autonomy and political integration. Indigenous peoples must be able to participate effectively in the decisions affecting their destiny at all levels, enjoying a large measure of control over their internal affairs, and an equitable sharing of power in national politics.

## Collective and Individual Rights

It should be clear from the foregoing discussion that there are both collective and individual aspects to the protection and exercise of the rights of indigenous peoples.[10] What I have called 'rights of equality', for instance, will ordinarily be asserted by individuals who feel that they have been denied equal benefits or privileges of national citizenship. Equality will be of special importance for indigenous people who are living and working away from their own communities and who are therefore dealing chiefly with non-indigenous authorities. The rights of identity claimed by indigenous peoples are mainly concerned with autonomy,[11] the use and control of a territory, and participation as a distinct group in regional and national political processes. Hence these rights are ordinarily exercised through collective institutions, such as local governments and locally selected leaders. They do not have practical meaning unless indigenous peoples are free to establish and maintain institutions of their own design for their exercise.

It may fairly be said, then, that indigenous peoples tend to demand legal equality as individuals, but exercise their identity as groups. There is another aspect to this individual/collective dimension which poses more difficulties, however, both in theory and in practice. The recognition of autonomous institutions will create a capacity for indigenous people to oppress one another: in particular, a potential for the group itself to mistreat some of its individual members. This should not be regarded as an internal affair of the group, any more than abuses of human rights by states are regarded as their internal affairs. Since at least the 1970s, an international consensus has emerged that Articles 1 and 55 of the Charter confer an affirmative duty on the international community to cooperate in the protection of human rights in all countries. If indigenous peoples are seeking the support of international institutions for their assertions of the right to exercise self-determination, it would seem that they should accept the responsibilities of exercising the powers they seek in conformity with international law.

Similar questions have arisen in the case of federal states, such as Canada, which, having ratified international human rights instruments, contend that they lack the constitutional authority to discipline their constituent subordinate governments. The two International Covenants on Human Rights apply *expressus verbis* to the constituent parts of a federal state, but the treaty bodies charged with the implementation of those instruments have yet to persuade the government of Canada that it must ensure compliance by its ten 'provincial' governments. The government of Australia was beset with the same problem until a decision of the national High Court upheld the constitutionality of imposing federal human rights laws on constituent 'state' governments.

These questions will no doubt be raised in future both by states and by the local authorities of indigenous people. Even among indigenous peoples, leaders may arise who abuse their position, and the states concerned preferring not to intervene may argue that non-intervention is required out of their respect for the indigenous people's right to self-determination. Individuals would then lack any recourse at the national or the international levels – an unacceptable situation.

This possibility is addressed by Articles 8 and 9 of the ILO Convention on Indigenous and Tribal Peoples, 1989, which requires an indigenous people's own autonomous institution to be compatible with 'internationally recognized human rights'. There is no like provision in the draft Declaration, thus reflecting strong opposition to such a provision from many of the indigenous organizations and activists who have participated in developing the text. They are understandably still preoccupied with oppression by their nation-states rather than their own leaders, and the Working Group has chosen to respect their position.

On other hand, the Working Group has heard tragic stories of abuses of individual human rights by local indigenous authorities created, financed and protected by the nation-state, whether as a mechanism of indirect rule or in a well-intentioned (but misguided) effort to devolve local responsibility to the peoples concerned. It seems implausible that the international community should or would exempt indigenous peoples' authorities from the fundamental principles enshrined in the International Bill of Human Rights. Nor is it likely that the human rights treaty bodies will look favourably on arguments by States Parties that they have no duty to carry out their treaty obligations in territories administered by indigenous peoples. The real issue is not whether individual indigenous people continue to enjoy the protection of international human rights law, but who interprets and applies these standards. There is a genuine concern, on the part of many indigenous leaders, that national governments could abuse their responsibility for protecting individuals, employing pretended human rights disputes to pressure and harass legitimate local governing bodies. It will be recalled that the same fears have been expressed by many developing countries, and that it has taken many years to persuade them that international human rights procedures are not simply a stick designed by the former colonial powers with which to continue to beat them.

The solution, in any event, is not a blanket exemption from universal principles of justice, but greater local responsibility for the interpretation and enforcement of these principles in the first instance. Allegations of abuses should be reviewed first by the indigenous authorities concerned. Member states should do everything possible to foster the development, within autonomous indigenous territories, of effective, culturally appropriate local machinery for the protection and enhancement of human rights. In addition, member states can encourage human rights education and the growth of independent NGOs, within indigenous communities, as a check on potential abuses. State officials and national human rights institutions should adopt the policy of deferring to local indigenous authorities and to their interpretations of relevant laws, just as United Nations treaty bodies require the exhaustion of domestic remedies and defer, to some extent, to national legal standards.

This approach would encourage autonomous communities to find culturally and socially appropriate ways of protecting the rights of individuals, without depriving individual indigenous people of access, where necessary, to national and international redress.

## Procedural Rights

The foregoing review has explored the various facets of the concept of self-determination, as understood by indigenous peoples. It should be clear to the reader that indigenous people view self-determination as a complex bundle of rights, balancing dialectically greater freedom from the nation-state with greater collective participation in state institutions and more security of individual equality with other citizens.

This would not necessarily differ, in results, from autonomy arrangements made in some countries, such as Belgium and Canada, to accommodate linguistically distinct regions. In fact, possibly the most interesting and significant dimension of indigenous peoples' claims is procedural rather than substantive in nature. Indigenous peoples assert, and to a growing extent are recognized as possessing, standing to negotiate their legal status with the nation-state, and standing to maintain some elements of their own international personality as a guarantee of their rights. It is this aspect of the emerging law of indigenous rights, and not the complex but familiar conception of autonomy within nation-states, which distinguishes the self-determination of indigenous peoples most clearly from the historical protection of minorities. Even the 'minorities treaties' which were negotiated at Versailles in the wake of the First World War did not confer legal standing at the national or international levels.[12]

The importance of procedural rights and standing in the case of indigenous peoples is certainly a reflection of the fact that these peoples have been directly involved in developing standards within the United Nations system. They fully understand the significance of collective participation in decision making as a guarantee of the genuine and free exercise of their substantive rights. They have little confidence in the interpretation and enforcement of their fundamental rights by others. At the same time, the traditional philosophies of indigenous peoples equate political relationships with social relationships or kinship.[13] Indigenous nations viewed treaties as marriages and adoptions, not business contracts; and they expected to revise their relationships with other nations and peoples continually. The legal status of each nation in the alliance was periodically adjusted and reaffirmed. From a traditional indigenous perspective, then, procedure is the source of rights. Consequently, indigenous peoples are highly sensitive to issues of standing and participation.

The procedural aspects of indigenous rights must be explored at both the national and international levels. In the pages which follow, the focus is on indigenous peoples' role in transforming the constitutional structure of the state, their continuing role in governing the state and their access to, and participation in, international fora.

*Constitutional Reform*

Self-determination, as indigenous peoples understand it, cannot be achieved in most states without constitutional amendments.[14] Qualitative changes are required in the distribution of political authority and legislative jurisdiction. In federal states, there is a need to define new constituents of the federation, while, in unitary states, there is a need to introduce a federal structure. Mutual guarantees of security, cooperation, respect for law and respect for the individual rights of one another's citizens will be demanded on both sides. National machinery will be needed for the enforcement of these arrangements. It is unlikely that these sweeping changes can be accomplished through ordinary legislation and, even if they could, all parties will almost certainly prefer the security and longevity of constitutional entrenchment.

It is, moreover, essential to the success of the project that indigenous peoples collaborate in preparing constitutional drafts and agree formally to their adoption. Successful reconciliation depends, in the long run, on developing a relationship of respect between indigenous peoples and their fellow citizens, as well as a shared national vision. Collaboration is an essential step in building a constructive relationship and ensuring that everyone is fully committed to maintaining the spirit and intent of their new political arrangements. Indigenous and non-indigenous people must not only share responsibility for restructuring their legal relationships but must each enjoy the opportunity to review and ratify the proposed changes, before they are adopted as constitutional law. Haste can only lead to resentment and will undermine the broad popular support for a new relationship which will protect it against future political reversals.

The true objective of these constitutional processes is to begin the long process of reconciliation. It is an opportunity to seat indigenous and non-indigenous people at the same table in a spirit of equality, with a shared purpose. The resulting agreements may not last for all time, for indeed no agreement made by human beings is so perfect as to settle matters forever. However, the experience of taking one step forward in a concrete political partnership is indispensable to persuading indigenous and non-indigenous people that they can live side by side as co-tenants of a single state.

The evolving relationship between Denmark and Greenland has much to teach us in this regard. The 'Home Rule' law which began the process of transferring political authority to the indigenous Inuit people of Greenland was the result of collaboration between Danish and Inuit leaders. There have been many adjustments since the enactment of the original legislation, but the trust that had been developed between Danes and Inuit facilitated these changes. It appears that Greenland Inuit feel very confident in their relationship with Denmark, and have no misgivings whatever about remaining a part of the Danish state. This may be attributed to the collaborative nature of the process of constitutional change. Paradoxically, the same can be said of the autonomy arrangements which were recently adopted for the Atlantic coast of Nicaragua. Although the parties had been at war, the negotiated character of the reintegration of indigenous territories into Nicaragua seems to have succeeded in restoring respect and cooperation.

There is another important dimension to collaborating on the project of constitutional reform. The reform process can lead to a broader rethinking of the nature of the state and society as a whole, with significant benefits for democratization and greater respect for the human rights of all citizens. Indigenous peoples were highly visible and especially active in the 1988 revision of the Brazilian Constitution. Their participation led to the adoption of a special chapter on the rights of indigenous peoples, but it also helped other social groups in Brazil to advance their rights and to broaden and deepen the roots of democracy in that state. One could say that the arduous and, as yet, inconclusive process of constitutional reform in Canada, beginning in 1978, is a close parallel. By highlighting the aspirations of indigenous peoples as well as of the French-speaking society of Quebec, these talks have confronted all Canadians with important questions about the history, nature and values of their country. One crucial result, at least, was the constitutional entrenchment of a national bill of human rights.

Negotiated constitutional reform is not explicitly required by existing international instruments, but is unavoidable if the express terms of these instruments are to be implemented fully in good faith. In particular, the ILO Indigenous and Tribal Peoples Convention, 1989, requires the adoption of appropriate procedures at the national level to seek the agreement of indigenous peoples 'through their representative institutions' to measures which may affect them. Furthermore, States Parties must respect the 'freely expressed wishes' of these peoples with regard to measures which distinguish between them and other citizens. The most reasonable means of satisfying these complementary requirements is to agree, with indigenous peoples, on a constitutional amendment which sets out plainly the procedures to be followed in future legislation.

On a more general level, the rights to autonomy, collective ownership and management of lands and resources necessarily imply the negotiation of agreements between indigenous authorities and national officials. These are very complex rights and cannot be realized except through a sequence of steps beginning with formal recognition of indigenous peoples' representative institutions as legal authorities, and the establishment of agreed procedures for consultation and agreement on specific matters, ranging from the demarcation of administrative borders to the financing of schools and hospitals. The authority and responsibility of the national authorities in this process will require a constitutional basis.

Although the right of indigenous peoples to self-government or autonomy, as a component of their right to self-determination, has not yet been universally recognized in the form of a legally binding instrument, General Assembly resolution 49/214 encourages governments to 'seek means, in consultation with indigenous people, of giving indigenous people greater responsibility for their own affairs, and an effective voice in decisions which affect them'.

It is precisely during this lengthy process of negotiations that the United Nations system may play its most supportive role. Technical assistance, in particular the dissemination of examples and expertise developed in other countries, such as the reconciliation procedure between indigenous peoples and the government of Australia or the Home Rule Government in Greenland, will help demonstrate the feasibility of negotiated constitutional reforms, and provide indigenous peoples and governments with a better sense of options for constructive change. Technical assistance could also play an important role in designing negotiation procedures, ensuring that they are followed in good faith. Ultimately, the United Nations system may be called upon for informal mediation. Strong commitments of United Nations technical resources to these procedural aspects of the realization of indigenous peoples' rights will be a better investment in the protection of these peoples over the long term than more resources devoted to monitoring and reporting abuses.

*International Procedures*

To guarantee their rights, indigenous peoples seek enhanced standing to petition and participate in United Nations bodies. To a limited extent, they have already achieved this goal in practice. At the Working Group on Indigenous Populations, they enjoy unrestricted access. In principle, they will enjoy the same degree of access to the Intergovernmental Working Group of the Commission on Human Rights, established to review the Draft Declaration on the Rights of Indigenous Peoples. Indigenous peoples have been able to take part in international conferences as a distinct 'major group' of civil society, and continue to participate as a distinct group in the work of the Commission on Sustainable Development. Although they are not 'non-governmental organizations' strictly speaking, indigenous peoples have been able to obtain and use NGO status in ECOSOC and its subsidiary bodies, as well as in the ILO and UNESCO, as a means of advancing their concerns as nations and peoples.

However, the most important procedural developments have taken place at a technical level, for example in meetings of experts organized by the United Nations Centre for Human Rights to discuss the rights of indigenous peoples, and the technical meetings convened under the authority of the General Assembly to plan the International Year and Decade of the World's Indigenous People. At these meetings, representatives of indigenous peoples and governments collaborate on the basis of equality, taking decisions by consensus. This is both a significant procedural precedent and compelling evidence that indigenous peoples and governments are capable of practical partnerships at the international level. Paragraph 13 of

General Assembly resolution 49/214 endorses even greater participation by indigenous peoples in the policy conferences and
operational work of the United Nations system.

The participation, albeit symbolic, of indigenous leaders in opening ceremonies for the International Year and Decade of the World's
Indigenous People, inside the General Assembly chamber, and in the
presence of the Secretary-General, other high-level United Nations
officials and representatives of governments, reflects acceptance in
United Nations practice of these peoples' unique character. While
this falls short of the aspirations of many indigenous peoples for
standing as observers, following the precedent of liberation organizations, it is nonetheless a significant departure from conventional
practices and a concession which has not been lightly made.

Three fields of procedural development merit our attention, because of their potential contributions to the protection of the rights of
indigenous peoples.

*Human rights treaty bodies*   It is of fundamental importance that all
existing supervisory mechanisms, under the International Covenants
on Human Rights and other human rights instruments, pay particular attention to the situation of indigenous peoples when they examine
the periodic reports of States Parties. The decision by the chairper-
sons of the various treaty bodies to request basic socioeconomic and
legal data in the form of 'core documents' from each state party was
a very constructive step, since it increases the likelihood that the
existence of indigenous peoples and their life circumstances will
come to the attention of treaty bodies in the regular course of their
work. Some governments had never even admitted that indigenous
peoples lived within their borders. General Assembly resolution 49/
214 also recognizes the need for a wider data-gathering effort by the
United Nations system, to establish basic facts about the distribution
and condition of indigenous peoples worldwide.

Treaty bodies increasingly request detailed explanations of the land
rights, internal self-government and national political participation
of indigenous peoples. This practice was begun by the Committee on
the Elimination of Racial Discrimination (CERD) a decade ago, particularly when it examined periodic reports from States Parties in the
Americas. Governments naturally pay greater attention to these issues when they expect to be questioned every time they report. They
are likely to include more relevant data in their periodic reports,
which offers the indigenous peoples in those countries an opportunity to respond with their own data and viewpoints. Ideally, the
treaty bodies can facilitate a dialogue between governments and
indigenous peoples, at the international level, focused on the adequacy and reform of domestic policies. This can only evolve,

however, if treaty bodies make a consistent practice of addressing indigenous peoples as a distinct concern.

*Monitoring mechanisms* Monitoring mechanisms are most effective when NGOs are fully involved. NGOs can participate officially in the meetings of the Committee on Economic, Social and Cultural Rights and the Committee on the Rights of the Child. They lack official standing but nevertheless participate informally as observers at public meetings of other treaty bodies such as CERD and the Human Rights Committee. Access to these meetings is restricted to NGOs in consultative status with ECOSOC, but there are at least 12 such organizations comprising indigenous peoples which have been able to sponsor the United Nations activities of indigenous peoples that lack ECOSOC accreditation. It is doubtful that greater levels of participation can be achieved without amending the relevant human rights treaties. However, treaty bodies themselves could greatly enhance the effectiveness of periodic reports, not only for indigenous peoples but for all sections of national society. They could achieve this by interpreting the duty of States Parties to submit reports as including an obligation to involve relevant groups directly in the preparation of reports. Evidence of this participatory process would be required as part of the reports.

In the case of indigenous peoples, this would contribute to development of partnerships with governments. It would encourage indigenous peoples and government officials to discuss and assess current policies and laws. They might continue to disagree, but they would be talking. The role of treaty bodies would simply be to ensure that this dialogue precedes each report and, by means of their comments on periodic reports, to suggest ways of making the dialogue more constructive.

This is an example of an indigenous perspective on protection of human rights, a perspective which stresses the significance of procedural rights. By enriching the procedures States Parties use to prepare their reports, treaty bodies can directly empower key groups in society, such as indigenous peoples, women, minorities or children. Treaty bodies would conceivably accomplish more by promoting and monitoring effective participation at the national level than by simply evaluating the extent to which substantive rights are enjoyed.

Before leaving the issue of monitoring, some consideration of the potential role of the existing Working Group on Indigenous Populations as a monitoring body is in order. Ever since 1985, when work began on the text of a declaration of rights, there has been support for eventually entrusting the Working Group with the mandate to monitor its implementation. There are two advantages to this approach. The Working Group has developed expertise over the years since its establishment in 1982, and it has earned the trust of a large number of interested governments. It has well-established procedures which offer indigenous peoples the greatest possible access to its meetings, as a result of which it has become the most popular central meeting-place of the world's indigenous peoples. With these advantages, the Working Group can easily reorient from standard-setting to oversight. Indeed, the most recent sessions of the Working Group have witnessed a number of candid and constructive exchanges of views between indigenous leaders and government officials, even at the ministerial level. There is more cause for confidence than ever that the Working Group can use the Declaration of the Rights of Indigenous Peoples to engage all of the relevant parties in an open, frank and pragmatic dialogue at the international level, and thereby encourage the development of a parallel dialogue within each country at the national level.

*The permanent forum for indigenous peoples*   One of the most important recommendations of the World Conference on Human Rights was the establishment of a permanent forum for indigenous peoples within the United Nations system.[15] The General Assembly endorsed this recommendation in its resolutions 48/163 and 49/214 and modalities for its implementation are currently being studied by the Commission on Human Rights with the advice of the Working Group.[16] In its resolution of 1999 the Commission on Human Rights decided to re-establish the open-ended inter-sessional working group to meet for eight working days prior to its fifty-sixth session with a view to submitting one or more proposals on the establishment of a permanent forum for indigenous people to the Commission at its next session in March/April 2000. The second session of the *ad hoc* working group was due to meet in Geneva from 7 to 17 February 2000.[17] Indigenous peoples clearly see this new institution as the key to gaining an effective direct voice in United Nations relevant decision making.

The permanent forum should be as open as the Working Group to the participation of indigenous peoples, without regard to the consultative status of their NGOs with ECOSOC. It also seems desirable that the official members of this new United Nations body should be equally divided between individual experts nominated by relevant member states, and experts nominated by those indigenous peoples who participate in its work. Above all, the permanent forum must be lodged at a high level in the United Nations system, most logically as one of the regular advisory committees reporting directly to ECOSOC. It would require the assistance of a special secretariat unit, to be made up as far as possible of indigenous professionals who can promote awareness and build administrative links throughout the United Nations system.

Unlike the existing Working Group, which is fundamentally a body of human rights experts concerned with legal standards, the permanent forum will have a broader and more operational mandate. Its first task will undoubtedly be implementation of the programme of action for the International Decade of the World's Indigenous People. This will evolve into continuing responsibility for setting goals and coordinating the relevant activities of United Nations operational bodies and specialized agencies. For example, it might organize technical workshops and strategy round tables for the personnel of specialized agencies and indigenous peoples, both at headquarters and at the national and regional levels. It could maintain links between indigenous communities in different regions, and help the communities locate the expertise they need in other countries. Also the permanent forum should promote recruitment of indigenous people for professional posts throughout the United Nations system, and ensure the employment of indigenous expertise in field projects.

It was suggested earlier that United Nations technical assistance could play a significant role in fostering constitutional reforms and other negotiated political settlements through which indigenous peoples concretely exercise their right to self-determination. Securing this constructive developmental role for the United Nations will be the task of the permanent forum. It should have the capacity to identify emergent situations where indigenous peoples and governments are willing to address problems cooperatively, and allocate resources to give these initiatives the greatest possible opportunity to succeed. If adequately financed and suitably respected by other United Nations bodies and agencies, the permanent forum could indeed become a kind of Trusteeship Council, to which indigenous peoples can turn for guidance and good offices in their efforts to exercise their vision of self-determination.

## Policy Considerations

This concluding part of the chapter will briefly explore the most compelling reasons why states should support the rights of indigenous peoples, both substantive and procedural, as they have been outlined above. The bundle of rights which indigenous peoples associate with self-determination has been gaining recognition in international fora and instruments, but this recognition remains incomplete and subject to challenges. It would be tragic for the countries concerned if this process of evolution were to be cut short.

*State Building*

We live today in a world of dangerously weak, tentative and unconsolidated states. The territorial reorganizations of Europe after the First and Second World Wars, and the subsequently rapid decolonization of other regions under United Nations auspices, have created a large number of multinational, multiethnic countries which have had little time or opportunity to build new, integrated societies upon a solid foundation of trust and cooperation. This is most especially true of states with large indigenous populations. Very few of these states have involved indigenous peoples in the formation of a modern national identity or in the design of the national economy and political system. This will continue to be a source of potential conflict until it has been addressed fully and effectively by the governments concerned. If we have learned nothing else from recent events in Europe, we have learned that peoples who have no reason to feel that they are full partners in the state can never be suppressed so completely that they will forget their own identity or feelings of exclusion.

The first reason why member states should support indigenous peoples in their conceptions of self-determination, then, is that constitutional reforms and partnerships in decision making dispel mistrust and build stronger nations. This approach to furthering the enjoyment of human rights by indigenous peoples also makes a contribution to maintaining international peace and security.

*Environmental Security*

The United Nations Conference on Environment and Development (UNCED) exposed two important truths. One was the absolute necessity of international cooperation to stabilize, renew and conserve the living resources and critical ecosystems of the planet. No state can pretend any longer that its destruction of fisheries, forests or the atmosphere is simply its own internal affair. Just as the 1970s brought an awareness of the connection between human rights and peace, and the 1980s an understanding of the linkages between peace and development, UNCED underscored the dependence of peace, human rights and development on basic environmental security. By diminishing our limited stock of planetary resources, we condemn ourselves and our children to poverty, ill-health, ignorance and wars of survival.

The second truth exposed by UNCED was the important role of indigenous peoples and their traditional knowledge in addressing global environmental challenges. As the people living closest to land and living resources, with the longest and richest memories of ecological processes and changes, indigenous societies must be able to maintain their expertise and apply it to the conservation of their own territories, which tend to be rich in biodiversity, fragile and, as yet, relatively undisturbed. They must also be included as partners in the search for solutions to national and international environmental problems. Protecting the territories of indigenous peoples from interference and enabling indigenous communities to manage their own lands and resources, in conformity with their values and experience, will be an indispensable source of insight and technology for the countries in which they live and, ultimately, for all peoples.

Thus the second reason why member states should support indigenous peoples in their conceptions of self-determination is the role of local autonomous management of resources in conserving ecosystems and maintaining expertise for global environmental security.

*Human Development*

A major revolution in economic thinking has taken place over the years between the United Nations Declaration on International Economic Co-operation[18] and the World Summit on Social Development. After the failure of finance-intensive strategies of development, with their legacy of environmental destruction, external debt and 'aid fatigue', economists and planners concluded that development requires a healthy, literate and skilled population that has the freedom and the means to participate actively in decision making. It is now generally agreed that human development, including the realization of human rights, is a strategy for development rather than simply one of the beneficial results of development.

Most of the countries in which indigenous peoples live today are relatively poor and underdeveloped. They have generally been accustomed to regarding indigenous people as an obstacle to their national development, not as an economic asset. By pursuing this philosophy, they will neglect the potential creativity and energy of a large portion of their national population and condemn them to becoming centres of poverty, despair and conflict which future generations will have to repair. Ignoring the human potential of indigenous communities is a waste of resources in the short term, and a source of high social and financial costs in the long term. In brief, it is very poor development policy, especially in view of the growing recognition of the commercial value of indigenous peoples' traditional knowledge of medicine and ecology.

Accordingly, the third reason why member states should support indigenous peoples in their pursuit of self-determination is the contribution that indigenous peoples can make, as free and equal partners, to national development.

## Some Concluding Remarks

The struggle of the world's indigenous peoples, which is of historic importance, has already reached a new significant stage. The issues related to an effective protection of their human rights and fundamental freedoms are on the agenda of the international community. However, further efforts should be made to: a) accelerate the elaboration of the draft Union Nations Declaration on Indigenous Rights, which is still pending before the *ad hoc* Working Group of the Commission on Human Rights, b) complete the work for the establishment of a Permanent Forum for Indigenous Peoples, which is also an issue before the competent Working Group of the Commission on Human Rights, c) continue future constructive dialogue and consultation at the annual meetings of the United Nations Working Group on Indigenous Populations, which should focus in particular on the degree of independence of the indigenous peoples from the states in which they have lived, and the extent to which indigenous peoples have standing to participate formally and actively in United Nations system's decision-making organs and bodies.

The hopes should be expressed that the indigenous peoples, united in their struggle, will achieve these goals at the dawn of the new millennium.

## Notes

1    Articles 73 and 74 of the Charter of the United Nations.
2    See the Statement by Boutros-Boutros Ghali, UN Secretary General, at the Inauguration of the International Year of the World's Indigenous People, General Assembly of the United Nations 47th session, Plenary, 82nd Meeting and Special Ceremony, *Transnational and Contemporary Problems*, 3, 1993, pp.168–71.
3    World Conference on Human Rights, The Vienna Declaration and Programme of Action, June 1993, UN, Declaration (DPI)/1394–39399, August 1993 – 20M, paras 20 and 28–32, pp.35 and 52–3.
4    Explanatory note concerning the Draft Declaration on the Rights of Indigenous Peoples by Erica-Irene A. Daes, Chairperson/Rapporteur of the Working Group on Indigenous Populations, E/CN.4/Sub.2/1993/26/Add.1 (1993). In connection with the right to self-determination of indigenous peoples, see, among others, Daes (1993) and (1995, p.92); Hannum (1990, pp.458–77) and (1993, pp.1–69). See also Anaya (1993, pp.131–64); Alfredsson (1993); Sanders (1993, pp.55–81); and Barsh (1994, pp.33–86).
5    See Daes (1995, pp.85–95).
6    Report of the United Nations Conference on Environment and Development, Vol. I, A/CONF.151/26/Rev.1 (Vol.I), Chapter 26, sub-paragraph 26–3(a)(ii).
7    Swepston (1990, pp.677–714).
8    In this respect, see Daes (1995, pp.493–9). The text of the United Nations Draft Declaration, as agreed upon by the Members of the Working Group on Indigenous Populations at its eleventh session, is included in Annex I of this *St*

*Thomas Law Review* issue, pp.500–515. This draft was presented to the Sub-Commission on Prevention of Discrimination and Protection of Minorities by the Chairperson/Rapporteur, Erica-Irene A. Daes (SR/CN.4/1994/ of August 1994). It was duly considered, adopted by the Sub-Commission and submitted to the Commission on Human Rights by its resolution 1994/45. See Daes (1995, pp.493–4). The Commission of Human Rights by its resolution 1995/32 decided to establish a working group to consider further the above-mentioned draft declaration. This resolution was endorsed by the relevant decision of ECOSOC, and the new established Working Group met in November 1995.

9 See Daes, *supra*, note 5. See also Gayim (1994, pp.1–72).

10 See Gayim and Myntti (1995, pp.16–45).

11 See, for example, Coombs (1994, pp.2–230).

12 In connection with a brief summary of the historical protection of minorities, see, among others, Daes (1973, pp.43–51).

13 See, for example, the excellent summary by Chief Oren Lyons in *Little Bear*, Copenhagen, Bold and Long, 1984.

14 See the relevant important proposals contained in the speeches from the Conference on 'The position of indigenous peoples in national constitutions' (Council for Aboriginal Reconciliation, 1994, pp.3–116).

15 The Vienna Declaration and Programme of Action in the World Conference on Human Rights, *supra*, note 3, para. 31, p.53, General Assembly resolutions 48/163 and 49/214 and Commission on Human Rights resolution 1995/30. See also the Note by the Chairperson/Rapporteur of the Working Group on Indigenous Populations, Erica-Irene A. Daes, on the Consideration of a Permanent Forum for Indigenous Peoples E/CN/Sub.2/AC.4/1994/13.

16 In this respect, the first Workshop on a Permanent Forum for Indigenous People was organized by the UN Centre of Human Rights in cooperation with the government of Denmark (Copenhagen, 26–28 June 1995), and the second one in cooperation with the government of Chile, in Santiago, 30 June–2 July 1997. See the Report of the Second Workshop on a Permanent Forum for Indigenous People within the United Nations system held in accordance with Commission on Human Rights resolution 1997/30, UN.DOC.E/CN.4/1998/11 of 19 September 1997. See also, Daes, E-I.A., Note on the future role of the Working Group by Erica-Irene Daes, Chairperson of the Working Group on Indigenous Populations, UN.DOC.E/CN.4/Sub.2/AC.4/1995/6, of 13 June 1995. Also the Report of the Second Workshop on a Permanent Forum for Indigenous People with the United Nations system held in accordance with Commission on Human Rights resolution 1997/30 (Santiago, 30 June–2 July 1997), Addendum contribution of Mrs Erica-Irene Daes, UN.DOC.E/CN.4/1998/11/Add.2, 17 March 1998, Chapter V, pp.1–5.

17 UN.DOC.E/CN.4/Sub.2/AC.4/1999/3, of 16 June 1999.

18 General Assembly resolution S-18/3 (1 May 1990), Annex.

# Bibliography

Aboriginal and Torres Strait Islander Commission (ATSIC) (1995), 'Recognition, Rights and Reform: Overview, Proposed Principles for Indigenous Social Justice', Report to Government on Native Title Social Justice Measures, Commonwealth of Australia.

Aboriginal and Torres Strait Islander Commission (ATSIC) (1995), 'Recognition, Rights and Reform–Report to Government on Native Title Social Justice Measures', Commonwealth of Australia.

Alfredsson, G. (1993), 'The right to self-determination and indigenous peoples', in C. Tomuschat (ed.), *Modern Law of Self-Determination*, Dordrecht/Boston/London, Martinus Nijhoff Publishers/Kluwer Academic Publishers, pp.41–54.

Anaya, S.J. (1993) 'A contemporary definition of the international norm of self-determination', *Transnational Law and Contemporary Problems* (a journal of the University of Iowa College of Law), **3**, Springs, 131–64.

Assies, W.J. and A.J. Hoekema (1994), 'Indigenous Peoples' Experiences with Self-Government', Proceedings of the Seminar on Arrangements for Self-Determination by Indigenous Peoples within National States, 10–11 February 1994, Law Faculty, University of Amsterdam, IWGIA, Doc. No. 76, Copenhagen, IWGIA and University of Amsterdam.

Barsh, R.L. (1994), 'Indigenous peoples in the 1990s: from object to subject of international law?' *Harvard Human Rights Journal*, **7**, 33–86.

Bear, L.L., M. Bold and A. Long (eds) (1984), *Path-Ways to Self-Determination*, Toronto, University of Toronto Press.

Brosten, J. *et al.* (eds) (1985), *Native Power: The Quest for Autonomy and Nationhood of Indigenous Peoples*, Bergen, Universitets for laget.

Brownlie I. (1992), *Treaties and Indigenous Peoples: The Robb Lectures, 1991*, F.M. Brookfield (ed.), Oxford, Clarendon Press.

Burger, J. (1987), *Report from the Frontier: The State of the World's Indigenous Peoples*, London/Cambridge, Mass., Zed Books.

Crawford J. (ed.) (1992), *The Rights of Peoples*, Oxford, Clarendon Paperbacks.

Coombs, H.C. (1994), *Aboriginal Autonomy – Issues and Strategies*, Diane Smith (ed.), Cambridge, Cambridge University Press.

Council for Aboriginal Reconciliation (ed.) (1993), *The Position of Indigenous Peoples in National Constitutions*, Speeches from the Conference, Constitutional Centenary Foundation, produced by the Australian Publishing Service, Canberra, 4–5 June, pp.1–116.

Daes, E-I.A. (1973), 'Protection of minorities under the International Bill of Human Rights and the Genocide Convention', in E. von Caemmerer *et al.* (eds), *Xenion, Festschrift fur Pan. J. Zepos*, Zweiter (II) Band, Athen-Freiburg/BR-Koln, Ch. Katsicalis Verfag, pp.35–86.

Daes, E-I.A. (1986), 'Native people's rights' in *Les Droits des minorités*, Actes du IIIe Colloque international de droit constitutionnel de la faculté de droit de l' Université Laval, Quebec, March 1985, *Les Cahiers de droit*, **27**, (1), Faculté de droit, Universite Laval, 123–33.

Daes, E-I.A. (1993), 'Some considerations on the rights of indigenous peoples to self-determination', *Transnational Law and Contemporary Problems* (a journal of the University of Iowa College of Law), **3**, Spring, 2–11.

Daes, E-I.A. (1995), 'The United Nations Declaration on Minority Rights: necessary, urgent and overdue', in Eco' Diagnostic (ed.), *International Geneva Yearbook, 1995*, Vol. IX, Geneva, Georg, pp.85–95.

Daes, E-I.A. (1995), 'The United Nations Draft Declaration on the Rights of Indigenous Peoples' (Symposium Tribal Sovereignty: Back to the Future?), *St. Thomas Law Review*, **7**, Summer, 493–519.

Dalee, S. (1994), 'A wave of change: the United Nations and indigenous peoples', *Cultural Survival Quarterly*, Spring.

Fliert, L. van de (ed.) (1994), *Indigenous Peoples and International Organization*, Nottingham, Russel Press.

Gayim, E. (ed.) (1994), 'The UN Draft Declaration on Indigenous Peoples – Assessment of the Draft. Prepared by the Working Group on Indigenous Populations', University of Lapland, Northern Institute for Environmental and Minority Law, Rovaniemi-Finland.

Gayim E. and K. Myntti (eds) (1995), *Indigenous and Tribal Peoples' Rights – 1993 and*

*After,* University of Lapland, Northern Institute for Environmental and Minority Law, Rovaniemi, University of Lapland's Printing Services.

Ghali, B-B. (1993) 'Statement on the International Year of the World's Indigenous Peoples at the United Nations General Assembly', 47th session, 82nd Plenary meeting, Special Ceremony, *Transnational Law and Contemporary Problems* (a journal of the University of Iowa College of Law), 3, Springs, 168–71.

Hannum, H. (1990), *Autonomy, Sovereignty and Self-Determination. The Accommodation of Conflicting Rights,* Philadelphia, University of Pennsylvania Press.

Hannum, H. (1993), 'Rethinking self-determination', *Virginia Journal of International Law,* **34,** (1), Fall, 1–69.

Heinz, W.S. (1991), *Indigenous Populations, Ethnic Minorities and Human Rights,* Saarbrucken/Fort Lauderdale, Verlag Breitenbach Publishers.

Marks, G.C. (1992), 'Indigenous peoples in international law. The significance of Francisco de Vitoria and Bartolome de Las Casas', *The Australian Year Book of International Law,* Vol. 13, The Australian National University, Faculty of Law, pp. 1–51.

McRae, H., G. Nettheim and L. Beacroft (1991), *Aboriginal Legal Issues,* Charlottsville, Virginia, Virginia Journal of International Law Association.

Mendelsohn, O. and U. Baxi (eds) (1994), *The Rights of Subordinated Peoples,* Delhi/ Bombay/Calcutta/Madras, Oxford University Press.

Ortiz, R.D. (1984), *Indians of the Americas. Human Rights and Self-Determination,* London, Zed Books.

Phillips A. and A. Rosas (1995), *Universal Minority Rights,* Turku-Åbo/London, Åbo Akademi University Institute for Human Rights/Minority Rights Group.

Sanders, D. (1993), 'Self-Determination and Indigenous Peoples', in C. Tomuschat (ed.), *Modern Law of Self-Determination,* Dordrecht/Boston/London, Martinus Nijhoff Publishers/Kluwer Academic Publishers, pp.55–82.

Suagee, D.B. (1992), 'Self-determination for indigenous peoples at the dawn of the Solar Age', *University of Michigan Journal of Law Reform,* **25,** (3 & 4), Spring and Summer, 671–749.

Swepston, L. (1990), 'A new step in the international law on indigenous and tribal peoples: ILO Convention No. 169 of 1989', *Oklahoma City University Law Review,* **15,** 677–714.

Tomuschat, C. (ed.) (1993), *Modern Law of Self-Determination,* Dordrecht/Boston/ London, Martinus Nijhoff Publishers.

Wilmer, F. (1993), *The Indigenous Voice in World Politics: Since Time Immemorial,* Newbury Park, Calif., Sage.

# 10 Migrant Workers' Rights

## FARUK ŞEN AND SEDEF KORAY

## Introduction

The history of mankind can be regarded as a history of migration. Labour mobility has been an important and essential feature of the economic and social development of societies throughout history. Despite this fact, migration is at present the cause of rising tension worldwide. The substantial increase in the pressure to migrate during the last two decades and the dramatic rise in the number of refugees and asylum seekers are two of the reasons for this. Consequently, there are uneasy and sometimes hostile feelings in sections of the population about migration and migrants.

As a result, international migration has become one of the most important and challenging issues for the international community today. Apart from traditional immigration countries such as the United States, Canada and Australia, many European countries and former sending countries, such as Italy and Spain, have become countries of immigration. Despite the restrictions of entry, particularly into Western European countries, reality moves in a different direction. First of all, traditional labour migration continues in the form of selective recruitment for special reasons on a bilateral basis. Second, a trend of increasing immigration is observed by way of family formation. Third, refugees continue to immigrate. In fact, the acceptance of refugees has become a major gate of entry by which gaps in the labour market are filled.

As a result of these developments, many receiving countries, and particularly those in Western Europe, are faced with a dilemma. On the one hand, the protection of human rights has gained weight in public discussion and political negotiation. On the other, aggressive nationalism, racism and xenophobia are gaining ground, and there are great deficiencies with regard to the rights of migrant workers in

many of these societies. Reflecting this dilemma, international opinion concerning labour migration has also evolved in two different
directions. First, the issue of migrant workers' rights has been increasingly linked to the concepts of democracy and human rights in
Europe and elsewhere. It is closely linked to the contemporary international law of human rights because it involves a clear test of the
relevance and enforceability of the international human rights norms
which have been developed since the Second World War. Second,
migratory movements, including labour migration, are increasingly
perceived as a matter of security and stability and less from a human
rights perspective: 'The predominant policy orientation in the field
of migration and refugees is not any longer the protection of rights,
but the control of migratory movements.'[1]

We can, indeed, note the following changes in international opinion
concerning international labour migration. After the Second World
War, the needs of the international labour market required changes in
the transfer of foreign workers between countries and mass labour
migration continued in the 1950s and 1960s. Beginning with the 1970s,
the negative effects of the uncontrolled increase in migration movements were beginning to be perceived by the countries of origin as
well as by migrants themselves, along with the emergence of economic, social and cultural problems in the host countries. Norms were
sought to remedy the detrimental effects of migration both in the
sending and receiving countries. In the 1990s, discouraging and combating illegal migration and employment have become the main
objectives of international instruments and norms. As a result of the
security aspect, migration and development policies have been closely
linked in the 1990s. Developed countries hosting large numbers of
migrants have been increasingly called upon to contribute to the economies and development of the countries of origin, so that migratory
pressures can be alleviated. This shows a clear preference for the transfer of capital and technology rather than the movement of persons.

## International Legal Instruments on Migrant Workers' Rights

The international community today witnesses a change in the way
the rights of migrant workers are protected. The traditional system
of diplomatic protection, invoking the international law governing
the treatment of foreigners (or 'non-nationals', as they may be called),
has been replaced by the direct protection of the rights of individual
foreigners by means of national and international instruments to
enforce a set of reformulated international norms.[2]

The problem of the rights of migrant workers and their families is
one of the most significant and difficult areas of the law governing

the treatment of non-nationals today. Part of the problem lies in that migrant workers are often perceived and treated as temporary guests who would eventually return to their country of origin. In reality, however, they have become permanent settlers who demand their status as a permanent component of the society in which they live.

Subject to various economic, political, social and humanitarian pressures and influences, governments face two tendencies with regard to the treatment of non-nationals. The first is the desire of many states to see further developments in the field of human rights. The second is the continuing insistence of states on the principle of sovereignty. In this connection, non-nationals are subject to the powers of exclusion and expulsion of the state. Nevertheless, reciprocity, internationally acknowledged principles of human rights and domestic support for migrants can be moderating factors in the practice of these powers.[3]

International law is of little use in the treatment of foreigners with regard to entry to a foreign territory. Entry and residence of foreigners continue to be regulated by the traditional concept of state sovereignty. States possess a broad competence in this domain, and access to territory and to citizenship is allowed as a privilege extended on its own terms. It is understandable that the state considers its own interests first of all and, to that end, will find some people more acceptable than others for economic, social, political and cultural reasons. Matters of entry and expulsion can then be taken up within the framework of international law, when treaties or international norms such as those concerning non-discrimination are operative. Despite the fact that such matters essentially fall within the domain of domestic jurisdiction, states are not completely free to act as they wish. As a result of increasing economic and political interdependence in the world, states have become aware of the significance of the existence of migrant workers as an indispensable factor for economic and social development.[4]

The rights of migrant workers are not confined to matters of entry and expulsion. International law provides legal instruments and remedies to protect the rights of migrant workers and their families. Bilateral and multilateral treaties are a primary source of obligations indicating the limits of state powers in matters of entry and expulsion and of safeguarding the rights of migrant workers and their families.

Today there is a large body of international instruments dealing directly and indirectly with the treatment of migrant workers. These instruments vary, from global ones, such as the United Nations International Covenants on Human Rights and International Labour Organisation (ILO) Conventions, to regional ones, such as the European Convention of Human Rights. Some of these instruments are of a non-binding character and can be considered as 'soft law'. Nevertheless, governments have become increasingly restrained in their actions, as these instruments have come to be used in domestic politics and by non-governmental organizations. There are, of course, other international instruments which are binding on States Parties to them.

The International Bill of Human Rights includes the Universal Declaration of Human Rights, which lists basic human rights that must be respected regardless of nationality or national origin, the International Covenant on Economic, Social and Cultural Rights and the International Covenant on Civil and Political Rights and its Optional Protocol.

### The International Convention on the Protection of the Rights of All Migrant Workers and Members of Their Families

In view of the weakness of legal instruments in force with regard to the rights of migrant workers and the need to regulate their employment, the United Nations adopted a new convention, the International Convention on the Protection of Rights of All Migrant Workers and Members of Their Families, on 18 December 1990. The purpose of this Convention was to discourage illegal migration. A 'migrant worker' is defined in the Convention as 'a person who is to be engaged, is engaged or has been engaged in a remunerated activity in a State of which he or she is not a national'.

In fact, this definition is highly simplified. The term 'migrant worker' represents a very heterogeneous and diverse group in reality. It includes highly skilled professional, managerial and technical workers on short-term assignments or in joint ventures, contract labour migrants recruited in groups for specific projects, individual contract workers, seasonal workers, domestic servants, au pairs, bar girls, entrepreneurs, family members who enter the labour market and become part of the migrant labour force, foreign students working temporarily, asylum seekers who enter the labour market illegally before acceptance and who stay and work illegally after rejection of the asylum application and, finally, refugees who enter the labour market legally after acceptance.[5]

The International Convention on the Protection of the Rights of All Migrant Workers and Members of Their Families introduces recognition by states of the competence of an international committee receiving and considering communications from individuals claiming that their individual rights have been violated by the State Party. It does not oblige Contracting Parties to admit migrant workers, but regulates recruitment and grants social, cultural and some civil rights to them. It was drafted in collaboration with the ILO and is now open for signature and ratification. It will enter into force when ratified by 20 states. Up to the present, only a small number of countries have ratified it. As of the end of 1995, four countries had ratified it and another three had signed it. By November 1999, 11 countries had ratified the convention and another six had signed it. This is worrying, particularly as several major migrant-sending and migrant-receiving countries have not yet ratified the ILO's conventions.

### Conventions of the International Labour Organisation (ILO)

Since its foundation, the ILO has pursued two objectives with regard to migrant workers. It has sought to establish the right of equality of treatment between nationals and foreigners in the field of social security through the Convention No. 19 and Recommendation No. 25, concerning Equality of Treatment (Accident Compensation), 1925; Convention No. 48 concerning Maintenance of Migrants' Pension Rights, 1935; and Convention No. 118 concerning Equality of Treatment (Social Security), 1962. It has also sought to find solutions to problems facing migrant workers in a broad range of issues. It also adopted the Convention No. 97 and Recommendation No. 86 concerning Migration for Employment, 1949; and Convention No. 143 and Recommendation No. 151 concerning Migrant Workers, 1975.

Conventions No. 97 and No. 143 in particular deal with practically all aspects of the working life of non-nationals, such as recruitment, access to information, contract conditions, medical attention, customs exemption for personal effects, assistance in settlement into the new environment, language and vocational training, promotion at work, job security, alternative employment, freedom of movement, participation in cultural life, maintenance of their own culture, transfer of earnings and savings, family reunification, appeal against unjustified termination of employment or expulsion and assistance in coping with return.

Both Conventions No. 97 and No. 143 aim at ensuring non-discrimination and equality of opportunity and treatment between migrant workers and nationals. The non-discrimination principle is basically of humanitarian and social inspiration, although it has some economic objectives as well. A state of origin does not wish its nationals to be the object of discrimination, whether this be due to statutory provisions, administrative practice or private behaviour. On the other hand, a host state and its workers do not wish to see non-nationals work under inferior conditions, because this may lead to displacement of national workers or to a reduction of their wages and deterioration of working conditions.

## European Human Rights Instruments

The European Convention of Human Rights of 1950, which entered into force in 1953 and is of a binding character, does not contain provisions specifically addressed to foreigners or migrant workers, but deals only incidentally with the treatment of foreigners. Therefore applications have been based on Article 3, which prohibits inhuman and degrading treatment, Articles 5 and 6, which protect the liberty of the person and the rights to a fair and public hearing, Article 8, which guarantees respect for private and family life, Article 12, which deals with the right to marry, and Article 14, which establishes the principle of non-discrimination.[6] As a result, European governments have found it difficult to introduce radical changes in the laws governing family reunification of migrant workers. The Convention does not create any right of asylum or the right to enter a country of which one is not a national, but a number of provisions do confer certain rights on foreigners and restrict state action in the field of expulsion. Article 2 of Protocol No. 7 to the Convention safeguards certain procedural rights of foreigners who are lawfully resident in the territory of a particular state. According to this article, lawfully resident foreigners may only be expelled in pursuance of a decision reached in accordance with law and, except in exceptional circumstances, after having been given an opportunity to submit reasons against expulsion and to have their case reviewed. However, not all states have ratified this Protocol.

The expulsion of a non-national may constitute a violation of the right to respect for the family based on Article 8, if the person concerned has all his family, and social and cultural ties, in the expelling country and has no connection, other than the formal one of nationality, with the country to which he is to be expelled. This view has been confirmed by the European Court of Justice.[7] However, there is a balancing between the individual's right and that of the state to control immigration and residence of non-nationals, particularly in the domains of public safety, economic well-being of the country and the prevention of disorder and crime. Thus there is no absolute right to protection and, under certain circumstances, even second-generation immigrants can be expelled.

Finally, Article 14 of the Convention prohibits discrimination on the grounds of sex, race, colour, language, religion, political or other opinion, national or social origin, association with a national minority, property, birth or other status. It should be noted that this article can only be invoked in connection with one of the rights and freedoms included in the Convention and does not constitute a prohibition of discrimination in general.

There are further restrictions on state action sponsored by the Council of Europe which supplement the limitations imposed by the European Convention of Human Rights. The most prominent ones are the European Social Charter of 1961 and the European Convention on the Legal Status of Migrant Workers of 1977. The European Social Charter, which has been in force since 1965, offers some degree of protection for migrant workers. The Appendix to the Charter states that foreigners who are either lawfully resident or employed regularly in the territory of a state are entitled to enumerated rights. Specifically, the general application of the Charter can be rendered in two ways to migrant workers:

1   the Preamble to the Charter states that the enjoyment of social rights must be secured without discrimination on grounds of race, colour, sex, religion, political opinion, national extraction or social origin;
2   the Appendix to the Charter states that Articles 1 to 17 'include foreigners only insofar as they are nationals of other Contracting Parties or fully resident or working regularly within the territory of the Contracting Party concerned, subject to the understanding that these articles are to be interpreted in the light of the provisions of Articles 18 and 19'.

It is thus generally agreed that the Appendix to the European Social Charter provides for equality of treatment between a contracting state's nationals and those of the other Contracting Parties. However, the principle of jurisdiction whereby the European Convention of Human Rights, for instance, can be applied to any person within the jurisdiction of each Contracting Party was not adopted for the European Social Charter. Consequently, this leads to a somewhat restrictive category of persons protected.[8]

Articles 18 and 19 of the Charter specifically concern migrant workers. Article 18 provides for the liberal application of existing regulations governing the employment of foreign workers, and Article 19 deals with the rights to protection and assistance of migrant workers and their families. More specifically, Article 18 is concerned with the right of nationals to leave the country in order to engage in a gainful activity in the territories of other Contracting Parties, and provides for a simplification of formalities and reduction of dues and charges as well as for the liberalization of regulations governing the employment of foreign workers.

Article 19 is concerned with the right of migrant workers and their families to protection and assistance, as mentioned above. It comprises ten undertakings. The first three paragraphs provide for information, combating misleading propaganda, travel assistance, reception facilities, cooperation between social services and so on for migrant workers. The next six paragraphs refer to specific commitments on the treatment of migrant workers being no less favourable than that of nationals in a range of fields, including employment conditions, trade union membership, housing, taxation, legal proceedings, family reunification, guarantees against expulsion and transfer of earnings and savings. The final provision of Article 19 extends all these guarantees to self-employed migrant workers.

Paragraph 6 of Article 19 concerns family reunification. The family of a foreign worker is defined in the Appendix to the Charter as 'at least his wife and dependent children under the age of 21 years'. In this respect, given the terms of the Appendix, establishing an age limit lower than 21 years is not permitted. However, since the persons concerned must also be 'dependent' on the migrant worker, meaning persons who depend for their existence on their family for economic reasons, for the continuation of education without remuneration or for reasons of health, those fulfilling the age condition could be deprived of the right of family reunification if it is established that they are no longer dependent on the migrant worker.

In the Convention on the Legal Status of Migrant Workers, which was designed to supplement the European Convention of Human Rights and the European Social Charter, the 'migrant worker' is defined as 'a national of a Contracting Party who has been authorized by another Contracting Party to reside in its territory in order to take up paid employment'. The Convention contains provisions concerning the main aspects of the legal status of migrant workers such as recruitment, travel, residence and work permits, family reunification, housing, medical examinations and vocational tests, conditions of work, transfer of savings, social security, expiry of the contract of employment, dismissal and re-employment and preparation for return to the country of origin.

In the matter of family reunification, according to the Convention, a European migrant worker resident in a contracting state which has ratified the Convention is entitled to be joined by his spouse and dependent children, the waiting period not exceeding 12 months (Article 12). The Convention also provides for the equality of treatment with regard to conditions of work and the right to organize (Articles 16, 21, 24 and 28). Another important provision in the Convention is the right of migrant workers who are involuntarily unemployed to remain in the territory of the receiving state for a certain period in order to look for another job (Articles 9 and 25).

The Convention also grants an effective right of appeal to a judicial or administrative authority in the receiving state (Article 9) for migrant workers whose residents' permits have been withdrawn for one of the reasons listed in the Convention. Lastly, the Convention contains provisions in the field of information (Article 6) which are designed to give migrant workers a feeling of greater security, as misinformation about rights and obligations in the host country often leads to the conflicts with which migrant workers are frequently faced.

There are other legal instruments in Europe, such as the European Interim Agreements on Social Security and the European Convention on Social Security, which contain provisions guaranteeing the equality of treatment between nationals and non-nationals. In particular, the European Convention on Social Security was designed as a multilateral instrument on social security for people moving within the territory of the Contracting Parties, especially migrant workers.

Being more specific at the European level, there also exist association agreements between the European Union and some third countries of the Mediterranean and Eastern Europe. These agreements include non-discrimination clauses with regard to migrant workers and bring some additional rights for the nationals of these third countries working within the territory of the European Union.

Regarding international legal instruments concerning the rights of migrant workers, it must be noted that not all have a binding effect on States Parties to them. The Universal Declaration of Human Rights, for instance, binds not only the States Parties to one or both of the International Covenants but also those which have neither ratified them nor acceded thereto. The Universal Declaration has provided the basis on which international instruments concerning the rights of migrant workers have been drafted both in and outside the United Nations. The Declaration is universal in its scope and applies to all humans regardless of whether their government has ratified the International Covenants and the other international conventions.

International conventions, on the other hand, are binding only on the states which have ratified them. Furthermore, the rights and freedoms for which they make provision may be subject to the limitations and restrictions which a government can introduce in order to protect national security or the rights and freedoms of others. For instance, the International Labour Standards of the ILO have binding effect when they are incorporated into national legislation or when an agreement between organizations representing workers and those representing employers in a field of occupational activity is concluded through collective bargaining.[9]

In reality, however, there is a contradiction between *de jure* and *de facto* situations. Despite the existence of anti-discrimination legislation, various studies show that discriminatory practice takes place against migrant workers in daily life, either directly or indirectly.[10] The difference between *de jure* and *de facto* discrimination can be attributed to a number of factors. These include the dispersal of legislative texts in various codes, the failure to incorporate them in a specific legislative instrument, the limited enforcement capability of anti-discrimination institutions and the difficulty of legal redress, particularly in those cases in which it is difficult to provide proof or in which the financial cost of proceedings is very high.[11] Therefore it can be said that the ratification of an international convention does not suffice to guarantee its application.

The international consensus embodied in the provisions of the ILO and UN conventions and in other conventions remains more theoretical than real as long as most major sending and receiving countries do not feel bound to adhere to them in law and in practice. In fact, various scholars in the field argue that there is no need to set new standards or to make new declarations in the field of international migration for employment. A strict application of the standards which have already been voted and their ratification are needed to cut down on irregular migration or employment as well as to ensure an acceptable standard level of rights for migrant workers.

## Migrant Workers' Rights under International Norms

The rights of migrant workers can be classified under certain headings: social rights, cultural rights, and civil and political rights. Social rights include the right to work, the right to social security and to an adequate standard of living, the right of access to health services, the right to rest and leisure, the right to housing, the right to family reunification for lawfully resident migrants, the right to transfer any part of their earnings and savings out of the country and the right of self-employed migrant workers to protection and assistance.

Migrants who are lawfully resident enjoy numerous legal rights with regard to the right to work, including the right to equal pay for equal work, the right to join trade unions, the right to access to unemployment benefits and the right to vocational training offered by unemployment offices. An important prerequisite for the integration of migrant workers in the labour market is equal pay for equal work, as well as equal work in the case of equal qualification between nationals and migrant workers. In order to obtain successful integration, material equality between nationals and migrant workers should be achieved under equal conditions. Legal rights with regard to work also include the right to vote and stand as candidates in trade union elections and, in some countries, the right to become workers' representatives.

The cultural rights of migrant workers include the right to education, the right to participate in the cultural life of the community freely, and the right to enjoy the arts and to participate in scientific progress.

Civil and political rights include the right to life, freedom of thought, conscience and religion, freedom of opinion and expression, the right to freedom of movement and to free choice of place of residence, the right to recognition as a person before the law, the right to freedom of association and peaceful assembly, the right to marry without any restriction on grounds of race, nationality and religion, the right to own property and, in some countries, the right to vote and stand as a candidate in local elections for those who have lived in the country for several years.

Even though the rights listed above are universally acknowledged norms, there are differences in the way they are practised from one country to another. Quite different views on labour migration are to be found worldwide and the difference in perceptions of labour migration leads to a variety of policy instruments. While countries like Australia, Canada, Israel and the United States consider themselves to be immigration countries, most Western European countries such as Germany do not acknowledge that they have become countries of immigration, and employ more restrictive regimes with regard to recruitment, residence, family reunion, naturalization and other social, civil and political rights.

The Ad Hoc Group on Immigration of the European Union drafted a resolution on admission for the purpose of employment in 1992. The amended version was approved in June 1994. Even though the resolution is not legally binding on member states, it sets out principles for the harmonization of national policies on admission for employment. The Resolution on Limitations on Admission of Third-Country Nationals to the Member States for Employment does not deal with the issue of third-country nationals who are permanent residents of a member state, but invites member states to refuse entry to third-country nationals for employment. According to the resolution, family reunification for migrant workers admitted to a member state is not a right, but a discretion reserved to host states. A development in the area of family reunification was the Resolution on Harmonization of National Policies on Family Reunification, adopted by the ministers of immigration of the European Union in June 1993. According to the principles of the resolution, which are not legally binding on the member states, the spouse and single, dependent children below 16 or 18 (depending on the member state) of people lawfully resident within the territory of a member state on a basis which affords them an expectation of permanent or long-term settlement are granted admission. The resolution provides member states with the right to impose waiting conditions and periods before allowing family reunification, the right to impose a primary purpose test for the admission of spouses, discretion as to the admission of step-children and adopted children, and so on.[12]

The European Union resolution adopted in June 1993 is a reflection of the tightening up of family reunification rules in Europe. Increasingly aware of the potential risk of liberal family reunification policies and the attached 'pull factor', countries such as Germany, France and the United Kingdom, which have experienced heavy inflows of family members, reviewed their policies with regard to family reunification in recent years. The restrictive European Union resolution contrasts with the liberal policies in North America and Australia, where family reunification is traditionally given a high priority and has a prominent role in immigration planning.[13]

In general, the application of rights, treatment of migrant workers and policies for integration of migrant workers differ greatly between Europe and the transatlantic states. For instance, Canada introduced a policy for the maintenance of languages and cultural traditions of migrants almost from the beginning, while, in the United States and the United Kingdom, emphasis has been placed on the development of harmonious race relations. Australia, Sweden, Norway, Denmark and the Netherlands adopted the Canadian policy in the 1970s, while integration in France is based on assimilation into French-speaking society.

With the Treaty on the European Union signed in Maastricht, the Schengen Agreement and the developments preceding the Intergovernmental Conference in 1996, the European Union presents a special situation for migrant workers. Currently, there are about ten million third-country nationals residing lawfully within the European Union. However, they are not recognized as having the same rights with regard to free movement, involving the right to take up paid employment in another member state, as European Union nationals. The draft Convention of the Member States of the European Community on Crossing External Borders of 1991 made a concession of three-months' visa-free travel in the Union to resident third-country nationals, but it is no longer on the agenda, and still remains as a draft convention. The Schengen Agreement, which is in force, brings some remedy to this situation by recognizing three-months' visa-free travel between Schengen countries, which nevertheless retain the right to carry out controls at internal frontiers.

The European Commission has asked for enlarged rights for long-term third-country residents in the Union since 1991. It intends to propose to the Council of Europe the granting of limited rights to third-country nationals legally resident in a member state to work in other member states. The idea in mind is to give third-country residents of the European Union priority over third-country intending immigrants for jobs. However, this is a rather restrictive approach, given the policies adopted on employment and the possibility of free movement for European Union nationals. A Council of Europe decision concerning travel facilities for school pupils from third-countries resident in a member state was adopted at the Council of Europe meeting on 30 November 1994. This is a very first step towards free movement for resident third-country nationals within the European Union. Schoolchildren on school excursions will not need visas for a short stay in other member states in the future, provided that their teacher can present a list of the pupils and documents concerning the purpose and circumstances of the intended stay or transit and that the pupil presents a valid travel document.

## Conclusions

Legislation constitutes an important instrument to ensure the effective equality of opportunity and treatment and often leads to a change in attitudes. Nevertheless, it must be noted that legislation is not by itself sufficient to eliminate prejudice and discrimination against migrant workers. A well-thought-out, coordinated strategy is needed to ensure the equality of migrant workers both before the law and in practice in everyday life. This requires that active information and education policies and dissemination of codes of practice be implemented in harmony with legal measures.

In order to reduce discrimination and combat xenophobia and racism giving rise to social conflicts, it is often proposed that migrant workers be granted the same rights as nationals. These rights would, of course, entail obligations. The present immigration policies in Europe and elsewhere are founded on the principle of equal obligations, that is full respect by migrant workers for legislation and other regulatory provisions on the same terms as nationals. However, their integration in society is not based on the principle of equal rights and equal opportunities. Although the lives of migrant workers are as affected by government decision making as those of any other residents, their participation in the decision-making process is very limited and often non-existent. If a substantial number of permanent residents cannot vote, the legitimacy of the political decision-making process is impaired. It must be noted that the existence of such disenfranchised groups in significant numbers throughout the world undermines democracy.

Political participation, such as the right to vote, would be an effective means of integrating migrant workers. It would also ensure an engagement among the political parties on the matter of migrant workers. Dual citizenship and enactment of anti-discrimination laws for those countries which have not recognized these rights would be another means of promoting the integration of and equal opportunities for migrant workers.

At a time of comparatively high unemployment, the difficulty of admitting migrant workers into many countries is widely recognized and accepted. Nevertheless, the importance of family reunification should be endorsed and migrant workers should be encouraged to apply for work in particular fields where they are needed. Furthermore, a recognition programme can be developed for illegal migrants who have been working in the country for at least five years. Freedom of movement is another important issue which should be recognized for migrant workers, particularly within the European Union.

Finally, it must be emphasized that it is just as important to enforce the numerous, existing international legal instruments as to draft new conventions or charters which are not always supported by control and recourse, unless states accede to them and incorporate them in their national legislation. To these ends, the ratification of the existing international conventions is an important step and should be encouraged.

## Notes

1   Niessen (1993, p 23).
2   R.B. Lillich, *The Human Rights of Aliens in Contemporary International Law*, Manchester, Manchester University Press, 1984, p.3.
3   Böhning (1984, pp.30–31).
4   Maillat (1987, p.50).
5   Salt (1993).
6   Robertson and Merrills (1993).
7   Case of Moustaquim, Judgment of 18 February 1991.
8   Council of Europe (1992, p.16).
9   Fonteneau (1992, p.61).
10  See Zegers de Beijl (1990).
11  Fonteneau, *supra*, note 9.
12  Churches Committee for Migrants in Europe (1995, pp.18–19).
13  International Centre for Migration Policy Development (1994, p.66).

## Bibliography

Böhning, W.R. (1984), *Studies in International Labour Migration*, London, Macmillan.
Churches Committee for Migrants in Europe (ed.) (1995), 'Intergovernmental Co-operation on Immigration and Asylum', CCME Briefing Paper No. 19, Brussels, April.
Council of Europe (1992), 'Activities of the Council of Europe in the Migration Field', CDMG (92), 1, Strasbourg, 20 January.
European Convention on the Legal Status of Migrant Workers (1977), European Treaty Series 93.

European Social Charter (1961), European Treaty Series 35; and Additional Protocol to the European Social Charter (1988), European Treaty Series 128.

European Union Migrants' Forum (1995), 'The European Union Migrants' Forum Proposals for the Revision of the Treaty on European Union at the Intergovernmental Conference of 1996', Brussels, May.

Falga, B., C. Withol de Wenden, and C. Leggewie (eds) (1994), *Au Miroir de l'autre – De l'immigration à l'intégration en France et en Allemagne*, Paris, Les Éditions du CERF.

Fonteneau, G. (1992), 'The rights of migrants, refugees or asylum seekers under international law', *International Migration*, Vol. XXX, Geneva, International Organization for Migration (IOM).

Friedrich Ebert Stiftung (1994), 'Einwanderungspolitik Kanadas und der USA', *Gesprächskreis Arbeit und Soziales*, **31**, Bonn, July.

International Centre for Migration Policy Development (1994), 'The Key to Europe – A Comparative Analysis of Entry and Asylum Policies in Western countries', prepared for the Swedish Parliamentary Immigrant and Refugee Commission, Stockholm.

International Labour Organisation/International Organization for Migration and United Nations High Commissioner for Refugees (eds) (1994), *Migrants, Refugees and International Co-operation. A Joint Contribution to the International Conference on Population and Development*, Geneva, ILO.

Maillat, D. (1987), 'The experience in the main geographical OECD areas: European receiving countries', *The Future of Migration*, Paris, OECD.

Niessen, J. (1993), 'Proposals for a comprehensive European immigration policy. Between the open and closed door approaches', in Churches Committee for Migrants in Europe (ed.), Report of the Seminar on Migratory Movements and European Policies, Brussels, 5–6 March.

Robertson, A.H. and J.G. Merrills (1993), *Human Rights in Europe*, 3rd edn, Manchester, Manchester University Press.

Salt, J. (1993), 'The future of international labour migration', *International Migration Review*, **100**.

Schoger, K. (1994), 'Zuwanderer und Politik. Ein deutsch-französischer Vergleich' *Reihe Völkervielfalt und Minderheitenrechte in Europa*, Vol. 4, Berlin, Hitit.

Schumacher, H. (1995), *Einwanderungsland BRD*, Düsseldorf, Zebulon Verlag.

Straubhaar, T. and K.F. Zimmermann (1993), 'Towards a European migration policy', *Population Research and Policy Review*, **12**, 225–41.

UN Centre for Human Rights (1987), *Status of International Instruments*, Geneva, UN Centre for Human Rights.

UN Centre for Human Rights (1990), *Chart of ratifications (updated)*, Geneva, UN Centre for Human Rights.

Werner, H. (1994), 'Integration of Foreign Workers into the Labour Market – France, Germany, the Netherlands and Sweden', Geneva, ILO, World Employment Programme, working paper (MIG WP.74 E).

Zegers de Beijl, R. (1990), 'Discrimination of Migrant Workers in Western Europe', Geneva, ILO, World Employment Programme, working paper (MIG WP.49).

Zimmermann, K.F. (1994), 'Immigration policies in Europe: an overview', in H. Siebert (ed.), *Migration: A Challenge for Europe*, Tübingen, J.C.B. Mohr, pp.227–58.

# PART IV
# HUMANITARIAN LAW

# 11 Humanitarian Law and Human Rights

### HÉCTOR GROS ESPIELL

## Introduction

The connection between human rights and humanitarian law must today be considered from two distinct viewpoints: first, analysis of the significance of humanitarian law with regard to the observance, promotion and defence of human rights: in other words, humanitarian law as it is today and as it is applied, and its contribution to the concrete existence of human rights and their observance as such in international and internal armed conflicts, within the framework of the provisions of the 1949 Geneva Conventions and the Protocols of 1977; second, the relation between humanitarian law and human rights law as two distinct branches, sectors or aspects of modern international law.

This method of analysis will allow us to bypass a number of approaches to the subject which are now obsolete. In the context of the present international situation and advances in legal theory in recent years, this question can no longer be addressed in the same way as it was 30 or 40 years ago.

Because the current international situation has a strong bearing on this issue, it is necessary to assess past and present world events in these final years of the twentieth century, including, of course, the new methods and rules of international organizations, in particular those of the United Nations, the International Committee of the Red Cross, case law and legal theory.

## Geneva Conventions of 1949 and Additional Protocols of 1977 and Human Rights

There is no doubt that international humanitarian law has always been an element of vital importance in the safeguarding and defence of human rights, both before and after the Geneva Conventions of 1949 and the Additional Protocols of 1977.

It is clear from the articles of the Conventions of 1949 that, in considering the wounded and the sick in armed forces in the field (Convention I), the wounded and shipwrecked members of the armed forces at sea (Convention II), prisoners of war (Convention III) and civilian persons in time of war (Convention IV), its provisions are essentially aimed at ensuring that the observance of certain human rights is guaranteed in specific situations. There is no need to review all the provisions of these conventions. Their common Article 3 enjoins humanitarian treatment without distinction of any kind, and prohibits violence to life and person, outrages upon personal dignity, cruel treatment and torture and humiliating and degrading treatment. Its aim is therefore to safeguard the human rights of such persons in the specific situations in which they find themselves. The wording of Article 3 is identical or similar to that used in the 1948 Universal Declaration of Human Rights, and adopted again in the 1966 International Covenants on Human Rights and, at a regional level, in the European Convention of Human Rights, the American Convention on Human Rights and the African Charter of Human and Peoples' Rights.

Many other provisions of the Conventions could be quoted to support this view. This is not necessary, but it is worth mentioning Article 27 of Convention IV, which, referring to the same principles as the common Article 3, includes among the rights of protected persons their entitlement to their honour, their family rights, their religious convictions and practices and their manners and customs.

The same principles are to be found in the two Protocols of 1977. In Protocol I, applicable to armed conflicts in which peoples are fighting against colonial or foreign domination and against racist regimes, the reference to the protection of the wounded, sick and shipwrecked and of persons who are in the power of the adverse party or who are interned, detained or deprived of liberty must be underlined (Articles 10 and 11). Article 75 (fundamental guarantees) is aimed at guaranteeing the protection of the fundamental human rights of persons who find themselves in situations referred to in Article 1 of the Protocol.

In Protocol II, applicable to international armed conflicts, Part II (humane treatment), which includes Article 4 (fundamental guarantees) and Article 5 (persons whose liberty has been restricted), is aimed at protecting and guaranteeing the rights of persons in such conflicts.

The application of international humanitarian law is steadily becoming more important for human rights law and for true observance of human rights. Conversely, human rights law is steadily becoming more important for international humanitarian law and its effective application. This conviction, born of the awareness of common principles and objectives and the common fundamental principle of the dignity of the human person which exists in both laws and which reinforce and support each other, is constantly growing, although international humanitarian law applies in specific situations and has its own instruments and organs of enforcement.

This conviction and awareness is also present and growing within the organs of the Red Cross and the Red Crescent, in the United Nations, in the United Nations specialized agencies and in regional systems for the protection of human rights, such as the European, American and African systems. It is also the prevailing position in the relevant non-governmental organizations, in particular the International Institute of Humanitarian Law, San Remo, Italy.

For this reason, the traditional theories on the connection between human rights and international law (separatist, complementarist and integrationist) have to some extent been transcended by the development of the political situation and of practice on the international scene. There is no doubt that specific international humanitarian law is aimed at protecting human rights in certain situations, by means of special procedures and for certain categories of persons. Thus it is part of what could be called international human rights law in the broad sense (*lato sensu*).

But it is also a parallel system to international human rights law in the strict sense, based on the same principles and the same objectives. These two parallel sectors of international law influence, support and reinforce each other. In the present international political situation, it is impossible to conceive of the existence of international law without human rights law. Conversely, human rights law would not be what it is today without international humanitarian law.

## Definition and Understanding of Human Rights and Humanitarian Law

An appropriate definition of both terms (human rights and humanitarian law) is clearly required today in order to determine their common elements and reciprocal connections. The fact that they are often used with different meanings on different occasions, that these meanings do not always coincide and that they are increasingly used in common parlance rather than restricted to specialized legal language, makes it necessary to clarify and define the terms and the concepts according to current legal practice and theory in this sphere.

The relationship between the two concepts and the identification of their common and distinct elements have been the subject of various legal works[1] which have undoubtedly helped to clarify the question and, above all, facilitate its study and analysis. Nevertheless, the doubts and uncertainties which remain fully warrant an effort to achieve greater clarity.

The term 'rights' in the expression 'human rights' refers to subjective rights, powers or faculties which human beings possess in virtue of their recognition by national law and/or international law. The term 'law' in international humanitarian law refers to an objective set of principles and rules which, in international law, govern the protection of individuals in international or internal armed conflicts in accordance specifically with the provisions of the Geneva Conventions of 1949 and the two Protocols of 1977 and the protection of refugees in accordance, notably, with the Convention relating to the Status of Refugees of 1951 and the Protocol relating to the Status of Refugees of 1967. While in English the confusion does not arise, this distinction and its conceptual significance is particularly important in Latin, Spanish, French, Italian, German and the Slavonic languages, where the same word (*ius, derecho, droit, diritto, recht, pravo*), derived from the objective concept of law,[2] has both meanings.

In order to standardize terminology in these languages, it is therefore necessary to refer to the objective meaning of the term '*Derecho*', for example, as '*Derecho Internacional de los Derechos Humanos*' (international human rights law) and '*Derecho Internacional Humano*' (international humanitarian law) and to refer to the subjective meaning of the term '*Derecho*' as '*Derechos Humanos*' or human rights and the rights (*derechos*) of combatants and civilian populations in armed conflicts.

In Spanish, Latin, French, Italian and German, a different meaning is given to the same word in the expressions 'human rights' and 'international humanitarian law'. Therefore, in order to standardize the expressions with a view to a homogeneous and common terminology, the terms 'international human rights law' and 'international humanitarian law' will have to be used.

While it does not provide us with any new information on the subject, this simple and obvious terminological clarification facilitates analysis by overcoming the confusion which usually arises.

Whatever the theoretical, philosophical, political or legal framework used as a basis for analysis, the term 'human rights' means the fundamental powers, responsibilities and requirements that a human being possesses, declared, recognized and conferred by the legal order and which, derived as they are from the inherent dignity of humankind (the general and universal bedrock of human rights), constitute today the indispensable and necessary basis of any organization or national political system, and indeed of the international community itself.

The assertion of the possibility of a common, universal ideal in the sphere of human rights, proclaimed in the Universal Declaration of Human Rights, must recognize the unavoidable fact that there are different conceptions of those rights, both in theory and in reality in the present international situation.[3]

The universal concept of human rights was reaffirmed by the 1993 Vienna World Conference on Human Rights in Articles 1 and 5 of the Vienna Declaration and Programme of Action, while recognizing the importance of national and regional differences and the diversity of historical, cultural and religious backgrounds, and bearing in mind that all states have the duty, whatever their political, economic and cultural systems, to promote and protect all human rights (Article 5).

Today, the concept of human rights includes the traditional civil and political rights or traditional public liberties, the economic, social and cultural rights which entail the state's positive duty to satisfy human economic, social and cultural needs and the new rights which have arisen from the demands of today's world, particularly with regard to development, the environment, peace, self-determination, and so forth.

As declared by the General Assembly of the United Nations, all these rights are interdependent, every right and every category of right requiring for its actual existence the recognition and enforcement of the others. Freedom exists only when it is exercised by a person who is free from fear, poverty, hunger, insecurity and lack of culture. On the other hand, economic, social and cultural rights have a strict meaning which fully respects human dignity if they are exercised by a free person who is not subjected to arbitrary acts, despotism and discrimination.

The rights of each human being can exist in reality only as a result of a legal order which is in force, and the exercise of those rights is limited by the rights of other human beings and the demands of social coexistence, in accordance with rules derived from a law established in the general interest, without discrimination of any kind.

The declaration, protection and promotion of human rights is the responsibility, first and foremost, of internal law, because it is in and for the state, whose existence and security constitute the condition of the actual existence of human rights, that the body of rules aimed at regulating and guaranteeing them is developed.

But faced with the risk of human rights violations resulting from the activities of the state (which is not, however, the only considerable source of such violations), international law, whether in its universal or its regional manifestations, also guarantees and promotes the enforcement and observance of human rights.

The question of human rights is therefore no longer the preserve of the domestic jurisdiction of states, but is now recognized as being governed by internal law and by international law, against which special internal law cannot be invoked.

The body of principles and rules in international law which currently governs the issue of human rights on the international plane is known as 'international human rights law'. It is derived from the Charter of the United Nations, the Universal Declaration of Human Rights, the two International Covenants on Human Rights, the Optional Protocol to the International Covenant on Civil and Political Rights and a long series of instruments, treaty-based or otherwise, developed within the framework of the United Nations[4] and some of its specialized agencies, in particular the International Labour Organisation (ILO) and the United Nations Educational, Scientific and Cultural Organization (UNESCO).

Besides these instruments of a universal nature, there are international regional instruments such as the European Convention on the Protection of Human Rights and Fundamental Freedoms and its Protocols, the European Social Charter, the American Declaration of Human Rights and Duties, the African Charter of Human and Peoples' Rights, and many others.

International human rights law, which is today one of the most dynamic and controversial branches of international law, encompasses various systems of operation with a complex organic structure in both the universal and the regional spheres. In a very broad sense, all the international rules and principles aimed at protecting and guaranteeing the rights of persons, whatever their legal status (civilian, military, national, alien, man, woman, combatant, non-combatant, and so on), at any time (peace, war, civil war, insurrection, and so on), both within the territory of which they are nationals or residents and outside it, whatever their reason for deciding to leave that country and settle in another, could be regarded as making up international human rights law.

However, this very broad and comprehensive notion, although not conceptually at fault, if its meaning is clearly stated, runs up against the existence of various branches of current international law aimed at protecting the rights of persons in different situations. Its use without the necessary qualifications could prove to be vague and controversial and lead to dangerous confusion.

However, taking into account these distinctive aspects, the dissimilarities in situation and the different systems of operation which are not always reconcilable, one must recognize that both the protection of human rights in general, based on the relevant universal and regional instruments in force, and the protection of the rights of persons under international humanitarian law constitute posts, specific sectors, of a general international legal system of essentially humanitarian origin, aimed at protecting human beings in the broadest and most comprehensive manner compatible with the existence of the established legal system of the state and the international community.

Although the scope of this general system, which makes the human being the subject of internationally guaranteed rights, varies according to the different cases and situations in international human rights law proper, in international humanitarian law it is based on general fundamental principles which influence the various branches of international law aimed at protecting and guaranteeing human rights. There may be specific principles and criteria which are applicable only in certain branches of international law, as in the special case of humanitarian law,[5] but there can be no denying the existence of general principles common to all sectors, linked and interrelated, with the essential aim of protecting and guaranteeing the dignity and integrity of human beings. Indeed, it would be extremely dangerous to deny this.[6]

Let us first examine the question of international humanitarian law. This law, which is sometimes called 'the Law of Geneva', is based essentially on the four Geneva Conventions of 1949 and the two Protocols of 1977. It can be considered to be a part of the law on armed conflicts, although strictly speaking this law, also called 'the Law of The Hague' and derived from the 1907 Fourth Hague Convention and its annex, lays down the rules which must be observed by the warring parties as a consequence of the principle that the parties in an armed conflict do not have an unlimited choice of means with which to fight the enemy. However, this law is not confined to the rules of The Hague, because it also includes the Geneva Protocol of 1925 for the Prohibition of the Use in War of Asphyxiating, Poisonous or other Gases and Bacteriological Methods of Warfare, the Convention on the Prohibition of the Development, Production and Stockpiling of Bacteriological (Biological) and Toxin Weapons and on their Destruction, of 10 April 1972, and the Convention on Prohibitions or Restrictions on the Use of Certain Conventional Weapons, of October 1980.

In a broad sense, the humanitarian provisions cover the conduct of military operations (methods and means of combat) as well as the protection of the victims of armed conflicts (wounded, sick, prisoners, civilian populations, and so on). But, strictly speaking, international humanitarian law is based on the Geneva Conventions of 1949 and the Additional Protocols of 1977, that is to say, the Law of Geneva, which differs from the Law of The Hague in its specific system of operation.

However, one should not make the mistake of placing these laws in opposition, because together they form the law of armed conflicts and, while their approach and their immediate objectives are different, they are based on the same principles and have a common final objective.[7] The link between international humanitarian law and international human rights law, and the acknowledgment of the fact that they are derived from the same general principles aimed at protecting human beings, has become established in current legal theory.[8] Although the Red Cross has only in exceptional circumstances invoked human rights,[9] and although its action has its own distinctive character, its work has always been aimed at achieving the observance of certain fundamental human rights.[10]

In contrast to the general character of international human rights law, which refers to the existence of rights possessed by all individuals in all situations,[11] international humanitarian law applies only in certain specific cases (international or internal armed conflicts and certain situations specifically provided for: Articles 2 and 3 common to the 1949 Conventions and articles of the 1977 Protocols I and II), and its rules apply only to those persons protected as a consequence of such situations in the cases expressly provided for in the Conventions of 1949 and the Protocols of 1977 (sick, shipwrecked, prisoners of war, wounded, civilian populations, refugees, stateless persons, and so on). Although international human rights law and international humanitarian law overlap to a certain extent, each also has its own substantive and specific field of application calling for different methods of implementation and monitoring.

International humanitarian law and international human rights law have developed along different lines historically. The former is derived from the 1864, 1899 and 1929 Geneva Conventions leading to the Conventions of 1949 and the Protocols of 1977, including the 1907 Hague Conventions and the other standards mentioned above and which, although they do not refer directly to the fate of human beings affected by armed conflict but to the conduct of military operations, also have the ultimate aim of protecting human beings.

International human rights law, on the other hand, is derived, notwithstanding certain earlier instruments, from the Charter of the United Nations, the Universal Declaration of Human Rights, the American Declaration of Human Rights and Duties, the European Convention, the American Convention, the two International Covenants on Human Rights, the Optional Protocol to the International Covenant on Civil and Political Rights and the African Charter on Human and Peoples' Rights. Also of importance are the Final Declarations of the Tehran and Vienna Conferences on Human Rights, adopted by agreement in 1968 and 1993, respectively, which crystallize the present thinking of the international community on human rights: the duty of their observance, the need for their international protection and other relevant themes.

Yet, despite these two distinct and parallel lines of development, which show nevertheless that the Geneva Convention of 1864 enshrines the essential principle of human rights and its necessary universal unbiased recognition, enjoining as it does the duty of equal treatment for all wounded, whether allies or enemies, more and more interconnections have developed, particularly in recent years,[12] owing to the existence of principles common to both. This has been achieved, nevertheless, while recognizing the usefulness of maintaining two different systems, with distinct criteria and methods of implementation.

One must also bear in mind that, in the event of armed conflict, the application of international humanitarian law does not necessarily exclude the application of international human rights law. Human beings can consider themselves protected by both sets of standards. In situations which are not governed by international humanitarian law, all human beings are protected by international human rights law, notwithstanding the fact that, 'in exceptional circumstances endangering the life of the nation', such as some cases of internal or international armed conflict, the duty to guarantee the exercise of certain rights may be waived 'to the extent strictly required by the exigencies of the situation'.[13] However, this emergency regime does not in any circumstances permit the suspension of the duty of all states to respect at all times the right to life, for example, not to use torture, cruel, humiliating and degrading punishments and treatments, not to allow slavery or servitude and to recognize the legal status of all human beings. These absolutely fundamental rights, which cannot be revoked and which must be observed at all times and in whatever situation, constitute the essential core of respect for human rights. They are true cases of *jus cogens* in the present international situation, or mandatory norms accepted by the international community as a whole, and whose violation entails the nullity of the legal act which infringes them, whatever its nature.[14]

In the specific situations provided for by international humanitarian law, the persons to whom it applies enjoy *ab initio* the guarantees specific to humanitarian law, notwithstanding the subsidiary protection of those same persons by international human rights law, which remains in force also for those individuals who, *rationae personae*, may not have been expressly protected by international humanitarian law.

The fundamental convergence and shared concerns of international human rights law proper and international humanitarian law are further borne out by the fact that the International Committee of the Red Cross has extended its sphere of protective action, on the basis of humanitarian principles but not on those of the Geneva Conventions, to political prisoners, even when they have been imprisoned, not as a consequence of an armed conflict, but as a result of political repression. This is an application of international humanitarian law aimed at protecting certain fundamental human rights (life, liberty, the right not to be tortured and not to suffer degrading treatment) by an organ of international humanitarian law such as the Red Cross, in a situation which differs from those which have traditionally determined the necessary practical and personal scope of this law.

This state of affairs and the efforts to extend the role of the Red Cross as regards the protection of human rights, expressed chiefly just before the 1981 Manila Conference and at the conference itself,[15] confirm the close and necessary connection between international human rights law and international humanitarian law.

This convergence, and the need to face up to the joint responsibility of international human rights law and international humanitarian law for the protection of the individual, have developed and grown more acute in recent decades. The United Nations has displayed a constant tendency to refer to and quote international humanitarian law when considering the issue of human rights in certain situations and cases.

This trend is apparent in the repeated references to the Geneva Conventions and international humanitarian law in successive resolutions of the General Assembly, the Security Council, the United Nations Commission on Human Rights, the Sub-Commission for Protection of Minorities and Prevention of Discrimination and the Human Rights Committee, created by the International Covenant on Civil and Political Rights. It acquired ultimate importance following the 1968 United Nations Conference on Human Rights held in Tehran, which adopted Resolution XXIII, entitled 'Protection of Human Rights in the Event of Armed Conflict'. The World Conference on Human Rights (Vienna, 1993), following the same course, proclaimed in paragraph 29 of the Vienna Declaration:

> The World Conference on Human Rights expresses grave concern about the continuing human rights violations in all parts of the world, in disregard of standards as contained in international human rights instruments and international humanitarian law, and about the lack of effective remedies for the victims.
> The World Conference on Human Rights is deeply concerned about violations of human rights during armed conflicts, affecting the civilian population, especially women, children, the elderly and the disabled. The Conference therefore calls upon States and all parties to armed conflicts strictly to observe international humanitarian law, as set forth in the Geneva Conventions of 1949 and other rules and principles of international law, as well as minimum standards for protection of human rights as laid down in international conventions. The World Conference on Human Rights reaffirms the right of the victims to be assisted by humanitarian organizations, as set forth in the Geneva Conventions of 1949 and other relevant instruments of

international humanitarian law, and calls for the safe and timely access to such assistance.

The International Court of Justice has also adopted this approach. In the case concerning the military and paramilitary activities in and against Nicaragua (*Nicaragua* v. *the United States*), the Court, in the ruling of 27 June 1986, referred to the general basic principles of humanitarian law, which the Geneva Conventions developed in some cases and in others limited themselves to expressing. The Court quoted Article 63 of the First Convention, Article 62 of the Second, Article 142 of the Third and Article 158 of the Fourth, which refer to the 'laws of humanity'. Likewise, it referred to Article 3, common to the four conventions, which prescribes the rules which it is at the discretion of the Court to apply, not only in armed conflicts which are not of an international nature, but also in international armed conflicts to which the detailed and specific norms of the four conventions apply. This identical prescription by the common Article 3 is based on the existence of 'elementary considerations of humanity', an expression which the Court had already used in 1949 in the Corfu Channel case.

The Court has also repeatedly invoked 'the general principles of humanitarian law of which the Conventions are none other than the concrete expression'. International humanitarian law, strictly speaking, has a system of implementation and monitoring established by (common) Articles 8–11 of the four 1949 Geneva Conventions. This system is essentially based on the establishment of the 'Protecting Powers' (Article 8), whose system of operation includes a *sui generis* procedure of good offices (Article 11), the International Committee of the Red Cross, any other neutral humanitarian organization with the consent of the parties (Article 9) and, in certain cases, neutral states (Article 10.2).

This system, and these organs of implementation and monitoring, are exclusive to international humanitarian law. The system cannot act through the organs of international human rights law in the strict sense, which has different universal and regional organs for the enforcement of its principles and rules. Neither the General Assembly of the United Nations, nor the Economic and Social Council, the Commission on Human Rights, the Sub-Commission for Protection of Minorities and Prevention of Discrimination, the Human Rights Committee, the Committee for the Elimination of Racial Discrimination or the European Commission and/or Court of Human Rights, for example, are strictly speaking organs for the implementation of international humanitarian law. Conversely, neither the Protecting Powers, nor the International Committee of the Red Cross, are organs for the implementation of international human rights law.

However, this does not imply that an organ of an international organization which includes in its jurisdiction instruments relating to the protection and promotion of human rights cannot invoke and adopt a position on a violation of international humanitarian law, or refer to this sector of international law, as the General Assembly[16] and the Commission on Human Rights have repeatedly done, or that an organ of the Red Cross such as the International Conference cannot invoke, as has often happened, the observance and guarantee of human rights in general.

Consequently, the differences in the legal systems and the terminology of these two branches of international law, their two distinct systems of operation and control and their individual characteristics must not cause us to overlook their fundamental unity. That unity is the result of common general principles and the fact that they both have their roots in defending, guaranteeing and safeguarding human rights generally and in situations which require specific treatment. With a common and global approach, but with different procedures according to different situations, current international law aims at constantly ensuring the effective application of human rights through the international law of human rights *strictu sensu* and international humanitarian law.

## Notes

1   Y. Dinstein, 'The Law of Armed Conflict and Human Rights: Convergence and Integration', International Institute of Human Rights, 6th Teaching Session, Strasbourg, 1976; E. Giraud, 'Le respect des droits de l'homme dans la guerre internationale et dans la guerre civile', *Revue de droit public et de la science politique*, July–August 1958, Paris; I.P. Blishchenko, 'Conflit armé et protection des droits de l'homme', *Revue de droit contemporain*, **177**, (1); Junod (1981); Swedish Red Cross (1981); Freymond (1979); J. Moreillon, *The Fundamental Principles of the Red Cross, Peace and Human Rights*, Geneva, The International Committee of the Red Cross, 1980; MacBride (1970); Patrnogic (1970); Pilloud (1949); Alexie and Ibriescu (1976); *International Lawyers Commission*, 35, 1968, Geneva; David (1977); Dinstein (1977); La Pradelle (1977); Meyrowitz (1972); Partsch (1974); Vasak (1965); Aldrich (1973); Gros Espiell (1984); Gros Espiell (1991); Patrnogic (1991); Meron (1991); Hampson (1991); Cornelio Sommaruga (1994); Karel Vasak, 'Conclusions', *The International Dimensions of Humanitarian Law*, Geneva/Paris, Henry Dunant Institute/UNESCO/Pedone, 1988; Meurant (1993); Daswald-Beck and Vité (1993); Weissbrodt and Hicks (1993); Hans Haug, *Humanity for All: The International Red Cross and Red Crescent Movement and Human Rights*, Geneva, Henry Dunant Institute/Bern, Paul Haupt Publishers, 1993; The United Nations, 'Human Rights, International Humanitarian Law and Human Rights', Fact Sheet no. 13.

2   In his *Common Sense in Law*, P. Vinogradoff has rightly said: 'Such coincidences should not be attributed to mere chance or to a misuse of language likely to obscure the real meaning of words; on the contrary, they point to a deep-rooted connection between the concepts in question. The expression

*Derecho* has two meanings: on the one hand, all rights are derived from the legal order; on the other, the legal order is, so to speak, the aggregate of all the rights which it co-ordinates' (3rd Spanish edn, Fondo de Cultura Economica, Mexico City, 1963, p.47, English edn, 1913, Oxford, Oxford University Press.

3   H. Gros Espiell, 'La evolución del concepto de los derechos humanos: criterios occidentales, socialistas y del tercer Mundo', *Anuario del Instituto Hispano Luso Americano de Derecho Internacional*, 5, Madrid, 1979, 80.

4   See *Human Rights, A Compilation of International Instruments*, Vol. I, First Part, Universal Instruments, United Nations, New York, 1993.

5   Pictet (1966). See 'The Proclamation of the Fundamental Principles of the Red Cross' (Twentieth International Conference of the Red Cross, Vienna 1965).

6   J. Patrnogic, 'Inter-relationship between general principles of international law and fundamental humanitarian principles applicable to the protection of refugees', *Annals of International Medical Law*, May 1977; Pictet, *supra*, note 5; J. Moreillon, *supra*, note 1; see Round Table on the Current Problems of International Humanitarian Law, San Remo, September 1979.

7   Nahlik (1978).

8   In addition to the works mentioned in note 1, the UNESCO manual on the teaching of human rights in universities (*The International Dimensions of Human Rights*, Paris, 1978) includes the study by Christian Dominicé, 'The implementation of humanitarian law', and many references on the subject in the work of T. Van Boven (*Survey of the Positive International Law of Human Rights*, paras 117–20) and S.P. Marks, *The Principles and Norms of Human Rights Applicable in Emergency Situations*).

9   For example, the Declaration of Istanbul, Resolution XIX, Twenty-First International Conference of the Red Cross, 1969.

10  Moreillon, *supra*, notes 1 and 6.

11  Inter-American Conference on the Security of the State, Human Rights and Humanitarian Law, San José, 27 September–2 October 1982, Inter-American Institute of Human Rights and International Committee of the Red Cross, General Comments for Participants 1–3, 'Human rights and international humanitarian law'.

12  Both the United Nations and the Red Cross have contributed to this rapprochement. For the opinions of the United Nations, see Respect for Human Rights in Armed Conflict, Report of the Secretary-General, doc. A7720, 1969; Respect for Human Rights in Armed Conflict: Third session of the Diplomatic Conference on the Reaffirmation and Development of International Humanitarian Law, Report of the Secretary-General, doc. A/31/163, 1976.

13  Many international instruments incorporate this criterion: in particular, Article 4 of the International Covenant on Civil and Political Rights, Article 15 of the European Convention, which refers expressly to armed conflict, and Article 27 of the American Convention, which also expressly refers to armed conflict.

14  H. Gros Espiell, 'No discriminación y libre determinación como normas imperativas de derecho internacional', *Anuario del Instituto Hispano Luso Americano de Derecho Internacional*, 6, Madrid, 1980; A. Gomez Robledo, *El Jus Cogens Internacional*, México, UNAM, 1982.

15  'Human rights. The need for a more active approach on the part of the Red Cross', working document presented by the Swedish Red Cross, International Institute of Humanitarian Law, San Remo, 1981.

16  See, for example, the resolutions of the General Assembly on Israeli practices with regard to human rights in occupied territories, in which it deplores the violation by Israel of the Geneva Convention relative to the Protection of Civilian Persons in Time of War (3525 (XXX), LA-B, 31/106 A-B-C), and the

resolutions of the General Assembly on the signing and ratification of the 1977 Protocols (32/44, 34/51 and others).

## Bibliography

Aldrich, G.H. (1973), 'Human Rights in Armed Conflicts', **68**, Washington.

Alexie, M. and P.H. Ibriescu (1976), 'Some considerations on the protection of human rights in times of armed conflict', *Romanian Review of International Studies*, **10**, (4), Bucharest.

Daswald-Beck, Louise and Sylvain Vité (1993), 'International humanitarian law and human rights law', *International Review of the Red Cross*, 800.

David, E. (1977), 'Human rights and humanitarian law', *Review of the Institute of Sociology*, 1, Brussels.

Dinstein, Y. (1977), 'The international law of inter-states war and human rights', *Israeli Yearbook of Human Rights*, **7**, Tel Aviv.

Freymond, J. (1979), *Security and Human Rights*, Geneva, ICRC.

Gros Espiell, Héctor (1984), 'Human rights, international humanitarian law and the international law of refugees', *Studies and Essays in International Humanitarian Law and the Principles of the Red Cross*, Geneva/Dordrecht, ICRC/Nijhoff.

Gros Espiell, Héctor (1991), 'Human rights and international humanitarian law', United Nations, *Bulletin of Human Rights*, 1.

Hampson, Françoise J. (1991), 'Human rights law and humanitarian law: two coins or two sides of the same coin?', United Nations, *Bulletin of Human Rights*, 1.

Junod, I.S. (1981), 'Human rights and Protocol II', International Institute of Humanitarian Law, San Remo Round Table.

La Pradelle, P. Geouffre de (1977) *Human Rights and Armed Conflicts: the 500th Anniversary of Las Casas*, Geneva, ICRC.

MacBride, S. (1970), 'Human rights in armed conflicts', *Review of Penal Military Law and the Law of Armed Conflict*, **IX**, (2), Brussels.

Meron, Theodor (1991), 'The protection of the human person under human rights law and humanitarian law', United Nations, *Bulletin of Human Rights*, 1.

Meurant, Jacques (1993), 'Humanitarian law and human rights: distinctive and common aspects ', *International Review of the Red Cross*, 800.

Meyrowitz, H. (1972), 'Droit de la guerre et les droits de l'homme', *Revue du droit public et de la science politique en France et à l'étranger*, September–October, Paris.

Nahlik, S.E. (1978), 'Droit dit de Genève et droit dit de La Haye: unicité ou dualité', *AFDI*, **XXIX**, Paris.

Partsch, K.J. (1974), 'The international protection of human rights and the Geneva Conventions of the Red Cross', *International Review of Comparative Law*, **26**, Paris.

Patrnogic, J. (1970), 'The United Nations and the respect for human rights in times of armed conflict ', *Jugoslovenska Revija za Medunarodno Pravo*, Belgrade, 263.

Patrnogic, J. (1991), 'Human rights and international humanitarian law', United Nations, *Bulletin of Human Rights*, 1.

Pictet, J. (1966), *The Principles of the Red Cross*, Geneva, ICRC.

Pilloud, C. (1949), *The Universal Declaration of Human Rights and the International Conventions Protecting Victims of War*, Geneva, ICRC.

Sommaruga, Cornelio (1994), *The ICRC in Current Conflicts: Human Rights, Humanitarian Law and Operational Actions*, Geneva/London, ICRC/British Institute of Human Rights.

Swedish Red Cross (1981), 'Human rights, the need for a more active approach on the part of the Red Cross', International Institute of Humanitarian Law, San Remo Round Table.

United Nations Educational, Scientific and Cultural Organization (1996), *Colloque international sur le droit à l'assistance humanitaire*, Paris, UNESCO.

Vasak, K. (1965), *The European Convention on Human Rights, Useful Complement to the Geneva Conventions*, Geneva, ICRC.

Weissbrodt, David and Peggy L. Hicks (1993), 'The implementation of human rights and humanitarian law in situations of armed conflict', *International Review of the Red Cross*, 800.

# Index